GUIDE TO LIBRARIES AND INFORMATION SOURCES

IN MEDICINE AND HEALTH CARE

Edited by **PETER DALE**
With the assistance of PAUL WILSON
and TONY ANTONIOU

THE BRITISH LIBRARY

Guide to Libraries and Information Sources in Medicine and Health Care
2nd edition February 1997
ISBN 0-7123-0839-3

Published by:

The British Library
Science Reference and Information Service (SRIS)
Marketing and Public Relations Section
25 Southampton Buildings
London
WC2A 1AW

British Library Cataloguing-in-Publication Data
A catalogue record for this book is available from The British Library

Cover photograph by David Griffiths

Desktop publishing by Samara Publishing

Printed by Hobbs the Printers Ltd, Totton, Hampshire S043 3YS

For further information on SRIS titles contact Tony Antoniou
on 0171-412 7471

CONTENTS

HEALTH CARE INFORMATION SERVICE
from THE BRITISH LIBRARY
offers

Free services

- An outstanding reference collection of printed and electronic material on biomedical and healthcare topics, patents and business information available in our London Reading Rooms
- Telephone enquiry line for quick queries

Ask your library about our fee-based services for

- **Keeping up to date** - our current awareness services include standard bulletins from Medline and the unique AMED database, compiled by the Library, as well as individually customised profiles
- **Checking what information is available** - we can search online databases for you through STMsearch, or BLAISE-LINK/Grateful Med subscribers can access the US National Library of Medicine's data bases direct
- **Getting hold of the articles, reports and other published material you need** - through our Document Supply Centre
- **Exploring the Internet** - we run regular courses on searching for biomedical sources

For more information contact:
The Health Care Information Service
The British Library
25 Southampton Buildings
London WC2A 1AW
Tel: 0171-412 7288
Fax: 0171-412 7217
or E-mail: hcis@bl.uk

Photo courtesy of Imperial Cancer Research Fund.

PREFACE

Introduction

This is the second edition of *Guide to Libraries and Information Sources in Medicine and Health Care*, a title in the Key Resources series which is published by the British Library Science Reference and Information Service (SRIS). The series aims to provide useful and informative coverage of leading sources of information in order to facilitate the work of librarians, information workers and researchers who need to know where specialist information can be obtained. Many librarians and information workers are already familiar with other titles in the series, most notably the *Guide to Libraries and Information Units in Government Departments and Other Organisations* (currently in its 32nd edition). This *Guide* is intended to complement the *Guide to Libraries and Information Units...* and so it follows a very similar style of layout and arrangement.

Inclusions policy

The *Guide* does not aim to be exhaustive in its coverage. Other directories provide good coverage of medical libraries in the UK, or in specific regions. This *Guide* aims to cover those libraries which are prepared to accept serious enquiries from outside, where a reasonable need exists. Consequently a significant number of medical libraries, but by no means all of them, are included here.

A highly significant feature of this *Guide*, and the one that does most to distinguish this work from others in similar fields, is that it has attempted to extend the scope of its coverage beyond the range of what might be described as the traditional sources of medical information. So, in addition to the 'orthodox' medical libraries this work contains a very high proportion of entries for non-library information sources. In the realm of medical information there is a wealth of material available from the many charities, support groups and voluntary bodies who can provide information for particular groups of people, or for sufferers of a specific disorder. It is the editor's belief that these groups represent invaluable sources of specialised information, and an attempt has been made to include as many of these groups as possible.

How the potential entries were identified

All of the organisations included in the first edition were invited to update their details, and the vast majority did so. A number of libraries and information services had closed down, or been merged, since the last edition, and these have been duly deleted. A significant number of organisations had undergone name changes in the intervening period, and these changes have been taken account of here. With regard to new entries, extensive research was carried out in the planning stages in order to identify as many potential inclusions as possible. The most recent editions of various other relevant directories were scanned, and all potential candidates for inclusion were mailed with an invitation to submit details. In addition, directories of voluntary bodies, charities and various other works were scanned in order to identify those organisations who appeared likely to be in a position to supply information related to some medical field. In all, nearly 1,500 organisations were approached. As a result, this edition features just under 160 completely new entries along with updated entries for most of the organisations who appeared in the first edition. Inevitably, a number of organisations declined to be included, indicated that they were not in a position to accept outside enquiries, or simply failed to respond. However, a good proportion of those approached did supply the required details, and the results are given in the following pages.

How the *Guide* is arranged

The main body of the *Guide* comprises a single alphabetic sequence of entries for the various organisations. This is followed by a small Stop Press list containing details which arrived too late for inclusion in the main sequence. An Appendix provides a summary of some of the more useful medical information resources that can be found on the Internet. This is followed by an Organisation Index and a Subject Index. Since many of the organisations included here are best known by the acronym for their name, there is also an Organisation Acronym Index listing all the organisations who use an acronymic form of their name.

The entries have been numbered sequentially, and the indexes refer to entry numbers rather than page numbers.

What information is provided?

Each entry begins with the name, address, telephone number and (where available) fax number and e-mail address for the organisation. An important new feature in this edition is the inclusion of a World Wide Web address for those organisations who have a site on the Internet. This is followed by a contact name, and a summary of the objectives and/or purposes of the organisation. The remainder of the entry provides details of the stock and subject coverage, services offered, terms of availability, hours of availability, publications produced by the organisation, and any linked organisations. It should be kept in mind that many of these organisations do not hold a formal library, so there is not necessarily any 'stock', or services other than the basic provision of information.

It must also be borne in mind that many of these organisations are operated by volunteers – sometimes by private individuals – so users of the *Guide* are requested to pay particular attention to the terms of availability indicated here and to respect any preferences that are indicated with regard to how requests for information should be submitted (e.g. the organisation may only be able to deal with written requests).

Future editions

Every effort has been made to be as comprehensive as possible with regard to the inclusion of appropriate organisations in this *Guide*. Nevertheless, some worthy organisations will have been overlooked, and some who failed to respond may feel more inclined to be included next time. SRIS, and the editor, are keen to include as many relevant entries as possible, so if any user of the *Guide* is in a position to make us aware of any potential new inclusions, please contact the Marketing and Public Relations Section at SRIS (address on the title page of this *Guide*). Similarly, all comments and suggestions are gratefully received, and considered carefully.

Peter Dale
British Library, February 1997

THE GUIDE

[1]
Abortion Law Reform Association (ALRA)

11-13 Charlotte Street
London W1P 1HD
Telephone: 0171 637 7264
Fax: 0171 580 4672
Contact: Jane Roe (Campaign Manager)
Objectives and Purposes: To campaign for a woman's right to safe, legal and free abortion, both in law and in practice
Stock and Subject Coverage: Material on unwanted pregnancy and abortion
Availability: Telephone and written enquiries only; nominal charge made for literature
Hours: Irregular
Publications: Newsletter (3 per year); annual report
Related Bodies: Part of Pro-Choice Alliance; linked with Education for Choice (educational charity)

[2]
Access Committee for England

12 City Forum
250 City Road
London EC1V 8AF
Telephone: 0171 250 0008
Fax: 0171 250 0212
Contact: Claire Goodridge (Policy Officer)
Objectives and Purposes: To challenge the environment which disables individuals, through policy work, training and information
Stock and Subject Coverage: Material on access to the built environment, and details of access groups and access officers
Services/Facilities: Library database
Availability: Telephone and written enquiries accepted; visits by prior arrangement
Hours: 09.00-17.00
Publications: Working Together for Access; Building Homes for Successive Generations

[3]
Acne Support Group (ASG)

PO Box 230
Hayes
Middlesex UB4 0UT
Telephone and Fax: 0181 561 6868
E-mail: asg@the-asg.demon.co.uk
World Wide Web: http://www.m2w3.com/acne/
Contact: Allison Dudley (Secretary/Co-ordinator)
Objectives and Purposes: To provide support and information for people and their families, and health professionals, on the causes and treatments of acne and rosacea
Services/Facilities: Various booklets, factsheets, etc. on acne and rosacea; Helpline - number as above
Availability: Telephone and written enquiries accepted; no visits
Hours: 09.00-17.00
Publications: List available

[4]
Action for Blind People

14-16 Verney Road
London SE16 3DZ
Telephone: 0171 732 8771
Fax: 0171 639 0948
E-mail: 100551.1531@compuserve.com
Contact: Enquiries to Information and Advice Centre; Ida Forster (Information and Advice Services Manager)
Objectives and Purposes: To answer enquiries on matters relating to visual impairment, in particular service provision and welfare rights
Stock and Subject Coverage: 700 pamphlets/books; 700 newspaper and journal articles; 10 periodicals; various leaflets, equipment catalogues, audio tapes and videos. Covers visual impairment and related topics, especially service provision for visually impaired people
Services/Facilities: Most publications available in large print, on tape and in Braille; photocopies; CCTV magnifier; database searches on VIS; mobile service around the country
Availability: Freely available; visits by appointment
Hours: 09.30-17.00 (answerphone available out of hours)
Publications: Newsletter (3 per year); annual report; various leaflets and information sheets - list available

[5]
Action for Dysphasic Adults (ADA)

1 Royal Street
London SE1 7LL
Telephone: 0171 261 9572
Fax: 0171 928 9542
Contact: Mrs Ruth Coles (Director)

Objectives and Purposes: ADA works to alleviate the frustration and social isolation of people who have language disability following stroke, head injury, etc. It campaigns to raise awareness of the condition among the general public and to improve the provision of services by professionals, and self-support through local groups

Stock and Subject Coverage: A range of booklets, audio cassettes and videos

Services/Facilities: Information service covering local facilities and overseas contacts

Availability: Open to dysphasic people, their families and professionals, for advice and information

Hours: 09.00-17.00

Publications: Series of booklets; annual report

---

[6]
Action for M.E. (AFME)

PO Box 1302
Wells
Somerset BA5 2WE
Telephone: 01749 670799
Fax: 01749 672561
Contact: Anthea Westlake (Office Manager)
Objectives and Purposes: To provide M.E./Post Viral Fatigue Syndrome/Chronic Fatigue Syndrome sufferers with information on self-help, therapies, and the process of medical research; to fund research; to campaign to Government and the medical profession for better understanding and treatment
Stock and Subject Coverage: Various factsheets, books, etc. are available
Services/Facilities: Advice and information for sufferers; list of both sympathetic and unsympathetic doctors and consultants
Availability: Open to anyone. Written enquiries accepted (with large s.a.e.)
Hours: 09.00-17.00
Publications: InterAction (3 per year); free to members or £5 to non-members
Related Bodies: There is a Scottish branch in Edinburgh, and a network of 120 local support groups throughout the UK

---

[7]
Action for Sick Children (NAWCH – National Association for the Welfare of Children in Hospital)

Argyle House
29-31 Euston Road
London NW1 2SD
Telephone: 0171 833 2041
Fax: 0171 837 2110
Contact: Cheryl Hooper (Operations Director); Anne Rivett (Development Director); Kay Hadwick (Librarian)

Objectives and Purposes: To raise the standards of health care for all children, whether in hospital or at home. To provide information and help for parents, professionals, policy makers and all those concerned with the needs and care of sick children
Stock and Subject Coverage: A unique collection of books, articles and reports covering the emotional and psychological needs of sick children and their welfare
Services/Facilities: Photocopies (£1 per article); free advice and information for parents; telephone and written enquiries accepted; visits by appointment; literature searches (£5)
Availability: Open freely to anyone (by appointment) for reference use only.
Hours: 09.00-17.00 Monday to Wednesday (Library staffed Monday-Tuesday)
Publications: 20 Keypoints factsheets and 12 reading lists on child health care; full list available on request

---

[8]
Action for Victims of Medical Accidents (AVMA)

Bank Chambers
1 London Road
Forest Hill
London SE23 3TP
Telephone: 0181 291 2793
Fax: 0181 699 0632
Contact: Arnold Simanowitz (Executive Director); Keith Miles (Assistant Director)
Objectives and Purposes: To assist and advise victims of medical accidents
Availability: Written requests accepted
Hours: 09.00-17.00
Publications: AVMA Medical and Legal Journal (quarterly); range of conference proceedings - list available

---

[9]
Action on Smoking and Health (ASH)

Devon House
12-15 Dartmouth Street
London SW1H 9BL
Telephone: 0171 314 1360
Fax: 0171 222 4343
E-mail: ashuk@ash.org.uk
World Wide Web: http://www.ash.org.uk
Contact: Information Department
Objectives and Purposes: ASH aims to alert the public about the dangers of smoking; to promote policies to discourage it and thereby reduce the level of disease, death and disability that it leads to
Stock and Subject Coverage: Material on tobacco control and related issues
Availability: Personal visits by appointment. Telephone and written enquiries accepted. Reference use only
Hours: 09.30-17.00
Publications: List available

---

[10]

Action on Smoking and Health Scotland (ASH Scotland)

8 Frederick Street
Edinburgh EH2 2HB
Telephone: 0131 225 4725
Fax: 0131 220 6604
E-mail: 101554.267@compuserve.com
Contact: Christine Sheehy (Information Officer); Wendy Ugolini (Assistant Information Officer)
Objectives and Purposes: To promote non-smoking as the norm in society and to keep the tobacco control issue on the public agenda. The Information Service supports this purpose by providing information and advice services on all aspects of smoking and health
Stock and Subject Coverage: Books, periodicals, press cuttings, etc. covering all aspects of smoking and health, with particular reference to Scotland
Services/Facilities: Advice and information on all aspects of smoking
Availability: Telephone and written enquiries accepted from anyone; visits by prior arrangement
Hours: 09.30-14.30
Publications: List available

[11]

AD/HD Family Support Group UK

1a High Street
Dilton Marsh
Westbury
Wiltshire BA13 4DL
Telephone: 01373 826045/01380 726710
Fax: 01373 825158
E-mail: 100131.2050@compuserve.com
Contact: Mrs G Mead; Mr B Tuffill; Mrs B Tuffill
Objectives and Purposes: To raise awareness of Attention Deficit Disorder plus Attention Deficit Hyperactivity Disorder and related disorders. To help sufferers and their families; and to link parents for mutual support
Services/Facilities: Information pack for parents and professionals (s.a.e. required); advice service; visits to schools and other organisations
Availability: No restrictions other than time constraints (staffed entirely by voluntary workers)
Hours: Variable
Publications: Basic information pack; more detailed information for professionals and educationalists
Related Bodies: Contact Parents and Support Groups around the country

[12]

AFASIC – Overcoming Speech Impairments

347 Central Markets
Smithfield
London EC1A 9NH
Telephone: 0171 236 3632/6487
Fax: 0171 236 8115
Contact: Tessa Sambrook (Information Line Manager)
Objectives and Purposes: To provide a support and information service on speech and language impairments for families, sufferers and professionals
Stock and Subject Coverage: Books and leaflets on speech and language impairment
Services: Limited translation service; free telephone helpline for families and sufferers;
Availability: Telephone and written enquiries accepted; limited visiting facilities, by appointment
Hours: 09.00-17.00 (closes 16.00 on Friday)
Publications: AFASIC News (3 per year); full list available on request

[13]

Age Concern Cymru

4th Floor
1 Cathedral Road
Cardiff CF1 9SD
Telephone: 01222 371566
Fax: 01222 399562
E-mail: accymru@ace.org.uk
Contact: Jackie Dix (Policy Officer); Debbie Meehan (Information Officer)
Objectives and Purposes: To improve the lives of older people throughout Wales by promoting positive attitudes and approaches to ageing, ensuring that older people have their needs addressed, their voices heard and that their later life is a fulfilling and enjoyable experience
Stock and Subject Coverage: Wide range of books and leaflets are available covering key aspects of older peoples' lives. List available on request
Services: The library system is being computerised at the time of compilation
Availability: Personal visits by appointment; loans at the Information Officer's discretion
Hours: 09.150-17.30
Publications: Monthly Digest to members; monthly newsletter to Age Concern groups; annual report; various books and leaflets (priced)

[14]

Age Concern England (ACE)

Astral House
1268 London Road
London SW16 4ER
Telephone: 0181 679 8000
Fax: 0181 679 6069
E-mail: wattsc@ace.org.uk
World Wide Web: http://www.ace.org.uk
Contact: Librarian
Objectives and Purposes: To promote the well-being of older people and to help make later life a fulfilling and enjoyable experience; to promote positive attitudes towards older people and ageing; to influence and develop public policies that affect older people; to campaign, provide information and advice, and act as a resource for Age Concern groups

Stock and Subject Coverage: 10,000 books; 164 periodicals covering all aspects of older people, including gerontology; social policy and social welfare. There is a small collection of videos, and a large collection of information files
Services/Facilities: Searches on internal database; photocopies (priced)
Availability: By prior appointment, for reference use only
Hours: 09.15–17.00
Publications: List available on request

[15]
Age Concern Northern Ireland (ACNI)

3 Lower Crescent
Belfast BT1 1NR
Telephone: 01232 245729
Fax: 01232 235497
Contact: James O'Hanlon (Librarian)
Objectives and Purposes: To promote the well-being of older people and help make life a fulfilling and enjoyable experience by all means that respect their rights and dignity
Stock and Subject Coverage: Material on the needs of older people and those who work with them. Includes welfare rights and benefits; social services; housing; heating; and transport
Services/Facilities: Free advice and information for older people; photocopies (at cost, but free to elderly persons). Factsheets and information packs are available. Computerised database
Availability: Telephone and written enquiries; visits by arrangement
Hours: 09.00–17.00 (closes 16.00 on Friday)
Publications: Newsletter; annual report; range of factsheets and briefing papers; books include Your Rights; Your Taxes and Savings; An A-Z Guide to Services; Winter Warmth Guide

[16]
Age Concern Scotland

113 Rose Steet
Edinburgh EH2 3DT
Telephone: 0131 220 3345
Fax: 0131 220 2779
Contact: John Urquhart (Librarian); Lucie McKenzie (Information Officer)
Objectives and Purposes: To support organisations and individuals working with older people by providing information, training and grants; to campaign for improvements in policies and services for older people
Stock and Subject Coverage: Books, periodicals, pamphlets, and audiovisual materials, covering all aspects of age and ageing
Availability: Telephone and written enquiries; visits by appointment. Lending and reference facilities; charge for photocopies
Hours: 09.00–17.00
Publications: List available on request

[17]
Aid for Children with Tracheostomies (ACT)

215A Perry Street
Billericay
Essex CN12 0NZ
Telephone and Fax: 01277 654425
Contact: Mrs Jenny Simmons (Secretary)
Objectives and Purposes: To give encouragement and support to families caring for a child with a tracheostomy; to promote a greater awareness within the community of the needs and problems of children with a tracheostomy. ACT is affiliated to Contact a Family (q.v.) and the Long Term Medical Conditions Alliance
Services/Facilities: Free advice to families and those professionals serving families caring for a child with a tracheostomy. Temporary hire of suction equipment and room humidifiers; holiday caravan for members
Availability: Telephone and written enquiries only
Hours: 09.00–21.00
Publications: Quarterly newsletter; Carers information booklet (£5.50)

[18]
AIDS Education and Research Trust (AVERT)

11-13 Denne Parade
Horsham
West Sussex RH12 1JD
Telephone: 01403 210202
Fax: 01403 211001
E-mail: avert@dial.pipex.com
World Wide Web: http://www.oneworld.org/avert/
Contact: Mrs L Lincoln (Information Officer)
Objectives and Purposes: To prevent people becoming infected with HIV; to work with others towards a cure; to improve the quality of life for those already infected
Stock and Subject Coverage: 800 books; 50 periodicals. Covers all aspects of AIDS and HIV. A file of press cuttings is maintained
Services/Facilities: Reading lists drawn up for various groups, and free information service on AIDS
Availability: Open to anyone for reference use. Written and telephone enquiries are welcome. Visits by appointment
Hours: 09.00–17.00
Publications: Annual report; leaflets; books; reports. List available on request

[19]
Airedale NHS Trust Library and Information Service

Department of Medical Education
Airedale General Hospital
Steeton
Keighley
West Yorkshire BD20 6TD
Telephone: 01535 651042

Fax: 01535 655907
Contact: Mrs Sue Thompson BA (Hons) ALA (Head of Service); Mrs Anne Troth BA (Hons) (Librarian)
Objectives and Purposes: To ensure the provision of quality health care to patients by organising and disseminating a knowledge base to support the education/training/information and R&D needs of the Trust
Stock and Subject Coverage: 8,000 books; 250 periodicals. Covers biomedicine and related fields
Services/Facilities: Database searches (MEDLINE, CINAHL and Cochrane); interlibrary loans; photocopies (charges apply)
Availability: By prior appointment, for reference use only
Hours: 08.30-17.00 (closes 16.00 on Friday)
Publications: Journal holdings list; accessions list; library guide

[20]

Alcohol Concern

Waterbridge House
32-36 Loman Street
London SE1 0EE
Telephone: 0171 928 7377
Fax: 0171 928 4644
E-mail: alccon@popmail.dircon.co.uk
World Wide Web: http://www.alcoholconcern.org.uk
Contact: Librarian or Information Officer
Objectives and Purposes: To reduce the cost of alcohol misuse and to develop the range and quantity of helping services available to problem drinkers and their families
Stock and Subject Coverage: Material covering the full spectrum of alcohol-related subjects including health and social issues, treatment, and workplace and community care
Services/Facilities: Database searches; photocopies (priced)
Availability: By prior appointment, for reference use only; telephone and written enquiries accepted
Hours: 09.30-17.00
Publications: Current awareness bulletin; quarterly information and research bulletin; magazine

[21]

Allergy Induced Autism Support and Research Network – UK (AiA)

3 Palmera Avenue
Calcot
Reading RG31 7DZ
Telephone: 0118 941 9460
Fax: 0118 961 5967
E-mail: autism_aia@piers.demon.co.uk
World Wide Web:
http://www.demon.co.uk/charities/AIA/aia.htm
Contact: Brenda O'Reilly (Director)
Objectives and Purposes: To support families with children with this condition; to initiate research; to disseminate information

Availability: Telephone and written enquiries; open access for researchers; small charge for photocopies if required
Hours: 09.30-15.00
Publications: Quarterly newsletter (£10 pa); information pack for parents (£3); professional information (£3)
Related Bodies: Affiliated to the Hyperactive Children's Support Group

[22]

Alzheimer Scotland – Action on Dementia

8 Hill Street
Edinburgh EH2 3JZ
Telephone: 0131 225 1453
Fax: 0131 225 8748
Contact: Kate Fearnley (Information Officer); Jim Jackson (Executive Director)
Stock and Subject Coverage: Material on all aspects of dementia and caring
Services/Facilities: Free advice and information to people with dementia, their carers and families through a 24-hour helpline on 0800 317817 (Scotland only)
Availability: Library open to members, staff and volunteers. Visits by appointment but staff help may not be available due to lack of resources
Hours: 09.00-17.00
Publications: Dementia in Scotland (quarterly newsletter); annual report; full list available on request
Related Bodies: Network of local branches and service provision projects

[23]

★Alzheimer's Disease Society

Gordon House
10 Greencoat Place
London SW1P 1PH
Telephone: 0171 306 0606
Fax: 0171 306 0808
E-mail: 101762.422@compuserve.com
World Wide Web:
http://www.vois.org.uk/alzheimers/
Contact: Clive Evers (Director, Information and Education); Miss Pia Chowdhury (Librarian)
Objectives and Purposes: The Alzheimer's Disease Society is the leading care and research charity for people with Alzheimer's Disease and other forms of dementia, and their families. It is a national membership organisation and works through nearly 300 branches and support groups. The Society has expertise in information and education for carers and professionals. It provides helplines and support for carers, runs quality day and home care through its Care Consortium, funds medical and scientific research and gives financial help to families in need. It campaigns for improved health and social services and greater public understanding of all aspects of dementia

Stock and Subject Coverage: Material on Alzheimer's
    Disease and other forms of dementia
Availability: By appointment with the Librarian
Hours: 09.00-17.00
Publications: List available on request

[24]
Amersham General Hospital, Staff Library

South Buckinghamshire NHS Trust
Whielden Street
Amersham
Buckinghamshire HP7 0JD
Telephone: 01494 734000
Fax: 01494 734293
E-mail: ju81@cityscape.co.uk
Contact: Ann Flood BA ALA
Objectives and Purposes: To provide, and help in the
    retrieval of, information in the field of health care,
    including mental health
Stock and Subject Coverage: 2,800 books; 75
    periodicals. Covers mental health (main subject),
    general medicine; nursing; and geriatrics
Services/Facilities: Online and CD-ROM searches;
    photocopies; fax; current awareness
Availability: By prior appointment, for reference use
    only
Hours: 09.15-17.00 Monday, Tuesday, Wednesday and
    Friday; 10.00-16.00 Thursday
Related Bodies: Linked to Chiltern Medical Library
    and to Buckinghamshire College of Nursing and
    Midwifery; part of the Anglia and Oxford RHA,
    and HeLIN

Anaesthetic Research Society
see **Stop Press on page 155**

[25]
★Anglia and Oxford RHA (AORHA)

Union Lane
Chesterton
Cambridge CB4 1RF
Telephone: 01223 375375
Fax: 01223 353209
Objectives and Purposes: Health administration,
    monitoring and planning
Stock and Subject Coverage: Collection of
    health-related journals
Availability: Staff only
Hours: 09.00-17.00

[26]
Anglia Polytechnic University

Bishop Hall Lane
Chelmsford
Essex CM1 1SQ
Telephone: 01245 493131
Fax: 01245 495920
World Wide Web: http://www.anglia.ac.uk

Contact: Nicola Kershaw (University Librarian);
    Maurice Wakeham or Simon Beard (Academic
    Liaison Librarians, Health and Social Work)
Objectives and Purposes: To meet the information
    needs of the university
Stock and Subject Coverage: Books, periodicals and
    videos on all aspects of nursing and health care;
    also some social studies, etc.
Availability: By appointment for reference use;
    membership available
Hours: Variable
Related Bodies: 4 "main" sites and 6 nursing libraries

[27]
Appropriate Health Resources and Technologies Action Group (AHRTAG)

Farringdon Point
29-35 Farringdon Road
London EC1M 3JB
Telephone: 0171 242 0606
Fax: 0171 242 0041
E-mail: ahrtag@gn.apc.org; ahrtag@geo2.geonet.de
Contact: Resource Centre Officer
Objectives and Purposes: AHRTAG aims to strengthen
    the management and practice of primary health
    care and community-based rehabilitation by
    maximising the use and impact of information.
    The Group provides technical support and
    training to organisations in developing countries,
    provides an information and enquiry service to
    health and development workers, undertakes small
    research projects, disseminates practical
    information through a publications programme
    and strengthens human resource and institutional
    capacities of organisations supporting primary
    health care
Stock and Subject Coverage: Materials on primary
    health care in developing countries. 19,000 books,
    journals, unpublished reports, slides, videos and
    other reference materials. Also a collection of
    2,000 World Health Organization photographs
Services/Facilities: Resource lists and bibliographies
    can be prepared. Written enquiries from
    developing countries are dealt with. Reference use
    only. AHRTAG bibliographic database available
    online via the Internet
Availability: Visitors by appointment 10.00-17.00
    Monday, Wednesday and Friday. Membership
    available
Publications: Various newsletters; free international
    newsletters; range of directories, booklets and
    resource lists; AHRTAG Update

[28]
Arthritis and Rheumatism Council (ARC)

Copeman House
St Mary's Court
Chesterfield
Derbyshire S41 7TD
Telephone: 01246 558033

Fax: 01246 558007
Contact: Dr Madeleine Devey (Scientific Secretary);
Mr James Norton (Chief Executive);
Mr Keir Windsor (Education Officer)
Objectives and Purposes: To fund research into rheumatic diseases, and to promote a better understanding of these diseases
Availability: Telephone and written enquiries as time permits; but no visits
Hours: 09.00-17.00
Publications: Arthritis Today (3 per year); Reports on Rheumatic Diseases (3 per year, for medical professionals); annual report; annual scientific report; medical student handbook; range of booklets, leaflets, teaching slides and conference proceedings. List available (s.a.e. required)
Related Bodies: ARC is the parent body of the Kennedy Institute for Rheumatology in London, and the Epidemiology Research Unit in Manchester; there is a trading and distribution warehouse, ARC Trading, in Newark

---

[29]

Arthritis Care

18 Stephenson Way
London NW1 2HD
Telephone: 0171 916 1500
Fax: 0171 916 1505
Contact: Cathy Irving (Information Officer)
Objectives and Purposes: Works with and for all people with arthritis; aims to promote their health, well-being and independence through services, support, self-help, campaigning and information
Stock and Subject Coverage: Books, periodicals, leaflets and factsheets covering all aspects of arthritis, including therapies, daily living, benefits, equipment and pain management
Services/Facilities: Free confidential support and information to people with arthritis, their friends, relatives and carers
Availability: Telephone and written enquiries; visits restricted, and by appointment only
Hours: 10.00-16.00 (Freephone helpline 12.00-16.00 on 0800 289170)
Publications: Wide range - list available

---

[30]

Ashford Hospital Medical and Health Care Library

London Road
Ashford
Middlesex TW15 3AA
Telephone: 01784 884370/884343
Fax: 01784 884815
E-mail: sandrawatt@ashlib.demon.co.uk
Contact: Sandra Watt (Health Sciences Librarian)
Objectives and Purposes: To contribute to the quality of health care by ensuring that all NHS staff have access to, and help in making use of, the knowledge and information base of health care

Stock and Subject Coverage: Books and periodicals covering medicine; surgery; nursing; and health care management
Services/Facilities: Online and CD-ROM searches; photocopies; word processing; literature searches; current awareness service; interlibrary loans. Charges for British Library requests
Availability: Telephone and written enquiries; visits by appointment
Hours: 09.00-17.00 (24-hour access for key-holders)
Publications: Monthly current awareness bulletins

---

[31]

Association for Continence Advice (ACA)

Winchester House
Kennington Park
Cranmer Road
The Oval
London SW9 6EJ
Telephone: 0171 820 8119
Fax: 0171 820 0442
Contact: Deborah Dawkins (Administrator)
Objectives and Purposes: To provide a means of communication and support between members and other interested groups; to promote educational activities; to promote research and disseminate the results; to liaise and maintain dialogue with relevant manufacturers; to promote public awareness and positive attitudes within society
Availability: Written and telephone enquiries. Members may visit by appointment
Hours: 09.00-17.00
Publications: Quarterly newsletter; bi-monthly journal; annual report
Related Bodies: ACA is affiliated to the Continence Foundation

---

[32]

Association for Glycogen Storage Disease, UK (AGSD(UK))

9 Lindop Road
Hale
Altrincham
Cheshire WA15 9DZ
Telephone: 0161 276 3323; after 18.00: 0161 980 7303
Fax: 0161 226 3813
E-mail: ae314@dial.pipex.com
World Wide Web: http://www.compulink.co.uk/nembra/agsdhome.html
Contact: Ann Phillips (President and Co-Founder)
Objectives and Purposes: A family contact and support group for all persons affected by GSD; it aims to encourage the provision of specialist centres for the diagnosis, monitoring and treatment of GSD and to act as a focus for scientific, educational and charitable activities concerning GSD
Publications: List available

---

[33]

Association for Post Natal Illness (APNI)

25 Jerdan Place
Fulham
London SW6 1BE
Telephone: 0171 386 0868
Fax: 0171 386 8885
Objectives and Purposes: Provides information, advice and support to women suffering from post natal illness. There is a network of volunteers (past sufferers) who offer telephone support, and the association offers specialist information to health professionals
Availability: Written and telephone enquiries only
Hours: 10.00-17.00 (answerphone at other times)
Publications: Newsletter (3 per year); various leaflets and booklets

[34]

Association for the Study of Obesity (ASO)

20 Brook Meadow Close
Woodford Green
Essex IG8 9NR
Telephone and Fax: 0181 503 2042
Contact: Mrs C Hawkins; Professor I Macdonald (Chairman); Mrs H Rose (Secretary/Treasurer)
Objectives and Purposes: To promote medical research into the causes, prevention and treatment of obesity. To facilitate contact between individuals and organisations interested in any aspect of the problem of obesity and body weight regulation. ASO is a member organisation of the International Association for the Study of Obesity
Availability: Telephone and written enquiries
Hours: 09.00-17.00
Publications: Newsletter for members
Related Bodies: Member of the International Association for the Study of Obesity

[35]

Association of Anaesthetists of Great Britain and Ireland (AAGBI)

incorporating the British Journal of Anaesthesia Library (BJA Library) and the British Oxygen Company Museum (BOC Museum)

9 Bedford Square
London WC1B 3RA
Telephone: 0171 631 1650
Fax: 0171 631 4352
E-mail: 100567.3364@compuserve.com
Contact: Dr Anna-Maria Rollin (Hon. Curator); Dr DJ Wilkinson (Hon. Archivist); Dr I McLellan and Dr N Adams (Hon. Librarians)

Objectives and Purposes: The Association exists to promote progress and safety in the practice of anaesthesia by seeking to improve the expertise, training and status of anaesthetists. The headquarters of the Association houses the BJA Library and the BOC Museum, which together constitute a resource base on the history of anaesthesia
Stock and Subject Coverage: The Library houses over 1,000 books, articles and technical literature, 300 films, and 700 photographs/slides covering all aspects of the history of anaesthesia. There is also a small archive of the history of the Association. The museum comprises a collection of historical anaesthetic apparatus. The display is changed annually. It is based on the original collection of Charles King but has been greatly increased by donations and purchases in recent years
Services/Facilities: Information on all the collections is maintained in an internal database. Free advice and information is given to enquirers. Materials are not generally available for loan. Photocopies; fax
Availability: Open to members; non-members by appointment
Hours: 09.30-17.00
Publications: Journal (Anaesthesia); annual report. Full list available
Related Bodies: The Association houses the BJA Library and the BOC Museum, which together constitute a resource base on the history of anaesthesia

[36]

Association of British Health Care Industries (ABHI)

St Georges House
195-203 Waterloo Road
London SE1 8WD
Telephone: 0171 787 3069
Fax: 0171 787 3061
Contact: Gordon Aylward (Director General); Michael Kreuzer (Technical Director); David Mackenzie (International Executive)
Objectives and Purposes: To serve the medical systems industry and to provide a health care forum for the industry, government the professions and others involved in the future of health care
Stock and Subject Coverage: Material on regulatory/technical topics relating to medical devices, export markets and NHS matters
Services/Facilities: Photocopies; fax (charges apply)
Availability: By prior appointment for reference use only
Hours: 09.00-17.00
Publications: Various newsletters; yearbook and directory

[37]

Association of Clinical Biochemists (ACB)

2 Carlton House Terrace
London SW1Y 5AF
Telephone: 0171 930 3333
Fax: 0171 930 3553
E-mail: 100673.3340@compuserve.com
World Wide Web:
  http://www.acb.wcl.bham.ac.uk/ACB/
Contact: Hilary Crosweller (Senior Administrator)
Objectives and Purposes: A professional body
  dedicated to the practice and promotion of
  clinical science. It has members, medical and
  non-medical, in district, general and teaching
  hospitals. It is consulted by government health
  departments and many other organisations
Hours: 09.30-17.00
Publications: Details available on request

[38]

Association of Clinical Pathologists (ACP)

221 Preston Road
Preston Old Village
Brighton BN1 6SA
Telephone: 01273 561188
Fax: 01273 541227
E-mail: admin@pathologists.org.uk
World Wide Web: http://www.pathologists.org.uk/
Contact: Mrs Jeanette Turner (General Secretary)
Objectives and Purposes: To promote and encourage
  the study and practice of clinical pathology
Stock and Subject Coverage: Archive material only
  relating to the history of pathology, and of the
  Association
Availability: By prior appointment, for reference use
  only; telephone, fax and written enquiries accepted
Hours: 09.00-17.30
Publications: Journal of Clinical Pathology (monthly);
  newsletter (3 per year); annual report; Programme
  of Postgraduate Education (annual)
Related Bodies: A network of local branches

[39]

Association of Community Health Councils for England and Wales (ACHCEW)

Earlsmead House
30 Drayton Park
London N5 1PB
Telephone: 0171 609 8405
Fax: 0171 700 1152
Contact: Information Officers
Objectives and Purposes: To provide information and
  advisory services to Community Health Councils
  and to represent the user of the health service at a
  national level

Stock and Subject Coverage: Material on health issues
  with a consumer perspective
Availability: Telephone and written enquiries; visits
  by appointment
Hours: By appointment
Publications: Various - list available
Related Bodies: 203 member councils

[40]

Association of Disabled Professionals (ADP)

170 Benton Hill
Wakefield Road
Horbury
West Yorkshire WF4 5HW
Telephone and Fax: 01924 283253; Minicom:
  01924 270335
E-mail: 76721.2160@compuserve.com
Contact: Sue Maynard-Campbell (Chairman)
Objectives and Purposes: The Association aims to
  improve the education, training and employment
  opportunities available to disabled people
Stock and Subject Coverage: Material on all aspects of
  disability, with special emphasis on employment
Availability: Telephone and written enquiries
Hours: 24-hour answerphone facility
Publications: Quarterly journal for members; annual
  report; leaflet

[41]

Association of Medical Research Charities (AMRC)

29-35 Farringdon Road
London EC1M 3JB
Telephone: 0171 404 6454
Fax: 0171 404 6448
E-mail: amrc@mailbox.ulcc.ac.uk
World Wide Web: http://www.amrc.org.uk
Contact: Diana Garnham (General Secretary)
Objectives and Purposes: To further medical research
  in the UK generally, and in particular the
  advancement of the effectiveness of these charities;
  to represent members collectively (currently 90
  charities are members)
Services/Facilities: General information on the charity
  sector in medical research
Availability: Open to member charities; others by
  written application
Hours: 09.30-17.30
Publications: AMRC Handbook (annual)

Association of Optometrists
see **Stop Press on page 155**

[42]
Association of Reflexologists

27 Old Gloucester Street
London WC1N 3XX
Telephone: 0990 673320
Contact: Geoffrey Woodward (Administrator)
World Wide Web: http://www.reflexology.org/aor/
Objectives and Purposes: To support members needs, and to provide information on reflexology to the public. Maintains a Register of Qualified Practitioners. Collaborates with other organisations in complementary medicine
Stock and Subject Coverage: Database of research projects (priced); database of case studies; files of press cuttings
Services/Facilities: Educational workshops and seminars for members; free information and advice to the public; information packs for nurses, students, researchers, etc.; offprints service (priced)
Availability: Telephone and written enquiries
Hours: 09.00-17.00
Publications: Quarterly journal; information leaflets; special subject leaflets; annual report; Register of Qualified Practitioners (3 per year); List of Accredited Practitioner Courses; Curriculum for a Practitioners Course
Related Bodies: International Council of Reflexologists; Reflexology in Europe Group; Parliamentary Group for Alternative and Complementary Medicine; network of regional branches

[43]
Association of the British Pharmaceutical Industry (ABPI)

12 Whitehall
London SW1A 2DY
Telephone: 0171 930 3477
Fax: 0171 747 1411
Contact: Miss Janet Ogleby (Librarian), ext 1441; Mrs Gail Turner (Health Industry Information Officer), ext 1471
Objectives and Purposes: Trade association for manufacturers of prescription medicines in the UK
Stock and Subject Coverage: Joint library between ABPI and the Office of Health Economics; ca. 600 books and 130 periodicals covering economics, general medicine, health care and pharmacy. Enquiries on pharmaceutical industry issues should be directed to the Health Industry Information Officer
Services/Facilities: Interlibrary loans; photocopies
Availability: Enquiries from other libraries welcome; loans only through libraries
Hours: 08.30-16.30
Publications: Details through the Publications Department - not the library
Related Bodies: Supports the Office of Health Economics and the Animals in Medicines Research Information Centre

[44]
Association of Welsh Health Librarians (AWHL)

The Library
Glan Clwyd DGH NHS Trust
Bodelwyddan
Rhyl
Denbighshire LL18 5UY
Telephone: 01745 583910, ext 4882
Fax: 01745 534938
Contact: Miss Nia Morris (Secretary)
Objectives and Purposes: To provide a co-operative and supportive network amongst all health librarians in Wales. Training and educational events/courses regularly organised
Availability: Membership open to all library service staff in any Welsh 'health' library
Publications: Newsletter; Union List of Periodicals

[45]
Avon Health Promotion

Central Health Clinic
Tower Hill
Bristol BS2 0JP
Telephone: 0117 929 1010
Fax: 0117 975 0607
Contact: Angelica Anderson (Information Manager)
Objectives and Purposes: Health promotion within the area served by Avon Health Commission
Stock and Subject Coverage: Books, videos, teaching packs, cassettes, models and equipment covering all aspects of health promotion
Services/Facilities: Telephone and written enquiries accepted; visits by appointment
Hours: 08.00-17.00 (closes 12.30 Wednesday and 16.00 Friday)
Publications: Health Promotion News; Sexual Health News
Related Bodies: Member of SWHESLinc and SWRLIN

[46]
Aylesbury Vale Healthcare (AVH)

Mental Health Services Library
Tindal Centre
Bierton Road
Aylesbury
Buckinghamshire HP20 1HU
Telephone: 01296 393363
Fax: 01296 399332
E-mail: ju75@cityscape.co.uk
Contact: Mrs Valerie Cahill (Librarian); Mrs Linda Brennan (Library Assistant)
Objectives and Purposes: To provide library and information services for Aylesbury Vale Healthcare Trust
Stock and Subject Coverage: 3,000 books; 66 periodicals. Covers psychiatry; mental health; mental handicap; and learning disabilities
Services/Facilities: Photocopies; CD-ROM searches; Internet access

Availability: Telephone and written enquiries accepted; visits by prior arrangement
Hours: 08.30-13.00 (open until 15.30 on Monday and Tuesday)
Publications: Library News; quarterly current awareness service

[47]

Barnsley District General Hospital NHS Trust, Staff Library

Education Centre
Gawber Road
Barnsley S75 2EP
Telephone: 01226 730000, ext 2653
Contact: Mrs RC Merrill (Librarian)
Objectives and Purposes: To promote and support the educational needs of employees of Barnsley Health Authority
Stock and Subject Coverage: 11,000 books; 140 periodicals; 150 videos. Covers medicine and nursing
Services/Facilities: CD-ROM searches; fax; photocopies
Availability: By prior appointment, for reference use only
Hours: 08.30-20.00 (closes 16.30 on Tuesday and Friday)
Publications: Quarterly newsletter
Related Bodies: Partly run by the University of Sheffield

[48]

Beatson Oncology Centre

Western Infirmary
Glasgow G11 6NT
Telephone: 0141 211 1917
Fax: 0141 337 1712
E-mail: gpra08@udcf.gla.ac.uk
Contact: Annette Thain (Librarian)
Objectives and Purposes: Cancer treatment. Part of the Department of Radiation Oncology, University of Glasgow, Western Infirmary, Glasgow
Stock and Subject Coverage: 40 current journal titles covering oncology; radiotherapy; chemotherapy; and cancer nursing. Book stock of about 750 items
Services/Facilities: Photocopying; CD-ROM workstation with MEDLINE; Online searching for university staff
Availability: Reference only, charges for photocopies and interlibrary loans for non BOC staff
Hours: 09.15-13.15

[49]

Bedford Medical Institute

Bedford Hospital NHS Trust
Ampthill Road
Bedford MK42 9DJ
Telephone: 01234 792114
Fax: 01234 792127
E-mail: er75@cityscape.co.uk

Contact: Mrs Yvette de Souza (Librarian)
Objectives and Purposes: A library and information service to support postgraduate medical and dental education and to provide for the library and information needs of hospital medical staff
Stock and Subject Coverage: 2,000 books; 100 periodicals; MEDLINE on CD-ROM; online access to DataStar
Services/Facilities: Photocopies; literature searches; current awareness service; Internet access (services are priced)
Availability: Telephone and written enquiries
Hours: 08.00-16.00
Publications: Annual report

[50]

Bell College of Technology, School of Nursing and Midwifery

Dumfries Campus
Crichton Hall
Glencaple Road
Dumfries DG1 4SG
Telephone: 01387 244063
Fax: 01387 265938
E-mail: gl55@dial.pipex.com
Contact: AC Little (Associate Dean); J Anderson (Campus Librarian)
Objectives and Purposes: To support nurse education
Stock and Subject Coverage: Material on nursing and allied health
Services/Facilities: CD-ROM searches; interlibrary loans; photocopies (priced)
Availability: By prior appointment, for reference use only
Hours: 08.30-19.30

[51]

Bio Products Laboratory (BPL)

Dagger Lane
Elstree
Hertfordshire WD6 3BX
Telephone: 0181 905 1818
Fax: 0181 207 4824
E-mail: lb20972@bpl.co.uk
Contact: Mrs Lorna Brook (Librarian)
Objectives and Purposes: To manufacture therapeutic products from donated blood plasma and to carry out research into improving them. BPL is part of the National Blood Authority
Stock and Subject Coverage: Ca. 2,200 books; 97 periodicals. Covers haematology; immunology, and allied subjects. An internal database of articles is maintained, and there is a press cuttings file
Services/Facilities: Photocopies (priced); CD-ROM searches
Availability: By appointment
Hours: 09.00-17.00 (closes 16.15 on Friday)
Publications: Annual report; National Blood Update (newsletter)

[52]

Birmingham Children's Hospital NHS Trust

Ladywood Middleway
Birmingham B16 8ET
Telephone: 0121 450 6612
Fax: 0121 455 7389
E-mail: medlib.bch@dial.pipex.com
Contact: Mrs Ursula Ison ALA (Medical Librarian);
Mrs Gloria James (Library Assistant)
Objectives and Purposes: To provide library and
information services to staff of the Trust
Stock and Subject Coverage: 3,000 books; 200
periodicals. Covers medicine, with an emphasis on
paediatrics
Services/Facilities: MEDLINE searches; photocopies
(priced)
Availability: By prior appointment, for reference use
only
Hours: 09.00–17.00

[53]

Birth Control Trust (BCT)

3rd Floor
16 Mortimer Street
London W1N 7RD
Telephone: 0171 580 9360
Fax: 0171 637 1378
E-mail: bct@birthcontroltrust.org.uk
Contact: David Nolan (Information Officer);
Ann Furedi (Director)
Objectives and Purposes: To provide legal, medical and
sociological information on contraception and
abortion for the public, the media, health
professionals, policy makers and parliamentarians
Stock and Subject Coverage: BCT administers the
Pamela Sheridan Resource Centre which contains
statistical, medical, social, demographic and
parliamentary material on abortion (including a
unique collection of parliamentary references),
alongside a collection of literature from the library
of abortion pioneer Alice Jenkins. BCT also has
anti-Choice material (mainly UK and USA), and
an historical survey of material on abortion
Services/Facilities: Free advice; use of Resource Centre
Availability: By prior appointment, for reference use
only (charges for large amounts of photocopying)
Hours: 09.30–17.30
Publications: Abortion Review (quarterly); periodic
briefings; various books and pamphlets

[54]

Blackburn, Hyndburn and Ribble Valley Healthcare NHS Trust (BHRV Healthcare NHS Trust)

Education Centre Library
Royal Infirmary
Blackburn
Lancashire BB2 3LR
Telephone: 01254 294308
Fax: 01254 687306

Contact: Mrs C Riley (District Librarian)
Objectives and Purposes: To support the staff of BHRV
Healthcare NHS Trust with book loans and
information facilities to meet their clinical and
educational needs
Stock and Subject Coverage: 7,000 books; 120
periodicals. Covers all aspects of health, social
welfare and medicine
Services/Facilities: CD-ROM searches; photocopies;
fax
Availability: To staff and other local health service
employees. Telephone and written enquiries.
Loans to members only
Hours: 08.30–16.00
Publications: Bi-monthly bulletin

[55]

Bradford University, Health Studies Library·

Unity Building
25 Trinity Road
Bradford BD5 0JJ
Telephone: 01274 386370
E-mail: name@bradford.ac.uk
Contact: Angela Hornby; Diane Kearns (Subject
Specialists)
Objectives and Purposes: To provide library and
information services to Bradford University
students and local NHS staff
Stock and Subject Coverage: 15,000 books; 200
periodicals covering all aspects of health care,
especially nursing; also covers radiography,
physiotherapy and related management studies
Availability: By prior appointment, for reference use
only
Hours: 08.30–19.00
Related Bodies: Part of University of Bradford

[56]

Breast Cancer Care

Kiln House
210 New Kings Road
London SW6 4NZ
Telephone: 0171 384 2984 (administration);
Helpline: 0171 384 23444;
Nationwide Freeline: 0500 245345
Fax: 0171 384 33873
Contact: Samia Al Qadhi (Director); Jan Murray
(Direct Services Manager)
Objectives and Purposes: To offer practical help,
medical information and emotional support to
women who have, or fear they have, breast cancer
or benign breast disease; to offer support to
families, partners and friends
Services/Facilities: Helplines; free leaflets; a prosthesis
fitting service; one-to-one emotional support
from volunteers who have themselves experienced
breast cancer; partner volunteer service; younger
women's network
Availability: Open to all sufferers
Hours: 09.00–17.00 (helpline 09.30–16.30; closes
16.00 on Friday)

Publications: Various - list available
Related Bodies: Cancer Relief MacMillan Fund;
branch offices in Glasgow, Edinburgh and Leeds

[57]
Breast Cancer Care, Glasgow

Suite 2/8
65 Bath Street
Glasgow G2 2BX
Telephone: 0141 353 0539; Helpline: 0500 245 345
Fax: 0141 353 0603
E-mail: 106226.167@compuserve.com
Contact: Fiona Sandford (Scottish Co-ordinator)
Objectives and Purposes: Breast Cancer Care is the
national charity which provides information and
support to anyone affected by breast cancer
Stock and Subject Coverage: A wide range of
internally-produced literature which covers most
aspects of breast disease for use by the general
public. Also holds copies of many breast cancer
papers for reference use
Services/Facilities: Freeline, free prosthesis fitting
service and a nationwide network of trained
volunteers with personal experience of breast
cancer. We also produce a wide range of literature
Availability: Prosthesis service is by appointment only.
The helpline is open Monday-Friday, 09.30 to
16.00. Answering machine at all other times. All
services are accessed via the helpline. Literature is
free to the public, but charged to health
professionals. Discounts on bulk orders
Hours: 09.30-16.00
Publications: List and order form available on request
Related Bodies: This is the Scottish section of a
national organisation. Breast Cancer Care's head
office is located in Kiln House, 210 New Kings
Road, London SW6 4NZ (q.v.)

[58]
Bridgend Postgraduate Medical Centre Library

Princess of Wales Hospital
Coity Road
Bridgend
Glamorgan CF31 1RQ
Telephone and Fax: 01656 752532
Contact: Barbara L Paullada (Medical Librarian);
Mr P Rawle (Librarian)
Objectives and Purposes: To provide a library service
for all staff in the Princess of Wales Hospital and
the Bridgend General Hospital, as well as for local
GPs and community health staff
Stock and Subject Coverage: Material covering all
aspects of medicine and related topics
Availability: Restricted to identified users. Telephone
and written enquiries. Material available for
reference or loan
Hours: Permanently open; staffed 09.00-17.00
Related Bodies: AWHILES; PLCS

[59]
BRIDGES

c/o Margot Carne (Chairperson)
23 Chigwell Park Drive
Chigwell
Essex IG7 5BD
Telephone: 0181 281 1454
Objectives and Purposes: To identify issues and
promote policies which will contribute to
effective services and a high quality of life
for people with learning disabilities, and their
families
Stock and Subject Coverage: Material on all aspects of
learning disabilities
Services/Facilities: Free information supplied to
enquirers, and assistance in locating information
that is not held within the charity's own resources
Availability: Written and telephone enquiries only
Hours: 09.00-17.00
Publications: Bi-annual newsletter; book list available
on request

[60]
Bristol Royal Infirmary

Postgraduate Library
Bristol
BS2 8HW
Telephone: 0117 928 2043
Fax: 0117 928 2192
E-mail: postgrad-lib@bbcnc.org.uk
Contact: Chrissy Jones (Library & Information
Services Manager); Jason Ovens (Deputy Librarian)
Objectives and Purposes: To contribute to the quality
of health care by assisting our staff
Stock and Subject Coverage: Multidisciplinary health
care, including a good management collection.
Ophthalmology and oncology at relevant
branches. PILLS (Patient Information, Leaflet and
Literature Service)
Services/Facilities: Photocopies; CD-ROM searches -
help available when needed; word processing;
ADAM; microfiche; video; Internet access
Availability: Full access to staff of United Bristol
Healthcare NHS Trust. Others for reference use
only at the Librarian's discretion
Hours: 09.00-17.00
Publications: User Guide; Guide to PILLS; quarterly
reports; new book list (monthly)
Related Bodies: Branches at Bristol General Hospital,
Bristol Eye Hospital, St Michael's Hospital,
Barrow Hospital & Bristol Oncology Centre

[61]
British Acupuncture Association and Register (BAAR)

34 Alderney Street
London SW1V 4EU
Telephone: 0171 834 1012

Contact: Dr AC Cecil Chen (Hon. President)
Objectives and Purposes: Holds seminars for members; aids in devising acupuncture curricula; participates in research; conducts a charitable programme; operates a speakers bureau; maintains a library and archive. Related to the British Acupuncture Council (formerly the Council for Acupuncture)
Stock and Subject Coverage: Library held by British Acupuncture College, 8 Hunter Street, London WC1N 1BN (Tel: 0171 833 8164)
Availability: To College personnel only
Publications: Handbook, with list of members
Related Bodies: Council for Acupuncture

[62]
British Acupuncture Council (BAcC)

Park House
206–208 Latimer Road
London W10 6RE
Telephone: 0181 964 0222
Fax: 0181 964 0333
Contact: The Secretary
Objectives and Purposes: Acts as a forum for five associations, which include The British Acupuncture Association and Register, The Chung San Acupuncture Society, The International Register of Oriental Medicine, The Register of Traditional Chinese Medicine, and The Traditional Acupuncture Society. Together they work to maintain common standards of education, ethics, discipline and codes of practice and to promote research
Availability: Telephone and written enquiries only
Hours: Staffed on Tuesday and Thursday (may vary)
Publications: Register of Practitioner Members (£3.50); booklet on CFA

[63]
British Association for Cancer Research (BACR)

20 Queensberry Place
London SW7 2DZ
Telephone: 0171 581 8333
Fax: 0171 823 9409
E-mail: info@iob.primex.ac.uk
World Wide Web:
   http://www.icr.ac.uk/bacr/home.htm
Contact: Ms Barbara Cavilla
Objectives and Purposes: To promote the advance of research in relation to all aspects of cancer and to encourage the exchange of information
Publications: The British Journal of Cancer

[64]
British Association in Forensic Medicine (BAFM)

Department of Forensic Medicine
Medico-Legal Centre
Watery Street
Sheffield S3 7ES
Telephone: 01142 738721
Fax: 01142 798942
E-mail: p.howson@sheffield.ac.uk
Contact: Dr John Clark (Secretary)
Objectives and Purposes: To advance the study and practice of forensic medicine and to act as a negotiating and advisory body
Stock and Subject Coverage: No library service, but the Association can advise on likely sources of material
Availability: Telephone and written enquiries
Hours: 09.00–17.00
Publications: List of members; constitution

[65]
British Association of Aesthetic Plastic Surgeons (BAAPS)

Royal College of Surgeons
Lincoln's Inn Fields
London WC2A 3PN
Telephone: 0171 405 2234
Fax: 0171 430 1840
Contact: Julia Martin (Administrative Secretary)
Subject Coverage: Factsheets on aesthetic procedures; list of members; basic information for GPs and members of the public
Publications: Membership booklet and factsheets available to anyone (send s.a.e.)

[66]
British Association of Cancer United Patients and Their Families and Friends (BACUP)

3 Bath Place
Rivington Street
London EC2A 3JR
Telephone: 0171 696 9003
Fax: 0171 696 9002
Contact: Frances Bennet (Librarian)
Objectives and Purposes: To offer information and support on all aspects of cancer through a telephone information service, a counselling service and a variety of publications
Services/Facilities: A computerised directory and a library of resources are used by specially trained cancer nurses to provide information to anyone who enquires about treatment, research, support groups, therapists, counsellors, financial assistance, insurance, home nursing services and much more
Availability: Only to cancer sufferers and their families/friends
Hours: 09.00–17.30

Publications: BACUP News (3 per year);
    Understanding Cancer (series of over 50
    booklets); annual report

[67]
★British Association of Dermatologists (BAD)

3 St Andrew's Place
Regents Park
London NW1 4LB
Telephone: 0171 935 8576
Fax: 0171 224 0321
Contact: Dr RA Marsden (Hon. Secretary);
    Michelle Hardwicke (Chief Administrative Officer)
Objectives and Purposes: A professional body formed
    to promote and represent the best interests of
    dermatologists and patients affected by diseases of
    the skin. It promotes greater knowledge and
    understanding of the condition and aims to
    improve the teaching of dermatology, to
    encourage research, and to disseminate the results
Availability: Telephone and written enquiries
Hours: 09.00-17.30
Publications: British Journal of Dermatology
    (monthly)

[68]
★British Association of Oral and Maxillofacial Surgeons (BAOMS)

The Royal College of Surgeons of England
35-43 Lincoln's Inn Fields
London WC2A 3PN
Telephone: 0171 405 8074
Fax: 0171 430 9997
Objectives and Purposes: To promote the advancement
    of education and research in oral and maxillofacial
    surgery in the British Isles
Publications: British Journal of Oral and Maxillofacial
    Surgery (6 per year)

[69]
British Association of Otorhinolaryngologists - Head and Neck Surgeons (BAO-HNS)

Royal College of Surgeons
35-43 Lincoln's Inn Fields
London WC2A 3PN
Telephone: 0171 404 8373
Fax: 0171 404 4200
Contact: Barbara Komoniewska BA (Administrative
    Secretary)
Objectives and Purposes: The British Association of
    Otorhinolaryngologists - Head and Neck
    Surgeons aims to promote the highest quality and
    standards of medical and surgical practice of the
    specialty for the benefit of patients and to
    encourage future advancement through education,
    research and audit. It is the only body which
    represents fully the views of Members of the
    Specialty within the United Kingdom.

Hours: 09.30-17.30 Monday to Thursday
Publications: Clinical Otolaryngology (6 per year);
    Newsletter (6 per year); annual report;
    membership list and constitution

[70]
British Association of Pharmaceutical Physicians (BrAPP)

1 Wimpole Street
London W1M 8AE
Telephone: 0171 491 8610
Fax: 0171 499 2405
Contact: Mrs Elizabeth Borg (Administrator)
Objectives and Purposes: A professional and medical
    association for physicians working in or on behalf
    of the pharmaceutical industry
Hours: 09.00-17.00
Publications: Pharmaceutical Physician (bi-monthly)

[71]
★British Association of Psychotherapists (BAP)

37 Mapesbury Road
London NW2 4HJ
Telephone: 0181 452 9823
Fax: 0181 452 5182
Contact: Linda Farley (Librarian)
Objectives and Purposes: To promote the knowledge
    and application of psychotherapy and the training
    and competence of psychotherapists
Stock and Subject Coverage: 2,000 books; 14
    periodicals; some audiovisual tapes and videos
    covering psychoanalytic psychotherapy; analytical
    psychology; and child psychotherapy
Services/Facilities: In-house literature searches; fax;
    photocopies
Availability: By prior appointment, for reference use
    only; external membership (priced) is possible
Hours: 09.15-17.00

[72]
British Association of Urological Surgeons (BAUS)

Royal College of Surgeons
35-43 Lincoln's Inn Fields
London WC2A 3PN
Telephone: 0171 405 1390
Fax: 0171 404 5048
Contact: Mrs Patricia Neville (Administrative
    Secretary)
Objectives and Purposes: To promote a high standard
    in the practice of urology
Availability: Through the Royal College of Surgeons
    Library
Hours: 09.00-17.00
Publications: Handbook for members; Handbook of
    Hospitals and Urological Departments

[73]

British Chiropody and Podiatry Association (BChA)

The New Hall
149 Bath Road
Maidenhead
Berkshire SL6 4LA
Telephone: 01628 32440
Fax: 01628 74483
E-mail: 106033.354@compuserve.com
World Wide Web: http://ourworld.compuserve.com/
    homepages/SMAE_INSTITUTE
Contact: MJ Batt (Hon. President - 01628 324440);
    MG Paynton (Chairman - 01295 273073)
Objectives and Purposes: Professional body
    representing over 10,000 members; to ensure high
    standards and to ensure that members are
    professionally insured
Stock and Subject Coverage: Factsheets on medical and
    surgical procedures in foot health, including
    chiropody; podiatry; physiotherapy; and osteopathy
Availability: Personal visits by appointment
Hours: 09.00-17.00
Publications: The SMAE Journal

[74]

British Colostomy Association (BCA)

15 Station Road
Reading RG1 1LG
Telephone: 0118 939 1537
Fax: 0118 956 9095
Contact: Mrs Olivia Reed (Association Secretary);
    Mrs Cathy Richards (Director of Services)
Objectives and Purposes: To help anyone who is about
    to have, or who has already had, a colostomy by
    providing advice, help or comfort from someone
    who has had the experience and has training in
    how to assist others
Stock and Subject Coverage: Booklets, leaflets, tapes
    and videos relating to all aspects of day to day
    living with a colostomy. Other helpful
    information (e.g. photocopied articles)
Availability: Available to anyone with an interest in
    stoma care or bowel cancer - students, nurses,
    researchers, etc.
Hours: 09.00-15.30 (closes 15.00 on Friday)
Publications: Range of booklets and leaflets
Related Bodies: Associated charity of the Cancer
    Relief MacMillan Fund

[75]

British Deaf Association, Health Promotion Services (BDA)

17 Macon Court
Herald Drive
Crewe
Cheshire CW1 1EA
Telephone: 01270 250736; Minicom: 01270 250743
Fax: 01270 250742

Contact: Michelle Simpson (Senior Health
    Promotion Adviser)
Objectives and Purposes: The promotion of and
    fostering of access to health promotion resources
    and primary health care facilities for deaf people
    and hard-of-hearing people in the UK
Stock and Subject Coverage: Collection of materials
    (including videos in BSL, with voiceover and
    subtitles) covering HIV/AIDS; well men and
    women; and alcohol awareness
Services/Facilities: Interpreters
Availability: Videos available for loan
Hours: 09.00-17.00 (Helpline 19.00-22.00 on
    Wednesday)
Publications: Newsletter; quarterly reports

[76]

British Dental Association (BDA)

64 Wimpole Street
London W1M 8AL
Telephone: 0171 935 0875
Fax: 0171 935 6492
E-mail: bdainfo@mailbox.ulcc.ac.uk
Contact: Roger Farbey (Information Centre
    Manager); Miss Helen Nield (Senior Information
    Officer)
Objectives and Purposes: The BDA is the national
    professional association for dentists. Its purpose is
    to promote the interests of dentists; to advance the
    science, arts and ethics of dentistry; and to
    improve the nation's oral health
Stock and Subject Coverage: Ca. 13,000 books; 200
    current periodicals. Covers clinical dentistry, oral
    health and oral surgery. In addition there are a
    number of packages consisting of recent journal
    articles on over 500 dental topics, and a rapidly
    expanding collection of slides and videos
Services/Facilities: MEDLINE searches; photocopies
    (priced). There is a multimedia room and
    computer-assisted learning facilities
Availability: Freely available to members; bona fide
    researchers by appointment; telephone and
    written enquiries accepted; reference facilities, and
    loans to members, are free
Hours: 09.00-18.00
Publications: Guide to Oral Health Libraries and
    Dental Collections

[77]

British Diabetic Association (BDA)

10 Queen Anne Street
London W1M 0BD
Telephone: 0171 323 1531
Fax: 0171 637 3644
Contact: Katy Griggs (Information Scientist)
Objectives and Purposes: To support people living
    with diabetes by providing information and
    advice; to act on their behalf by making
    representations to government, and working to
    dispel prejudice and ignorance about diabetes; and
    to support research into diabetes

Stock and Subject Coverage: Books and periodicals about diabetes and related subjects; a range of leaflets and reports on diabetes for lay people and health professionals

Services/Facilities: Diabetes database; searches carried out on request

Availability: Telephone and written enquiries only

Hours: 09.00-17.00

Publications: Balance (6 per year; magazine for members); Diabetes Contents (quarterly); Diabetes Update (newsletter - twice yearly); Diabetic Medicine (12 per year); full list available on request

[78]
British Digestive Foundation (BDF)

3 St Andrew's Place
London NW1 4LB

Telephone: 0171 486 0341

Fax: 0171 224 2012

World Wide Web: http://www.bdf.org.uk

Contact: Geraldine Oliver (Administrator)

Objectives and Purposes: To fund research into digestive diseases and to provide information leaflets to the public covering the most common disorders of the digestive system. The BDF is the charitable arm of the British Society of Gastroenterology

Stock and Subject Coverage: Material on diverticular disease; gallstones; Gilbert's Syndrome; heartburn and hiatus hernia; indigestion; irritable bowel syndrome; travellers' diarrhoea; ulcers; food poisoning; and viral hepatitis. Includes - Maintaining Bowel Control; Who Needs the Hepatitis B Vaccine; and General Guidelines on Looking After Your Insides

Availability: Telephone and written enquiries only; (s.a.e. required for leaflet requests)

Hours: 09.00-17.30

Publications: Annual review; information leaflets - list available on request

Related Bodies: Independent local branches in Hull, Wolverhampton and Suffolk

[79]
British Geriatrics Society (BGS)

1 St Andrew's Place
Regents Park
London NW1 4LB

Telephone: 0171 935 4004

Fax: 0171 224 0454

E-mail: britishgeriatrics@dial.pipex.com

Contact: Richard Lynham (Administrative Director)

Objectives and Purposes: To set and promote high standards of health for elderly people; to promote the training of medical and paramedical staff in geriatric medicine and the care of elderly people; to research into age-related disease and methods of care; to provide a forum for the exchange and dissemination of scientific information

Availability: Free advice and information to medical and lay carers; postal requests preferred

Hours: 09.00-12.00 and 14.00-16.00

Publications: Age and ageing (quarterly scientific journal); bi-monthly internal newsletter

[80]
British Heart Foundation (BHF)

14 Fitzhardinge Street
London W1H 4DH

Telephone: 0171 935 0185

Fax: 0171 486 5820

Contact: Major General Leslie FH Busk CB (Director General); Maxine Smith (Director of Communications)

Objectives and Purposes: To play a leading role in the fight against heart disease by creating centres of excellence for research; by supporting research; by informing the medical profession of advances, and encouraging discussion of current research; by informing members of the public of the ways in which they may reduce the risk of heart disease; by promoting training in cardiopulmonary resuscitation; by offering practical help to patients; and by providing essential equipment for hospitals and other health providers

Availability: Written enquiries preferred; donations or stamps are welcomed when information is requested

Hours: 09.00-17.00

Publications: Wide range - list available

Related Bodies: A network of regional offices:

Bath
6 Terrace Walk, Bath BA1 1LN
(Tel: 01225 463616)

Cardiff
21 Cathedral Road, Cardiff CF1 9HA
(Tel: 01222 382368)

Edinburgh
45a Moray Place, Edinburgh EH3 6BQ
(Tel: 0131 226 3705)

Liverpool
7 Queen Avenue, Dale Street, Liverpool L2 4TZ
(Tel: 0151 236 6988)

London
1st Floor, Towpath Link, Limehouse Court,
3-11 Dod Street, London E14 7EQ
(Tel: 0171 987 2088)

Nottingham
16 The Ropewalk, Nottingham NG1 5DT
(Tel: 0115 941 7835)

Saffron Walden
25a Church Street, Saffron Walden,
Essex CB10 1JW
(Tel: 01799 521420)

Tadcaster
4-6 Bridge Street, Tadcaster,
North Yorkshire LS24 9AL
(Tel: 01937 835421)

Wadhurst
33 High Street, Ticehurst, Wadhurst,
East Sussex TN5 7AS
(Tel: 01580 200443)

[81]
British Herbal Medicine Association (BHMA)

Sun House
Church Street
Stroud
Gloucestershire GL5 1JL
Telephone: 01453 751389
Fax: 01453 751402
Contact: Mr RA Hill
Objectives and Purposes: To defend the right of the public to choose herbal remedies and to be able to obtain them freely; to encourage wider knowledge and recognition of the value of herbal medicine; and to advance the science and practice of herbal medicine by modern techniques
Services/Facilities: Advice service on most aspects of herbal medicine
Hours: 09.00-17.00
Publications: British Herbal Pharmacopeia 1983; British Herbal Pharmacopeia 1990; British Herbal Compendium; British Herbal Pharmacopeia 1996
Related Bodies: European Scientific Cooperative for Phytotherapy

[82]
British Holistic Medical Association (BHMA)

Rowland Thomas House
Royal Shrewsbury Hospital South
Shrewsbury SY3 8XF
Telephone: 01743 261155
Fax: 01743 353637
Contact: Mrs Yvette Wright (Membership Secretary)
Objectives and Purposes: To educate doctors and other health care practitioners in the principles and practice of holistic medicine; to encourage research studies in the field of holistic medicine; to bring together holistic health care professionals for mutual support and further personal and professional development
Stock and Subject Coverage: Information and educational materials on holistic approaches to health care, and on complementary therapies
Services/Facilities: Training seminars; conferences; GP referrals (limited to members' approval)
Availability: Telephone and written enquiries
Hours: 09.00-17.00
Publications: Quarterly newsletter. Full list available on request

[83]
British Homoeopathic Association (BHA)

27a Devonshire Street
London W1N 1RJ
Telephone: 0171 935 2163
Contact: Mrs Enid Segall (General Secretary)
Objectives and Purposes: To promote homoeopathy and provide information on the availability of homoeopathic treatment

Stock and Subject Coverage: Ca. 1,500 books and a number of periodicals, both historical and contemporary, on homoeopathy in general. Listings of homoeopathic doctors and hospitals are available
Services/Facilities: Photocopies
Availability: Open to members for loans and reference use on payment of an annual fee (£15). Visits for reference purposes by bona fide researchers are permitted - £5 per day
Hours: 09.30-17.00
Publications: Homoeopathy (bi-monthly journal)

[84]
British Hypnotherapy Association (BHA)

67 Upper Berkeley Street
London W1H 7DH
Telephone: 0171 723 4443
Contact: Mrs Alison Wookey (Secretary and Librarian)
Objectives and Purposes: To maintain a register of competent qualified practitioners, raise standards in the treatment of nervous problems, care for the interests of patients and members, collate and disseminate information on hypnotherapy
Stock and Subject Coverage: 1,500 books, periodicals reports, videos and audiotapes. Covers psychology; upbringing; personal development; emotional problems; psychotherapy; hypnotherapy; and related subjects
Services/Facilities: Advice and information to members and trainees
Availability: Telephone enquiries accepted; visits by appointment; loans to members only
Publications: Occasional special reports; list available

[85]
British Institute for Brain Injured Children (BIBIC)

Knowle Hall
Bridgwater
Somerset TA7 8PJ
Telephone: 01278 684060
Fax: 01278 685573
Contact: Dr S Wood (Medical Director); Miss J Rugg (Head of External Affairs); Mrs C Lane (Head of Clinic)
Objectives and Purposes: To improve the functions, performance and behaviour of children with brain injury who have been variously diagnosed as spastic, autistic, cerebral palsied, mentally handicapped, epileptic, dyslexic, retarded or as Down's Syndrome
Stock and Subject Coverage: Details of treatment to aid development are provided
Services/Facilities: Individually designed programmes of intensive sensory stimulation therapy, and follow up courses
Availability: Telephone and written enquiries accepted; visits by arrangement. Open to anyone involved with brain injured children
Hours: 09.00-17.00

[86]

British Institute of Learning Disabilities (BILD)

Wolverhampton Road
Kidderminster DY10 3PP
Telephone: 01562 850251
Fax: 01562 851970
E-mail: bild@bild.demon.co.uk
Contact: Dr John Harris (Chief Executive);
Mrs Linda Averill (Information Officer)
Objectives and Purposes: To improve the lifestyles of
people with learning disabilities
Stock and Subject Coverage: 3,000 books; 70 periodicals;
60 videos. Covers all aspects of learning disability
and multiple handicap
Services/Facilities: Internal database; current
awareness service
Availability: By appointment for reference use only
Hours: 09.00-13.00 and 14.00-16.00
Publications: List available

---

[87]

British Institute of Musculoskeletal Medicine (BIMM)

27 Green Lane
Northwood
Middlesex HA6 2PX
Telephone and Fax: 01923 820110
Contact: Dr Peter Skew (Hon. Secretary);
Deena Harris (Secretary - for enquiries)
Objectives and Purposes: The promotion of education
and research in the science and art of
musculoskeletal medicine for the ultimate benefit
of the public
Stock and Subject Coverage: Video library on
manipulative techniques
Services/Facilities: Slide and OHP presentation
production
Availability: Members only
Hours: 08.30-16.30
Publications: Journal of Orthopaedic Medicine (4 per
year)
Related Bodies: Associated with the Society of
Orthopaedic Medicine, American Association of
Orthopaedic Medicine, the British League Against
Rheumatism (BLAR) and the Fédération
International de Médecine Manuel (FIMM)

---

[88]

British Institute of Radiology (BIR)

36 Portland Place
London W1N 4AT
Telephone: 0171 580 4085
Fax: 0171 255 3209
Contact: Mrs Kate Sanders (Library and Information
Systems Manager)
Objectives and Purposes: A charitable organisation
aiming to promote the science of radiology and its
allied disciplines through its library, conference
facilities and membership. Related to the College

of Radiographers (COR) and the Royal College of
Radiologists (RCR)
Stock and Subject Coverage: Material on radiology;
and allied sciences. Ca. 100 current periodicals
and a selective collection of monographs and
textbooks. Special collections, include the KC
Clark Slide Collection, Thurston Holland and
William Maynlord
Services/Facilities: CD-ROM searches; fax;
photocopies
Availability: By prior appointment, for reference use
only; charges apply
Hours: 09.00-17.00 Monday, Wednesday and Friday;
10.00-18.00 Tuesday and Thursday
Publications: Library produces a library information
leaflet and a list of current journals. BIR produces
the British Journal of Radiology (monthly) and
various other publications

---

[89]

British Kidney Patient Association (BKPA)

Bordon
Hampshire GU35 9JZ
Telephone: 01420 472021/2
Fax: 01420 475831
Contact: Mrs Elizabeth Ward OBE (Founder
President)
Objectives and Purposes: Dedicated to the benefit and
welfare of kidney patients throughout the UK. To
create awareness of the need for kidney donors
and to lobby for more improved facilities and
funding
Services/Facilities: Information, support, advice and
financial help is available for renal patients and
their relatives. Also, a much needed break at the
BKPA Holiday Dialysis Centre at Portelet Bay,
Jersey
Availability: Services available to members
(membership £1)
Hours: 09.00-17.30
Publications: Various question and answer leaflets;
annual appeal brochure; Timbo - A Struggle for
Survival (by Elizabeth Ward); The Home Dialysis
Patient (by Elizabeth Ward)

---

[90]

British League Against Rheumatism (BLAR)

41 Eagle Street
London WC1R 4AR
Telephone: 0171 242 3313
Fax: 0171 242 3277
E-mail: blar@rheumatology.org.uk
Contact: Anne Mansfield (Chief Executive);
Sophie Edwards (Information/Marketing
Manager); Kevin Rowan (BLAR Audit Assistant)
Objectives and Purposes: An umbrella group, and
registered charity, representing the interests of
professionals and support groups for people with
rheumatic complaints

Stock and Subject Coverage: Patient information from a range of organisations. Information for professionals, including guidelines, subject to some restrictions

Services/Facilities: Fax; Internet; meeting rooms available for hire

Availability: Telephone and written enquiries accepted; visits by prior arrangement

Hours: By arrangement

Publications: Purchasers Pack (of leaflets and documents); Disability and Arthritis Report (1994)

Related Bodies: There are 23 member groups, including the British Society for Rheumatology, and a network of regional groups (details on request)

---

[91]

British Library, Health Care Information Service (HCIS)

25 Southampton Buildings
London WC2A 1AW

Telephone: 0171 412 7477

Fax: 0171 412 7947

E-mail: hcis@bl.uk

World Wide Web:
http://portico.bl.uk/sris/leadmed.html

Contact: Bruce Madge (Head of HCIS - 0171 412 7433); Dave Roberts (AMED - 01937 546520); Tony McCulloch (MEDLINE Indexing - 01937 546039); Ann Rotherham (BLAISE-LINK - 01937 546364); Fiona McLean (STMSearch - 0171 412 7489)

Objectives and Purposes: To provide a focus for all health care information handled by the British Library

Services/Facilities: Online searches; fax; BLAISE-LINK online database service providing access to MEDLINE and other NLM databases; AMED internal database on alternative medicine; Current Awareness Topics Searches (CATS); training and consultancy; document delivery. Online searches in science, technology and medicine are available through STMSearch (0171 412 7477/7478)

Availability: By subscription

Hours: 09.00-17.00

Publications: CATS listings; NLM publications

Related Bodies: The British Library, Document Supply Centre

---

[92]

British Library, Science Reference and Information Service (SRIS)

Aldwych Reading Room
9 Kean Street
London WC2B 4AT

Telephone: 0171 412 7288

Fax: 0171 412 7217

E-mail: sris-aldwych-desk@bl.uk

World Wide Web: http://portico.bl.uk/sris/

Contact: Andrea Reid (Aldwych Reading Room Manager)

Objectives and Purposes: To provide access to the British Library's reference collections in the life sciences (including medicine), earth sciences and mathematics

Stock and Subject Coverage: Material on the life sciences, including medicine but excluding nursing and health service administration (stock is aimed at postgraduate research level)

Services/Facilities: Photocopies; CD-ROM, online and Internet searches; charged research services

Availability: Freely available for reference use; telephone and written enquiries accepted

Hours: 09.30-17.30

Publications: List available on request (0171 412 7472)

Related Bodies: Holborn Reading Room (physical sciences, business information and patents). Part of the British Library

---

[93]

British Liver Trust

Central House
Central Avenue
Ransomes Europark
Ipswich IP3 9QG

Telephone: Information Line (14.00-17.30): 01473 276328; Administration: 01473 276326

Fax: 01473 276327

E-mail: info@liver-t.demon.co.uk

Contact: Information Line

Objectives and Purposes: To provide information and support for people with liver disease, and their families and carers

Stock and Subject Coverage: Range of factsheets on liver disease

Services/Facilities: Information Line operated by medically trained staff, weekdays 14.00-17.30

Availability: Freely available

Hours: 09.00-17.30

Publications: Bi-annual newsletter

Related Bodies: Local support groups

---

[94]

British Lung Foundation (BLF)

78 Hatton Garden
London EC1N 8JR

Telephone: 0171 831 5831

Fax: 0171 831 5832

Contact: Sarah Clarke (Publications); Ms Alex Mazzetta (Grants Administrator) (Fundraising and Publications Officer)

Objectives and Purposes: To raise funds for research into the prevention, diagnosis and treatment of all kinds of lung disease; to provide public information on lung disease; to support sufferers

Stock and Subject Coverage: A growing collection of predominantly lay information on lung disease from newspapers, magazines, and journals

Services/Facilities: Breathe Easy club for people with lung disease

Availability: Telephone and written enquiries

Hours: 09.00-17.30
Publications: Various – list available
Related Bodies: Branches in Birmingham, Cheltenham, Glasgow, Liverpool and Newcastle

[95]

British Medical Acupuncture Society (BMAS)

Newton House
Newton Lane
Whitley
Warrington WA4 4JA
Telephone: 01925 730727
Fax: 01925 730491
E-mail: drcalewis@aol.com
World Wide Web:
http://users.aol.com/acubmas/bmas.html
Contact: The Administrator/Assistant
Objectives and Purposes: To further research and training in medical acupuncture for use alongside western medicine. To provide training in acupuncture for medically qualified doctors and dentists
Services/Facilities: Area lists of practitioners are available, and a leaflet
Availability: Telephone and written enquiries
Publications: Newsletter for members; Acupuncture in Medicine (twice-yearly journal)

[96]

British Medical Association Library (BMA Library)

BMA House
Tavistock Square
London WC1H 9JP
Telephone: 0171 383 6625
Fax: 0171 388 2544
E-mail: library@bma.org.uk
World Wide Web: http://www.bma.org.uk
Contact: Mr Tony McSean (Librarian); Ms Jane South (Deputy Librarian)
Objectives and Purposes: To provide medical information for members
Stock and Subject Coverage: 50,000 books; 3,200 periodicals; 1,500 videos specialising in clinical medicine and allied sciences, and the social aspects of medicine
Services/Facilities: Literature searches; online information network; photocopies
Availability: By prior appointment, for reference use only (fee payable)
Hours: 09.00-18.00

[97]

British Migraine Association

178A High Road
Byfleet
West Byfleet
Surrey KT14 7ED
Telephone: 01932 352468
Fax: 01932 351257

Contact: Mrs Brenda Jones (Secretary)
Objectives and Purposes: To encourage and support research into the cause and treatment of migraine; to gather and pass on information about drugs and treatments available for the control and relief of migraine
Services/Facilities: Information to sufferers and their families
Availability: Enquiries by letter
Hours: 09.30-16.00
Publications: Migraine Handbook (£8.75); newsletter (3 per year); leaflets on all aspects of migraine

[98]

British Nutrition Foundation (BNF)

High Holborn House
52-54 High Holborn
London WC1V 6RQ
Telephone: 0171 404 6504
Fax: 0171 404 6747
Contact: Dr Michele Sadler (Nutrition Scientist)
Objectives and Purposes: To help individuals understand what a good diet is and how they may best match diet and lifestyle. The main field of interest is diet and health, with particular interest in nutrition/food education
Stock and Subject Coverage: Material on nutrition and related health matters
Availability: Information on request. The Foundation is unable to provide individual dietary advice
Hours: 09.00-17.00
Publications: BNF Journal (4 per year); BNF News (newsletter – 3 per year); BNF Briefing Papers (ca. 2 per year); annual report

[99]

British Optical Association Library

College of Optometrists
10 Knaresborough Place
London SW5 0TG
Telephone: 0171 373 7765
Fax: 0171 373 1143
Contact: Miss JM Taylor (Librarian)
Objectives and Purposes: The main professional body and examining body for optometrists in the UK. Its aims are the improvement and conservation of human vision, the promotion of research, the promotion and maintenance of high standards in optometry for the public benefit
Stock and Subject Coverage: 10,000 books; 100 periodicals covering optics; vision science; optometry; and ophthalmology. Special collection of early books on optics and vision
Services/Facilities: MEDLINE on CD-ROM; enquiry service; interlibrary loans; photocopies (priced)
Availability: By prior appointment, for reference use only; subscription membership available
Hours: 09.00-13.00 and 14.00-17.00

[100]

★British Orthopaedic Association (BOA)

35-43 Lincoln's Inn Fields
London WC2A 3PN
Telephone: 0171 405 6507
Fax: 0171 831 2676
Contact: Mr DC Adams (Chief Executive)
Objectives and Purposes: The advancement of the Science, Art and Practice of Orthopaedic Surgery with the aim of bringing relief to patients of all ages suffering from the effects of injury or disease of the musculoskeletal system including arthritis
Stock and Subject Coverage: Information available on all aspects of orthopaedic surgery and the provision of an orthopaedic service in the UK
Availability: To non-members by special application; a charge may be levied
Hours: 09.00-17.00
Publications: Occasional publications on matters of orthopaedic significance; bi-annual newsletter; annual report and members handbook
Related Bodies: Links by affiliation with a number of subspecialty societies, e.g. British Association for Surgery of the Knee, British Hip Society, etc.

[101]

British Orthoptic Society (BOS)

Tavistock House
Tavistock Square
London WC1H 9HX
Telephone: 0171 387 7992
Fax: 0171 383 2584
Contact: Joanna Brown (Executive Secretary)
Objectives and Purposes: A professional body and trade union for orthoptists
Availability: Telephone and written enquiries
Hours: 09.00-17.00
Publications: British Orthoptic Journal (annual); directory of members; The Role of the Orthoptist (booklet)
Related Bodies: Member of International and European Orthoptic Associations, and of the Health and Care Professions Education Forum

[102]

British Osteopathic Association (BOA)

8-10 Boston Place
London NW1 6QH
Telephone: 0171 262 5250
Contact: Dr R MacDonald (Hon. Secretary)
Objectives and Purposes: A professional association of medically qualified osteopaths representing the interests of those practising osteopathy integrated into the medical specialty of musculoskeletal medicine
Hours: 09.00-17.00

[103]

British Pharmacological Society (BPS)

16 Angel Gate
City Road
London EC1V 2PT
Telephone: 0171 417 0113
Fax: 0171 417 0114
E-mail: sjs@bphs.org.uk
Contact: Sarah-Jane Stagg (Executive Officer)
Objectives and Purposes: A learned society with the objective of promoting and advancing pharmacology, including clinical pharmacology. No library
Availability: Telephone, e-mail and written enquiries from press and other media only
Hours: 09.00-17.30
Publications: British Journal of Pharmacology (fortnightly); British Journal of Clinical Pharmacology (monthly); What is Pharmacology? (leaflet); Pharmacology - a career in research (booklet)

[104]

British Polio Fellowship (BPF)

Eagle Office Centre
The Runway
South Ruislip
Middlesex HA4 6SE
Telephone: 0181 842 1898
Fax: 0181 842 0555
Contact: Andrew Kemp (Acting Chief Executive)
Objectives and Purposes: To support people who have had polio, and their carers
Stock and Subject Coverage: Material on the late effects of polio/post polio syndrome. General information on issues affecting people who have had polio
Availability: Details on request
Hours: 09.00-17.00
Publications: The Bulletin (bi-monthly)

[105]

British Pregnancy Advisory Service (BPAS)

Austy Manor
Wootton Wawen
Solihull
West Midlands B95 6BX
Telephone: 01564 794935
Fax: 01564 794935
Contact: Ian Jones (Director); enquiries to Marketing Department
Objectives and Purposes: A charity-based organisation with 30 branches throughout the UK offering information, counselling and treatment and a range of services linked with pregnancy and contraception

Availability: Enquiries accepted by telephone, fax or letter. Free leaflets usually available

Hours: 09.00-17.00

[106]

British Psychological Society (BPS)

St Andrew's House
48 Princess Road East
Leicester LE1 7DR
(NB The Library is housed in the Senate House Library, University of London –
Tel: 0171 636 8000; Fax: 0171 436 1494)

Telephone: 0116 254 9568

Fax: 0116 247 0787

Contact: Colin V Newman (Executive Secretary, BPS); Susan Tarrant (Psychology Librarian, Senate House Library)

Objectives and Purposes: The professional body and learned society incorporated by Royal Charter to promote the advancement and diffusion of a knowledge of psychology, pure and applied, within the United Kingdom

Stock and Subject Coverage: The BPS maintains an extensive library of mainly scientific periodicals in psychology, housed within the Senate House Library at the University of London, alongside Senate House's own psychology journals. The merged collection represents one of the world's largest collections of scientific journal publications

Services/Facilities: Photocopying and other facilities are provided courtesy of the University of London Library

Availability: Restricted to BPS members and bona fide users of the University of London Library

Hours: As published by the University of London Library

Publications: The Psychologist (monthly); Register of Chartered Psychologists; Directory of Chartered Psychologists; annual report; a range of other scientific journals (list available)

[107]

British Retinitis Pigmentosa Society (BRPS)

PO Box 350
Buckingham MK18 5EL

Telephone: 01280 860363

Fax: 01280 860515

Contact: Mrs Lynda M Cantor MBE (Hon. Secretary)

Objectives and Purposes: To find a cure and treatment for Retinitis Pigmentosa, and to provide a support and welfare service throughout the UK for people with RP

Publications: Quarterly newsletter; annual handbook with report and accounts

[108]

British School of Osteopathy (BSO)

1-4 Suffolk Street
London SW1Y 4HG

Telephone: 0171 930 9254

Fax: 0171 839 1098

E-mail: name@bso.co.uk

World Wide Web: http://www.bso.co.uk

Contact: Will Podmore (Librarian); Adele Walton (Assistant Librarian)

Objectives and Purposes: To promote osteopathy and its contribution to the provision of contemporary health care by providing learning opportunities for undergraduate and qualified practitioners; enhancing the quality of osteopathic patient care and management; maintaining a commitment to using research to facilitate continuing improvement in professional practice

Stock and Subject Coverage: Covers osteopathy and complementary medicine, with some general medicine. Special collection on the history of osteopathy

Services/Facilities: Photocopies at cost; CD-ROM searches on MEDLINE

Availability: Open access for researchers, for reference use. Visits by arrangement

Hours: Termtime: 09.00-19.30 Monday and Tuesday; 09.00-21.30 Wednesday and Thursday; 09.00-17.00 Friday. Holidays: 09.00-17.00

Publications: Articles proving that spinal manipulation works; How to do Research; subject bibliographies

[109]

British Society for Immunology

Triangle House
Broomhill Road
London SW18 4HX

Telephone: 0181 875 2400

Fax: 0181 877 9308

E-mail: bsi@immunology.org

Internet: http://immunology.org

Contact: Kevin Horlock (Chief Executive); Kirstie Urquhart (Public Relations)

Objectives and Purposes: To advance the science of immunology for the benefit of the public

Stock and Subject Coverage: Material on general immunology and clinical/experimental immunology

Availability: Telephone and written enquiries only; some services charged

Hours: 09.00-17.00

Publications: Immunology (monthly); Immunology News (6 per year); Immunology (monthly); Clinical and Experimental Immunology (monthly); annual report

[110]

British Society for Research on Ageing (BSRA)

University of Manchester
School of Biological Sciences
Stopford Building
Oxford Road
Manchester M13 9PT
Telephone: 0161 275 5252
Fax: 0161 275 5252 or 5363
E-mail: Ioan.Davies@man.ac.uk
Contact: Dr Ioan Davies (enquiries - Hon. General Secretary); Professor Tom Kirkwood (Chairman)
Objectives and Purposes: The BSRA is an academic Society for the promotion of research in biological and biomedical gerontology. Its main activity is the organisation of scientific meetings
Publications: Lifespan - a twice yearly journal, with other newsletters as required
Related Bodies: The BSRA does not have a library. The BSRA has close links with the British Society of Gerontology (social/behavioural issues) and the British Geriatrics Society. The BSRA is affiliated to the International Association for Gerontology

[111]

British Society for Restorative Dentistry (BSRD)

c/o Turner Dental School
Higher Cambridge Street
Manchester M15 6FH
Telephone: 0161 275 6797
Fax: 0161 275 6797
E-mail: shearera@fsl.den.man.ac.uk
Contact: Miss Ann Shearer (Hon. Secretary); Mrs Janet Harlow (Administrative Secretary)
Objectives and Purposes: To promote and advance the study of and research into restorative dentistry; to further the interests of restorative dentistry; to instruct and advise dentists in the practice of restorative dentistry
Publications: Annual newsletter

[112]

British Society for Rheumatology (BSR)

41 Eagle Street
London WC1R 4AR
Telephone: 0171 242 3313
Fax: 0171 242 3277
E-mail: BSR@rheumatology.org.uk
Contact: Anne Mansfield (Chief Executive)
Objectives and Purposes: A professional organisation (and registered charity) for clinicians and others concerned with rheumatic diseases. Part of the British League Against Rheumatism
Stock and Subject Coverage: The Heberden Library comprises an antiquarian and contemporary library covering the whole field of rheumatic diseases

Services/Facilities: Fax; photocopies. Meeting rooms available for hire
Availability: On special request
Hours: By arrangement
Publications: Annual report; BLAR Diary of Events
Related Bodies: The Library is based within the Royal College of Physicians

[113]

British Society for the Study of Infection (BSSI)

Dr NC Weightman
Hon. Secretary BSSI
Department of Microbiology
Friarage Hospital
Northallerton
North Yorkshire DL6 1JG
Telephone: 01609 763033
Fax: 01609 778656
E-mail: hon.sec@bssi.octacon.co.uk
Contact: Dr NC Weightman
Objectives and Purposes: A registered charity whose aim is to relieve human sickness by the study of all types of infection and to promote the wide dissemination of relevant knowledge
Publications: The Journal of Infection (6 per year)

[114]

British Society of Audiology (BSA)

80 Brighton Road
Reading RG6 1PS
Telephone: 01189 660622
Fax: 01189 351915
E-mail: bsa@cityscape.co.uk
World Wide Web:
http://www.gold.net/users/hh97/index.html
Contact: Dr Valerie Cleaver (Chairman); Mrs Ann Allen (Administrative Secretary); Mr Andrew Reid (Hon. Secretary)
Objectives and Purposes: A voluntary non-profit making body for the promotion and advancement of audiology
Stock and Subject Coverage: No library, but the Society houses the National Hearing Aid Museum
Services/Facilities: Advice about audiology in Britain
Availability: Telephone and written enquiries; no visits
Publications: British Journal of Audiology; BSA newsletter

[115]

British Society of Gastroenterology (BSG)

3 St Andrew's Place
London NW1 4LB
Telephone: 0171 387 3534
Fax: 0171 487 3734
World Wide Web: http://www.bsg.org.uk
Contact: Ms Di Tolfree (Administrative Secretary)

Objectives and Purposes: To set standards and arrange training, audit and research in gastroenterology

Stock and Subject Coverage: Limited in-house library covering gastroenterology. Patient information is dealt with by the British Digestive Foundation

Publications: Gut (journal); BSG News (quarterly)

Related Bodies: British Digestive Foundation

---

[116]
British Society of Periodontology (BSP)

Administrative Secretary
44 Pool Road
Hartley Wintney
Hook
Hampshire RG27 8RD

Telephone: 01252 843598
Fax: 01252 844018
E-mail: 101547.1774@compuserve.com

Contact: Administrative Secretary for enquiries. President (September 1996 to September 1997): Professor FC Smales; President (September 1997 to September 1998): Professor RA Seymour; Honorary Secretary: Dr GS Griffiths; Honorary Treasurer: Dr MS Saxby

Objectives and Purposes: To promote for the benefit of the public the art and science of dentistry, and in particular the art and science of periodontology and in furtherance thereof to advance all aspects of periodontology and to promote improvements in the teaching of the same

Services/Facilities: Referral service offered

Availability: No visits; telephone and written enquiries accepted

Hours: 09.00-17.30

Publications: Journal of Clinical Periodontology (monthly); Annual newsletter

Related Bodies: Member of the European Federation of Periodontology

---

[117]
British Thyroid Foundation

PO Box 97
Clifford
Wetherby
West Yorkshire LS23 6XD

Contact: Mrs J Hickey (National Co-ordinator); Mrs B Nevens (Membership Secretary)

Objectives and Purposes: To offer support and understanding of thyroid disorders to sufferers and their families; to provide information and to raise awareness; to raise funds for research; to help establish local support groups

Stock and Subject Coverage: Pamphlets and books aimed at the lay reader

Services/Facilities: Advice and information; information pack available

Availability: By appointment for reference use; written enquiries in the first instance

Hours: 10.00-14.30

Publications: Newsletter; pamphlets. Full list available

---

[118]
British Tinnitus Association (BTA)

4th Floor, White Building
Fitzalan Square
Sheffield S1 2AZ

Telephone: 0114 273 0122
Fax: 0114 279 6222

Contact: Miss V Rose (Operations/Publications Manager)

Objectives and Purposes: To help and advise tinnitus sufferers, promote public and medical awareness, work for the relief and cure of permanent head noise

Stock and Subject Coverage: Material on tinnitus in general

Availability: Written and telephone enquiries accepted; most material free of charge

Hours: 09.30-16.45 (Answerphone at other times)

Publications: Quiet (quarterly journal); annual report

Related Bodies: Local self-help affiliated groups

---

[119]
Brittle Bone Society

30 Guthrie Street
Dundee DD1 5BS

Telephone: 01382 204446/7
Fax: 01382 206771

Contact: Miss Morna Wilson (Administrator)

Objectives and Purposes: To promote research into the causes, inheritance and treatment of osteogenesis imperfecta and similar disorders characterised by excessive fragility of the bones. The Society also provides advice, encouragement and practical help for patients and their relatives facing the difficulties of living with brittle bones

Availability: Telephone and written enquiries

Hours: 09.00-16.30

Publications: Newsletter (3 per year); various leaflets

---

[120]
Broadmoor Hospital, Patrick McGrath Library

Crowthorne
Berkshire RG11 7EG

Telephone: 01344 754400; Librarian: 754404
Fax: 01344 754296

Contact: Mrs Alison Farrar (Librarian); Mrs Judy Phillips (Deputy Librarian)

Stock and Subject Coverage: 6,000 books; 50 periodicals; 3,000 documents, topic boxes covering psychiatry; forensic psychiatry; and nursing

Services/Facilities: Internal database searches (priced other than to staff); photocopies (priced)

Availability: By prior appointment, for reference use only (a charge applies)

Hours: 09.00-17.00 (closes 16.30 on Friday)

Publications: Additions to Stock (monthly)

Related Bodies: Cooperates with HeLIN, and members of PLCS

[121]

Bronglais General Hospital Library Services

Postgraduate Centre
Aberystwyth
Ceredigion SY23 1ER
Telephone: 01970 635803
Fax: 01970 635923
Contact: Ms P Chapman (Library Services Manager)
Objectives and Purposes: To serve the staff and patients of Ceredigion and Mid Wales NHS Trust by providing appropriate library and information services in the field of medicine and health care
Stock and Subject Coverage: 3,500 books; 150 current periodicals; pamphlets; indexes; bibliographies covering medicine; nursing; allied health subjects; and consumer health
Services/Facilities: Online and CD-ROM searches; interlibrary loans; photocopies
Availability: By prior appointment, for reference use only (subject to charges for non-members)
Hours: 09.00-17.00
Related Bodies: Member of Association of Welsh Health Librarians and All Wales Health Information and Library Extension Service

[122]

Broomfield Hospital

Warner Library
Court Road
Chelmsford
Essex CM7 5ET
Telephone: 01245 443651/2
Fax: 01245 442140
E-mail: carol.warner.lib@dial.pipex.com
Contact: Carol Roberts (Librarian); Jane Hayes (Assistant Librarian)
Objectives and Purposes: To provide library and information services for staff of local NHS Trusts
Stock and Subject Coverage: 2,000 books; 100 periodicals. Covers all aspects of clinical medicine
Services/Facilities: Online and CD-ROM searches; Internet access; word processing; fax; current awareness; photocopies (priced)
Availability: By prior appointment, for reference use only; telephone and written enquiries accepted
Hours: 09.00-18.00 (closes 17.30 on Friday; open until 19.00 on Monday)

[123]

Brunel University College

Osterley Campus Library
Borough Road
Isleworth
Middlesex TW7 5DU
Telephone: 0181 891 0121
Fax: 0181 891 8251
E-mail: library@brunel.ac.uk
World Wide Web: http://www.brunel.ac.uk/depts/lib/
Contact: Polly Wharram (Director of Library Services); Robert Elves (Information Services Librarian)

Objectives and Purposes: Library serving a university
Stock and Subject Coverage: The Osterley Campus Library holds material relevant to courses taught on that site, being: physiotherapy, occupational therapy, and health studies; physical education and sport; earth sciences; and business and computing
Services/Facilities: Photocopiers; online and CD-ROM services for registered users
Availability: Free access to registered staff and students of the University. Open to others for reference use. External users can join the Library for a fee
Hours: Semester time: 09.00-21.00 Monday to Thursday; 09.00-17.00 Friday; 09.00-12.00 Saturday. Vacations: 09.00-17.00 Monday to Friday
Related Bodies: Part of Brunel University, expected to merge fully in 1997/8

[124]

Buckinghamshire College

Newland Park Library
Gorelands Lane
Chalfont St Giles
Buckinghamshire HP8 4AD
Telephone: 01494 874441, ext 2249
Fax: 01494 603082
E-mail: nplib@buckscol.ac.uk
World Wide Web:
http://www.buckscoll.ac.uk/library/library.html
Contact: Louise Cooke (Campus Librarian); Michael King (Health Studies Faculty Librarian)
Objectives and Purposes: To provide a quality reference, lending and information service to staff and students, assisting and supporting teaching staff and student-centred learning programmes
Stock and Subject Coverage: 40,000 books; 350 periodicals covering all aspects of nursing; allied health; sociology; social sciences and business studies
Services/Facilities: Printed abstracts, indexes and bibliographies are available; database searches; fax; photocopies; CD-ROM searches
Availability: By prior appointment, for reference use only; external membership is available for a fee
Hours: 08.30-21.00 Monday to Thursday; 08.30-17.30 Friday; 10.00-17.00 Saturday. Vacation: 09.00-16.30 Monday to Friday
Related Bodies: Site library at Buckinghamshire College, Queen Alexandra Road, High Wycombe (Tel: 01494 522141)

[125]

Burton Graduate Medical Centre

Belvedere Road
Burton on Trent
Staffordshire DE13 0RB
Telephone: 01283 566333, ext 2104
Fax: 01283 510347
E-mail: bgmc.lib@dial.pipex.com
Contact: David Rogers (Librarian)
Objectives and Purposes: Medical and dental education
Stock and Subject Coverage: 2,000 books; 80 videos. Covers medicine; dentistry; psychiatry; psychology; and NHS management

Services/Facilities: MEDLINE on CD-ROM;
photocopies (5p per sheet); fax; PC for audit work
Availability: By written request for reference only
Hours: 09.00–17.00 Monday and Friday; 09.00–21.00
Tuesday to Thursday

[126]

Bury General Hospital Postgraduate Centre

Medical Library
Bury BL9 6PG
Telephone: 0161 705 3375
Fax: 0161 761 4702
E-mail: ae54@cityscape.co.uk
Contact: Jean Williams (Librarian)
Objectives and Purposes: To supply the information
and educational needs of doctors and other NHS
staff. Linked with the University of Manchester
Stock and Subject Coverage: General medical texts and
periodicals
Services/Facilities: Online, Internet and CD-ROM
searches; fax; photocopies
Availability: By prior appointment, for reference use
only
Hours: 09.00–17.00

[127]

Cairns Library

The John Radcliffe
Oxford Radcliffe Hospital
Headington
Oxford OX3 9DN
Telephone: 01865 221936
Fax: 01865 221941
E-mail: maureen.forest@cairns-library.ox.ac.uk
Contact: Maureen Forest (Librarian); Anne Lusher
(Reader Services Librarian); Karen Henderson
(Systems Librarian); Robin Snowball (Site
Librarian Radcliffe Infirmary)
Objectives and Purposes: To provide library and
information services in all aspects of health care
Stock and Subject Coverage: Material covering health
care in general
Services/Facilities: Online and CD-ROM searches;
interlibrary loans; photocopies
Availability: By prior appointment, for reference use
only
Hours: 09.00–21.00 (09.00–17.00 in vacations)
Publications: Library guide; Guide to Searching on
CD-ROM
Related Bodies: Oxford University; member of HeLIN

[128]

Cancer Care Society (CARE)

Jane Scarth House
39 The Hundred
Romsey
Hampshire SO51 8GE
Telephone: 01794 830374
Fax: 01794 518133

Contact: Kim Fielder (Director/Oncology
Counsellor); Julie Perkin (National Administrator)
Objectives and Purposes: Free confidential counselling
for anyone whose life has been affected by cancer
Services/Facilities: Information and resource centre;
cancer literature/booklets; wig fitting service;
reflexology
Availability: Available, freely, to anyone. Counselling
by appointment
Hours: 10.00–16.30
Publications: Quarterly newsletter

[129]

*Cancer Relief MacMillan Fund

15–19 Britten Street
London SW3 3TZ
Telephone: 0171 351 7811
Fax: 0171 376 8098
World Wide Web:
http://www.easynet.co.uk/aware/contacts/
macmillan/index.html
Contact: Susan Butler (Director of Public Affairs)
Objectives and Purposes: A national charity devoted to
the care of people with cancer; funds the
MacMillan nurses, MacMillan cancer care doctors,
in-patient units and day care centres
Services/Facilities: Leaflets – Help Is There: Contacts
For People With Cancer; and Breast Cancer: How
to Help Yourself
Availability: Written enquiries only
Hours: 09.00–17.30
Publications: Directory of Breast Cancer Services in
the UK; annual report
Related Bodies: Associated charities are Breast Cancer
Care, Cancerlink, British Colostomy Association,
and BACUP

[130]

Cancer Research Campaign (CRC)

10 Cambridge Terrace
London NW1 4JL
Telephone: 0171 224 1333
Fax: 0171 487 4302
E-mail: thince@crcsd.demon.co.uk
Contact: Ms Joanna Meadows or Ms Holly Ellson;
Ms Jean King (Head of Education);
Dr Lesley Walker (Scientific Secretary,
Information)
Objectives and Purposes: To attack and defeat the
disease of cancer in all its forms; to investigate its
causes, distribution, symptoms, pathology and
treatment, and to promote its cure. The Education
Department aims to provide comprehensive
health information and education resources for
health professionals, academics and teachers
Availability: Telephone and written enquiries
accepted (no formal library unit)
Publications: Factsheets on Cancer; various
educational resources (catalogue available);
scientific yearbook; annual review; directory of
research

[131]
Cancerlink
11-21 Northdown Street
London N1 9BN
Telephone: 0171 833 2818; Asian Helpline:
    0800 5904157; Macline (for young people):
    0800 591028
Fax: 0171 833 4963
E-mail: cancerlink@canlink.demon.co.uk
Contact: Angela Hayes (Director); Maggie Alexander
    (Information Services Manager)
Objectives and Purposes: To provide information and
    support for people with cancer, their families,
    friends and professionals, and to act as a resource
    for independent self-help groups, providing
    training, information and support to the groups
Stock and Subject Coverage: Reference books; medical
    journals; booklets and articles covering all aspects
    of cancer
Services/Facilities: Special helplines for Asian people
    and young people (numbers given above);
    (Minicom: 0171 833 2451)
Availability: Telephone and written enquiries;
    booklets supplied free to sufferers, although a
    charge may be made for multiple copies
Hours: 09.30-17.30 (answerphone available out of
    hours)
Publications: Range of publications - list available;
    Link Up (quarterly magazine)

[132]
*Cancerlink in Scotland
9 Castle Terrace
Edinburgh EH1 2DP
Telephone: 0131 228 5567; Helpline: 0131 228 5557;
    Freephone: 0800 132905
Fax: 0131 228 8956
Contact: Evelyn Smillie (Manager)
Objectives and Purposes: To provide information and
    support for people with cancer, their families,
    friends and professionals, and to act as a resource
    for independent self-help groups, providing
    training, information and support to the groups
Stock and Subject Coverage: Reference books; medical
    journals; booklets and articles covering all aspects
    of cancer
Services/Facilities: Minicom: 0131 228 5557
Availability: Telephone and written enquiries;
    booklets supplied free to sufferers, although a
    charge may be made for multiple copies
Hours: 09.30-17.30 (answerphone available out of
    hours)
Publications: Range of publications - list available;
    Link Up (quarterly magazine)

[133]
Canterbury and Thanet Community NHS Trust Library
Education Centre
St Martins Hospital
Littlebourne Road
Canterbury CT1 1TD
Telephone: 01227 812360
Fax: 01227 812005
Contact: Joy Sharman ALA
Objectives and Purposes: To provide library and
    information services to Trust staff
Stock and Subject Coverage: Material on mental health,
    with some holdings on community care and NHS
    legislation
Services/Facilities: Online and CD-ROM searches;
    photocopies; fax
Availability: By prior appointment, for reference use
    only
Hours: 09.00-15.00 (open until 16.00 on Monday)
Publications: Bi-monthly bulletin
Related Bodies: South Thames Regional Library Service

[134]
Capability Scotland
formerly Scottish Council for Spastics, External Therapy and Advisory Services (SCS-ETAS)
11 Ellersly Road
Edinburgh EH12 6HY
Telephone: 0131 313 5510
Fax: 0131 346 7864
Contact: Sheila Williams (Senior Advice Worker)
Objectives and Purposes: To enable the needs of
    people with cerebral palsy, and those with a
    disability resulting in similar needs, to be met
Stock and Subject Coverage: 1,700 items covering
    cerebral palsy, disability and related resources
Availability: Freely available to anyone
Hours: 09.00-17.00
Publications: List available on request

[135]
Carers National Association (CNA)
20-25 Glasshouse Yard
London EC1A 4JS
Telephone: 0171 490 8818; Carers Helpline
    (13.00-16.00 Monday to Friday): 0171 490 8898
Fax: 0171 490 8824
Contact: Gail Elkington (Policy and Information
    Officer); Jill Pitkeathley (Executive Officer)
Objectives and Purposes: CNA aims to encourage
    carers to recognise their own needs; to develop
    appropriate support for carers; to provide advice
    and information to carers; to bring the needs of
    carers to the attention of government and other
    policy makers. As a membership organisation it
    offers information and advice to professionals,
    students, etc.

Stock and Subject Coverage: An internal library on many aspects of carers issues; information sheets; professional journals

Availability: Telephone and written enquiries. No loans. Access to carers, professionals, students and researchers

Hours: 09.00-17.00

Publications: The Carer (bi-monthly); Carers Workers Information Bulletin. Full list available on request

Related Bodies: Network of area and local offices

[136]
Carlisle Hospitals NHS Trust

Library
Education Centre
Cumberland Infirmary
Carlisle CA2 7HY

Telephone: 01228 814878/9

Fax: 01228 814822

Contact: Mrs P Goundry (Librarian)

Objectives and Purposes: The provision of library and information services to staff and to support the teaching requirements of staff and students of the University College of St Martin at Carlisle

Stock and Subject Coverage: 10,000 books; 273 periodicals. Covers health sciences specialising in medicine and nursing

Services/Facilities: Online and CD-ROM searches (MEDLINE, CINAHL, Cochrane); current awareness service; photocopies (priced)

Availability: By prior written application

Hours: 09.00-17.00 (closes 16.30 on Friday)

Publications: Library guides; recent additions list

Related Bodies: Part of Health Libraries North

[137]
Carmarthen District NHS Trust Library

West Wales General Hospital
Glangwili
Carmarthen SA31 2AF

Telephone: 01267 227076

Fax: 01267 223710

Contact: Mrs VE Bisnath (Senior Librarian)

Objectives and Purposes: To provide information support to the work of the Trust

Stock and Subject Coverage: Material on medicine, nursing and therapies

Services/Facilities: Photocopies; fax; CD-ROM searches; Internet access

Availability: By prior appointment, for reference use only

Hours: 09.00-17.00 (closes 16.30 on Friday)

[138]
Central Middlesex Postgraduate Centre Library

Central Middlesex Hospital NHS Trust
Acton Lane
London NW10 7NS

Telephone: 0181 453 2503/4

Fax: 0181 453 2763

E-mail: 1101527.635@compuserve.com

Contact: Barbara Cumbers; Bridget Farrant; Susan Golder

Objectives and Purposes: To provide a service to Central Middlesex Hospital NHS Trust and the North West London Mental Health Trust, in conjunction with St Mary's Hospital Medical School Library and the North Thames (West) Medical Library and Information Service

Stock and Subject Coverage: 3,000 books; 140 current periodicals in the fields of medicine, psychiatry and allied subjects

Services/Facilities: CD-ROM searches; photocopies;

Availability: Full service to registered users

Hours: 09.30-19.00 Monday to Wednesday; 09.00-17.00 Thursday and Friday

Publications: Newsletter (quarterly); library guide; database guides

[139]
Centre for Accessible Environments (CAE)

60 Gainsford Street
London SE1 2NY

Telephone and Minicom: 0171 357 8182

Fax: 0171 357 8183

Contact: Ann Sawyer (Head of Technical Information)

Objectives and Purposes: To act as an information and training resource on accessibility for the construction industry, care professions and disabled people; committed to the provision of buildings and environments that are accessible to all people, including disabled and older people

Stock and Subject Coverage: A library with a wide range of books and journals covering access to the built environment; current awareness files are maintained

Services/Facilities: Access audits and appraisals; training and seminars; and an Architectural Advisory Service - register of architects experienced in designing accessible buildings

Availability: By prior appointment, for reference use only; enquiries by personal visit, telephone or letter are handled

Hours: 09.00-17.00

Publications: Access by Design (3 per year); other ad hoc publications, the most recent being Reading and Using Plans, Access Audits (a guide and checklists), and Designing for Accessibility (an introductory guide)

[140]

Centre for Health Studies, University of Durham (CHS)

Centre for Health Studies
University of Durham
Elvet Riverside
New Elvet
Durham DH1 3JT

Telephone: Direct: 0191 374 4734; Office: 0191 374 2313

Fax: 0191 374 7010

E-mail: s.m.childs@durham.ac.uk (Health Information Officer)

World Wide Web: http://www.dur.ac.uk/~dss0zz2/index.htm

Contact: Director: Dr Philip Cheung; Health Information Officer: Susan Childs

Objectives and Purposes: The Centre for Health Studies is the focus for health-related research and graduate studies at the University of Durham. The principal activity is research and the Centre is developing a diverse and expanding range of projects in collaboration with health and community care agencies

Stock and Subject Coverage: The role of the Health Information Officer within the Centre of Health Studies is to: (a) provide information support for the Centre's research activities, (b) produce a bi-monthly health research/health information bulletin for circulation to local health-related personnel and information centres, (c) assist the Centre's support of the research activities of local health-related personnel by LIS skills training and (d) develop health information research projects and consultancies. There is no library service

Availability: People interested in developing contacts with the Centre for research, consultancy or training activities can access the Centre by post or IT routes. No material is available for loan or reference. Any charge for services would depend on the nature of the request

Hours: 10.00-17.00

Publications: Health Facts. Bulletin of the Centre for Health Studies (bi-monthly); Centre for Health Studies flyer

[141]

Centre for Pregnancy Nutrition

Department of Obstetrics and Gynaecology
Clinical Sciences Centre
Northern General Hospital
Herries Road
Sheffield S5 7AU

Telephone: 0114 242 4084

Fax: 0114 261 7584

E-mail: pregnancynutrition@sheffield.ac.uk

Contact: Mrs Fiona Ford (Research Dietician); Ms Charlotte Evans (Dietician)

Objectives and Purposes: To provide a focal point for continuing research programmes into nutritional physiology of human pregnancy; to develop a database of national observations and interventions in pregnancy and lactation for electronic publication; to house a national 'Eating in Pregnancy' helpline to answer queries from the public, media, health professionals, and fellow scientists

Stock and Subject Coverage: 4,000 original articles on nutritional observations and interventions relating to pregnancy and lactation, dating back over 40 years. There is a computerised citation index. Also various health education materials (booklets, leaflets, posters, etc.)

Services/Facilities: Helpline service; information also supplied by post or fax; database searches

Availability: Telephone and written enquiries; freely available

Hours: 09.00-14.00 (answerphone available out of hours)

Publications: Healthy Eating for You and Your Baby; research papers; annual report

Related Bodies: University of Sheffield

[142]

Centre for Women's Health

6 Sandyford Place
Sauchiehall Street
Glasgow G3 7NB

Telephone: 0141 211 670

Fax: 0141 211 6702

E-mail: cfwh@cqm.co.uk

Contact: Jenni Campbell (Information Worker)

Objectives and Purposes: To provide free information, self-help and suport groups, training and development, a lesbian health service, counselling, current awareness bulletin and a helpline database

Stock and Subject Coverage: Material on women's physical, emotional and mental health

Availability: Free membership; women only

Hours: 10.00-21.00 Tuesday to Thursday (Monday and Friday by appointment only)

[143]

Chace Postgraduate Medical Centre Library

Chase Farm Hospital
The Ridgeway
Enfield
Middlesex EN2 8JL

Telephone: 0181 366 6600, ext 5500; Direct line: 0181 364 5502

Fax: 0181 363 4662

Contact: Mrs H Frankel (Librarian)

Objectives and Purposes: To provide a library service within the postgraduate educational service provided by the Centre to junior hospital doctors and local medical/dental professionals

Stock and Subject Coverage: Clinical and pre-clinical books (excluding nursing), and 80 journals

Services/Facilities: MEDLINE on CD-ROM; interlibrary loans

Availability: To hospital staff and other local professionals; personal visits preferred; most material may be borrowed; charges for interlibrary photocopies are passed on to readers

Hours: 09.00-17.00

Publications: Library guide; new books list

---

[144]

Charing Cross and Westminster Medical School, University of London

(1) The Reynolds Building
St Dunstans Road
London W6 8RP

(2) Chelsea and Westminster
369 Fulham Road
London SW10 9NH

Telephone: Charing Cross: 0181 846 7159; Chelsea and Westminster: 0181 746 8107

Fax: Charing Cross: 0181 846 7565; Chelsea and Westminster: 0181 746 8215

E-mail: library@cxwms.ac.uk

Contact: Mrs Susan V Howard (Charing Cross); Mr Reinhard Wentz (Chelsea and Westminster)

Objectives and Purposes: To provide a multidisciplinary service for staff and students of the medical school, and staff of the associated hospitals

Stock and Subject Coverage: 20,000 books; 500 current periodicals covering all aspects of pre-clinical and clinical medicine; there is a growing collection in the fields of nursing, midwifery and professions allied to medicine. There is an extensive audio-visual collection and a CAL laboratory. A number of bibliographic databases, including MEDLINE (which is networked), are available on CD-ROM

Services/Facilities: Photocopies; fax; word processing

Availability: Researchers who are not members may use the facilities for reference, free of charge, up to five times per year. For more extensive use they should become associate members (fee charged)

Hours: 09.00-21.00 Monday to Thursday; 09.00-20.00 Friday; 09.00-12.00 Saturday

Publications: Various library guides; newsletter; Medical School Annual Report

---

[145]

Chest, Heart and Stroke Scotland (CHSS)

65 North Castle Street
Edinburgh EH2 3LT

Telephone: 0131 225 6963; Adviceline: 0345 720720; answerphone out of office hours

Fax: 0131 220 6313

Contact: Lesley Munro (Education and Development Director)

Objectives and Purposes: A medical charity, CHSS aims to improve the quality of life for people affected by chest, heart or stroke illness through programmes of medical research, health promotion and the provision of services

Services/Facilities: Enquiry/information service; health promotion programmes; details of over 100 groups for chest, heart or stroke patients in Scotland

Hours: 09.00-16.30

Publications: List available for over 40 titles, mainly patient-carer related; directory of groups; newsletter (quarterly); annual report

---

[146]

CHILD

Charter House
43 St Leonards Road
Bexhill-on-Sea
East Sussex TN40 1JA

Telephone: 01424 732361

Fax: 01424 731858

E-mail: office@email2.child.org.uk

World Wide Web: www: http://www.child.org.uk

Contact: Clare Brown (Executive Director)

Objectives and Purposes: To encourage the exchange of information and mutual support between couples themselves; e.g. by setting up local support groups. To promote public awareness as to the extent of infertility in the UK and the severe impact it can have on a couple's quality of life

Stock and Subject Coverage: Material on infertility, together with linked subjects such as adoption

Services/Facilities: LINKLINE - When the office is not staffed, the telephone number of a volunteer is provided, who is usually available to talk to both non-members and members alike. Please note that the linkline is not manned by medically qualified personnel

Availability: Telephone and written enquiries; membership available for £15 annually

Hours: 24 hour services through Telephone Helpline, run by volunteers to provide advice seven days a week. This service offers help to those who need to talk to someone with both knowledge and personal experience in a particular area of infertility. Please note that these lines are not manned by qualified personnel

Publications: Range of factsheets; CHILDchat - quarterly magazine free to members. Full list available

Related Bodies: National Infertility Awareness Campaign (NIAC), PO Box 9399, London SW9 0ZE (Freephone: 0800 716345). Local CHILD Groups - A network of contacts around the country providing local support and/or group meetings

---

[147]

Child Accident Prevention Trust (CAPT)

4th Floor
18-20 Farringdon Lane
London EC1R 3AU
Telephone: 0171 608 3828
Fax: 0171 608 3674
E-mail: safe@capt.demon.co.uk
Contact: Carol Sherriff (Director); Susan Pinckney (Press and Information Officer - Enquiries)
Objectives and Purposes: Research into childhood accidents and the dissemination of information to professionals and the public. Campaigns aimed at accident prevention, such as Child Safety Week
Stock and Subject Coverage: Ca. 10,000 items, mostly papers and journal articles, covering all aspects of childhood accidents - their background, outcome and prevention
Services/Facilities: Fax; photocopies (priced)
Availability: Freely available to anyone by prior appointment. Written enquiries accepted, but please enclose s.a.e. No loans. Complex searches may be charged for if CAPT staff are heavily involved
Hours: 10.00-16.00
Publications: List available on request

[148]

Child Growth Foundation (CGF)

2 Mayfield Avenue
London W4 1PW
Telephone: 0181 994 7625/995 0257
Fax: 0181 995 9075
E-mail: cgf.london@aol.com
Contact: Tam Fry; Lynne Norris; Rita Chesney
Objectives and Purposes: To ensure that every child's growth is regularly assessed throughout its childhood against the new UK growth charts, and to ensure that any child growing too slowly or too much is referred for medical attention. It maintains a pateint support network for families of children under treatment
Stock and Subject Coverage: Material on all kinds of growth disorders (no library facility)
Publications: List available

[149]

Children's Liver Disease Foundation

1st Floor
138 Digbeth
Birmingham B5 6DR
Telephone: 0121 643 7282
Fax: 0121 643 8262
World Wide Web:
    http://www.nahat.net/childliverdisease
Contact: Mrs Catherine Arkley (Director); Mrs Sue Davis (Family Support Officer)
Objectives and Purposes: To fund research into all aspects of paediatric liver disease; to promote awareness of paediatric liver disease; to provide education for the public and medical profession on paediatric liver disease; to provide information; to provide an emotional support service for families
Stock and Subject Coverage: Wide range of patient literature
Hours: 09.00-17.00 (Answerphone out of hours)

[150]

★Chiltern Medical Library

Chiltern Postgraduate Medical Centre
Wycombe General Hospital
High Wycombe
Buckinghamshire HP11 2TT
Telephone: 01494 425573
Fax: 01494 425975
Contact: Mrs L Martyn (Library Services Manager); Mrs J Kendell (Library Assistant)
Objectives and Purposes: To provide library and information services for staff and GPs in the area
Stock and Subject Coverage: 3,700 books; 120 periodicals covering medicine and related health care, including health service management
Services/Facilities: Online and CD-ROM searches; photocopies; interlibrary loans; fax
Availability: By prior appointment, for reference use only
Hours: 09.00-17.30
Publications: Library guide; accessions lists
Related Bodies: Sub-library at Amersham General Hospital; part of HeLIN

[151]

Christie Hospital NHS Trust and Paterson Institute for Cancer Research

Wilmslow Road
Withington
Manchester M20 4BX
Telephone: 0161 446 3452/3455/3456
Fax: 0161 446 3454
E-mail: libmh@picr.cr.man.ac.uk
Contact: Mr N Rainford (Systems Librarian)
Objectives and Purposes: To provide oncology related information to staff of the hospital and research laboratories
Stock and Subject Coverage: 3,000 books; 120 current periodicals covering oncology and related fields
Availability: NHS staff and bona fide researchers by appointment. Loans to site staff only. Enquiries by telephone, fax or letter. Reference facilities. Photocopies (5p per page). Proof of identity may be requested
Hours: 09.00-19.00 Monday to Wednesday; 08.00-17.30 Thursday; 08.00-17.00 Friday; 09.00-13.00 Saturday

[152]

CIBA Foundation

41 Portland Place
London W1N 4BN
Telephone: 0171 637 2127
Fax: 0171 436 2840
E-mail: mrs@cibafound.org.uk
Contact: Dr Chris Langley (Head of Information)
Objectives and Purposes: The Foundation exists to organise scientific meetings; to provide library and information services; and generally to promote international co-operation in medical and chemical research
Stock and Subject Coverage: Textbooks, journals and key reference volumes in biomedicine and allied subjects
Services/Facilities: Photocopies; fax; CD-ROM searches; Science Citation Index
Availability: Open to any graduate. Visits or telephone enquiries welcomed. Charges levied for photocopies, faxes and CD-ROM searches
Hours: 09.00-18.00
Publications: Foundation Quarterly Bulletin; annual handbook; Media Resource Service newsletter (2 per year)

[153]

City Hospital NHS Trust
formerly Dudley Road Hospital

Peter Gilroy Bevan Library
Postgraduate Centre
Dudley Road
Birmingham B18 7QH
Telephone: 0121 507 4491
Fax: 0121 523 4562
E-mail: karen@drhmelib.demon.co.uk
Contact: Mrs Karen Bowen (Librarian)
Objectives and Purposes: To provide a library service to medical, paramedical and other hospital specialist staff. Also covers the Department of Geriatric Medicine Library, City Hospital NHS Trust
Stock and Subject Coverage: 4,000 books; 130 periodicals covering general medicine, surgery, dermatology, ophthalmology and geriatric medicine
Services/Facilities: Photocopies (at cost); CD-ROM and Internet searches; fax (at cost)
Availability: To staff, and by appointment to other hospital staff from the West Midlands Region. Enquiries by telephone, fax, e-mail or letter are accepted. Reference enquiries. Loans to staff only
Hours: 08.30-20.00 (closes 19.00 on Friday)
Publications: Weekly current awareness bulletin; new books list (quarterly); library leaflet

[154]

Coeliac Society

PO Box 220
High Wycombe
Buckinghamshire HP11 2HY
Telephone: 01494 437278
Fax: 01494 474349
Contact: Mrs J Wilson (Office Manager)
Objectives and Purposes: Self-help charity for those who have been medically diagnosed as having the coeliac condition, or dermatisis herpetiformis. Its aim is to advance education in and understanding of these conditions for patients, their families, friends and carers. Advice is given on how to cope with these life-long medical conditions, the main treatment for which is a strict gluten-free diet. The Coeliac Society promotes research into the nature, causes, treatment and cure of the two conditions
Services/Facilities: Information on the coeliac condition and dermatitis herpetiformis; leaflets; food lists; handbook recipe book; holiday guide (UK); a video is also available
Hours: 09.15-15.00
Publications: Annual list of gluten-free manufactured foods; bi-annual magazine
Related Bodies: Network of local support groups

[155]

Colchester and North East Essex Postgraduate Medical Library

Colchester General Hospital
Colchester CO4 5JL
Telephone: 01206 832146
Fax: 01206 851231
Contact: Ruth Fosker (District Librarian)
Objectives and Purposes: To support the training needs of doctors in the local NHS Trusts
Stock and Subject Coverage: 4,000 books; 120 periodicals covering general medicine, and related disciplines
Services/Facilities: Multidisciplinary library in the afternoons
Availability: By prior appointment, for reference use only (fee charged)
Hours: 09.00-17.00 Monday, Thursday and Friday; 09.00-20.00 Tuesday and Wednesday

[156]

College of Occupational Therapists, Disability Information and Study Centre (COT)

6-8 Marshalsea Road
Southwark
London SE1 1HL
Telephone: 0171 357 6480
Fax: 0171 207 9612
Contact: Sandra Harwood (Information Services Officer)

Objectives and Purposes: The professional association for occupational therapists in the UK

Stock and Subject Coverage: Specialist library covering occupational therapy, and other related literature

Services/Facilities: Current awareness service (priced); photocopies; postal loans; literature searches

Availability: Telephone and written enquiries (£5 charge for services to non-members)

Hours: 09.00–17.00

Publications: List available

[157]

Common Services Agency for the NHS in Scotland, Information and Statistics Division (CSA)

Library B044
Trinity Park House
South Trinity Road
Edinburgh EH5 3SE

Telephone: 0131 551 8087

Fax: 0131 551 1392

E-mail: alanj@isdlib.demon.co.uk

Contact: AH Jamieson (Manager, Information Services)

Objectives and Purposes: To collect, validate, collate, summarise, promulgate, interpret and advise on Scottish health statistics

Stock and Subject Coverage: Health and population statistics. Special collection of NHS in Scotland circulars

Services/Facilities: The Library acts as the national centre for information and advice on health statistics. Information is provided in the appropriate format - photocopy; fax; computer disk; or loan of books

Availability: All approaches considered

Hours: 09.00–17.00

Publications: Annual journals list

[158]

Confederation of Healing Organisations (CHO)

The Red and White House
113 High Street
Berkhamsted
Hertfordshire HP4 2DJ

Telephone: 01442 870660

Fax: 01442 870667

Contact: Cdr JDL Repard OBE DSC FIMgt

Objectives and Purposes: To make healing available (as a complementary therapy) on the NHS and in private medicine

Availability: Those seeking referral to a healer may telephone or write (s.a.e. required); some healers charge a reasonable fee, others accept a donation, and some make no charge

Hours: 09.30–14.00 Monday to Thursday

Related Bodies: CHO has 12 self-administering member associations (all registered charities) with ca. 7,000 contact and distant healers

[159]

Contact a Family (CaF)

170 Tottenham Court Road
London W1P 0HA

Telephone: 0171 383 3555

Fax: 0171 383 0259

Contact: Harry Marsh (Director); Carol Youngs (Assistant Director)

Objectives and Purposes: To support the families of children with any kind of special need or disability and to encourage the establishment of mutual support groups

Stock and Subject Coverage: Collection of 1,000 books and pamphlets, plus grey literature and periodicals covering specific conditions, family networks, etc.

Services/Facilities: The collection is uncatalogued as there is not yet a library service, or librarian. Advice available to families who need it

Availability: CaF is not yet in a position to handle bibliographic enquiries

Publications: Range of books, pamphlets, directories, factsheets, etc. List available

[160]

Cookridge Hospital Postgraduate Medical Library

Hospital Lane
Leeds LS16 6QB

Telephone: 0113 267 3411

Contact: Ms JR Walker (Librarian)

Objectives and Purposes: To provide library and information services for postgraduate staff employed by United Leeds Teaching Hospitals Trust, and other personnel employed at Cookridge

Stock and Subject Coverage: 700 books; 88 periodicals. Mainly covers oncology and radiotherapy, with some material on nursing, management, etc.

Services/Facilities: CD-ROM searches; computerised catalogue; photocopies (priced)

Availability: Staff only

Hours: 24 hours

Related Bodies: United Leeds Teaching Hospitals Trust

[161]

Coronary Artery Disease Research Association (CORDA)

121 Sydney Street
London SW3 6NR

Telephone: 0171 349 8686

Fax: 0171 349 9414

Contact: Anthony Burns (Executive Director); Sheila James (Information)

Objectives and Purposes: A medical research charity raising and applying funds for research into the prevention of premature death and disability from cardiovascular diseases by early diagnosis and non-surgical treatment

Availability: Telephone and written enquiries accepted

Hours: 09.30–17.00

[162]

Council for Professions Supplementary to Medicine (CPSM)

Park House
184 Kennington Park Road
London SE11 4BU
Telephone: 0171 582 0866
Fax: 0171 820 9684
Contact: Mr MD Hall (Registrar); Peter Burley and Miss G Malcolm (Deputy Registrars)
Objectives and Purposes: To provide state registration for the professions of chiropody, dietetics, medical laboratory service, occupational therapy, orthotics, physiotherapy and radiography by the maintenance of registers, approval of educational arrangements, and the maintenance of high professional and personal standards
Availability: Freely available
Hours: 09.00-17.00
Publications: Registers for the above-mentioned professions; annual report

[163]

Coventry University Nursing and Midwifery Library

Walsgrave Hospital
Clifford Bridge Road
Walsgrave
Coventry CV2 2DX
Telephone: 01203 602020, ext 8366
Fax: 01203 538838
Contact: DA Guest (Nursing and Midwifery Librarian)
Objectives and Purposes: To provide library and information services for nursing and midwifery education
Stock and Subject Coverage: 25,000 books; 120 periodicals. Covers nursing and allied health subjects
Services/Facilities: CD-ROM searches; photocopies
Availability: Freely available for reference use
Hours: 09.00-17.00
Publications: Bi-annual newsletter; annual report

[164]

CRC Beatson Laboratories

Garscube Estate
Switchback Road
Bearsden
Glasgow G61 1BD
Telephone: 0141 942 9361
Fax: 0141 942 6521
E-mail: gpma16@udcf.gla.ac.uk
Contact: Mrs E Gordon (Librarian)
Objectives and Purposes: Cancer research
Stock and Subject Coverage: Mainly periodicals, some books, covering cancer; genetics; virology; molecular and cell biology; and drugs/therapeutics
Services/Facilities: Online and CD-ROM searches; photocopies; fax
Availability: By prior appointment, for reference use only
Hours: 09.00-17.00
Publications: CRC Beatson Laboratories Scientific Report (annual); CRC Beatson Laboratories Prospectus (irregular)
Related Bodies: Linked with the Beatson Oncology Centre, Western Infirmary, Glasgow, and with Glasgow University Library

[165]

Crosshouse Hospital

Medical Library
Kilmarnock KA2 0BE
Telephone: 01563 577092
Fax: 01563 577096
Contact: Susan Cuthbertson (Library Services Manager); Betty Kerr and Iris McMahon (Library Assistants)
Objectives and Purposes: To provide library and information services for Trust staff
Stock and Subject Coverage: Material on medicine; nursing; paramedical professions; occupational therapy; speech therapy; pharmacology; and health service management
Services/Facilities: Literature searches; fax; photocopies
Availability: By prior appointment, for reference use only. Telephone and written enquiries accepted
Hours: 09.45-17.00 (closes 16.30 on Friday)
Publications: Library Update
Related Bodies: North Ayrshire and Arran NHS Trust

[166]

Cystic Fibrosis Trust (CF Trust)

5 Blyth Road
Bromley
Kent BR1 3RS
Telephone: 0181 464 7211
Fax: 0181 313 0472
Contact: Mrs R Barnes (Executive Director); Dr MT Scott (Medical and Scientific Administrator); Mr P Kent (Director, Family and Adult Support Services)
Objectives and Purposes: To raise funds to finance research to find a cure for cystic fibrosis (CF) and to improve the care and treatment of people with CF; to provide support for those affected by CF, their families and carers. To educate and raise public awareness of CF
Stock and Subject Coverage: A range of factsheets, booklets, videos and audiocassettes on CF and CF treatment
Availability: Telephone and written enquiries
Hours: 09.00-17.00 (answerphone out of hours)
Publications: CF News (4 per year); Research Grants List (annual); annual report
Related Bodies: Member of International CF Association

[167]
Darlington Memorial Hospital NHS Trust

Hollyhurst Road
Darlington
Co. Durham DL3 6HX
Telephone: 01325 380100
Fax: 01325 743622
Contact: Mrs Barbara Mais (Medical Librarian);
Mrs Carol Houghton (Assistant Librarian)
Objectives and Purposes: To provide library and
information services to medical staff
Stock and Subject Coverage: 5,000 books; 80
periodicals; covering all medical subjects, and
psychiatry. Collection of videos
Services/Facilities: Online and CD-ROM searches;
photocopies (priced); interlibrary loans
Availability: By prior appointment, for reference use
only
Hours: 09.30-17.30
Publications: Darlington Postgraduate Journal (2 per
year)

[168]
Dementia Services Development Centre (DSDC)

University of Stirling
Stirling FK9 4LA
Telephone: 01786 467740
Fax: 01786 466846
E-mail: mtm1@stir.ac.uk
World Wide Web: http://www.stir.ac.uk/dsdc
Contact: Mrs Averil Harrison or Mrs Anne
McCulloch (Information Officers); James Grant
(IT Manager)
Objectives and Purposes: DSDC exists to extend and
improve services for people with dementia and
their carers by providing information,
development assistance, conferences and seminars,
publications, research and training to any manager,
planner or provider of services in the statutory,
voluntary or private sector
Stock and Subject Coverage: A specialist library on
dementia care and related topics. There are two
databases: library material, and specialist services
Services/Facilities: Database searches for anyone
working in the field of dementia service
provision (£10 outside Scotland). Books and
reports available for loan, and journal articles
photocopied subject to copyright restrictions.
Remote databases may be searched through the
University Library
Availability: Loans within Scotland, otherwise
reference use only
Hours: 10.00-16.00
Publications: List available
Related Bodies: Close relationship with Alzheimer
Scotland - Action on Dementia

[169]
Department of Experimental Psychology

Downing Street
Cambridge CB2 3EB
Telephone: 01223 333554
Fax: 01223 333564
Contact: Mrs E Ingle (Library Assistant in Charge);
Dr A Dickinson (Honorary Academic Librarian)
Objectives and Purposes: Teaching and research within
the University of Cambridge
Stock and Subject Coverage: 10,000 books; 110 current
periodicals. Covers experimental psychology and
psychopathology. Oldfield Collection (mostly on
VISION)
Services/Facilities: Photocopies; interlibrary loans
(members only); database searches (members
only); access to online catalogue
Availability: To all members of the University; others
by arrangement. Telephone and written enquiries
accepted when time permits
Hours: 09.00-17.30 (closes 17.15 out of Term);
09.00-13.00 Saturday (termtime only)

[170]
Department of Health Library and Information Service (DH)

(1) Room G17C
Skipton House
80 London Road
London SE1 6LW
Telephone: 0171 972 6541
Fax: 0171 972 5976/1609
Contact: Mr M Lees

(2) Room 5/C/05
Quarry House
Quarry Hill
Leeds LS2 7UE
Telephone: 0113 254 5080
Fax: 0113 254 5084
Contact: Mrs PL Bower

(3) Room G12
Wellington House
133-135 Waterloo Road
London SE1 8UG
Telephone: 0171 972 4204
Fax: 0171 972 4209
Contact: Ms M Peffer

Contact: Ian Snowley (Head, Library and
Information Services)
Objectives and Purposes: Responsible (in England) for
the administration of the NHS; for the social
services provided by local authorities; and for
certain aspects of public health. It also makes
reciprocal arrangements with other countries, and
represents the UK in the World Health
Organization and other fora

Stock and Subject Coverage: Ca. 200,000 books and pamphlets; ca. 2,000 current periodicals on health service management; public health; and the personal social services

Availability: By prior appointment, for reference use only; general enquiries about the Department should be made to the Public Enquiry Office on 0171 210 4850

Hours: 09.00-17.00

Publications: Health Service Abstracts (monthly); DHSS-Data (bibliographic database of library stock)

Related Bodies: Departmental agencies - Medicines Control Agency, NHS Estates Agency, and Medical Devices Agency

[171]

Derby City General Hospital NHS Trust, Medical Library

Postgraduate Medical Education Centre
Uttoxeter Road
Derby DE22 3NE
Telephone: 01332 340131, ext 5192
Fax: 01332 200318
Contact: Mrs JH Padmore (Medical Librarian)
Objectives and Purposes: To provide library and information services for local staff
Stock and Subject Coverage: 2,100 books; 98 periodicals covering medicine in general
Services/Facilities: Current awareness service; CD-ROM literature searches; photocopies; fax
Availability: By prior appointment, for reference use only
Hours: 09.00-17.00

[172]

Derbyshire Royal Infirmary Medical Library

London Road
Derby DE1 2QY
Telephone: 01332 254788
Fax: 01332 254608
Contact: Mrs MGT Lathbury (Medical Librarian)
Objectives and Purposes: Provision of information to the medical community within the hospital, and to the local community. A postgraduate medical library
Stock and Subject Coverage: 5,000 books; 150 periodicals. Covers all aspects of medicine (except nursing)
Services/Facilities: Online and CD-ROM searches; fax (services for members only)
Availability: By prior appointment, for reference use only
Hours: 08.00-17.00; 09.00-12.30 Saturday
Publications: Newsletter; weekly current awareness publication

[173]

Dermatomyositis and Polymyositis Support Group (D&P Support Group)

146 Newtown Road
Woolston
Southampton SO19 9HR
Telephone: 01703 449708
Fax: 01703 396402
Contact: Mr Les Oakley (Chairman); Mrs Irene Oakley (Secretary)
Objectives and Purposes: To give support and information to sufferers and their families and to help give them a better understanding of their illness, to relieve the isolation felt when a rare illness is diagnosed and to guide sufferers in the right direction for treatment; to promote research by fundraising
Stock and Subject Coverage: Research information and reports on D&P; seminar transcripts
Availability: Telephone and written enquiries; visits by prior arrangement; information supplied to anyone with an interest in D&P
Hours: 09.00-17.00 (answerphone available out of hours)
Publications: Booklet on Dermatomyositis and Polymyositis; quarterly newsletter; medical updates

[174]

Dewsbury Health Care Staff Library

Education Centre
Dewsbury and District Hospital
Healds Road
Dewsbury
West Yorkshire WF13 4HS
Telephone: 01924 465105, ext 3463
Fax: 01924 816127
Contact: Mrs Francesca Pendino (Librarian);
Objectives and Purposes: To provide library and information services for all employees of Dewsbury Health Care
Stock and Subject Coverage: 12,000 books; 200 periodicals covering all aspects of medicine, nursing and health care in general
Services/Facilities: Online and CD-ROM searches; computerised catalogue; photocopies; current awareness service
Availability: Telephone and written enquiries; by prior appointment, for reference use only (charges for some services)
Hours: 09.00-17.00 (opens 09.30 on Monday; closes 16.30 on Friday)

[175]

Diabetes Foundation

177A Tennison Road
London SE25 5NF
Telephone: 0181 656 5467
Contact: Arthur Bennett (Co-ordinator)
Objectives and Purposes: To raise funds so that grants can be made to doctors and scientists in their quest to find the cure for diabetes in the shortest time possible; the Foundation promotes diabetes education and is doing everything possible so that diabetics can avoid the long-term complications of the disease. The provision of blood glucose monitor packs free of charge to diabetic children
Publications: List available

[176]

Disability Action

2 Annadale Avenue
Belfast BT7 3JH
Telephone: 01232 491011
Fax: 01232 491627
Contact: Brigid Heggarty (Information Officer)
Objectives and Purposes: To ensure that people with disabilities attain their full rights as citizens. This is an umbrella organisation with 180 member groups
Stock and Subject Coverage: Books, reports, periodicals, statistics, legislation and videos on disability related health and welfare matters (non-medical)
Services/Facilities: Information service on benefits, access, holidays, employment, transport, etc. to disabled people, carers and service providers; photocopies (priced). Material available in audio and large print formats
Availability: Telephone and written enquiries; visits by appointment
Hours: By appointment
Publications: Monthly bulletin; annual report

[177]

Disability Information Service Surrey (DISS)

Harrowlands Centre
Harrowlands Park
Dorking
Surrey RH4 2RA
Telephone: 01306 875156; Minicom: 0306 742128
Fax: 01306 741740
E-mail: diss@dial.pipex.com
World Wide Web:
    http://dspace.dial.pipex.com/town/square/ad544
Contact: Judy Walker (Manager); Hazel Plastow (Deputy and IT Manager)
Objectives and Purposes: To provide a free, confidential, independent information and advice service covering all aspects of disability

Stock and Subject Coverage: Large library of leaflets, booklets, articles, catalogues and brochures on all aspects of disability, including treatments and therapies, equipment, benefits, health and welfare, sport and leisure, recreation, transport, and access. A large internal database of 4,500 national disability service providers and suppliers
Services/Facilities: Minicom text telephone; fax; cassettes for visually-impaired persons; enquiry service; photocopies; database searches
Availability: Open to disabled people, carers, relatives, service providers - anyone with an interest in disability. Access by visit, telephone, fax or letter; building is completely accessible. Appointments required
Hours: 10.00-13.00 and 14.00-16.00 (answerphone out of hours)
Publications: Paperchase (bi-monthly newsletter); various directories, databases, etc. (list available)
Related Bodies: DISS is a unit of the Queen Elizabeth's Foundation for Disabled People; there are six satellite units in Surrey

[178]

Disability Scotland

Princes House
5 Shandwick Place
Edinburgh EH2 4RE
Telephone: 0131 229 8632
Fax: 0131 229 5168
Contact: David Dunsmuir (Director); Kirsten Anne Ferguson
Objectives and Purposes: To improve the active participation of people with disabilities in mainstream society and to reduce their isolation
Stock and Subject Coverage: Material on all aspects of disability. Most information supplied through a new bibliographic database which will focus on all of Disability Scotland's areas of interest
Services/Facilities: Enquiry service; CD-ROM searches
Availability: To anyone with a need, through the Enquiry Service
Hours: 10.00-16.00
Publications: List available

[179]

Disability Wales (DW)

Llys Ifor
Crescent Road
Caerphilly CF83 1XL
Telephone: 01222 887325
Fax: 01222 888702
E-mail: dw-ac@mcri.poptel.org.uk
Contact: Howard John (Director); Clive Curtis (Information Manager)
Objectives and Purposes: To promote the rights, recognition and support of all disabled people in Wales
Stock and Subject Coverage: Collection of books, magazines and periodicals covering disability-related subjects. Limited library material for reference use

Services/Facilities: Free information to all disabled people in Wales; regular mailings

Availability: To all with an interest in disability in Wales

Hours: 09.00-13.00 and 14.00-17.00

Publications: Newsletter; journals; annual report; various ad hoc publications

Related Bodies: DW is the umbrella organisation of disability organisations in Wales

[180]

Disablement Income Group (DIG)

Unit 5
Archway Business Centre
19-23 Wedmore Street
London N19 4RZ

Telephone: 0171 263 3981

Fax: 0171 561 1300

Contact: Pauline Thompson MBE (Director); Pauline Greaves (Information Services Manager)

Objectives and Purposes: To improve the financial circumstances of disabled people through advice, advocacy, information and research

Stock and Subject Coverage: Material on Social Security benefits and other financial issues, e.g. local authority charging policies, pension arrangements, etc. Small library and a comprehensive filing system

Services/Facilities: Free advice and information

Availability: Telephone and written enquiries accepted; visits by prior arrangement

Hours: 10.30-16.30

Publications: Quarterly journal; range of research studies and information practice guides (list available)

[181]

Disfigurement Guidance Centre/Laserfair/Childfriend

PO Box 7
Cupar
Fife KY15 4PF

Telephone: 01337 870281/839084

Fax: 01337 870310/839105

Contact: Doreen Trust or Peter Trust

Objectives and Purposes: To provide support in relation to all aspects of disfigurement; Laserfair funds research into and promotes medical lasers and responsible usage; Childfriend funds and establishes child-friendly treatment environments in hospitals

Stock and Subject Coverage: Material covering treatments; science; technology; psychology; social, educational, and research aspects; professional and patient liaison; and management, all with regard to disfigurement. Specialist interest in skin lasers

Services/Facilities: Database searches; photocopies. This is the UK's only specialist skin laser resource

Availability: Telephone and written enquiries (s.a.e. required). Visits by appointment only

Hours: 09.00-16.00

Publications: Skinlaser Today (quarterly); Skinlaser Directory (annual); full list available

[182]

Doncaster Royal Infirmary, Child Health Information Centre Library (CHIC)

Thorne Road
Doncaster DN2 5LT

Telephone: 01302 553233

Contact: Mrs C Franks (Librarian, Welfare Services)

Objectives and Purposes: An extension of the Health Information Service specialising in material on child health; the objective is to act as an information resource for parents, families, carers, children and health professionals

Stock and Subject Coverage: Books and leaflets on various childhood diseases and disabilities for children and adults, literature on local and national self-help groups, subject files, specialist toy and supplier catalogues, and a number of specialist toys

Services/Facilities: Photocopies; fax

Availability: Open to any child with a special need, or to parents, families or carers of such a child

Hours: Under review

Related Bodies: Part of Health and Welfare Library and Information Services, provided by Doncaster Library and Information Services

[183]

Doncaster Royal Infirmary, Medical and Professional Library

Armthorpe Road
Doncaster DN2 8LT

Telephone: 01302 553118

Contact: Miss Margaret Evans (Principal Librarian, Hospital and Welfare Services); Mrs Chris Gamage (Medical Librarian)

Objectives and Purposes: To provide comprehensive library and information services to all employees within Doncaster Health Authority

Stock and Subject Coverage: 15,000 books; 163 periodicals covering all aspects of health care, but especially medicine

Services/Facilities: Online and CD-ROM searches; photocopies; fax

Availability: By prior appointment, for reference use only

Hours: 09.00-17.00

Related Bodies: Part of Trent Regional Association of Health Care Libraries and Information Specialists

[184]

Doncaster Royal Infirmary, Patients Library

Armthorpe Road
Doncaster DN2 5LT

Telephone: 01302 553233

Contact: Mrs C Franks (Librarian, Welfare Services)

Objectives and Purposes: To aid patient rehabilitation by the provision of health information material, written in a format that can be understood by the layman, in addition to recreational and educational reading

Stock and Subject Coverage: A range of recreational and educational material, and a specialist collection of books, leaflets and subject files on all aspects of health information

Services/Facilities: Helpbox - database of health information

Availability: Via Doncaster Library and Information Services

Hours: 09.00-17.00

Related Bodies: Part of Health and Welfare Library and Information Services, provided by Doncaster Library and Information Services

[185]

Down's Syndrome Association (DSA)

155 Mitcham Road
London SW17 9PG
Telephone: 0181 682 4001
Fax: 0181 682 4012
Contact: Sarah Rutter; Susannah Symon
Objectives and Purposes: To provide information, support and advice on all aspects of Down's Syndrome. To support a network of parent-led branches

Stock and Subject Coverage: Material on all aspects of Down's Syndrome; leaflets and books for sale

Services/Facilities: Free advice and information to people with the condition, and to carers

Availability: Telephone and written enquiries; visits by appointment

Hours: 09.00-17.00

Publications: List available

[186]

Dr Jan de Winter Clinic for Cancer Prevention Advice (CPA)

6 New Road
Brighton BN1 1UF
Telephone: 01273 727213 (24-hour Helpline)
Fax: 01273 748915
Contact: Dr Jan de Winter (Hon. Medical Director)
Objectives and Purposes: A shop-fronted High Street walk-in clinic where anyone with a worry about cancer can walk in and receive instant advice and reassurance, as well as guidance on what steps, if any, will be necessary to elucidate the particular problem

Services/Facilities: Various facilities for people who are unable to obtain them under the NHS. These include x-ray mammography or ultrasound screening of breasts; ultrasound of testes and ovaries for silent cancer; cervical smear tests; estimation of blood concentration of the prostatic specific antigen; ultrasound of aorta, kidneys, liver, etc.; meditation classes; psychotherapy; slimming advice; ultrasound assessment of bone density for brittle bones (osteoporosis) with counselling on the advisability of HRT; blood cholesterol estimation; 24-hour telephone helpline

Availability: Open to anyone. Telephone and written enquiries; a modest charge is made for more complex investigations to people who can afford to pay, otherwise the services are free

Hours: 10.00-15.00

Publications: How to Avoid Cancer, and How to Die Young at Ninety (both by Dr Jan de Winter); What the Doctor Ordered (by Daniele de Winter and Joanna Read); various information leaflets

Related Bodies: This is the executive arm of the Dr Jan de Winter Cancer Prevention Foundation

[187]

Dudley Health Authority

12 Bull Street
Dudley
West Midlands DY1 2DD
Telephone: 01384 239376
Fax: 01384 455068
E-mail: JanB@DudleyHA.demon.co.uk
Contact: Mrs Jan Brown (Librarian)
Objectives and Purposes: To provide library and information services to all Health Authority staff

Stock and Subject Coverage: 1,000 books; 35 periodicals. Covers health service management and public health medicine

Services/Facilities: Online and CD-ROM searches; photocopies; interlibrary loans

Availability: Visits by prior arrangement

Hours: 09.30-13.30

Publications: Library guide; newsletter

[188]

Dunn Nutrition Centre (Medical Research Council)

Downhams Lane
Milton Road
Cambridge CB4 1XJ
Telephone: 01223 426356
Fax: 01223 426617
E-mail: rebecca.sewell@mrc-dunn.cam.ac.uk
World Wide Web: http://www.mrc-dunn.cam.ac.uk
Contact: Rebecca Sewell (Librarian)
Objectives and Purposes: Engages in basic and applied research into nutritional problems in the UK and the developing countries. The work includes the elucidation of biochemical and physiological processes involved in pregnancy, lactation, premature babies, growth during infancy and childhood, energy balance, obesity, the control of fermentation in the large intestine, and vitamins metabolism

Stock and Subject Coverage: 9,500 books; 160 periodicals. Covers nutrition; medicine; dietetics; chemistry; and biochemistry

Services/Facilities: Online database searches; interlibrary loans; photocopies

Availability: By prior appointment, for reference use only

Hours: 09.00-17.00
Publications: History of the Dunn; publications lists; various reports. List available
Related Bodies: Medical Research Council Unit Library

[189]
Dyslexia Institute (DI)

133 Gresham Road
Staines
Middlesex TW18 2AJ
Telephone: 01784 463851
Fax: 01784 460747
Contact: Reception, for information; Mrs Liz Brooks MA (Executive Director); Martin Turner MA Msc (Head of Psychology); Margaret Rooms MA (Head of Teaching Development); Janet Townend MA (Head of Training)
Objectives and Purposes: To be foremost in the provision of high quality psychological and educational assessment services for people who may be dyslexic; to be a leader in the teaching of people with dyslexia; to be a leader in the training of specialist and classroom teachers in the skills required to help people with dyslexia; to contribute to the enlargement and development of the body of knowledge and understanding about dyslexia, its origins and treatment, by informing and facilitating exchange of thinking
Stock and Subject Coverage: Material on dyslexia in general
Availability: On site reference only
Hours: 09.00-17.00
Publications: Dyslexia Review (4 per year); full list available on request

[190]
Dystonia Society

Weddel House
13-14 West Smithfield
London EC1A 9JJ
Telephone: 0171 329 0797
Fax: 0171 329 0689
Contact: Jutta Mason (Office Manager/Welfare Co-ordinator)
Objectives and Purposes: To support people who have any form of the neurological movement disorder known as dystonia; and their families, through the promotion of awareness, research and welfare
Stock and Subject Coverage: Material giving details about dystonia
Availability: By prior appointment, for reference use only
Hours: 08.30-16.30
Publications: Newsletter (3 per year); What is Dystonia?; video; annual report; Young Dystonia - newsletter

[191]
Dystrophic Epidermolysis Bullosa Research Association (DEBRA)

DEBRA House
13 Wellington Business Park
Dukes Ride
Crowthorne
Berkshire RG11 6LS
Telephone: 01344 771961
Fax: 01344 762661
Contact: John Dart (Director)
Objectives and Purposes: Patient Support Group for people with Epidermolysis Bullosa (EB) and their families. DEBRA supports research into EB and provides a number of welfare services including information, advocacy and nursing/paramedical advice
Stock and Subject Coverage: Material on all aspects of Epidermolysis Bullosa
Availability: Freely available on request
Hours: 09.00-17.30
Publications: Range of information booklets (free) for use by professionals and affected individuals; quarterly newsletter for members; DEBRA News (quarterly, for supporters)

[192]
East and North Hertfordshire Health Authority

Charter House
Parkway
Welwyn Garden City
Hertfordshire AL8 6JL
Telephone: 01707 390855
Fax: 01707 390864
Contact: Mrs Patti Bristow; Miss Helen Strappe; Mrs Yvonne Davies
Objectives and Purposes: To provide library and information services for health authority staff
Stock and Subject Coverage: Material on health care in general. Particular strength in grey literature
Availability: Telephone and written enquiries accepted; visits by prior arrangement
Hours: 09.00-17.00
Publications: List available
Related Bodies: West Hertfordshire Health Authority

[193]
East Cheshire Association for Medical Education

Postgraduate Medical Centre
Macclesfield District General Hospital
Victoria Road
Macclesfield
Cheshire SK10 3BL
Telephone: 01625 661362
Fax: 01625 663145
Contact: Mrs M Perry (Medical Librarian)

Objectives and Purposes: To provide medical library and information services for all doctors and dentists who live or work within the district
Stock and Subject Coverage: Books, periodicals and videos covering general medicine and dentistry
Services/Facilities: MEDLINE on CD-ROM; fax
Availability: By prior appointment, for reference use only
Hours: 09.00-17.00

[194]
East Glamorgan Hospital NHS Trust, Medical Staff Library

Church Village
Nr Pontypridd
Mid Glamorgan CF38 1AB
Telephone: 01443 216064
Fax: 01433 203697
Contact: Mrs PJ Evans BA FLA
Objectives and Purposes: To provide a library and information service for doctors in the area
Stock and Subject Coverage: 3,000 books; 120 periodicals in all fields of medicine
Services/Facilities: Online and CD-ROM searches; photocopies (priced); fax
Availability: Free to local doctors; other health professionals by arrangement; telephone and written enquiries accepted
Hours: 08.30-17.00 Monday, Wednesday and Friday; 13.00-20.00 Tuesday and Thursday
Publications: AWHL Union list

[195]
East Surrey Library and Information Service (ESLIS)

East Surrey Healthcare NHS Trust
East Surrey Hospital
Canada Avenue
Redhill RH1 5RH
Telephone: 01737 768511
Fax: 01737 782924
E-mail: sheila.ditchfield@dm.krinfo.ch
Contact: Sheila Ditchfield (Library and Information Services Manager); Fred Knight (Deputy Library and Information Services Manager)
Objectives and Purposes: To ensure the rapid and convenient access to reliable, up-to-date information on all aspects of health care and current best practice for all medical and non-medical staff of the Trust
Stock and Subject Coverage: 10,000 books; 200 periodicals covering medicine; nursing; health and NHS management. Merged with East Surrey Priority Healthcare in 1996 and so has now a strong collection in the fields of mental health and learning disabilities
Services/Facilities: Photocopies; fax; Internet access; multi-media training facility. Some charges apply
Availability: To NHS staff and local students; external membership available
Hours: 09.00-17.00

Publications: Newsletter; annual report; information sheet
Related Bodies: Part of South Thames Regional Library Network

[196]
Eastman Dental Institute and Hospital (EDI)

Library
Eastman Dental Hospital
256 Grays Inn Road
London WC1X 8LD
Telephone: 0171 915 1045
Fax: 0171 915 1012
E-mail: m.hunt@eastman.ucl.ac.uk
Contact: Sally Jacobs (main contact); Matt Hunt (Librarian)
Objectives and Purposes: To conduct research into oral and dental health care services
Stock and Subject Coverage: Material on dentistry, oral health care and oral surgery
Services/Facilities: Photocopies
Availability: Reference use available to researchers in relevant subjects, by appointment
Hours: 08.00-20.00 (closes 17.30 on Friday)
Publications: Library Guide; newsletter
Related Bodies: University of London; North East Thames RHA

[197]
Eating Disorders Association (EDA)

Sackville Place
44 Magdalen Street
Norwich NR3 1JE
Telephone: Administration: 01603 619090; Helpline: 01603 621414; Youth Helpline: 01603 765050
Fax: 01603 664915
Contact: Joanna Vincent (Director); Gaye Hailstone (Enquiries)
Objectives and Purposes: To promote help and understanding about anorexia and bulima nervosa for sufferers, their families, carers and professionals
Hours: 09.00-17.30 (Helpline: 09.00-18.30; Youth helpline: 16.00-18.00)

[198]
Edge Hill University College, School of Health Studies

Library
Aintree Complex
Fazakerley Hospital
Longmoor Lane
Liverpool L9 7AL
Telephone: 0151 529 3609
Fax: 0151 529 3088
Contact: Mrs MJ Carney (Library Learning Resource Manager); Mrs SC Astley; Miss Z Summerskill

Objectives and Purposes: To ensure that the information needs of all readers are provided

Stock and Subject Coverage: 25,000 books; 134 periodicals covering all aspects of health care and related disciplines. An internal database is maintained, and a weekly current awareness bulletin is produced

Services/Facilities: Loans; photocopies; free searches on internal database; CD-ROM searches (priced at cost); interlibrary loans; lecturers available for talks

Availability: Telephone and written enquiries; reference facilities available by appointment

Hours: 08.15-19.15 (closes 16.15 on Friday)

Related Bodies: Networked to Edge Hill College of Higher Education, Hanley Library, and the Hesketh Centre Library

---

[199]

Edinburgh and South East Scotland Dyslexia Association

The Flat
7 Napier Road
Edinburgh

Telephone and Fax: 0131 229 1865

Contact: Mrs Gillian Thompson MBE (Chairman); Mrs Jennifer Allison (Secretary)

Objectives and Purposes: To provide professional services of psychological assessment for dyslexia to school children and adults in Scotland; to provide tutoring, advisory services, and awareness in dyslexia; to provide a small resource centre for specific use in dyslexia

Stock and Subject Coverage: Material on dyslexia for use by psychologists, tutors and members

Availability: Restricted

Publications: Various - list available

Related Bodies: Scottish Dyslexia Association

---

[200]

ENABLE (Scottish Society for the Mentally Handicapped)

6th Floor
7 Buchanan Street
Glasgow G1 3HL

Telephone: 0141 226 4541

Fax: 0141 204 4398

Contact: Information Service

Objectives and Purposes: To provide mutual support to people with learning disabilities and their families; to campaign for their rights and for improved services

Stock and Subject Coverage: 1,500 books and reports; 70 periodicals; file of press cuttings. All material relates to learning disabilities with emphasis on family issues and educational and social services

Services/Facilities: Current awareness service (priced); literature searches; photocopies (priced); free enquiries; some books available for loan

Availability: Freely available. Most enquiries are by telephone or letter. Visits by prior appointment

Hours: 08.45-16.45 (closes 15.55 on Friday)

Publications: Newslink (quarterly newsletter); Infoline (current awareness bulletin, 10 per year); annual report; ad hoc books/reports - list available

Related Bodies: There is a network of local branches across Scotland

---

[201]

Encephalitis Support Group (ESG)

Pasture House
Normanby
Sinnington
York YO6 6RH

Telephone and Fax: 01751 433318

E-mail: 101750.730@compuserve.com

World Wide Web:
http://www.connect.org.uk/merseyworld/glaxo

Contact: Elaine Dowell (National Contact)

Objectives and Purposes: To support sufferers and their families by listening, providing information, linking families; to increase awareness about the condition; and to support research

Availability: Telephone and written enquiries accepted

Hours: 10.00-15.00

Publications: Newsletter; annual report; various leaflets. Full list available

---

[202]

★EPDATA (British Epilepsy Association)

Anstey House
40 Hanover Square
Leeds LS3 1BE

Telephone: 0113 244 4798

Fax: 0113 242 8804

E-mail: epilepsy@bea.org.uk

Contact: Shelley Wagstaff

Objectives and Purposes: To provide an information service in response to specific requests from all those involved with epilepsy

Services/Facilities: CD-ROM searches (MEDLINE and Embase: Neurosciences) lists of literature, abstracts and references are provided; membership of EPDATA Club is available

Availability: Telephone and written enquiries

Hours: 09.00-13.00

Publications: EPDATA Bulletin (quarterly)

Related Bodies: British Epilepsy Association; sponsorship by Marion Merrell Dow

---

[203]

Epilepsy Association of Scotland (EAS)

48 Govan Road
Glasgow G51 1JL

Telephone: 0141 427 4911

Fax: 0141 427 2747

Contact: Mrs Judy Cochrane (Director of Education, Training and Information)

Objectives and Purposes: To work on behalf of people with epilepsy in Scotland

Stock and Subject Coverage: An epilepsy resource centre including a reference library and an epilepsy video library

Services/Facilities: Information, support, advice and counselling for people with epilepsy, their families, carers and the professionals who work with these groups. Also acts as a consultancy and advisory body, promotes public awareness and provides an extensive professional training programme

Availability: By prior appointment, for reference use only; telephone and written enquiries accepted; visits welcomed; videos may be hired, and literature is available at a small charge

Hours: 09.30-16.30

Publications: Newsletter (2 or 3 per year); annual report. Full list available

Related Bodies: There are regional resource centres and a network of local groups and branches

[204]

Epsom General Hospital

Sally Howell Library
Bradbury Centre
Dorking Road
Epsom
Surrey KT18 7EG
Telephone: 01372 735735, ext 6250
Fax: 01372 749502 (mark "FAO Librarian")
Contact: Gordon Smith BA ALA; Marion Morrison MA ALA; Fiona Rees BLib
Objectives and Purposes: To contribute to the quality of health care by helping all NHS staff to make effective use of the knowledge and information base of health care
Stock and Subject Coverage: 4,000 books; 115 periodicals. A multidisciplinary medical collection. Incorporates the former West Park Postgraduate Medical Library (psychiatry)
Services/Facilities: Online and CD-ROM searches; photocopies; fax
Availability: By prior appointment, for reference use only
Hours: 08.45-16.45
Publications: Induction handouts; journals list; CD-ROM tutorial
Related Bodies: South Thames Library and Information Service; Psychiatric Libraries Co-operative Scheme

[205]

European School of Osteopathy (ESO)

Boxley House
Boxley
Nr Maidstone
Kent ME14 3DZ
Telephone: 01622 671558
Fax: 01622 662165
E-mail: eso.m.stone@dm.krinfo.ch
Contact: Ray Smith (Librarian)

Objectives and Purposes: To train osteopaths through formal study and practical work in adult, children and sports injuries clinics

Stock and Subject Coverage: 3,000 books; 50 periodicals; reports; dissertations; case studies; audiovisual materials; 200 videos; slide sets; anatomical models. Covers osteopathy and relevant orthodox medical subjects, and other alternative therapies. Some material in French, German and Russian

Services/Facilities: CD-ROM and online searches; photocopies; contents page distribution to faculty members. Charges levied to non-ESO personnel

Availability: Loans to staff and students only; reference facilities to others by arrangement; enquiries handled as time permits

Hours: 09.00-17.00

Publications: E.S.O. (2 per year, in English and French)

[206]

Exeter Medical Library

Exeter Postgraduate Medical Centre
Barrack Road
Exeter EX2 5DW
Telephone: 01392 403002
Fax: 01392 403007
E-mail: v.b.newton@exeter.ac.uk
Contact: Virginia Newton BSc DipLib ALA; Jill Maxted ALA
Objectives and Purposes: To contribute to the quality of health care by helping all accredited staff make effective use of the knowledge and information base of health care
Stock and Subject Coverage: 8,000 books; 200 periodicals covering general medicine
Services/Facilities: CD-ROM searches and online MEDLINE searches
Availability: Available for reference use by prior appointment
Hours: 09.00-17.30
Related Bodies: University of Exeter; member of South and West Regional Library and Information Network (SWRLIN)

[207]

Eyecare Information Service (EIS)

PO Box 3597
London SE1 6DY
Telephone: 0171 357 7730
Fax: 0171 357 7155
E-mail: 100531.3717@compuserve.com
World Wide Web: http://www.vois.org.uk/eyeinfo
Contact: Tanya Susilovic
Objectives and Purposes: The general public relations body for the whole of the optical sector. It aims to educate the public on the importance of good eye care and a regular eye examination, as well as raising awareness of the modern optical products and technologies available
Stock and Subject Coverage: Material on eye care and optical subjects in general

Availability: Telephone and written enquiries
  accepted; no visits
Hours: 09.00-17.00
Publications: List available on request

[208]
Family Heart Association (FHA)

PO Box 303
Maidenhead SL6 1DL
Telephone: 01628 522177
Fax: 01628 522197
Contact: Dr Michael Turner (Chief Executive);
  Miss Jacqui Lynas (Dietician); Mrs Julie Foxton
  (Administrator)
Objectives and Purposes: To provide support and
  information for patients and others with or at a
  high risk of coronary heart disease, especially
  when hyperlipidaemia is a factor; the detection of
  families prone to premature angina or heart
  attack. Specialises in blood lipid (cholesterol)
  disorders including inherited high cholesterol and
  dietary/lifestyle aspects of the management of
  these conditions. Committed to the early
  detection in the community of families with
  genetic disorders and those prone to angina or
  heart attack for other reasons. Also participates in
  the post-registration training of nurses
Hours: 09.30-16.30
Publications: Family Heart Digest (6 per year - 16
  pages); occasional factsheets, leaflets and books

[209]
Family Planning Association (FPA)

2-12 Pentonville Road
London N1 9FP
Telephone: 0171 837 5432 (switchboard);
  Library: 0171 923 5228
Fax: 0171 837 3034
Contact: Mrs T Belfield (Head of Information and
  Research); Mrs M McGovern (Information and
  Library Officer)
Objectives and Purposes: To promote sexual health
  and family planning by means of information,
  research, education, training, publications and
  publicity
Stock and Subject Coverage: 3,500 books; 100
  periodicals covering all aspects of family planning,
  contraception, and sexual/reproductive health
Services/Facilities: Selected references from internal
  database; photocopies (priced)
Availability: Telephone and written enquiries;
  reference library available to all, by appointment
Hours: 09.00-17.00
Publications: Range of materials - list available
Related Bodies: Offices in Scotland, Wales and
  Northern Ireland

[210]
Federation of Ophthalmic and Dispensing Opticians (FODO)

113 Eastbourne Mews
London W2 6LQ
Telephone: 0171 258 0240
Fax: 0171 724 1175
Contact: Judith Payne (Director General)
Objectives and Purposes: To represent optical
  employers
Availability: Telephone and written enquiries
  accepted
Hours: 09.00-17.00
Publications: Optics at a Glance (statistical factsheet);
  FODO News (quarterly); annual report

[211]
Fibromyalgia Association UK

8 Rochester Grove
Hazel Grove
Stockport SK7 4JD
Telephone: 0161 483 3155
Fax: 0161 483 7512
Contact: Secretary
Objectives and Purposes: To relieve the suffering of
  people with fibromyalgia through the provision of
  counselling, advice, information and support; to
  promote medical research into the condition, and
  disseminate the results
Stock and Subject Coverage: Leaflets, booklets, a video
  and a newsletter on all aspects of fibromyalgia
Availability: Medical professionals only, by
  appointment
Hours: 11.30-14.00 (closed on Wednesday)
Publications: List available

[212]
Fife Healthcare NHS Trust Health Promotion Department

Glenrothes House
North Street
Glenrothes
Fife KY7 5PB
Telephone: 01592 754355
Fax: 01592 611423
E-mail: library@fife-hpd.demon.co.uk
Contact: Mr H Black (Health Promotion Manager);
  Miss H Cross and Miss D Palmer (Library
  Assistants)
Objectives and Purposes: To improve the health of the
  people of Fife through the provision of
  information and assistance to help people develop
  skills so that they can make informed choices
  about their health
Stock and Subject Coverage: Books and periodicals
  covering all aspects of health promotion; a wide
  range of issue-specific materials, e.g. on drugs,
  food and health, mental health, etc. Also has a
  wide range of posters and leaflets, and teaching
  and learning resources

Services/Facilities: Online and CD-ROM searches; photocopies (priced); infant car seat scheme
Availability: Telephone and written enquiries accepted; visits by arrangement. Charges apply to some services
Hours: 08.45–17.00

[213]

Food and Chemical Allergy Association

27 Ferringham Lane
Ferring
West Sussex BN12 5NB
Telephone: 01903 241178 (written contact preferred)
Contact: Mrs E Rothera; Mrs B Rogers
Objectives and Purposes: An information and advisory service covering all aspects of allergic reaction. Sufferers are shown how to discover the causes of their own allergies and advised on how to build up their own immune systems
Services/Facilities: Free advice and information to sufferers and their families
Availability: Anyone may enquire. Letters are preferred to telephone calls
Hours: 09.00–22.00 (optimum time for telephone calls is 20.00–22.00)
Publications: Understanding Allergies (booklet £2, plus s.a.e.); information sheets on asthma, eczema and other common allergy-related conditions are available

[214]

Forensic Science Society

Clarke House
18A Mount Parade
Harrogate
North Yorkshire HG1 1BX
Telephone: 01423 506068
Fax: 01423 566391
Contact: Mrs C Houseman (Office Manager)
Services/Facilities: List of independent consultants
Availability: Telephone and written enquiries from bona fide researchers
Hours: 09.30–16.00
Publications: Science and Justice (quarterly journal); Word List of Forensic Science Laboratories and Practices
Related Bodies: Affiliated to the California Association of Criminalists

[215]

FORESIGHT, The Association for the Promotion of Preconception Care

28 The Paddock
Godalming
Surrey GU7 1XD
Telephone: 01483 427839
Fax: 01483 427668
Contact: Mrs Belinda Barnes; Miss Julia Martin

Objectives and Purposes: Care of both parents before conception to minimise the dangers of miscarriage, perinatal death, malformation, prematurity and compromised health in mother and baby. Also help with infertility
Stock and Subject Coverage: Range of books, booklets, leaflets, videos and posters on preconception and pregnancy
Services/Facilities: Photocopies; fax
Availability: Telephone and written enquiries (s.a.e. appreciated); visits can be arranged (in either direction); talks or symposia can be given
Hours: Variable (answerphone when office is unattended)
Publications: List available on request

[216]

Forest Healthcare NHS Trust

Library
Medical Education Centre
Whipps Cross Hospital
Leytonstone
London E11 1NR
Telephone and Fax: 0181 535 6973
E-mail: library@fhcare.demon.co.uk
World Wide Web:
    http://www.nthames-health.tpmde.ac.uk/ntrl/forest.htm
Contact: Ann Weist (Librarian); Susan Kerslake and Colin Lynch (Assistant Librarians); Alma Quinn (Library Assistant)
Objectives and Purposes: To support the work of Trust staff
Stock and Subject Coverage: 4,000 books; 130 periodicals. Mainly covers clinical medicine
Services/Facilities: Online and CD-ROM searches; Internet access; CAL facility
Availability: Staff only
Hours: 09.00–17.00 (open until 19.00 on Tuesday and Thursday, and 18.30 on Friday)
Related Bodies: North Thames Regional Library Network

[217]

Foundation for the Study of Infant Deaths (FSID)

14 Halkin Street
London SW1X 7DP
Telephone: 0171 235 0965; 24-hour Cot Death Helpline: 0171 235 1721
Fax: 0171 823 1986
E-mail: fsia@dial.pipex.com
Contact: Kate Seeley (Media and Information Assistant)
Objectives and Purposes: To raise funds for research into the causes and prevention of cot death; to support bereaved families; and to provide information for parents and professionals
Stock and Subject Coverage: Collection books, periodicals and videos on grief, loss of a baby and cot death

Services/Facilities: Free advice and information to bereaved families and all parents; database searches on internal database (priced); 24-hour helpline; photocopies (priced)

Availability: Telephone and written enquiries; information leaflets available

Hours: 09.00-17.00 (helpline available 24 hours per day, every day)

Publications: FSID News (3 per year); range of leaflets; annual report

[218]
Foundation for Women's Health Organisation (FORWARD)

38 King Street
Covent Garden
London WC2E 8JT
Telephone: 0171 379 6889
Fax: 0171 379 6199
E-mail: forward@dircon.co.uk
Contact: Amira Kariem; Rahmat Mohammad; Ruhma Yusuf Rinaldi (main contact)
Objectives and Purposes: To promote good health amongst African women and their children, with specific focus on reproductive health; to assist national groups and individuals at their request with community support services; to provide training for professionals; and to provide advocacy work
Stock and Subject Coverage: Material on female genital mutilation and vesico vaginal fistulae
Availability: Telephone and written enquiries; visits welcomed; no loans or reference facilities
Hours: 09.30-16.30
Publications: Various - list available

[219]
Fragile X Society

53 Winchelsea Lane
Hastings
East Sussex TN35 4LG
Telephone: 01424 813147
Contact: Mrs L Walker (National Contact)
Objectives and Purposes: To provide information and mutual support to families with Fragile X Syndrome; to provide greater professional and public awareness of the condition; to encourage families to assist in research; and to encourage the transmission of research findings from abroad
Stock and Subject Coverage: Range of information on the condition
Services/Facilities: Free advice and information to families affected by the condition; photocopies (some priced); Link Network scheme; conferences, training programmes, etc. arranged
Availability: Open to all with an interest in the condition; diagnosed families can become members for free; professionals for £10 pa
Hours: 09.00-17.00
Publications: Newsletter (2 per year); What is Fragile X (booklet); An Introduction to Fragile X Syndrome (booklet); An Introduction to Educational Needs (booklet); annual report

Related Bodies: Affiliated to Contact a Family, Society for the Study of Behavioural Phenotypes, and the Genetic Interest Group

[220]
Freeman Hospital, Teaching Centre Library

High Heaton
Newcastle-upon-Tyne NE7 7DN
Telephone: 0191 284 3111, ext 26200
Fax: 0191 284 3783
Contact: Mrs M Valentine (Librarian); Mrs J Dyson (Assistant Librarian)
Objectives and Purposes: To provide multidisciplinary library and information services for the Freeman Group of Hospitals and the University of Northumbria at Newcastle
Stock and Subject Coverage: 15,000 books; 170 periodicals covering medical, health and nursing subjects. Specialises in transplantation; cardiothoracic; and ENT
Services/Facilities: Online and CD-ROM searches (MEDLINE and CINAHL); photocopies
Availability: By prior appointment, for reference use only
Hours: 09.00-19.00 Monday to Wednesday; 09.00-17.00 Thursday and Friday; 09.00-13.00 Saturday
Publications: Library bulletin; periodicals list; various library guides

[221]
Frenchay Healthcare NHS Trust

Library and Information Service
Postgraduate Medical Centre
Frenchay Hospital
Bristol BS16 1LE
Telephone: 0117 970 1212, exts 2634/7
Fax: 0117 970 1691
E-mail: wendy@frelais.demon.co.uk
Contact: Wendy Saywood Librarian; Sheila Headford Senior Library Assistant; Joan Sparke, Madeleine Hill and Jane Lewis (Library Assistants)
Objectives and Purposes: Hospital - specialities include Neurosurgery and Plastic surgery. An acute and community trust
Stock and Subject Coverage: Approximately 200 journal titles - specialist areas include: Plastic surgery, neurosurgery. Also general medical/surgical book stock of approximately 6,000 items
Services/Facilities: CD-ROM searching for MEDLINE, CINAHL, and Embase Neuroscience and Psychiatry; photocopyies; fax; word processing facilities all available. Online searching available at a charge by appointment with Librarian
Availability: Personal visit by prior agreement with the Librarian
Hours: 08.00-17.00

[222]
Friarage Hospital Library
Study Centre
Northallerton
North Yorkshire DL6 1JG
Telephone: 01609 762526
Fax: 01609 777144
E-mail: m.snowdon@pulse.york.ac.uk
Contact: Mrs Meri Snowdon
Objectives and Purposes: To supply relevant information to hospital employees and to students of York University Department of Health Studies
Stock and Subject Coverage: 6,000 books; 120 periodicals covering medicine and health care
Services/Facilities: CD-ROM searches; photocopies (priced)
Availability: Staff and students only; external membership available
Hours: 09.00-17.00
Publications: Library guides

[223]
Frimley Park Hospital NHS Trust
Health Sciences Library
Portsmouth Road
Frimley
Surrey GU16 5UJ
Telephone: 01276 604168
Fax: 01276 684247
E-mail: fphlib@dsk.co.uk
Contact: Librarian
Objectives and Purposes: To contribute to the quality of health care by helping all NHS staff make effective use of the knowledge and information of health care
Stock and Subject Coverage: 4,000 books; 115 current periodicals on all aspects of medicine
Services/Facilities: Online searches; CD-ROM searches; Internet connection
Availability: Open to NHS employees; others may become affiliated members (fee required)
Hours: 09.00-17.00
Related Bodies: Part of the South Thames (West) Library Service

[224]
Fulbourn Hospital Medical Library (Addenbrookes NHS Trust)
PGME Centre
Cambridge CB1 5EF
Telephone: 01223 218630
Fax: 01223 218708
Contact: Ian Preston (Librarian)
Objectives and Purposes: To provide core texts and periodicals in the fields of psychiatry, psychology and related subjects as part of the Hospital's educational facilities, and to provide library and information services for staff
Stock and Subject Coverage: Material covering psychiatry; psychology; and related disciplines; archive collection relating to Fulbourn Hospital; partner libraries at the Developmental Psychiatry and Psychotherapy departments
Services/Facilities: CD-ROM searches; photocopies (priced); fax (at cost); Internet access
Availability: By prior appointment, for reference use only
Hours: 09.30-17.30 (closes 17.00 on Friday)
Publications: Annual report
Related Bodies: University of Cambridge Medical Library, at Addenbrookes Hospital

[225]
Furness Hospitals NHS Trust, Education Centre Library
Furness General Hospital
Dalton Lane
Barrow-in-Furness
Cumbria LA14 4LF
Telephone: 01229 870870, ext 2127
Fax: 01229 431744
Contact: Pam Rigden BEd (Hons) PG DipLib (Librarian)
Objectives and Purposes: To provide an easily accessible range of resources for funded user groups in order to support their clinical and educational requirements; to assist them ultimately to deliver high quality patient care
Stock and Subject Coverage: Material covering all aspects of medicine, nursing and health care. Small collection of old medical and nursing texts
Services/Facilities: CD-ROM searches (MEDLINE, CINAHL, Cochrane and RCN Database); photocopies
Availability: Funded user groups only
Hours: 09.00-17.00
Related Bodies: Furness Hospitals NHS Trust

[226]
Garlands Hospital
Hospital Library
Garlands
Carlisle CA1 3SX
Telephone: 01228 602107
Contact: Valerie Bys (Librarian)
Objectives and Purposes: To provide material and information for hospital staff and also for community staff
Stock and Subject Coverage: Books and periodicals covering psychiatry; psychology; and geriatrics
Services/Facilities: Photocopies
Availability: Open to hospital and community staff; in person, by telephone or in writing
Hours: 09.00-12.00 and 13.00-16.00 Tuesday and Friday; 09.00-12.00 Wednesday and Thursday; closed Monday

[227]

Gaucher's Association

25 West Cottages
London NW6 1RS
Telephone: 0171 433 1121
World Wide Web: http://www.gaucher.org.uk
Contact: Mrs Susan Lewis (Secretary)
Objectives and Purposes: To provide information about Gaucher's Disease and to keep families and medical advisers up-to-date with the latest developments; to encourage the availability of treatment, including enzyme replacement therapy; to keep families in touch for support; and to compile a register of those affected by the disease
Stock and Subject Coverage: Material covering all matters relating to Gaucher's Disease
Availability: Telephone and written enquiries, from bona fide researchers only (photocopies of articles available, £1 each)
Hours: 10.00–17.00 (answerphone available out of hours)
Publications: Information pack; bi-annual newsletter

[228]

General Dental Council (GDC)

37 Wimpole Street
London W1M 8DQ
Telephone: 0171 486 2171
Fax: 0171 224 3294
Contact: The Registrar
Objectives and Purposes: To maintain and publish the Dentists Register and to promote high standards of dental education at all its stages and high standards of professional conduct among dentists. Also has responsibilities in relation to the training, enrolment and conduct of dental auxiliaries
Hours: 09.15–16.00
Publications: Dentists Register (annual); The Rolls of Dental Auxiliaries; GDC Gazette

[229]

General Optical Council (GOC)

41 Harley Street
London W1N 2DJ
Telephone: 0171 580 3898
Fax: 01436 3525
E-mail: optical@globalnet.co.uk
World Wide Web:
http://www.healthworks.co.uk/hw/orgs/ GOC.html
Contact: Mr RD Wilshin (Registrar); Mrs Dian Taylor (Deputy Registrar); Mr David Watt (Assistant Registrar)
Objectives and Purposes: Registration of opticians and companies carrying on the business of opticians, and promoting high standards of professional education and professional conduct among opticians
Stock and Subject Coverage: Printed register of all opticians registered to practice in the UK

Services/Facilities: Register database available for purchase as address labels, printout, or on magnetic media
Availability: Telephone and written enquiries; visits by appointment
Hours: 09.30–16.30
Publications: Register; information about careers and the work of the GOC; annual report

[230]

Gifted Children's Information Centre (GCIC)

Hampton Grange
21 Hampton Lane
Solihull
West Midlands B91 2QJ
Telephone and Fax: 0121 705 4547
Contact: Dr Peter Congdon
Objectives and Purposes: To publish and disseminate information on the subject of gifted and talented children
Stock and Subject Coverage: Material about gifted, dyslexic and left-handed children
Services/Facilities: Legal guidance for children with special educational needs; teaching materials for such children
Availability: Personal visits accepted
Hours: 24-hour helpline
Publications: List available

[231]

Glan Hafren NHS Trust

South Gwent Postgraduate Medical Centre
The Friars
Friars Road
Newport
Gwent NP9 4EZ
Telephone: 01633 238133/238134
Fax: 01633 238123
E-mail: jgllo1@gwent.nhs.gov.uk
Contact: Mrs Joanna Grey-Lloyd (Librarian);
Objectives and Purposes: To provide information and support for the educational, clinical and research needs of local staff
Stock and Subject Coverage: 3,000 books; 151 periodicals; 200 videos. Covers medicine and surgery, dentistry, nursing and management; special collection of archive material written by Trust staff
Services/Facilities: Online and CD-ROM searches (MEDLINE, CINAHL, Cochrane, etc.); video viewing facility; microfiche; fax; photocopies (priced); Internet access; current awareness
Availability: By prior appointment, for reference use only (some services may be restricted)
Hours: 09.00–18.00 (closes 17.00 on Friday)
Publications: Library guide; journal holdings list; video collection list

[232]

Glasgow Caledonian University Library

City Campus
Cowcaddens Road
Glasgow G4 0BA
Telephone: 0141 331 3859 (Librarian's Office)
Fax: 0141 331 3005
E-mail: M.Miller@gcal.ac.uk
World Wide Web:
   http://www.gcal.ac.uk/library/index.html
   (Library Health page: http://www.gcal.ac.uk/
   library/subject/foh/sub-foh.html)
Contact: Professor Jo Haythornthwaite (Chief
   Librarian); Marian Miller (Faculty of Health
   Librarian); Marion Kelt (Assistant Librarian -
   Faculty of Health, Southbrae)
Objectives and Purposes: Institution of Higher
   Education with largest Faculty of Health in the
   UK. Only degree programme for optometry in
   Scotland
Stock and Subject Coverage: Total book stock at City
   and Southbrae is 230,000 books and 2,300
   periodicals. The main Library at City Campus is a
   multi-disciplinary University Library looking after
   the Faculties of Business; Health; Science and
   Technology. The Health Faculty subjects taught at
   City are Biomedical Sciences; Nursing and
   Midwifery; Vision Sciences (Orthoptics and
   Optometry); Psychology; Social Sciences; Social
   Work. The Health Faculty subjects taught at
   Southbrae are Dietetics; Occupational Therapy;
   Physiotherapy; Podiatry; Radiography
Services/Facilities: CD-ROM searches (Assia;
   Biological Abstracts; RCN; Cochrane; Hebs);
   networked databases: MEDLINE; CINAHL;
   PsycLit; Bids; ISI; and IBSS; at Southbrae only -
   CancerLit and Human Nutrition Internet Access
   using Netscape; photocopying available
Availability: Charged external membership available
   (restricted services). Further information on
   membership from the Chief Librarian
Hours: Details on request
Publications: Librarian's Annual Report; Guide to
   Electronic Services; Student Guide etc. List
   available on request
Related Bodies: Smaller Southbrae Campus also in
   Glasgow will be integrated in 1998. As from
   September 1996 the University is running the
   contract for Nursing and Midwifery Diploma
   courses in Glasgow. The former Glasgow Colleges
   of Nursing and Midwifery- Eastern Division is
   now St James' Campus Library. The former
   Glasgow Colleges of Nursing and Midwifery -
   Northern Division is now Stobhill Campus
   Library. It is planned that both these libraries will
   move to City Campus in 1998

[233]

Glasgow Caledonian University, St James' Campus

110 St James' Road
Glasgow G4 0PS
Telephone: 0141 552 1562
Fax: 0141 552 4349
E-mail: ssutherland@gcal.ac.uk
Contact: Jan Howden (Librarian); Mrs S Sutherland
   (Senior Librarian)
Objectives and Purposes: Education and training of
   nurses and midwives, and continuing professional
   development
Stock and Subject Coverage: Ca. 30,000 books; 130
   periodicals covering nursing and midwifery
Services/Facilities: Photocopies; interlibrary loans
Availability: By arrangement
Hours: 08.15-18.30 (closes 16.00 on Friday)
Publications: Library guide; library bulletin; annual
   report
Related Bodies: North Division of the College

[234]

Glasgow Caledonian University, Stobhill Campus

300 Balgrayhill Road
Glasgow G21 3UR
Telephone: 0141 557 3443
Fax: 0141 558 9069
Contact: Sylvia Dickie; Jane Wilkins
Objectives and Purposes: Education and training of
   nurses and midwives, and continuing professional
   development
Stock and Subject Coverage: Material covering nursing
   and allied health subjects
Services/Facilities: CD-ROM searches; photocopies
   (priced); interlibrary loans; word processing facilities
Availability: By prior appointment, for reference use
   only; loans to staff, students and local nurses only
Hours: 08.15-18.00 Monday and Wednesday;
   08.15-19.45 Tuesday and Thursday; 08.15-16.00
   Friday
Related Bodies: Glasgow Caledonian University

[235]

Glasgow Dental Hospital and School

James Ireland Memorial Library
378 Sauchiehall Street
Glasgow G2 3JZ
Telephone: 0141 211 9705
E-mail: gzlx02@udcf.gla.ac.uk
Contact: Ms B Rankin (Librarian); Ms C Leitch
   (Library Assistant)
Objectives and Purposes: To serve the needs of
   University staff, students, and others working in
   the field of dentistry
Stock and Subject Coverage: 5,000 books; 217
   periodicals (139 current); 90 videos/tape slide sets.

Covers dentistry and related subjects. Glasgow University theses. Special collection on the history of dentistry

Services/Facilities: Online and CD-ROM searches; photocopies (at cost); current awareness service; cluster of 6 PCs with word-processing, dental CAL packages and Internet access

Availability: Freely available for reference, but loans to members only. Written, faxed and telephone enquiries accepted, as time permits

Hours: 09.00-21.00 (closes 17.00 on Friday and in vacations)

Related Bodies: Glasgow University Library

---

[236]

Glasgow Royal Infirmary University NHS Trust (GRI)

Trust Library
8-16 Alexandra Parade
Glasgow G31 2ER
Telephone: 0141 211 4760/5975
Fax: 0141 211 4802
E-mail: library@grilib.demon.co.uk
World Wide Web: http://www.gla.ac.uk:80/Library/
Contact: Dr Ann Wales (Library Services Manager); Mrs Lesley Robertson (Assistant Librarian); Mrs Sarah Brown (Library Assistant)

Objectives and Purposes: To support the highest possible standards of clinical care, service management, education, training and research, by providing all staff who work for the Trust with access to, and help in making effective use of, the knowledge and information base of health care

Stock and Subject Coverage: 5,000 books; 200 periodicals; videos. Covers medicine, nursing and allied health; TF Elias-Jones Collection on bacteriology, public health and hygiene (some items in this special collection date from the late 19th Century)

Services/Facilities: Online and CD-ROM and multimedia searches (MEDLINE, CINAHL, RCN-Nurse, Cochrane, etc.); photocopies; video players; BIDS, EDINA and OCLC datasets

Availability: By prior appointment, for reference use only

Hours: 09.30-19.00 (closes 17.30 on Friday)

Publications: Contents pages; various update services

---

[237]

Glasgow University Library

Hillhead Street
Glasgow G12 8QE
Telephone: 0141 339 8855, ext 6704/5
Fax: 0141 330 4952
E-mail: library@gla.ac.uk
World Wide Web: http://www.gla.ac.uk/Library/
Contact: Dr F Grainger (Medicine); Dr H Marlborough (Dentistry)

Objectives and Purposes: To provide library and information services to members of the university and to other bona fide researchers as appropriate

Stock and Subject Coverage: The collections support teaching and research needs and cover all aspects of medicine and public health. There is also material on specific aspects of health care such as community care, social policy, nursing and midwifery. Copies of Glasgow University theses are held. Additionally, important historical collections of books and manuscripts up to the end of the 18th Century (particularly strong in anatomy and obstetrics)

Services/Facilities: Online and CD-ROM searches; current awareness service; interlibrary loans; photocopies (most services charged)

Availability: Telephone and written enquiries accepted; brief visits by prior appointment for bona fide researchers. Membership available

Hours: 09.00-21.30 Monday to Thursday; 09-00-17.00 Friday and Saturday. Reduced hours in summer and Christmas vacations

Related Bodies: There is a separate branch library for Dentistry

---

[238]

Gloucestershire Royal NHS Trust

Gloucestershire Royal Hospital Library
Tower Block
Gloucestershire Royal Hospital
Great Western Road
Gloucester GL1 3NN
Telephone: 01452 394495
Fax: 01452 394170
E-mail: library@grhlib.demon.co.uk
World Wide Web:
http://www.netlink.co.uk/users/sharkli/
Contact: Trust Librarian: Helga Perry (helga@grhlib.demon.co.uk) Senior Library Assistant: Chloe George (chloe@grhlib.demon.co.uk)

Objectives and Purposes: The purpose of the Library is to contribute to the quality of health care in accordance with the aims and objectives of the Gloucestershire Royal NHS Trust by helping all NHS staff make effective use of the knowledge and information base of health care. The Library has a particular responsibility towards the provision of resources for Postgraduate Medical Education, in consultation with the Postgraduate Clinical Tutors

Stock and Subject Coverage: Ca. 3,900 books; 180 current journals. Covers clinical medicine; surgery; orthopaedics; some postgraduate-level nursing and allied health

Services/Facilities: Photocopies (card- and coin-operated); use of computers for word processing; CD-ROM databases (MEDLINE, CINAHL); fax

Availability: All library services available to staff employed by Gloucestershire Royal NHS Trust. Other health care staff, students, researchers may use the Library by prior arrangement. Telephone enquiries are welcome. This may involve charges for some services (e.g. interlibrary loans, photocopying, database use)

Hours: 08.30-17.00 (opens 09.00 on Friday)
Publications: See list on World Wide Web page

[239]

Grantham and District Hospital NHS Trust

101 Manthorpe Road
Grantham
Lincolnshire NG31 8DG
Telephone: 01476 565232
Contact: Mrs SL Taylor (Librarian)
Objectives and Purposes: To provide multidisciplinary library and information services to Trust staff
Stock and Subject Coverage: Material on medicine; nursing; paramedical professions; and management
Services/Facilities: CD-ROM searches; photocopies
Availability: By prior appointment, for reference use only
Hours: 09.00-17.00

[240]

Greenwich Healthcare Trust

Library and Information Service
Greenwich District Hospital
Vanbrugh Hill
London SE10 9HE
Telephone: 0181 312 6055
Fax: 0181 858 5717
Contact: Mrs Rosemary Bremer (Librarian, Print and Information); Miss Gillian Edwards (Librarian, Systems and Information)
Objectives and Purposes: To provide postgraduate medical and dental training, and access to information resources
Stock and Subject Coverage: 4,500 books; 250 periodicals covering medicine, dentistry and health management; recently expanded to serve the needs of trained nurses and professions allied to medicine
Services/Facilities: Photocopies; online and CD-ROM searches; interlibrary loans
Availability: Staff and local GPs; others may use the library for reference purposes by appointment with the Librarian
Hours: 09.00-17.00
Publications: Guide to the Library; holdings list; annual report
Related Bodies: Part of South Thames (East) Library and Information Service

[241]

Guide Dogs for the Blind Association (GDBA)

Hillfields
Burghfield
Reading RG7 3YG
Telephone: 0118 983 5555
Fax: 0118 983 5433
Contact: Alison Radevsky (Public Relations and Marketing Manager); JC Oxley (Director General)

Objectives and Purposes: Breeding, training and providing guide dogs; instructing visually impaired persons in the safe use of guide dogs; providing other services to visually impaired persons
Stock and Subject Coverage: Leaflets, posters, videos, etc.
Availability: Information free on request for all interested persons
Hours: 09.00-17.00
Publications: Forward (quarterly magazine); annual review

[242]

Guild Community Healthcare NHS Trust

Medical Library
Academic Unit
Royal Preston Hospital
Fulwood
Preston PR2 4HT
Telephone: 01772 710270
Fax: 01772 710772
Contact: Mrs Norma Blackburn (Librarian); Mrs Karen Kin (Library Assistant)
Objectives and Purposes: Library and information service to medical and multidisciplinary staff in the field of community psychiatry. Part of the University of Manchester Department of Community Psychiatry
Stock and Subject Coverage: 2,500 books; 39 periodicals covering medicine, psychiatry, psychotherapy, social work and occupational therapy. Collection of newsletters, press releases and a wide range of report literature
Services/Facilities: Photocopies; literature searches from CD-ROM databases
Availability: To staff, and to the public for reference purposes
Hours: 09.00-17.00
Publications: Library bulletin (quarterly); information pack; annual report
Related Bodies: University of Manchester Department of Community Psychiatry

[243]

Guillain-Barré Syndrome Support Group of the United Kingdom (GBS Support Group)

Room 4
Lincolnshire County Council Offices
Eastgate
Sleaford
Lincolnshire NG34 8NR
Telephone and Fax: 01529 304615
Contact: Glennys Sanders (Hon. President); Jane Tempest Roe
Objectives and Purposes: To provide emotional support to sufferers and their relatives/friends; to provide personal visits to sufferers where possible; to provide literature; to educate the public and the medical community about the illness; to promote research; to encourage special interest groups, e.g. pregnancy/children

Stock and Subject Coverage: Research papers; updates on the illness; information pack available on request

Services/Facilities: Video (£11 including p&p)

Availability: Telephone and written enquiries

Hours: 09.00-13.00 (answerphone out of hours)

Publications: Reaching Out (quarterly support group newsletter); Quick Guide; Short Guide for the Patient, Relative and Friend; The Guillain-Barré Syndrome Patient in Intensive Care; annual report

[244]
Haemochromatosis Society

Hollybush House
Hadley Green Road
Barnet
Hertfordshire EN5 5PR

Telephone and Fax: 0181 449 1363

E-mail: 106147.1054@compuserve.com

Contact: Mrs Janet Fernay

Objectives and Purposes: To support members and families; to promote awareness; to encourage research

Stock and Subject Coverage: Leaflets; videos; general information on haemochromatosis

Availability: Telephone and written enquiries accepted; membership available

Hours: 09.00-17.00

Publications: Quarterly newsletter

Related Bodies: International Association of HS

[245]
Haemophilia Society

123 Westminster Bridge Road
London SE1 7HR

Telephone: 0171 928 2020

Fax: 0171 620 1416

Contact: Mr Graham Barker (Director of Services and Development)

Objectives and Purposes: To support the needs of people with haemophilia and Von Willebrands Disease, and those of their families

Availability: By prior appointment, for reference use only; written enquiries are preferred

Hours: 09.00-17.00

Publications: Various - list available

[246]
Hairline International: The Alopecia Patients Society

Lyons Court
168 High Street
Knowle
West Midlands B93 0LY

Telephone: 01564 775281

Fax: 01564 782270

Contact: Elizabeth Steel (Director/Founder); Valerie Amies

Objectives and Purposes: A support network for alopecia patients and their families, providing information on treatment, contacts, etc.

Availability: Telephone and written enquiries

Hours: 09.00-15.30

Publications: Coping With Sudden Hair Loss; Hair Loss (both by Elizabeth Steel); newsletter (3 per year)

Related Bodies: The Hair Trust

[247]
Halifax General Hospital, Postgraduate Library

Halifax HX3 0PW

Telephone: 01422 357171, ext 4191

Fax: 01422 366889

Contact: Helen Curtis; Chris Jackson

Objectives and Purposes: To provide an information service to junior medical staff, and to all Trust employees

Stock and Subject Coverage: 4,000 books; 93 periodicals covering all aspects of medicine

Services/Facilities: Online searches; Cochrane database; CD-ROM searches; photocopies; fax

Availability: Telephone and written enquiries dealt with as time permits. Public access occasionally possible, subject to a charge

Hours: 09.00-17.00 (closes 16.30 on Friday)

Related Bodies: Member of Yorkshire Regional Association of Health Care and Information Services

[248]
Harefield Hospital NHS Trust

Library
Hill End Road
Harefield
Middlesex UB9 6JH

Telephone and Fax: 01895 828947

E-mail: gillian.poller@dm.rs.ch

Contact: Richard M Osborn (Library and Information Services Manager); Gill Poller (Trust Librarian)

Objectives and Purposes: To provide library and information services in support of the work, education and training of all health care staff

Stock and Subject Coverage: 800 books; 110 periodicals. Covers general medicine, but particular strengths in cardiothoracic medicine and surgery

Services/Facilities: Online and CD-ROM searches; word processing; fax; photocopies

Availability: By prior appointment, for reference use only

Hours: 09.00-17.00

Publications: Newsletter; annual report; periodicals holdings list

Related Bodies: Mount Vernon Postgraduate Centre Library

[249]

Hastings and Rother NHS Trust Library

Rosewell Library
Education Centre
Conquest Hospital
The Ridge
St Leonard's-on-Sea
East Sussex TN37 7RD
Telephone: 01424 755255, ext 8672
Fax: 01424 758040
Contact: Miss Jenny Turner
Objectives and Purposes: To provide a library and information service for members of the Trust and other approved users
Stock and Subject Coverage: Books, periodicals and multimedia covering medicine, nursing and some management
Services/Facilities: Online and CD-ROM searches; photocopies; fax; word-processing; audio/video facilities
Availability: Restricted to members of the Trust and organisations involved in health care in the area
Hours: 08.30-17.30
Related Bodies: Part of South East Thames Regional Library and Information Service (SETRLIS)

[250]

Health and Safety Executive (HSE)

Public Information Network
Broad Lane
Sheffield S3 7HQ
Telephone: 0541 545500
Fax: 0114 289 2333
World Wide Web:
  http://www.open.gov.uk/hse/hsehome.htm
Contact: Public Information Network
Objectives and Purposes: To ensure that risks to peoples health and safety from work activities are properly controlled
Stock and Subject Coverage: Material on all aspects of occupational health and safety
Services/Facilities: CD-ROM searches; photocopies
Availability: Open to the public for reference use; written enquiries accepted
Hours: 09.00-17.00
Publications: Catalogue on request

[251]

*Health Care Information West Sussex

PO Box 122
Chichester
West Sussex PO14 4XZ
Telephone: 01243 536962; Helpline: 0345 678565
Contact: Mike Roddham (Manager); Iris Booth and Mavis Hobs (Information Officers)
Objectives and Purposes: To provide a public helpline on health and health care for West Sussex

Stock and Subject Coverage: Consumer health information; leaflets and books; databases on local health groups and self-help groups
Services/Facilities: Telephone helpline
Availability: Telephone and written enquiries; visits by NHS staff only; not available for coursework or school/college projects
Hours: 10.00-17.00 (answerphone out of hours)
Publications: Analysis of enquiries; annual report

[252]

Health Education Authority (HEA)

Health Promotion Centre
Hamilton House
Mabledon Place
London WC1H 9TX
Telephone: 0171 413 1995
Fax: 0171 413 1834
E-mail: hpic.enquiry@hea.org.uk
Contact: Catherine Herman; Fiona Martin
Objectives and Purposes: To ensure that by the year 2000 the people of England are more knowledgeable, better motivated and more able to acquire and maintain good health
Stock and Subject Coverage: Books, reports, periodicals, videos, teaching packs, CD-ROMs and software in the areas of coronary heart disease and stroke; cancers – initially lung, breast, cervical and skin; mental health; HIV, AIDS and sexual health; accidents; tobacco smoking; diet and nutrition; alcohol consumption; injecting drug use; and other areas of priority such as immunisation, for health professionals and the public
Services/Facilities: Photocopies
Availability: Access by appointment only to health professionals, academics and educationalists researching health promotion issues
Hours: 09.00-17.00 (opens 11.00 on Friday)
Publications: Catalogue of new publications – HEA publishes a wide range of books and videos; annual report

[253]

Health Education Board for Scotland (HEBS)

Health Promotion Library Scotland
The Priory
Canaan Lane
Edinburgh EH10 4SG
Telephone: 0345 125 442 (for reader enquiries); 0131 447 6180 (other calls)
Fax: 0131 447 6180
E-mail: ah56@cityscape.co.uk
World Wide Web: http://www.hebs.scot.nhs.uk
Contact: Margaret Forrest; Donald M Mackay; Ailsa Anderson; Margaret Didcock; Paul Gray
Objectives and Purposes: To provide the most comprehensive, accessible and up-to-date source of health information in Scotland. The library service is aimed at professionals and members of the public interested and involved in promoting and educating for health

Stock and Subject Coverage: 12,000 books; 350 periodicals covering all aspects of health promotion and the behavioural sciences. 30 CD-ROM titles are held, including an in-house CD-ROM containing 5 separate databases on journal articles, patient education leaflets, self-help groups in health, Scottish HIV/AIDS initiatives register, and health education videos

Services/Facilities: Online and CD-ROM searches; photocopies

Availability: Free information service to all people living in Scotland (except for photocopies, which are priced). Enquiries accepted by personal visit, telephone, fax, e-mail or letter

Hours: 09.00–16.30 (closes 16.00 on Friday)

Publications: HEBS produces various publications on health education, and an annual report; the Library produces a bi-monthly bulletin

Related Bodies: Member of the Association of Scottish Health Sciences Librarians

[254]

Health Information First

Lister Hospital
Corey's Mill Lane
Stevenage
Hertfordshire SG1 4AB

Telephone: 01438 781092/01438 314333, ext 5520; Freephone: 0800 665544

Fax: 01438 312498

E-mail: sklister@demon.co.uk

World Wide Web: http://www.sklister.demon.co.uk

Contact: Sally Knight; Julia Mackenzie

Objectives and Purposes: To provide a health information service for all residents in the North Thames (West) region

Stock and Subject Coverage: Material on medicine and allied disciplines

Services/Facilities: Photocopies; online and CD-ROM searches

Availability: Freely available; telephone and written enquiries accepted

Hours: 09.00–17.00

Publications: Annual report

Related Bodies: Hertfordshire Libraries Arts and Information

[255]

Health Information Matters

795 Avebury Boulevard
Food Centre
Central Milton Keynes MK9 3NW

Telephone: 01908 677200

Fax: 01908 677301

Contact: Mrs M Muller (Information Manager)

Objectives and Purposes: To provide information on all aspects of health and health care, illnesses, treatments, disability, support groups and services to the public

Stock and Subject Coverage: Consumer health information

Services/Facilities: Databases of voluntary and self-care groups and services; online searches; photocopies (priced); fax; research undertaken for individual enquiries

Availability: Freely available to the public and to professionals on behalf of their patients/clients. Personal help available. Enquiries accepted by personal call, telephone and fax, and materials can be sent out if required. Some materials available for loan. Reference facilities for students. All services free

Hours: 10.00–16.00 (closed Wednesday)

Publications: Annual report

Related Bodies: Close liaison with Aylesbury Vale Health Information Service (01296 397647) and South Buckinghamshire Health Information Service (01494 432735)

[256]

Health Information Service – Trent Healthline

Victoria Health Centre
Glasshouse Street
Nottingham NG1 3LW

Telephone: 0115 924 3328; Freephone: 0800 665544 (covers Trent area – East Midlands and South Yorkshire)

Fax: 0115 941 3371

Contact: Jackie Chapman (Manager)

Objectives and Purposes: To provide information on any health issue in lay language. More specifically, information on diseases and conditions, the NHS and other caring services, self-help groups, voluntary organisations, waiting times for hospital treatment, how to complain about NHS services, national and local Charter standards, and how to maintain and improve health. There is a small library and periodical collection in lay language, and various databases

Stock and Subject Coverage: Books, periodicals, leaflets and databases covering consumer health information

Services/Facilities: Access to MEDLINE, Cochrane, etc. for members of the public

Availability: Freely available for reference use

Hours: 09.30–17.00 (answerphone available out of hours)

Publications: Annual report

Health Promotion Wales

see **Stop Press on page 156**

[257]

Health Visitors Association (HVA)

50 Southwark Street
London SE1 1UN

Telephone: 0171 717 4000

Fax: 0171 717 4040

Contact: Dougal McKechnie (Library); Garth Halliday (Publications)

Objectives and Purposes: A professional
association/trade union for health visitors, school
nurses and all qualified nurses working in the
community

Stock and Subject Coverage: 5,000 books; 100
periodicals covering health visiting; school and
community nursing; and all aspects of women's
and children's health, development and care

Services/Facilities: Photocopies (priced); library
database; literature searches (priced)

Availability: By prior appointment, for reference use
only; external enquiries handled as time permits

Hours: 09.00-17.00

Publications: Health Visitor (monthly); various ad hoc
publications - list available

---

[258]
Healthworks Ltd

30-38 Dock Street
Leeds LS10 1JF

Telephone: 0113 234 6624

Fax: 0113 242 7782

E-mail: info@d-access.demon.co.uk

World Wide Web: http://www.healthworks.co.uk

Contact: Stephen McCann (Managingg Director);
Simon Chapman (Systems Manager)

Objectives and Purposes: An information resource for
medical/health professionals. Contains free
MEDLINE access, a medical CD-ROM shop and
information on many UK medical organisations
and journals

Services/Facilities: Free access to MEDLINE,
AIDSLINE, TOXLINE, CANCERLIT and
Current Contents databases; document delivery

Availability: Open to anyone with Internet access

Hours: 24 hours

Publications: Health on the Internet (newsletter, £85
annually for 11 issues); Medical Computing
(newsletter, £175 annually for 8 issues)

---

[259]
Hearing Aid Council

Witan Court
305 Upper Fourth Street
Central Milton Keynes MK9 1EH

Telephone: 01908 235700

Fax: 01908 233770

Contact: Christopher Reid (Registrar)

Objectives and Purposes: To regulate trade practices.
The Council is a statutory body established under
the Hearing Aid Council Act, 1968 to regulate
those who dispense hearing aids in the private
sector in the United Kingdom. In effect, the
Council issues licences to practice

Availability: By law, the Register of Dispensers and
Employers of Dispensers is open for inspection
during business hours. Written and telephone
enquiries accepted

Hours: 09.00-17.30

Publications: Annual report; Buying a Hearing Aid

---

[260]
Hearing Concern

7/11 Armstrong Road
London W3 7JL

Telephone: 0181 743 1110

Fax: 0181 742 9151

E-mail: hearing.concern@ukonline.co.uk

World Wide Web:
http://web.ukonline.co.uk/hearing.concern

Contact: Cliff Docherty (Head of Hearing Advice
Services)

Objectives and Purposes: To represent and further the
interests of hard of hearing and late deafened
people

Stock and Subject Coverage: Extensive range of
factsheets covering all aspects of deafness
including medical, social, vocational and
rehabilitive materials. Range of leaflets and
booklets.

Availability: All materials are available to researchers,
but large quantities of material necessitate a small
cover charge. Special student pack available for
£3.75

Hours: 09.00-17.00

Publications: Hearing Concern Magazine is available
quarterly for £10 annually. Full up-to-date list
available on request

---

[261]
Heartlands Education Centre Library

Birmingham Heartlands & Solihull NHS Trust
(Teaching)
Bordesley Green East
Birmingham B9 5SS

Telephone: 0121 766 6611, ext 4790/4843

Fax: 0121 773 6349

Contact: Lesley Allen (Medical Librarian); Lisa Carter
and Doreen Skeene (Library Assistants)

Objectives and Purposes: To support improving
standards of health care by supplying high quality
library and information services to designated
users

Stock and Subject Coverage: Books; periodicals;
reports; directories. Covers medicine, nursing and
related areas. There is a separate GP collection

Services/Facilities: CD-ROM searches; interlibrary
loans; photocopies; list of translators; various
educational computer packages

Availability: By prior appointment, for reference use
only

Hours: 09.00-19.30

Publications: Quarterly bulletin; annual report

Related Bodies: Part of the West Midlands Regional
Health Libraries Network

[262]

Heatherwood and Wexham Park Hospitals Trust (Heatherwood Hospital)

Heatherwood Hospital Library
London Road
Ascot
Berkshire SL5 8AA
Telephone: 01344 23333, ext 7574
Fax: 01344 877547
Contact: Sarah Pallot (Library Services Manager)
Objectives and Purposes: To be the prime library and information resource for all health care staff in East Berkshire
Stock and Subject Coverage: Books and journals covering health and medicine in general. Some nursing coverage. Two special collections are housed at other local hospitals
Services/Facilities: CD-ROM and online searches; current awareness service
Availability: Open to anyone, although the level of service, and charges, may vary according to the category of user; access to special collections by arrangement
Hours: 09.00–14.00 (24-hour access to Trust staff; answerphone out of hours)
Publications: Business plan; library guide; annual report
Related Bodies: Parent organisation is Heatherwood and Wexham Park Hospitals Trust; part of HeLIN (Health Libraries and Information Network) of the former Oxford Region; member of Berkshire Libraries and Information Partnership

[263]

Heatherwood and Wexham Park Hospitals Trust (Wexham Park Hospital)

John Jamison Library
Wexham Park Hospital
Slough
Berkshire SL2 4HL
Telephone: 01753 634856/7
Fax: 01753 634189
E-mail: dl77@cityscape.co.uk
Contact: Sarah Pallot (Library Services Manager); Judy Herridge (Heatherwood Hospital)
Objectives and Purposes: To support health care education and training
Stock and Subject Coverage: Material on health care in general. Special collections on ophthalmology and management
Services/Facilities: Usual library services
Availability: Reference use only
Hours: 09.00–17.30
Publications: Library guides and leaflets
Related Bodies: Branch at Heatherwood Hospital

[264]

Help for Health Trust

Highcroft Cottage
Romsey Road
Winchester
Hampshire SO22 5DH
Telephone: 01962 849100; Helpline for Wessex residents: 0800 665544
Fax: 01962 840454
E-mail: gann@hfht.demon.co.uk
World Wide Web: http://www.hfht.demon.co.uk
Contact: Robert Gann (Director); Fiona Stobie (Health Information Service Manager)
Objectives and Purposes: To help people to become active partners in their own health care by providing them with information
Stock and Subject Coverage: Consumer health information including a range of databases, e.g. Helpbox with details of national and Wessex support/self-help organisations, books, leaflets. Large resources collection including books, journals, leaflets and audiovisual material
Services/Facilities: CD-ROM searches (MEDLINE); Minicom facility; enquiry monitoring; benchmarking
Availability: Regional telephone helpline; telephone and written enquiries accepted; visits by appointment
Hours: 09.00–17.00
Publications: NHS A-Z (compiled by R Gann); annual report

[265]

Help the Aged

St James's Walk
Clerkenwell Green
London EC1R 0BE
Telephone: 0171 253 0253
Fax: 0171 250 4474
World Wide Web: http://www.HelptheAged.org.uk
Contact: John Mayo (Director General); Sandra Chalmers (Director of Communications)
Objectives and Purposes: Help the Aged works to improve the quality of life of elderly people in the UK and internationally, particularly those who are frail, isolated or poor. The organisation is part of Helpage International
Stock and Subject Coverage: Range of advice and information leaflets, including health and finance
Services/Facilities: Free telephone advice line: 0800 650065
Availability: Open to all elderly people, their relatives, carers and friends
Hours: 10.00–16.00
Publications: Annual review

[266]

Hemel Hempstead Hospital Library

St Albans and Hemel Hempstead NHS Trust
Hillfield Road
Hemel Hempstead HP2 4AD
Telephone: 01442 287185
Fax: 01442 287992
E-mail: hemlis@dial.pipex.com
Contact: Mrs Liz Trounce
Stock and Subject Coverage: Material on general medicine and health care
Services/Facilities: CD-ROM searches; Internet access; fax; photocopies (priced)
Availability: By prior appointment, for reference use only
Hours: 09.00-17.00
Publications: Library guide; biannual bulletin
Related Bodies: St Albans City Hospital Library

[267]

Herpes Viruses Association (HVA-SPHERE)

41 North Road
London N7 9DP
Telephone: 0171 607 9661
Contact: Marian Nicholson (Co-ordinator)
Objectives and Purposes: To provide information and advice on herpes simplex, both genital and facial (cold sores) and herpes zoster (shingles)
Stock and Subject Coverage: Archives consist of 40 journals (spanning 12 years) with authoritative articles and personal case histories by members of the Association and medical professionals on herpes simplex, books and articles from medical journals (indexed) on the subject of herpes simplex
Services/Facilities: Members receive a journal, have access to the helpline, and have get-togethers, seminars, workshops, local contacts, etc.
Availability: Telephone and written enquiries; anyone may make an appointment during office hours; photocopies (priced)
Hours: 10.00-18.00
Publications: Sphere (quarterly journal); Herpes Simplex, a Guide (booklet - £1); various leaflets

[268]

Hexham General Hospital

Ryder PGMC Library
Hexham
Northumberland NE46 1QJ
Telephone: 01434 606161, ext 3252
Fax: 01434 607920
Contact: Mrs Susanne Ellingham (PGMC Administrator/Librarian)
Objectives and Purposes: To provide library and information services to local medical practitioners
Stock and Subject Coverage: 300 books; 40 periodicals covering medicine in general
Services/Facilities: CD-ROM searches (MEDLINE); photocopies

Availability: Restricted to staff and students
Hours: 24-hour availability to staff
Related Bodies: Member of Health Libraries North

[269]

Highland Health Sciences Library

University of Stirling
Highland Campus
Old Perth Road
Inverness IV2 3FG
Telephone: 01463 705269
Fax: 01463 713471
Contact: Rebecca Higgins (Area and Campus Librarian); Anne Gillespie (Deputy Librarian)
Objectives and Purposes: To provide library and information services for its users work, developmental and educational needs and to provide that service in a variety of media for all parts of the Highlands and Islands
Stock and Subject Coverage: 25,000 books and pamphlets; 300 periodicals. Covers medicine and its specialities, including nursing; social sciences; management; education; laboratory sciences and computing. Special collections - Royal Northern Infirmary Archives, from 1789 onwards; the Health Service archives for the area; and the Highland Health Board Archives
Services/Facilities: Photocopies (priced); online and CD-ROM searches (MEDLINE, CINAHL, etc.); video and tape slide viewers; word processing stations
Availability: Mainly for NHS employees, but others may become members for a fee, and the public may use the facilities for reference only
Hours: 09.00-21.00; 10.00-17.00 Saturday
Publications: Holdings lists; acquisitions lists; library guides
Related Bodies: Part of Stirling University Library; four branch libraries

[270]

Hinchingbrooke Health Care NHS Trust

Education Centre Library
Huntingdon
Cambridgeshire PE18 8NT
Telephone: 01480 416114
Fax: 01480 416299
Contact: Mrs L Edmonds (Library Services Manager)
Objectives and Purposes: The provision of multidisciplinary health care information
Stock and Subject Coverage: Books and periodicals covering all aspects of health care
Services/Facilities: CD-ROM searches; microfiche; special Healthlink service, plus the provision of patient health information to the general public; photocopies
Availability: By prior appointment, for reference use only
Hours: 09.00-17.00
Publications: Library guide; new books list; current periodicals list

[271]

Hodgkin's Disease and Lymphoma Association (HDLA)

PO Box 275
Haddenham
Aylesbury
Buckinghamshire HP17 8JJ
Telephone: Helpline: 01844 291500; Administration: 01844 291479
Fax: 01844 292757
World Wide Web: http://www.nahat.net/hodgkins
Contact: Mrs Celine Nicholls (Director); Nicola Felstead (Head of Lymphoma Support Services)
Objectives and Purposes: To provide information and emotional support to lymphoma patients (Hodgkin's Disease and non-Hodgkin's Lymphoma), their families and carers
Stock and Subject Coverage: Material covering all aspects of the condition, with particular emphasis on the effects on individual lives, and the ways in which it can be coped with
Availability: Open to all those affected by lymphomas. Telephone and written enquiries accepted; personal visits are not possible
Hours: 10.00-20.00
Publications: Quarterly newsletter; annual report; various leaflets and booklets. List available on request

[272]

Homerton School of Health Studies (HSHS) - (Addenbrookes Hospital)

Education Centre Library
Addenbrookes Hospital
Hills Road
Cambridge CB2 2QQ
Telephone: 01223 216258
Contact: Mr G Haldane (College Librarian); Mrs Kathy Cook and Mr Richard Parker (Library Assistants)
Objectives and Purposes: The School provides pre- and post-registration courses in nursing and midwifery. The library service aims to meet the academic and professional resource needs of students, tutorial staff and local clinical staff
Stock and Subject Coverage: 5,000 books; 70 periodicals on all aspects of nursing and health. Access to resources of other site libraries
Services/Facilities: CD-ROM searches (ASSIA, CINAHL, ChildData); photocopies (priced); interlibrary loans (priced)
Availability: By prior appointment, for reference purposes (01480 415267)
Hours: 08.30-16.30 (closes 16.00 on Friday)
Publications: Study Skills: a Guide for Students, by G Haldane (4th ed 1996); library guide
Related Bodies: Homerton College, Cambridge

[273]

Homerton School of Health Studies (HSHS) - (Fulbourn/IDA Darwin Hospital)

Education Centre Library
Fulbourn/IDA Darwin Hospital
Fulbourn
Cambridgeshire CB1 5EE
Telephone: 01223 884101
Fax: 01223 880128
Contact: Mr Graham Haldane (College Librarian); Ms Pauline Desborough (Secretary)
Objectives and Purposes: The School provides pre- and post-registration courses in nursing and midwifery. The library service aims to meet the academic and professional resource needs of students, tutorial staff and local clinical staff
Stock and Subject Coverage: 750 books; 30 periodicals on subjects relating to mental health and learning disabilities nursing. Access to resources of other site libraries
Services/Facilities: Photocopies; CD-ROM searches (ASSIA; Cochrane; Embase Psychiatry)
Availability: By prior appointment, for reference purposes
Hours: 09.00-16.00
Publications: Study Skills: a Guide for Students, by G Haldane (4th ed 1996); library guide
Related Bodies: Homerton College, Cambridge

[274]

Homerton School of Health Studies (HSHS) - (Papworth Hospital)

Education Centre Library
Papworth Hospital
Papworth Everard
Cambridgeshire CB3 8PE
Telephone: 01480 830541, ext 4294
Fax: 01480 831154
Contact: Mr Graham Haldane (College Librarian); Mrs Marina Balgobin (Secretary); Mrs J Coates
Objectives and Purposes: The School provides pre- and post-registration courses in nursing and midwifery. The library service aims to meet the academic and professional resource needs of students, tutorial staff and local clinical staff
Stock and Subject Coverage: 350 books; 10 periodicals mainly related to cardiovascular and coronary care nursing. Access to resources of other site libraries
Services/Facilities: MEDLINE on CD-ROM; photocopies (priced); interlibrary loans (priced)
Availability: By prior appointment, for reference purposes
Hours: 08.30-16.00
Publications: Study Skills: a Guide for Students, by G Haldane (4th ed 1996)
Related Bodies: Homerton College, Cambridge

[275]

Homerton School of Health Studies (HSHS) – (Peterborough District Hospital)

Education Centre Library
Peterborough District Hospital
Thorpe Road
Peterborough PE3 6DA
Telephone: 01733 67451, ext 4766
Fax: 01733 64603
Contact: Mr Graham Haldane (College Librarian);
Mrs Pat Billyard (Centre Librarian)
Objectives and Purposes: The School provides pre-
and post-registration courses in nursing and
midwifery. The library service aims to meet the
academic and professional resource needs of
students, tutorial staff and local clinical staff
Stock and Subject Coverage: 5,500 books; 70
periodicals on a wide range of topics in nursing,
midwifery and health. Access to resources of other
site libraries
Services/Facilities: CD-ROM searches (ASSIA,
CINAHL; ChildData; Cochrane; Embase
Psychiatry); online catalogue (from 1995);
photocopies; interlibrary loans
Availability: By prior appointment, for reference
purposes
Hours: 08.30-20.30 (closes 17.00 on Monday and
Friday); 09.00-13.00 Saturday
Publications: Study Skills: a Guide for Students, by
G Haldane (4th ed 1996); library guide
Related Bodies: Homerton College, Cambridge

[276]

Homerton School of Health Studies (HSHS) – (Rosie Maternity Hospital)

Education Centre Library
Rosie Maternity Hospital
Robinson Way
Cambridge CB2 2SW
Telephone: 01223 217755/213893
Contact: Mr Graham Haldane (College Librarian);
Mrs Caroline Carey (Secretary)
Objectives and Purposes: The School provides pre-
and post-registration courses in nursing and
midwifery. The library service aims to meet the
academic and professional resource needs of
students, tutorial staff and local clinical staff
Stock and Subject Coverage: 900 books; 19 periodicals
on midwifery, maternal care and family planning.
Access to resources of other site libraries
Services/Facilities: Photocopies; CD-ROM searches
(Cochrane)
Availability: By prior appointment, for reference
purposes
Hours: 08.30-16.30
Publications: Study Skills: a Guide for Students, by
G Haldane (4th ed 1996); library guide
Related Bodies: Homerton College, Cambridge

[277]

Homerton School of Health Studies (HSHS) – (Community Unit)

School Management Centre
Community Unit
Primrose Lane
Huntingdon PE18 6SE
Telephone: 01480 415267
Fax: 01480 456129
E-mail: ju84@cityscape.co.uk
Contact: Mr Graham Haldane (College Librarian);
Mrs Marina Balgobin (Clerical Assistant)
Objectives and Purposes: The School provides pre-
and post-registration courses in nursing and
midwifery. The library service aims to meet the
academic and professional resource needs of
students, tutorial staff and local clinical staff
Stock and Subject Coverage: Small stock on
librarianship and nurse education at this location.
The Management Centre co-ordinates the service
at five sites which have 15,000 books and 150
journal titles across the School
Services/Facilities: Photocopies; interlibrary loans;
CD-ROM searches
Availability: By appointment
Hours: 08.30-16.30
Publications: Study Skills: a Guide for Students, by
G Haldane (4th ed 1996)
Related Bodies: Homerton College, Cambridge

[278]

Homoeopathic Bicycle Company

2 Exeter Road
London NW2 4SP
Telephone and Fax: 0181 450 6564
E-mail: fran@gn.apc.org
Contact: Francis Treuherz
Stock and Subject Coverage: Computer databases on
homoeopathic materia medica known as
Reference Works, Zizia and MacRepertory. These
contain the best of 200 years of homoeopathic
clinical literature and are available for searching.
There is also a library of 4,000 books, periodicals
and grey literature
Services/Facilities: Literature searches; bibliographical
and study advice
Availability: By appointment
Publications: Occasional descriptive brochures;
academic and professional journal articles
Related Bodies: Kent Homoeopathic Associates, USA;
Homoeonet (electronic mail network – e-mail to
support@gn.apc.org for details)

[279]

Horder Centre for Arthritis

St John's Road
Crowborough
East Sussex TN6 1XP
Telephone: 01892 665577
Fax: 01892 662142
Contact: Mr JE Ball (Chief Executive)
Objectives and Purposes: To improve the quality of life for people stricken with arthritis
Availability: Referral from medical practitioners
Hours: 24 hours
Publications: Various - list available

[280]

Horton General Hospital NHS Trust

Library and Information Service
Terence Mortimer Postgraduate Education Centre
Oxford Road
Banbury
Oxfordshire OX16 9AL
Telephone: 01295 229316
Fax: 01295 254437
E-mail: cv83@horton.cityscape.ac.uk
Contact: Mrs CA Mortimer; Mrs K Davies (Library Assistant); Mrs RA Bosley (Library Assistant)
Objectives and Purposes: A multidisciplinary library for all NHS staff and undergraduate nurses
Stock and Subject Coverage: Books, reference materials and periodicals covering medicine; nursing; and management
Services/Facilities: CD-ROM searches; photocopies
Availability: By prior appointment, for reference use only
Hours: 09.00-17.00

[281]

Huddersfield Health Staff Library

Royal Infirmary
Acre Street
Lindley
Huddersfield HD3 3EA
Telephone: 01484 482869
Fax: 01484 482022
Contact: Richard Heywood (Librarian)
Objectives and Purposes: To support the objectives of the Huddersfield NHS Trust by providing materials and facilities for the education, training and development of staff, and enhancing patient care by providing access to the knowledge and evidence base of health care
Stock and Subject Coverage: 9,000 books; 200 periodicals. Covers clinical medicine, nursing and health care
Services/Facilities: Online and CD-ROM searches; fax; photocopies; computer facilities; audiovisual equipment
Availability: Open to all for reference use
Hours: 09.15 16.45
Publications: Various guides to resources

[282]

Hull Medical Library

Postgraduate Education Centre
Hull Royal Infirmary
Anlaby Road
Hull HU3 2JZ
Telephone: 01482 674337
Fax: 01482 586587
Contact: Mr DI Thompson (Librarian)
Objectives and Purposes: To provide information and materials in all health service, medical and related fields
Stock and Subject Coverage: 11,500 books; 5,800 bound periodicals; 230 current periodicals, covering all aspects of medicine; nursing; professions allied to medicine; history of medicine; and management; topic files are kept on many subjects
Services/Facilities: Online and CD-ROM searches; fax; photocopies
Availability: Restricted to NHS employees and Hull University staff and students; membership available (priced)
Hours: 09.00-20.00 Monday to Thursday; 10.00-20.00 Friday; 09.00-12.00 Saturday
Related Bodies: Branch at Castle Hill Hospital

[283]

Huntershill Marie Curie Centre

The Library
Belmont Road
Glasgow G21 3AY
Telephone: 0141 558 2555
Fax: 0141 558 5880
Contact: Ms Fiona McLeod MA DipLib ALA (Librarian)
Objectives and Purposes: To provide library and information services to staff and students of the hospice
Stock and Subject Coverage: Small collection of books, periodicals and audiovisual materials concentrating on palliative care of terminally ill patients
Services/Facilities: Photocopies (priced)
Availability: By prior appointment
Hours: 09.30-11.30 Monday and Thursday
Related Bodies: Member of the Scottish Association of Health Science Libraries

[284]

Huntington's Disease Association (HDA)

108 Battersea High Street
London SW11 3HP
Telephone: 0171 223 7000
Fax: 0171 223 9489
Contact: Eileen Cook (Senior Secretary); Laureen Bartlet (Secretary)
Objectives and Purposes: To offer help, support, advice and information to sufferers of Huntington's Disease, and their families

Services/Facilities: Factsheets available on all aspects of Huntington's Disease, and advice given on the condition. List of publications available on request (some charges are made)
Availability: Drop-in clinic on Friday; by appointment
Hours: 09.00-17.00
Related Bodies: There is a network of regional advisers, local groups and branches - details on request

---

[285]
Hyperactive Children's Support Group

71 Whyke Lane
Chichester
Westt Sussex PO10 2LD
Telephone and Fax: 01903 725182
World Wide Web:
http://www.geocities.com/hotsprings/2125
Contact: Mrs Sally Bunday (Founder)
Objectives and Purposes: To support and help parents of hyperactive/ADHD children using dietary/nutritional therapies as opposed to medication. Offer information to professionals when requested to assist with the care and control of hyperactive/ADHD children. To research into the causes and treatments, and to disseminate the information
Availability: Telephone and written enquiries accepted; membership available
Hours: 10.00-15.00
Publications: List available on request

---

[286]
IBS Network

St John's House
Hither Green Hospital
Hither Green Lane
London SE13 6RU
Telephone: 0181 698 4611, ext 8194
Fax: 0181 698 5655
Objectives and Purposes: A voluntary and support organisation to alleviate the distress and suffering caused through living with this condition. To offer help, support, advice and information to people with irritable bowel syndrome, and to other interested parties
Availability: Telephone and written enquiries (large s.a.e. required)
Hours: 10.30-13.30 Monday, Wednesday and Friday
Publications: Quarterly newsletter, Gut Reaction; information sheets; factsheets; full list available on request

---

[287]
Ileostomy and Internal Pouch Support Group (IA)

PO Box 23
Mansfield
Nottinghamshire NG18 4TT
Telephone and Fax: 01623 28099
E-mail: ia@dayveedz.demon.co.uk
Contact: David Eades
Objectives and Purposes: To help anyone whose colon has been, or is about to be, surgically removed or who has an ileostomy; to promote and co-ordinate research into bowel disease and other conditions, and into surgery of such; to keep ileostomists and others informed on all matters of interest to the IA by means of a journal, conferences, seminars and courses on topics of interest
Stock and Subject Coverage: Leaflets relating to ileostomy and internal pouch surgery and life thereafter
Services/Facilities: Hospital and home visits; meetings; advisory and information services
Availability: Telephone enquiries accepted from anyone (no charges)
Hours: 09.00-17.00 (answerphone out of hours)
Publications: IA Journal (quarterly)

---

[288]
Imperial College School of Medicine (ICSM)

Biomedical Sciences Collection
Central Library
Imperial College
South Kensington
London SW7 2AZ
Telephone: 0171 594 8840
Fax: 0171 584 3763
E-mail: j.yeadon@ic.ac.uk
Contact: Janice Yeadon (Sub Librarian Collection Development)
Objectives and Purposes: Multi site medical school in process of organisation. Provision for Basic Medical Sciences will be at the South Kensington Site. Other sites are/will be St Mary's, National Heart and Lung Institute, Charing Cross and Westminster Medical School, Royal Postgraduate Medical School. First intake of students sceduled for October 1998
Stock and Subject Coverage: BMS will incorporate and extend the present Life Sciences Collection. It will cover biochemistry and biology (including ecology, etc.) as well as the material to support the new medical curriculum at present being devised. This will include biomedical engineering
Services/Facilities: Photocopies (priced)
Availability: Will be open to bona fide researchers for reference only. Many electronic services are restricted to members of Imperial College
Hours: Termtime: 09.00-21.00; 09.30-17.30 Saturday. Vacations: 09.30-17.30

Publications: General leaflets on the Library's services available in the foyer
Related Bodies: Imperial College London

---

[289]

Imperial College School of Medicine at National Heart and Lung Institute

Dovehouse Street
London SW3 6LY
Telephone: 0171 351 8185
Fax: 0171 376 3442
E-mail: nhli.lib@ic.ac.uk
World Wide Web:
   http://libserver.lib.ac.uk/depts/nhindex.htm
Contact: Linda Dorrington (Librarian);
   Frances Parker (Information Services)
Objectives and Purposes: To carry out research into the causes, prevention and treatment of heart and lung disease; to provide education and training in this field
Stock and Subject Coverage: 10,000 books; 300 periodicals covering heart and lung disease; nursing; and allied health. There are rare book collections
Services/Facilities: CD-ROM searches on MEDLINE, CINAHL and Current Contents - Life Sciences; BIDS available to academic staff; photocopies (priced)
Availability: By prior appointment, for reference use only
Hours: 09.00-21.00 (restricted service after 18.00)
Publications: Annual report; library guides; reading lists; recent acquisitions; catalogue of rare books collection
Related Bodies: Merged with Imperial College, London, in 1995

---

[290]

Imperial College School of Medicine at St Mary's Hospital

Norfolk Place
London W2 1PG
Telephone: 0171 594 3692
Fax: 0171 723 7349
E-mail: n.palmer@sm.ic.ac.uk
World Wide Web:
   http://www.lib.ic.ac.uk/depts/stindex.htm
Contact: Mr ND Palmer (Librarian); Miss SE Smith (Senior Assistant Librarian - Enquiries);
   Miss RC Shipton (Assistant Librarian)
Objectives and Purposes: To provide library and information services for all staff and students of IC, for the medical staff of St Mary's NHS Trust and its associated health district
Stock and Subject Coverage: 5,000 books; 350 current periodicals; 33,000 bound periodicals covering undergraduate and postgraduate medicine
Services/Facilities: Online and CD-ROM searches

Availability: By prior appointment, for reference use only
Hours: Termtime: 09.00-21.00; 09.00-13.00 Saturday. Vacations: 09.00-13.00
Publications: A Bibliography of Sir Alexander Fleming 1881-1955 (1993)
Related Bodies: Part of Imperial College of Science, Technology and Medicine

---

[291]

Independent Doctors Forum (IDF)

1 Wimpole Street
London W1M 8AE
Telephone: 0171 290 2968
Fax: 0171 290 2989
Contact: The Secretariat
Objectives and Purposes: To provide a forum for, and represent the interests of, registered medical practitioners engaged in full time private medical practice

---

[292]

Independent Healthcare Association (IHA)

22 Little Russell Street
London WC1A 2HT
Telephone: 0171 430 0537
Fax: 0171 242 2681
Contact: Barry Hassell (Chief Executive)
Objectives and Purposes: To promote and protect standards of health care within the independent sector
Stock and Subject Coverage: Articles and statistics on the independent health care sector in the United Kingdom
Availability: Visits by arrangement; most items free to students; some charges for commercial enquiries
Hours: 09.00-17.30
Publications: List available on request

---

[293]

Industrial Injuries Advisory Council (IIAC)

DSS Library
Room 637
The Adelphi
1-11 John Adam Street
London WC2N 6HY
Telephone: 0171 962 8665
Fax: 0171 962 8491
E-mail: peter.banks@dial.pipex.com
Contact: John Goodier (Technical Secretary)
Objectives and Purposes: To advise the Secretary of State for Social Security on the operation of the Industrial Injuries Scheme
Stock and Subject Coverage: Uses the stock of the DSS library
Availability: Telephone and written enquiries only

Hours: 10.00-17.00
Publications: Periodic reports; series of command
papers on occupational diseases
Related Bodies: Part of the Department of Social
Security Library Service

[294]
*Institute for the Study of Drug Dependence (ISDD)

Waterbridge House
32-36 Loman Street
London SE1 0EE
Telephone: 0171 928 1211
Fax: 0171 928 7171
Contact: John Witton (Enquiries); Anna Bradley
(Director); Phil Defriel (Librarian)
Objectives and Purposes: To advance knowledge,
understanding and policy making about drugs
Stock and Subject Coverage: Material on all aspects of
drug use in any form; an audiovisual collection;
press cuttings date back to 1967
Services/Facilities: Database searches; fax; photocopies;
audiovisual materials
Availability: Telephone and written enquiries
accepted; visits welcome, for reference use only
Hours: 09.30-17.30
Publications: Druglink (bi-monthly journal); Drug
Abstracts (monthly); Audit of Drug Misuse in
Britain; various others - list available
Related Bodies: Member of Standing Conference on
Drug Abuse

[295]
Institute of Alcohol Studies (IAS)

Alliance House
12 Caxton Street
London SW1H OQS
Telephone: 0171 222 4001
Fax: 0171 799 2510
E-mail: info@ias.org.uk
World Wide Web: http://www.ias.org.uk
Contact: Lesley Webster (Librarian); Andrew McNeill
(Director of Studies)
Objectives and Purposes: Alcohol-related issues, such
as health policy, treatment methods and resources,
drink driving, alcohol education and the media
Stock and Subject Coverage: 7,000 books and
pamphlets; 1,700 papers, including much grey
literature. Special collection on historic
temperance literature
Services/Facilities: Computerised catalogue from
1989 onwards, photocopies (priced), searches on
internal databases
Availability: Personal visits by appointment, for
reference use only
Hours: 09.30-16.30
Publications: Monthly digest of press cuttings and
statsistics; Alcohol Alert and The Globe magazines,
both quarterly; occasional papers and conference
reports. Catalogue of books etc. for sale available
on request

[296]
Institute of Allergy Therapists

Ffynnonwen Natural Therapy Centre
Llangwyryfon
Aberystwyth
Ceredigion SY23 4EY
Telephone: 01974 241376
Fax: 01974 241376
Contact: Donald M Harrison
Objectives and Purposes: To maintain a register of
qualified allergy therapists for referral purposes; to
provide an information source for members; to act
as a regulatory body for the membership
Availability: Telephone and written enquiries
accepted
Hours: 09.00-17.00
Related Bodies: Member of Kinesiology Federation

[297]
Institute of Child Health, University College London (ICH)

30 Guilford Street
London WC1N 1EH
Telephone: 0171 242 9789, ext 2424
Fax: 0171 831 0488
E-mail: library@ich.ucl.ac.uk
World Wide Web:
http://www.ich.bpmf.ac.uk/libguide.htm
Contact: John Clarke (Librarian); Owen Stephens
(Assistant Librarian)
Objectives and Purposes: Postgraduate medical
education, and research into diseases of children.
Closely supports the work of Great Ormond
Street Hospital
Stock and Subject Coverage: Material on paediatrics,
including a historical collection. Collection of
staff publications (1945-1975). Library includes
the Resource Centre for International Child
Health
Services/Facilities: Database searches; photocopies
(priced); Internet access; interlibrary loans
(priced); Braille reader/printer
Availability: By prior appointment, for reference use
only
Hours: 09.30-18.00
Related Bodies: Part of University College London

[298]
Institute of Chiropodists

27 Wright Street
Southport
Merseyside PR9 0TL
Telephone: 01704 546141
Fax: 01704 500477
Contact: Mrs SM Kirkham (Secretary)
Objectives and Purposes: To promote the
standardisation throughout the profession of the
practice, research and instruction of and in
chiropody, and to establish and maintain
chiropody as a self-governing profession

Stock and Subject Coverage: Books; periodicals; photographs and slides. Covers all subjects related to chiropody

Availability: By prior appointment, for reference use only; telephone and written enquiries accepted (charges may be made)

Hours: 09.00-17.00

Publications: Chiropody Review (bi-monthly)

---

[299]
Institute of Health Education

University Dental Hospital
Department of Oral Health and Development
Higher Cambridge Street
Manchester M15 6FH

Telephone and Fax: 0161 275 6610

E-mail: anthony.blinkhorn@man.ac.uk

World Wide Web:
http://www.ucsalf.ac.uk/hs/hscience/jihevols.htm

Contact: Professor AS Blinkhorn (Hon. Secretary); Helen Draper (Secretary)

Objectives and Purposes: To promote the scientific basis of health education, through scientific meetings and a quarterly journal

Availability: Telephone and written enquiries accepted

Hours: 09.00-17.00

Publications: Quarterly newsletter; Journal of the Institute of Health Education (quarterly)

---

[300]
Institute of Health Sciences Library (IHS)

University of Oxford
PO Box 777
Oxford OX3 7LF

Telephone: 01865 226688

Fax: 01865 226619

E-mail: andre.tomlin@ihs.ox.ac.uk

World Wide Web: http://www. ihs.ox.ac.uk/

Contact: Mary Montague (Librarian); Andre Tomlin (Senior Library Assistant - enquiries)

Objectives and Purposes: To provide high quality library and information services to all library users; to promote developments in information technology, especially focusing on the importance of the Internet; to provide an information gateway ensuring access to any useful sources of evidence; to ensure that library users are aware of recent developments in their field, particularly focusing on trends in evidence based medicine and primary health care

Stock and Subject Coverage: Material on health management/policy; primary care; evidence based health care. Large collection of grey literature and DH circulars

Services/Facilities: Connected to JANET; Electronic Reference Library (WinSPIRS); various CD-ROM databases; photocopies; fax; online searching; current awareness services

Availability: Access restricted to employees of organisations who have a service level agreement with the Library. Short term usage of service is available (charges on request). All types of enquiries accepted

Hours: 09.00-17.00

Publications: Monthly booklist; journals list; IHS Newsletter (also available via WWW)

Related Bodies: Managed by HCLU (Health Care Libraries Unit) - University of Oxford; Member of HeLIN (Health Libraries Information Network)

---

[301]
Institute of Health Services Management (IHSM)

39 Chalton Street
London NW1 1JD

Telephone: 0171 388 2626

Fax: 0171 388 2386

E-mail: mailbox@ihsm.co.uk

World Wide Web: http://www.ihsm.co.uk

Contact: Karen Caines (Director)

Objectives and Purposes: To promote excellence in health services management; to affect health service policy and its implementation; to create, sustain and represent a professional community of health service managers

Stock and Subject Coverage: Health-related material including government documents, Hansard, policy reports from various organisations

Availability: By appointment; a small charge may be levied on non-members; telephone and written enquiries accepted

Hours: 09.15-17.30

Publications: The IHSM Health and Social Services Year Book

---

[302]
Institute of Laryngology and Otology

Library
330-332 Gray's Inn Road
London WC1X 8EE

Telephone: 0171 837 8855, ext 4145

E-mail: p.zwarts@ucl.ac.uk

World Wide Web: http://www.ucl.ac.uk/library/iol/

Contact: Peter Zwarts; Paul Pearson; Helen Dunning

Objectives and Purposes: Education in otology, rhinology and laryngology

Stock and Subject Coverage: Material covering otology, rhinology and laryngology

Services/Facilities: Online searches; photocopies

Availability: Bona fide researchers by appointment

Hours: 09.30-17.30 Monday and Friday; 09.30-19.00 Tuesday to Thursday

[303]

Institute of Naval Medicine (INM)

Crescent Road
Alverstone
Gosport
Hampshire PO12 2DL
Telephone: 01705 722351, ext 68738
Fax: 01705 504823
Contact: The Librarian
Objectives and Purposes: Biomedical research, and medical support to the Royal Navy. Material covering environmental medicine, including submarine and undersea medicine; health and safety; physiology; noise and vibration; toxicology; and radiation protection
Stock and Subject Coverage: Online and CD-ROM searches; photocopies
Services/Facilities: By prior appointment, for reference use only
Hours: 09.00-16.30
Publications: Various reports; annual report
Related Bodies: Ministry of Defence medical libraries

[304]

Institute of Neurology

Rockefeller Medical Library
National Hospital for Neurology and
    Neurosurgery
Queen Square
London WC1N 3BG
Telephone: 0171 829 8709
Fax: 0171 278 5069
E-mail: library@ion.ucl.ac.uk
World Wide Web:
    http://www.ion.ucl.ac.uk/~admin/library.html
Contact: Louise Shepherd (Librarian); Sam Duerden (Assistant Librarian)
Objectives and Purposes: To provide teaching and research of the highest quality in neurology, neurosurgery and neurosciences, and professional training for clinical careers in these fields
Stock and Subject Coverage: Material on neurology and its associated disciplines, and the basic neurosciences. Special collection on historical neurology; Queen Square Collection of publications by hospital and Institute staff
Services/Facilities: Photocopies (priced); CD-ROM searches
Availability: Open to all bona fide researchers on proof of identity, for reference only
Hours: 09.00-18.00
Publications: Newsletter
Related Bodies: Affiliated to University College London

[305]

Institute of Occupational Medicine (IOM)

8 Roxburgh Place
Edinburgh EH8 9SU
Telephone: 0131 667 5131
Fax: 0131 667 0136
E-mail: iom@iomhq.org.uk
Contact: Ann Boyle (Technical Information Officer)
Objectives and Purposes: To conduct research, consultancy work and training on occupational health, hygiene and safety
Stock and Subject Coverage: Material on occupational medicine; health, safety and hygiene; environmental health; toxicology; and ergonomics. Special collection of asbestos literature
Services/Facilities: Online and CD-ROM searches; photocopies; interlibrary laons
Availability: Telephone and written enquiries accepted; visits by prior arrangement
Hours: 09.00-17.00
Publications: Research papers, etc. List available

[306]

Institute of Ophthalmology

Bath Street
London EC1V 9EL
Telephone: 0171 608 6814/6815
Fax: 0171 608 6859
E-mail: s.lawrence@ucl.ac.uk
World Wide Web: http://www.ucl.ac.uk/ioo
Contact: Mrs CS Lawrence (Librarian)
Objectives and Purposes: Postgraduate research and teaching in the fields of ophthalmology, visual science and related disciplines; closely supports and collaborates with the work, teaching and research of Moorfields Eye Hospital NHS Trust. The Institute has been merged with University College London
Stock and Subject Coverage: Two libraries are maintained: the Institute Library holds 9,000 books and 8,000 bound volumes of periodicals (153 current titles) in visual science and ophthalmology, including historical works; the Hospital Library holds 3,000 books and 2,200 bound volumes of periodicals (59 current titles) in clinical ophthalmology, nursing and related disciplines. There is a collection of theses, a small historical collection and a large reprint/offprint collection (indexed)
Services/Facilities: Database searches (at cost); photocopies (at cost); interlibrary loans; no visitor access to computer facilities
Availability: No access to Hospital Library. Bona fide researchers may apply for short-term reference access to the Institute library. Telephone and written enquiries to the Librarian will be dealt with as time permits. Charges made for written replies, photocopies, etc.
Hours: 09.00-17.00
Publications: Institute Library: Reports and leaflets (e.g. Fight for Sight); annual reports. Hospital Library: Annual reports; Fight for Sight (related charity)

[307]

Institute of Orthopaedics

Francis Costello Library
Robert Jones and Agnes Hunt Orthopaedic and
    District Hospital NHS Trust
Oswestry
Shropshire SY10 7AG
Telephone: 01691 404388
Fax: 01691 404071
E-mail: mcarter@ortholib.demon.co.uk
Contact: Miss MF Carter (Librarian)
Objectives and Purposes: To serve the information
    needs of staff and students at the hospital
Stock and Subject Coverage: 3,300 books; 120
    periodicals; and 150 videos. Covers all aspects of
    orthopaedics. Other medical topics are covered in
    less depth. Special collection on the history of the
    hospital and historical books on orthopaedics
Services/Facilities: CD-ROM searches on MEDLINE;
    Internet access; photocopies
Availability: By prior appointment, for reference use
    only
Hours: 08.45–17.00 (closes 16.00 on Friday)
Publications: Quarterly bulletin; library guide
Related Bodies: Linked to Staffordshire University
    School of Health for nursing resources; part of
    West Midlands Health Libraries Network

[308]

Institute of Psychiatry

De Crespigny Park
London SE5 8AF
Telephone: 0171 919 3204
Fax: 0171 703 4515
E-mail: spyllib@iop.bpmf.ac.uk
World Wide Web: http://www.iop.bpmf.ac.uk/home/
    depts/library/library.htm
Contact: Martin Guha (Librarian)
Objectives and Purposes: To promote mental health
Stock and Subject Coverage: Range of material on
    psychiatry; psychology; neurosciences; and
    neurology. Mayer-Gross Collection on the history
    of psychiatry. Guttman-McLay Collection on art
    and mental illness. Maudsley Collection (founder
    of the Maudsley Hospital)
Availability: Not normally open to non-members
Hours: 09.00–20.00; 09.00–13.00 Saturday
Related Bodies: Linked to King's College, London;
    Branch library at Bethlem Royal Hospital

[309]

Institute of Psycho-Analysis

63 New Cavendish Street
London W1M 7RD
Telephone: 0171 580 4452
Fax: 0171 323 5312
Contact: Jill Duncan
Objectives and Purposes: A learned society whose aims
    are to promote creative discussion and
    communication between its members, with allied
    professions, and with the general public. Oversees
    training in the discipline

Stock and Subject Coverage: Books and journals on all
    aspects of psychoanalysis
Services/Facilities: Photocopies
Availability: By written application to the Hon.
    Librarian
Hours: 09.30–17.30

[310]

International Autistic Research Organisation/Autism Research Ltd

49 Orchard Avenue
Shirley
Croydon CR0 7NE
Telephone: 0181 777 0095
Fax: 0181 776 2362
E-mail: 106130.217@compuserve.com
World Wide Web: http://www.vois.org.uk/iaro
Contact: Mrs Gerda McCarthy; Mrs Patricia Moya;
    Mr Brian McCarthy
Objectives and Purposes: To carry out and to
    encourage all manner of research into the mental
    and emotional condition of autism and any other
    conditions that might be associated with autism,
    of whatever nature, and to disseminate the useful
    results of such research
Stock and Subject Coverage: Material on autism
Availability: Telephone, fax and written enquiries;
    open to all researchers who require support;
    personal visits by appointment; material available
    for research at nominal charge (10p per sheet) for
    photocopies
Hours: 09.00–17.00 (can be flexible)
Publications: Newsletter (5 per year); annual report

[311]

International Confederation of Midwives (ICM)

10 Barley Mow Passage
Chiswick
London W4 4PH
Telephone: 0181 994 6477
Fax: 0181 995 1332
E-mail: 100702.2405@compuserve.com
Contact: Miss Joan Walker (Secretary General)
Objectives and Purposes: To advance education in
    midwifery; to spread knowledge of the art and
    science of midwifery with the purpose of
    improving standards of care provided to mothers,
    babies and their families around the world. There
    are member associations in 60 countries
Stock and Subject Coverage: Books, pamphlets, reports
    (especially of WHO and UN Bodies), and journals
    and newsletters (including those of member
    organisations). Covers midwifery; maternal and
    child health; social, economic and cultural status
    of women and children - all with a strong
    international bias
Services/Facilities: Photocopies (limited by staff time,
    and priced)

Availability: Bona fide researchers, especially
  midwives; personal visits by appointment, for
  reference use only; written or fax enquiries
  preferred
Hours: 08.30-16.30
Publications: Newsletter (3 per year); annual report;
  list of other publications available on request
Related Bodies: Member associations in 60 countries.
  Co-operates with a wide range of related
  organisations

[312]

International Glaucoma Association (IGA)

King's College Hospital
Denmark Hill
London SE5 9RS
Telephone: 0171 737 3265/0171 737 4000, ext 2934
Fax: 0171 737 3265
E-mail: iga@kcl.ac.uk
World Wide Web: http://www.iga.org.uk/iga/
Contact: Mrs V Greatorex
Objectives and Purposes: To prevent blindness from
  glaucoma by providing information about
  glaucoma in a clear manner to patients and others
  with an interest; to promote better understanding
  and awareness of glaucoma; to encourage
  improved detection and treatment; to fund
  research into aspects of detection and treatment
Stock and Subject Coverage: Patient information about
  glaucoma; various research papers
Availability: Freely available; visits by prior
  arrangement only; all patient information is free
  (s.a.e. is appreciated); telephone and written
  enquiries accepted
Hours: 09.30-17.00
Publications: Newsletter (2 per year); full list available

[313]

International Hospital Federation (IHF)

4 Abbots Place
London NW6 4NP
Telephone: 0171 372 7181
Fax: 0171 328 7433
E:mail: 10166.1262@compuserve.com
World Wide Web: http://www.powertek.co.uk/ihf
Contact: Dr Errol Pickering; Mr Carl Richmond
Objectives and Purposes: The main aim of the IHF is
  to promote improvements in the planning and
  management of hospital and health services
  through international conferences, field study
  courses, management training courses,
  publications and research projects
Stock and Subject Coverage: Materials on health policy,
  environment, finance in health care, hospital
  statistics, management practice and training, law
  and legislation relating to health
Availability: By appointment to bona fide researchers
  for reference use only. Enquiries accepted by
  telephone, fax or letter

Hours: 09.00-18.00
Publications: List available on request

[314]

International Planned Parenthood Federation (IPPF)

Regents College
Inner Circle
Regents Park
London NW1 4NS
Telephone: 0171 486 0741
Fax: 0171 487 7950
E-mail: rward@ippf.attmail.com;
  ftait@ippf.attmail.com
World Wide Web: http://www.oneworld.org/ippf
Contact: Rita Ward and Frances Tait (Librarians)
Objectives and Purposes: A federation of autonomous
  national family planning associations (FPAs) in
  over 140 countries worldwide. It is concerned
  with family planning and sexual and reproductive
  health
Stock and Subject Coverage: 6,000 books; 100
  periodicals and newsletters; 400 videos. Covers
  demography; family planning; sex education; status
  of women; and reproductive rights
Services/Facilities: Free information service via
  telephone or letter; free database searches on
  CD-ROM (POPLINE, AIDSLINE, MEDLINE,
  BIRD)
Availability: By appointment, for reference use only
Hours: 10.00-17.00
Publications: Challenges (biennial); People and the
  Planet (quarterly); Medical Bulletin (6 per year);
  annual report; occasional publications (list
  available)

[315]

International Stress Management Association (UK) (ISMA)

South Bank University
LPSS
103 Borough Road
London SE1 0AA
Fax: 01702 584025
E-mail: 101752.744@compuserve.com
Contact: Janet Williams (UK Chair); David Moore
  (Membership Secretary)
Objectives and Purposes: An organisation for those
  with an interest in stress management. ISMA
  exists to spread sound knowledge, the
  maintenance of quality and to resource its
  members. It is the UK arm of the International
  Stress Management Association
Stock and Subject Coverage: Books, cassettes and
  videos dealing with stress
Services/Facilities: Seminars and conferences for
  members; material and resources for purchase only
Availability: Telephone and written enquiries accepted
Hours: 09.00-17.30
Publications: Stress News (bi-monthly); full list
  available

[316]
Inverclyde Royal NHS Trust

Robert Lamb Medical Library
Larkfield Road
Greenock PA16 0XN
Telephone: 01475 656011
Fax: 01475 635810
E-mail: mwright@rlmedlib.demon.co.uk
Contact: Dr R Brown (Hon. Librarian);
Mrs M Wright (Librarian)
Objectives and Purposes: To provide library and
information services to medical, paramedical and
management staff
Stock and Subject Coverage: 1,500 books; 110
periodicals; 2,000 bound journals; videotapes and
slides covering all medical and paramedical
subjects and management. UK National Slide
Bank on videodisc
Services/Facilities: CD-ROM and online searches;
literature searches; current awareness service;
microfiche reader; PC software available;
photocopies (priced); fax (priced)
Availability: By prior appointment, for reference use
only
Hours: 24 hours
Publications: Library information leaflet

[317]
*Ipswich Medical Library

Education Centre
Ipswich Hospital NHS Trust
Ipswich
Suffolk IP4 5PD
Telephone: 01473 702545
Fax: 01473 702548
Contact: Mrs P Althorpe (Librarian)
Objectives and Purposes: To support postgraduate
medical education and research
Stock and Subject Coverage: 7,000 books; 280 journals
in clinical medicine. Specialist collections in
psychiatry and family psychiatry held in satellite
libraries
Services/Facilities: MEDLINE searches on CD-ROM;
photocopies; video player; Cochrane database;
computer assisted learning for dentistry
Availability: By appointment. Loans to members only.
Enquiries accepted by telephone, fax or in person
Hours: 09.00-17.00
Publications: Library guide; annual report
Related Bodies: Oxford and Anglia Health Care
Libraries

[318]
Isle of Man Postgraduate Medical Library

PG Medical Centre
Nobles Hospital
Westmoreland Street
Douglas
Isle of Man IM1 4QA
Telephone: 01624 642377
Fax: 01624 611922

Contact: Mrs C Sugden (Medical Librarian)
Objectives and Purposes: To provide library and
information services to local medical staff
Stock and Subject Coverage: Material on clinical
medicine; 50 current periodicals
Services/Facilities: MEDLINE on CD-ROM;
photocopies
Availability: Telephone and written enquiries
accepted; by prior appointment, for reference use
only
Hours: 08.30-17.00 (closes 16.30 on Friday)

[319]
ISSUE – The National Fertility Association

509 Aldridge Road
Great Barr
Birmingham B44 8NA
Telephone: 0121 344 4414
Fax: 0121 344 4336
E-mail: issue@hedgley.thegap.com
World Wide Web: http://www.gpl.net/users/hedgley
Contact: Mrs J Susan Rice (Chief Executive)
Objectives and Purposes: To provide information; to
support and represent people with fertility
difficulties and those who work with them; to
raise awareness of infertility and to educate the
public; to work with self-help groups and others
interested in infertility
Stock and Subject Coverage: Small library of books on
infertility
Services/Facilities: 34 factsheets are produced;
telephone and written enquiries welcomed;
telephone counselling; self-help groups; access to
medical advice; full information and support
service is a priced facility
Availability: By prior appointment
Hours: 09.00-16.30 (closes 16.00 on Friday).
Answering service: 07.00-09.00 and 16.30-19.00;
09.00-12.00 Saturday
Publications: Issue (4 per year)

[320]
*Jersey General Hospital

Education Centre Library
St Helier
Jersey JE2 3QS
Telephone: 01534 59000, ext 2664; Direct line:
01534 34363
Fax: 01534 59805
Contact: Mrs S Tillman ALA
Objectives and Purposes: To provide library and
information services supporting the training and
practice of Jersey's health personnel
Stock and Subject Coverage: 5,000 books; 150
periodicals covering all general medical and
nursing subjects
Services/Facilities: Online and CD-ROM searches
(MEDLINE and CINAHL); photocopies (priced)
Availability: All island health personnel for reference
and loans; charges for interlibrary loans to
non-hospital employees

Hours: 09.00-17.30 (closes 17.00 on Friday)
Related Bodies: Member of Wessex Regional Library
and Information Network

[321]

Kennedy Institute of Rheumatology (KI)

1 Aspenlea Road
Hammersmith
London W6 8LH
Telephone: 0181 383 4444
Fax: 0181 383 4499
Contact: Miss K Bull (Librarian)
Objectives and Purposes: To carry out research into
the causes and treatment of rheumatic diseases and
to promote public education and teaching about
rheumatic diseases
Stock and Subject Coverage: 1,000 books; 80
periodicals covering rheumatology and
immunology
Services/Facilities: Photocopies (at cost)
Availability: By prior appointment, for reference use
only
Hours: 09.15-16.45
Publications: Annual report
Related Bodies: Associated with Charing Cross and
Westminster Medical School

[322]

Kent and Sussex Weald NHS Trust (KSWT)

Library
Kent and Sussex Hospital
Tunbridge Wells
Kent TN4 8AT
Telephone: 01892 526111, ext 2384
Fax: 01892 531975
E-mail: tunwells.health@dm.krinfo.ch
Contact: Mrs Jennifer Blackburn (Head of Library
Services)
Objectives and Purposes: A library and information
service for employees of the Trust supporting
professional education and clinical practice in the
health care professions
Stock and Subject Coverage: 2,700 books; 120
periodicals covering general medicine; surgery,
nursing; and some allied health literature
Services/Facilities: Online and CD-ROM searches;
literature searches; photocopies (fees charged to
external users)
Availability: By prior arrangement
Hours: 09.00-17.00 (open until 20.00 on Wednesday)
Related Bodies: Libraries at Pembury Hospital and
Sevenoaks Hospital

[323]

Kent Postgraduate Medical Centre

Kent and Canterbury Hospital
Canterbury
Kent CT1 3NG
Telephone: 01227 761849
Fax: 01227 453581
Contact: Mrs Sue Cover (Librarian); Mrs Kim Lee
and Mrs Val White (Library Assistants)
Objectives and Purposes: To provide library and
information services to local medical professionals
Stock and Subject Coverage: 5,000 books; 200
periodicals. Covers medicine, dentistry and
veterinary medicine
Services/Facilities: CD-ROM searches; interlibrary
loans (priced); fax; photocopies (priced)
Availability: By prior appointment, for reference use
only; telephone and written enquiries accepted
Hours: 09.00-17.00

[324]

Kilner Library of Plastic Surgery

Radcliffe Infirmary
Oxford OX2 6HE
Telephone: 01865 224864
Fax: 01865 311673
Contact: Dr Geraldine Ashworth (Hon. Librarian)
Stock and Subject Coverage: Material on plastic and
craniofacial surgery
Availability: This specialised material is only of
interest to plastic and reconstructive surgeons.
There are very limited staff resources for dealing
with enquiries
Hours: 09.00-17.00
Related Bodies: University of Oxford; Cairns Library

[325]

King's College London Library, Centre of Medical Law and Ethics

Strand
London WC2R 2LS
Telephone: 0171 873 2313/2424
Fax: 0171 873 0207
E-mail: vivien.robertson@kcl.ac.uk
World Wide Web: http://www.kcl.ac.uk
Contact: Mrs Vivien Robertson BA ALA;
Miss Caitriona Boulton BA; Ms Karen Driver BA
Objectives and Purposes: To support the research and
teaching programmes of the Centre of Medical
Law and Ethics, which is part of the School of Law
Stock and Subject Coverage: Material on medical law
and medical ethics, focusing on the UK, USA and
Commonwealth
Services/Facilities: Photocopies
Availability: By prior appointment, for reference use
only; borrowing facilities on payment of a fee
Hours: 09.00-21.00 (closes 19.00 on Friday);
09.30-17.30 Saturday. Shorter hours in vacations
Related Bodies: Part of King's College London

[326]
King's College School of Medicine and Dentistry Library (KCSMD Library)

Bessemer Road
London SE5 9PJ
Telephone: 0171 346 3003/737 4000, exts
  4022/4024
Fax: 0171 346 3001
E-mail: c.hogg@kcl.ac.uk
Contact: Ms CG Hogg (Librarian); Ms A Tobin and
  Mr GJ Horrocks (Assistant Librarians)
Objectives and Purposes: Medical and dental education
  and research
Stock and Subject Coverage: Ca. 10,000 books; 500
  current periodicals on clinical medicine and
  dentistry; health service matters; sciences and
  professions associated with medicine and dentistry.
  Slide bank on video disc; videos and multimedia
  programs. Historical collection from 16th Century
  to the 20th Century
Services/Facilities: Self-service photocopies; online
  and CD-ROM database searches (mediated
  searches charged at cost); educational/training
  programme on electronic resources
Availability: Reference facilities for visitors
Hours: 09.00-20.00
Publications: Newsletter
Related Bodies: Part of King's College London Library

[327]
King's Fund

11-13 Cavendish Square
London W1M 0AN
Telephone: 0171 307 2568/2569
Fax: 0171 307 2805
E-mail: libenqz@kehf.org.uk
Contact: Lynette Cawthra (Library and Information
  Services Manager); Valerie Wildridge (Reader
  Services)
Objectives and Purposes: To provide a public reference
  collection and library enquiry service to support
  the needs of managers working within the field of
  health and social care, and those training in related
  management areas
Stock and Subject Coverage: 30,000 books; 350
  periodicals; a World Health Organization
  documentation centre. Covers the management
  and delivery of health and social care services,
  primarily in the UK but with some international
  coverage. Material includes government
  documents, books, journals, and a major emphasis
  on informally published (i.e. grey) literature
Services/Facilities: Internal and external database
  searches; interlibrary loans (priced); photocopies
  (priced)
Availability: Telephone and written enquiries; visits
  by appointment; full-time students and nursing
  students are requested to use the services via their
  own institution's library; material is for reference
  use only

Hours: 09.30-17.30; 09.30-17.00 Saturday, by
  appointment only
Publications: Library Guide; journals holdings list;
  annual report
Related Bodies: Parent body is King Edward's
  Hospital Fund

[328]
Kings Lynn Health Science Library

The Queen Elizabeth Hospital
Gayton Road
Kings Lynn
Norfolk PE30 4ET
Telephone: 01553 613792
Fax: 01553 613683
E-mail: qelib@dial.pipex.com
Contact: Ms Ann Osborn (Librarian)
Objectives and Purposes: To provide a comprehensive
  library and information service to all staff of the
  parent organisation
Stock and Subject Coverage: Material on clinical
  medicine and nursing
Services/Facilities: CD-ROM searches (MEDLINE
  and CINAHL); photocopies; computer index to
  journals not covered by CD-ROM; current
  awareness service
Availability: Restricted to staff only
Hours: 08.30-17.30
Publications: Annual report; monthly current
  awareness bulletin

[329]
Kirkcaldy Acute Hospitals NHS Trust

Postgraduate Medical Centre
Victoria Hospital
Hayfield Road
Kirkcaldy
Fife KY2 5AH
Telephone: 01592 643355
Contact: Marie Smith; Ann Sheach
Objectives and Purposes: To provide library and
  information services to local medical staff
Stock and Subject Coverage: Material on general
  medicine and surgery
Services/Facilities: Online and CD-ROM searches;
  photocopies
Availability: To staff and doctors
Hours: 08.30-17.00 (closes 16.30 on Friday)

[330]

Klinefelter's Syndrome Association (KSA)

Parents Group:
56 Little Yeldham Road
Halstead
Essex CO9 4QT
Adults Group:
6 Borrowdale
Cambridge CB4 3HU

Telephone: Parents Group: 01787 237460;
Adults Group: 01223 311661
Contact: Sue Cook (Parents Group); David Hames
(Adults Group)
Objectives and Purposes: To provide information on
Klinefelter's Syndrome to all who seek it and to
facilitate contact between affected adults and the
parents of affected boys/teenagers
Availability: Members only
Hours: Evenings only
Publications: Newletter
Related Bodies: Network of regional contact groups

[331]

Lambeth Healthcare (NHS) Trust

108 Landor Road
Stockwell
London SW9 9NT
Telephone: 0171 346 5400/01, exts 5636/5762
Fax: 0171 346 5448
Contact: Catherine Ebenezer (Trust Librarian)
Objectives and Purposes: A community care NHS
Trust covering the fields of mental health/adult
learning disabilities, community paediatrics,
primary health care and elderly care (frail and
mentally ill) for the population of Lambeth. The
Library exists to provide information related to all
aspects of the Trust's activities and to provide
recreational reading for staff and patients
Stock and Subject Coverage: Health sciences books
(ca. 3,000) and journals (70 current titles). Covers
social sciences; management; education; primary
health care; social work; public health; health
promotion; nursing; psychology; neurology;
psychiatry (largest area); community paediatrics;
health service administration;
geriatrics/gerontology; general non-fiction;
general fiction; recreational patient/staff
collection; magazines; newspapers
Services/Facilities: CD-ROM databases (CINAHL,
MEDLINE, EMBASE Psychiatry, HealthSTAR)
Card-operated photocopier. Online searching
(chargeable at cost)
Availability: Serves Trust staff and patients, and
UMDS medical students; provides reference access
for Nightingale Institute or South Bank
University students, and other health professionals
at the Librarian's discretion. Ordinary members
may borrow up to four books for a maximum of
four weeks. Online searching is chargeable at cost.
Photocopying is chargeable at 5p per sheet.
Telephone enquiries accepted

Hours: 09.00–17.00
Publications: Library accessions list

[332]

Lambeth, Southwark and Lewisham Health Authority (LSLHA)

1 Lower Marsh
London SE1 7RJ
Telephone: 0171 716 7002
Fax: 0171 716 7039
Contact: David Bates (Librarian)
Objectives and Purposes: Purchasing health care for
the residents of Lambeth, Southwark and
Lewisham
Stock and Subject Coverage: Material on health service
management; epidemiology; public health; and
health economics. Special collection of
Department of Health circulars
Services/Facilities: Photocopies
Availability: Visits by appointment, for reference use
only
Hours: 09.00–17.00
Publications: Public Health Annual Report;
Purchasing Intentions

[333]

Lancaster Postgraduate Medical Centre Library

Royal Lancaster Infirmary
Ashton Road
Lancaster LA1 4RR
Telephone: 01524 583954
Fax: 01524 848289
E-mail: ow52@dial.pipex.com
Contact: Melanie Weeks (Librarian)
Objectives and Purposes: A resource centre for
postgraduate medical education
Stock and Subject Coverage: 1,500 books; 70
periodicals; small video collection. Covers general
medicine
Services/Facilities: CD-ROM searches; photocopies;
Internet access; word processing
Availability: Telephone and written enquiries
accepted; visits by prior arrangement
Hours: 09.00–17.00
Publications: Lancaster and Westmorland Medical
Journal
Related Bodies: Sister Library at Westmorland General
Hospital

[334]

Law Hospital NHS Trust

Alistair MacKenzie Library
Carluke
Lanarkshire ML8 5ER
Telephone: 01698 361100
Fax: 01698 376671
E-mail: 101574.114@compuserve.com

Contact: Julian Hodgson (Librarian); Janice Bryson (Postgraduate Secretary)

Objectives and Purposes: To provide library and information services to NHS staff in Lanarkshire Health Board

Stock and Subject Coverage: 3,000 books; 120 periodicals; 50 audiovisual items. Covers all aspects of medicine, nursing and related fields including health services management

Services/Facilities: CD-ROM searches on MEDLINE; photocopies; fax

Availability: By prior arrangement with the Librarian; most material available for loan

Hours: 09.00–17.00 Monday, Tuesday and Thursday; 09.00–13.30 Wednesday and Friday

Publications: Reviews of current awareness service (monthly); Addiction, Therapy, Child and Family Psychiatry (quarterly); The Law – Law Hospital 1939-1989: A Memoir (£2.50)

[335]
Leeds Health Promotion Service

St Mary's Hospital
Greenhill Road
Armley
Leeds LS12 3QE
Telephone: 0113 279 0121, ext 4581
Fax: 0113 231 0185
E-mail: 10513.2471@compuserve.com
Contact: Jane Carlton (Information and Resources Manager); Audrey Tate and Denise Moran (Information and Resources Officers)
Objectives and Purposes: To support organisations and health educators to develop effective health promotion at a strategic, policy and field level
Stock and Subject Coverage: A wide range of materials and equipment relating to health promotion work, in particular Health of the Nation programme areas
Services/Facilities: Advisory and consultancy service
Availability: Access for health professionals, or anyone undertaking a health promotion role within the Leeds District
Hours: 09.00–17.00 (closes 16.30 on Friday)
Publications: Newsletter; project reports

[336]
Leeds Medical Information

University of Leeds
Leeds LS2 9JT
Telephone: 0113 233 5550
Fax: 0113 233 5568
E-mail: lmi@leeds.ac.uk
World Wide Web: http://www.leeds.ac.uk/ library/mdl/lmi/intro.html
Contact: Robert Hall (Manager - Enquiries); Mark Cooney (Information Officer); Caroline Valleley (Information Officer)
Objectives and Purposes: The provision of printed current awareness services in AIDS/cancer (currently nine titles); the provision of literature search and retrieval services

Stock and Subject Coverage: Material on AIDS; cancer therapy; cancer virology; clinical cancer; palliative care; tumour markers

Services/Facilities: Document delivery; online search services; printed publications

Availability: Access by personal visit, telephone, fax, or e-mail; a charge is made for all services

Hours: 08.45–17.00

Publications: List available on request

[337]
Leicester General Hospital, Education Centre Library

Gwendolen Road
Leicester LE5 4PW
Telephone: 0116 258 4245
Fax: 0116 258 4666
E-mail: 106173.64@compuserve.com
Contact: Claire Honeybourne (Librarian); Robert Marsden; Anne Currie; Charlotte Timson
Objectives and Purposes: To provide library and information services with relevant and up-to-date materials to support staff and students at the hospital
Stock and Subject Coverage: 3,500 books; 114 periodicals in medical subjects. The Library has multidisciplinary coverage and serves the needs of nurses, physiotherapists, dieticians, managers, etc.
Services/Facilities: CD-ROM searches (MEDLINE and CINAHL); interlibrary loans; photocopies; Internet access
Availability: Telephone and written enquiries accepted
Hours: 08.30–20.00 (closes 18.00 on Friday); 09.00–13.00 Saturday
Publications: Annual report

[338]
Leukaemia Care Society (LCS)

14 Kingfisher Court
Venny Bridge
Pinhoe
Exeter EX4 8JN
Telephone: 01392 464848
Fax: 01392 460331
Contact: Mrs SJ Brown (Chief Administrative Officer)
Objectives and Purposes: To support those suffering from leukaemia and allied blood disorders via volunteers throughout the UK, many of whom have experience of the illness
Availability: Open to all interested persons and members. Telephone and written enquiries accepted; visits by arrangement. Free membership, but donations welcomed
Hours: 09.00–16.30
Publications: Newsletter; range of leaflets

[339]
Leukaemia Research Fund (LRF)
43 Great Ormond Street
London WC1N 3JJ
Telephone: 0171 405 0101
Fax: 0171 242 1488
E-mail: lrf@leukres.demon.co.uk
World Wide Web: http://www.leukres.demon.co.uk
Contact: Mr DL Osborne (Executive Director);
   Mr K Campbell (Information Officer)
Objectives and Purposes: The Leukaemia Research
   Fund is the only national charity devoted
   exclusively to finding ways to prevent, improve
   diagnosis and cure all forms of leukaemia,
   myeloma, the lymphomas and Hodgkin's Disease
   and related blood disorders such as aplastic
   anaemia and myelodysplasia. The charity funds
   research, trains specialist doctors and provides
   patient information
Services/Facilities: Free publications; information
   supplied to media sources, and where appropriate
   the Fund will identify a scientist for
   interview/comment on leukaemia topics
Availability: Telephone and written enquiries
   accepted; no visits
Hours: 09.30-17.30
Publications: Various - list available

[340]
*Lewisham Hospital NHS Trust
Lewisham High Street
London SE13 6LH
Telephone: 0181 690 4311, ext 6454
Fax: 0181 690 9829
Contact: Jane Coyte and Julia Jamieson (Librarians)
Objectives and Purposes: To provide library and
   information services to Trust members
Stock and Subject Coverage: 2,000 books; 100
   periodicals covering clinical medicine
Services/Facilities: Online and CD-ROM searches;
   photocopies
Availability: By prior appointment, for reference use
   only; charges to non-Trust members
Hours: 09.00-17.00

[341]
Library Association Health Libraries Group (HLG)
The Library Association
7 Ridgmount Street
London WC1E 7AE
Telephone: 0171 636 7543
Fax: 0171 436 7218
World Wide Web:
   http://www.nthames-health.tpmcle.ac.uk/
   ntrl/hlg/hlg.htm
Contact: Bruce Madge (Chair - 0171 412 7933)
Objectives and Purposes: To unite members of the
   Library Association who are working or interested
   in medical, health and community care issues as
   they apply to library and information services

Services/Facilities: Advice and information on matters
   relevant to the objectives; organisation of various
   events
Availability: Open to all personal members of the
   LA, and to others at the discretion of the
   committee
Publications: Health Libraries Review (quarterly);
   newsletter
Related Bodies: 3 sub-groups (IFM Healthcare,
   Libraries for Nursing, Community Care
   Network); parent body is the Library Association.
   Links with other professional and employer-based
   organisations

[342]
LIFE
LIFE House
Newbold Terrace
Leamington Spa CV32 6JG
Telephone: 01926 42158
Fax: 01926 336497
E-mail: life@lifehq.demon.co.uk
Contact: Professor JJ Scarisbrcek; Peter Garrett (Main
   Contact)
Objectives and Purposes: A national charity that
   provides a comprehensive care service for
   pregnant women, unmarried mothers, women
   with problems relating to pregnancy, fertility or
   infertility, or suffering from the effects of abortion;
   to provide educational support for students; to
   uphold the utmost respect for all human life from
   fertilisation onwards
Stock and Subject Coverage: Reproductions of material
   on ethical, moral and medical issues; genetics;
   population concerns; euthanasia; and general
   right-to-life issues
Services/Facilities: Speakers can be provided for
   schools, etc.
Availability: Telephone and written enquiries
   accepted; visits not possible
Hours: 09.00-17.00
Publications: Newsletter; briefing sheets (priced);
   leaflets. Full list available on request

[343]
Limbless Association
Roehampton Rehabilitation Centre
Roehampton Lane
London SW15 5PNl
Telephone: 0181 579 1758
Contact: Information Officer; Director/General
   Secretary
Objectives and Purposes: A charity devoted to giving
   advice on prosthetics and orthotics to limbless
   persons

[344]
Lincoln and Louth NHS Trust

County Hospital
Greetwell Road
Lincoln LN2 5QY
Telephone: 01522 573952
Fax: 01522 511709
Contact: Mr Philip Williams (Head Librarian)
Objectives and Purposes: To provide library and information service to staff, students and patients of Lincoln hospitals
Stock and Subject Coverage: 10,000 books; 200 periodicals covering medicine, nursing and allied health disciplines, and recreational reading materials
Availability: Full service to staff only; visits by prior appointment, for reference use only
Hours: 08.45-19.00 (closes 17.00 on Friday)

[345]
Liverpool John Moores University, School of Healthcare

The Library
Whiston Hospital
Prescot
Merseyside L35 5DR
Telephone: 0151 430 1342
Fax: 0151 430 8018
E-mail: c.m.benny@livjm.ac.uk
Contact: Miss Carolyn Benny (Librarian); Miss Suzanne Ford (Assistant Librarian)
Objectives and Purposes: A multidisciplinary library service specialising in psychiatry. Aims to serve the reference, reading, information, and research needs of its staff and users
Stock and Subject Coverage: 10,000 books; 105 periodicals covering nursing and psychiatry
Services/Facilities: CD-ROM searches (CINAHL, MEDLINE); photocopies; fax; Internet access
Availability: Freely available for reference use
Hours: 09.00-17.00
Related Bodies: Member of the Psychiatric Libraries Cooperative Scheme

[346]
Liverpool Medical Institution (LMI)

114 Mount Pleasant
Liverpool L3 5SR
Telephone: 0151 709 9125
Fax: 0151 707 2810
Contact: Mrs M Pierce Moulton (Librarian)
Objectives and Purposes: A medical society providing its membership with a postgraduate medical library and a venue for scientific meetings
Stock and Subject Coverage: 35,000 medical books and periodicals; some dating back to the 16th Century
Services/Facilities: Fax; photocopies (priced)
Availability: Bona fide researchers by prior appointment for reference use only

Hours: 09.30-18.00
Publications: Transactions of the LMI (annual)

[347]
Liverpool School of Tropical Medicine (LSTM)

Pembroke Place
Liverpool L3 5QA
Telephone: 0151 708 9393
Fax: 0151 708 9833
E-mail: cmdcar1@liverpool.ac.uk
World Wide Web:
http://www.liv.ac.uk/lstm/lstm.html
Contact: Dr CM Deering (Librarian)
Objectives and Purposes: To promote improved health, particularly for people of less developed countries in the tropics by providing high quality teaching, research, technical assistance, clinical services and appropriate consultancy services
Stock and Subject Coverage: Books and periodicals in the fields of infectious diseases; tropical medicine; parasitology; entomology; veterinary parasitology; and international community health; special collection of archives of the School
Services/Facilities: CD-ROM searches; Internet access; photocopies (priced)
Availability: Bona fide researchers by prior appointment, for reference use only
Hours: 09.00-16.45
Related Bodies: Affiliated to the University of Liverpool

[348]
Llandaff Campus Library, University of Wales Institute, Cardiff (UWIC)

Western Ave
Cardiff CF5 2YB
Telephone: 01222 551111, ext 6244
Fax: 01222 506911
World Wide Web: http://www.cihe.ac.uk
Contact: Jennifer Welsh (Centre Librarian); Alison Harding (Community Health Sciences Librarian)
Stock and Subject Coverage: Material on speech and language therapy; environmental health; environmental risk management; nutrition and dietetics; podiatry; nursing; biomedical sciences and social work
Special Collections: Clinical Practice - Speech and Language Therapy. Types of Material: periodicals; CD-ROMS; monographs; loose leaf encyclopaedias; Barbour microfiche
Services/Facilities: Photocopying (priced); multi-media access (Internet, etc.); lift for disabled students/users
Availability: UWIC is part of the WALIA scheme which ensures access/borrowing rights for any Welsh academic/researcher who belongs to any other Welsh academic institution, to any other academic library within Wales. Speech and language therapists can obtain the same privileges only if they are part of an organisation which

takes UWIC S & L therapy students for clinical practice. Researchers outside these groupings should apply in writing to the Centre Librarian for borrowing rights, but reference use is welcomed. Charges for external users are as follows: for borrowing rights £30 annually, any interlibrary loan requested by an external borrower £5.50 each

Hours: Termtime: 08.40-21.00 (closes 17.00 on Friday); 09.00-13.00 Saturday. Vacations: 08.45-17.00 (not open Saturday)

Publications: Publication list available on request from the Central Administration

Related Bodies: World Health Organization Collaboration Centre on site - only centre of its type concerned with chemical hazards. Llandaff Campus Library is one of 4 site libraries at UWIC; but the Llandaff Campus Library is the Community Health Sciences Faculty Library

---

[349]

London Foot Hospital and School of Podiatric Medicine

33 Fitzroy Square
London W1P 6AY
Telephone: 0171 530 4500
Fax: 0171 530 4540
Contact: Richard Peacock (Librarian)
Objectives and Purposes: To support research, clinical work and study by students and tutors of the hospital, school and Camden and Islington Community Health Services NHS Trust
Stock and Subject Coverage: Material on medicine in general, but especially subjects associated with the foot, including podiatry; orthotics; biomechanics; and dermatology
Services/Facilities: CD-ROM searches (MEDLINE); fax; photocopies
Availability: By prior appointment, for reference use (Wednesday and Thursday only)
Hours: 09.00-17.00

---

[350]

London School of Hygiene and Tropical Medicine (LSHTM)

Keppel Street
London WC1E 7HT
Telephone: 0171 927 2283
Fax: 0171 927 2273
E-mail: library@lshtm.a.uk
World Wide Web:
    http://www.lshtm.ac.uk/as/library/libintro.htm
Contact: Brian Furner (Librarian and Director of Information Services)
Objectives and Purposes: The London School's mission is to contribute to the improvement of health worldwide through research, postgraduate teaching, advanced training and consultancy in international public health and tropical medicine

Stock and Subject Coverage: 30,000 books; 4,000 periodicals. Covers public health and tropical medicine including: epidemiology, medical statistics, demography, infectious disease, medical microbiology, virology, medical parasitology, medical entomology, public health policy, health services and financing, health promotion, human nutrition, tropical and international public health. Special collections: Ross Archives; Reece Collection on Vaccination
Services/Facilities: Photocopies (postal; self-service); literature searching, by appointment for a fee
Availability: Open to personal visits from bona fide researchers for reference. Access to networked services (other than library catalogues) not permitted. External membership, which includes limited borrowing privileges, available on payment of a refundable deposit and an annual fee
Hours: 08.30-20.25; 09.00-12.30 Saturday

---

[351]

Lothian Health

Deaconess House
148 The Pleasance
Edinburgh EH8 9RS
Telephone: 0131 650 2608
Fax: 0131 662 0580
Contact: Anne Hogarth (Librarian)
Objectives and Purposes: To provide library and information service for employees and NHS Trusts in Lothian
Stock and Subject Coverage: Material on health care administration, planning and management
Services/Facilities: Online database searches; interlibrary loans; in-house journal article database
Availability: Bona fide researchers, for reference use only
Hours: 09.00-17.00
Publications: Liblist (bi-monthly listing of health care-related journal articles)

---

[352]

Luton and Dunstable Hospital NHS Trust

Lewsey Road
Luton LU4 0DZ
Telephone: 01582 497201
Fax: 01582 497389
E-mail: david-lq@david-lq.demon.co.uk
Contact: David Johnson (Medical Librarian)
Objectives and Purposes: To provide postgraduate medical library services
Stock and Subject Coverage: Material on postgraduate medicine and related subjects
Services/Facilities: Photocopies (priced); online searches; Internet access; interlibrary loans
Availability: By prior appointment, for reference use only
Hours: 08.30-18.00
Related Bodies: East Anglian Regional Library Service Psychiatric Libraries Cooperative Scheme

[353]

*Malcolm Sargent Cancer Fund for Children

14 Abingdon Road
London W8 6AF
Telephone: 0171 397 4548
Fax: 0171 376 1193
Contact: Sylvia Darley OBE (Chief Executive);
Mary Murphy (Finance Director)
Objectives and Purposes: To provide support –
financial and counselling – to people under 21
suffering from cancer, leukaemia or Hodgkin's
Disease
Services/Facilities: Leaflets given to parents when a
child is diagnosed; books for children, explaining
these conditions
Availability: Initial enquiries by letter or telephone
(these are subsequently referred to a local contact)
Hours: 09.30–17.30
Publications: Annual newsletter

[354]

Mackenzie Postgraduate Medical Centre

Burnley General Hospital
Casterton Avenue
Burnley BB10 2PQ
Telephone: 01282 474720
Fax: 01282 474254
E-mail: mackpgc@mackpgc.demon.co.uk
Contact: Librarian (post vacant at time of
compilation)
Objectives and Purposes: To provide postgraduate and
continuing medical education facilities for local
doctors and dentists
Stock and Subject Coverage: Books, periodicals and
videos covering all aspects of postgraduate
medicine
Services/Facilities: Database searches (priced for
external databases); photocopies (at cost); fax
Availability: By prior appointment, for reference use
only
Hours: 08.30–16.30
*Publications:*Bi-monthly bulletin; annual report

[355]

Manchester Childrens Hospitals NHS Trust, Booth Hall Childrens Hospital

Medical Library
Booth Hall Childrens Hospital
Charlestown Road
Blackley
Manchester M9 2AA
Telephone: 0161 741 5018
Contact: Mrs Jennifer Kelly BA ALA (Medical
Librarian); Miss Carol McGrath (Library Assistant)
Objectives and Purposes: To provide library and
information services to members of the Trust

Stock and Subject Coverage: 1,200 books; 30 periodicals.
Covers paediatrics and general medicine
Services/Facilities: CD-ROM MEDLINE searches
Availability: Staff only
Hours: 24 hours
Publications: New books; journals list
Related Bodies: Royal Manchester Childrens Hospital;
member of North West Health Service Librarians
Association (NWHSLA)

[356]

Manchester Childrens Hospitals NHS Trust, Royal Manchester Childrens Hospital

Medical Library
Giving for Living Research and Postgraduate Centre
Royal Manchester Childrens Hospital
Hospital Road
Manchester M27 4HA
Telephone and Fax: 0161 727 2387
Contact: Mrs Jennifer Kelly BA ALA (Medical
Librarian); Miss Pamela Oxley (Library Assistant);
Mrs Denise Parry (Library Assistant)
Objectives and Purposes: To provide library and
information services to Trust staff in paediatrics
and general medicine and to act as a resource
centre for postgraduate medical education
Stock and Subject Coverage: 2,000 books; 90
periodicals. Covers paediatrics and general
medicine
Services/Facilities: Photocopies (priced); current
awareness service; CD-ROM MEDLINE searches;
statistician available on Wednesday mornings
Availability: Bona fide researchers, by prior
appointment; telephone enquiries accepted
Hours: 09.00–19.30 (closes 16.30 on Friday)
Publications: Library bulletin; journals list
Related Bodies: Booth Hall Childrens Hospital;
member of North West Health Service Librarians
Association (NWHSLA)

[357]

Manchester Royal Infirmary, Jefferson Library

Oxford Road
Manchester M13 9WL
Telephone and Fax: 0161 276 4344
Contact: Mrs S Reddy (Chief Librarian)
Objectives and Purposes: To teach medical staff and
help in research
Stock and Subject Coverage: Materials covering
medicine, nursing and paramedical subjects
Services/Facilities: Online searches; photocopies; fax;
medical video watching facilities
Availability: By prior appointment, for reference use
only (charges for photocopies)
Hours: 10.00–19.00 (closes 17.00 on Tuesday and
Thursday)
Publications: Acquisitions list
Related Bodies: Barnes Library

[358]
Manor House Hospital
North End Road
Golders Green
London NW11 7HX
Telephone: 0181 455 6601
Fax: 0181 458 4991
Contact: Mrs G Holt (Part Time Librarian, ext 250);
Secretary, ext 222
Stock and Subject Coverage: Small collection covering
medicine and surgery (but excluding obstetrics
and paediatrics)
Services/Facilities: Usual library services
Availability: Staff only
Hours: 09.30-17.30
Related Bodies: Connections with the Royal Free
Hospital

[359]
*Marfan Association UK
6 Queens Road
Farnborough
Hampshire GU14 6DH
Telephone: 01252 54744; Answerphone:
01252 617320
Fax: 01252 523585
World Wide Web:
http://www.thenet.co.uk/~marfan/pubs.html
Contact: Diane Rust (Chairman/Support
Co-ordinator)
Objectives and Purposes: To help people suffering
from Marfan Syndrome by offering support and
educational literature, by fostering research, and by
liaising with the medical professions
Stock and Subject Coverage: A range of booklets,
pamphlets and research results covering Marfan
Syndrome (a disorder of the connective tissue)
Services/Facilities: A national awareness campaign in
schools, colleges, hospitals, etc. Information stands
mounted at various events, and literature provided
for symposiums, etc.
Availability: Limited scope for visits, but an attempt
will be made to find a suitable arrangement.
Donations welcomed
Hours: 09.00-17.00
Publications: In Touch magazine (2 per year)

[360]
Marie Curie Cancer Care
28 Belgrave Square
London SW1X 8QG
Telephone: 0171 235 3325
Fax: 0171 823 2380
Objectives and Purposes: To provide nursing and
medical care for people with cancer through 11
nation-wide hospice centres, and 5,000 Marie
Curie nurses providing care at home. To operate
its own research centre, and to provide education
and training for health professionals involved in
cancer care
Services/Facilities: Information leaflets; day care;
physiotherapy; occupational therapy

Availability: To anyone with cancer
Hours: 24 hours
Publications: Marie Curie News; annual review;
various leaflets
Related Bodies: Scottish office at: Marie Curie
Cancer Care, 21 Rutland Street, Edinburgh
EH1 2AE

[361]
Marylebone Library Information Service
Marylebone Road
London NW1 5PS
Telephone and Fax: 0171 641 1039/1028
Contact: Mrs SE Stallion (Information Services
Librarian); Miss VA Perkins (Librarian)
Objectives and Purposes: The provision of medical
literature for public loan, and general reference
facilities
Stock and Subject Coverage: Medical collection -
material in general medicine, allied biological
subjects (e.g. biochemistry; enzymology; genetics),
and the health service
Services/Facilities: MEDLINE on CD-ROM; other
CD-ROMs; photocopies
Availability: Freely available on proof of identity and
permanent address
Hours: 09.30-20.00 (opens 10.00 on Wednesday);
09.30-17.00 Saturday; 13.30-17.00 Sunday
Related Bodies: Westminster City Libraries

[362]
Maudsley Hospital, Professional Development Centre
Denmark Hill
London SE5 8AZ
Telephone: 0171 919 2595
Fax: 0171 252 5281
E-mail: 100162.1076@compuserve.com
Contact: Marco Isetta (Librarian)
Objectives and Purposes: The provision of a
multidisciplinary information service in the
Lambeth and Southwark area, and the provision of
specialist mental health facilities at regional and
national level
Stock and Subject Coverage: Material on psychiatry;
psychiatric nursing; and social science as related to
mental health
Services/Facilities: Online and CD-ROM searches;
photocopies; fax; Internet access
Availability: By prior appointment, for reference use
only
Hours: 08.30-16.30 (opens 12.30 on Thursday)
Publications: Monthly library bulletin
Related Bodies: This is a satellite library of the
Institute of Psychiatry; member of South Thames
Regional Library Service and Psychiatric Libraries
Co-operative Scheme

[363]
Mayday University Hospital

Medical Library
London Road
Thornton Heath
Surrey CR7 7YE
Telephone: 0181 401 3197
Fax: 0181 401 3583
Contact: Barbara Hartley (Medical Librarian)
Objectives and Purposes: Providing library and information services to the staff of the Trust
Stock and Subject Coverage: 4,500 books; 120 periodicals. Covers clinical medicine and nursing
Services/Facilities: Online and CD-ROM database searches; photocopies; fax; Internet
Availability: By prior appointment, for reference use only. Membership available
Hours: 09.00-19.00 (closes 17.00 on Friday)
Related Bodies: Part of South West Thames Regional Library Service; branches at Warlingham Park Hospital (mental illness) and Lifecare NHS Trust (mental handicap)

[364]
Medic Alert Foundation – British Isles and Ireland

12 Bridge Wharf
156 Caledonian Road
London N1 9UU
Telephone: 0171 833 3034
Fax: 0171 278 0647
Contact: Miss Julie Tamsin Ellis (Chief Executive)
Objectives and Purposes: The provision of emergency body worn identification (bracelets or necklaces) for people with hidden medical conditions, e.g. diabetes, allergies, asthma
Services/Facilities: Information leaflets for professional bodies; posters
Availability: Telephone or written contact is preferred in the first instance
Hours: 09.00-17.00 (answerphone out of hours)
Publications: Annual report
Related Bodies: Supported by Lions Clubs in the British Isles. Affiliated to Medic Alert Foundation International

[365]
Medical Devices Agency (MDA)

Room 1001, Hannibal House
Elephant and Castle
London SE1 6TQ
Telephone: 0171 972 8341
Fax: 0171 972 8079
E-mail: mdalib@mdalibrary.win-uk.net
World Wide Web:
  http://www.open.gov.uk/mda/mdahome.htm
Contact: Paul Woods (Librarian)
Objectives and Purposes: To ensure that medical devices for sale or use in the UK meet acceptable standards of safety, quality and effectiveness

Stock and Subject Coverage: 2,000 books and reports; 150 periodicals covering all aspects of medical devices and biotechnology; also includes titles of general medical interest
Availability: By prior appointment, for reference use only
Hours: 08.30-17.00
Related Bodies: An executive agency of the Department of Health

[366]
Medical Research Council

Harwell
Didcot
Oxfordshire OX11 0RD
Telephone: 01235 834393, ext 342
Fax: 01235 834776
E-mail: bulman@har-mrc.ac.uk
Contact: Mrs MJ Bulman
Stock and Subject Coverage: 5,000 books; 100 periodicals covering genetics; radiobiology
Services/Facilities: Online, CD-ROM and BIDS searches (these services for staff only)
Availability: By prior appointment, for reference use only
Hours: 08.30-17.00
Publications: Accessions list (bi-monthly)

[367]
Medical Research Council, Human Genetics Unit (MRC HGU)

Western General Hospital
Crewe Road
Edinburgh EH4 2XU
Telephone: 0131 332 2471
Fax: 0131 343 2620
E-mail: library@hgu.mrc.ac.uk
World Wide Web: http://www.hgu.mrc.ac.uk
Contact: Librarian
Objectives and Purposes: Provides library and information services to all MRC staff, postgraduate students and MRC visitors within the scope of Unit projects in human genetics
Stock and Subject Coverage: 3,000 books; 4,000 bound journals; 100 current periodicals covering the broad area of genetics; cytogenetics; human genetics; and molecular genetics; special collection of theses; special collection of Unit reprints from 1948 onwards
Services/Facilities: Online searches; photocopies
Availability: Open to bona fide researchers; book loans available; journals for reference only
Hours: Open 24 hours; staffed 08.50-17.15
Publications: Minutes of Library Committe meetings; annual report
Related Bodies: This is one of 43 MRC units

[368]

Medical Society for the Study of Venereal Diseases (MSSVD)

1 Wimpole Street
London W1M 8AE
Telephone: 0171 290 2968
Fax: 0171 290 2989
Contact: Dr AJ Robinson (Hon. Secretary)
Objectives and Purposes: To promote, encourage and improve the study and practice of the art and science of diagnosing and treating venereal diseases
Hours: 09.30–17.30

[369]

Medical Toxicology Unit

Avonley Road
New Cross
London SE14 5ER
Telephone: 0171 771 5364
Fax: 0171 771 5363
E-mail: h.checketts@umds.ac.uk
Contact: Helaina Checketts (Librarian)
Objectives and Purposes: To provide a library service to the National Poisons Information Service and to the Medical Toxicology Unit laboratories
Stock and Subject Coverage: Books and periodicals in the fields of clinical toxicology and analytical chemistry
Services/Facilities: Photocopies; fax (both services priced)
Availability: By appointment only; charges imposed
Hours: 09.00–17.00
Related Bodies: Part of the National Poisons Information Service

[370]

*Medical Women's Federation

Tavistock House (North)
Tavistock Square
London WC1H 9HX
Telephone and Fax: 0171 387 7765
Contact: Ms Lyn Perry (Executive Secretary)
Objectives and Purposes: To promote equal opportunities for women doctors and patients
Stock and Subject Coverage: Federation archives held at the Contemporary Archives Centre, Wellcome Institute for the History of Medicine, 183 Euston Road, London NW1 2BE (Tel: 0171 611 8482)
Availability: Telephone and written enquiries dealt with as time permits
Hours: 10.00–17.00
Publications: Medical Woman (3 per year); annual report
Related Bodies: Network of local associations

[371]

Medicines Control Agency Information Centre (MCA)

Room 1208
Market Towers
1 Nine Elms Lane
London SW8 5NQ
Telephone: 0171 273 0344/0346
Fax: 0171 273 0353
Contact: Juliet Male Mlib ALA (Head of Information Centre); Edward Scully BA ALA (Librarian)
Objectives and Purposes: The licencing authority for medicines in the UK
Stock and Subject Coverage: 10,000 books and pamphlets; 200 current periodicals. Specialises in the safety, quality and efficacy of medicines
Availability: Primarily for staff only; postgraduate researchers may be admitted by appointment
Hours: 09.00–17.00
Related Bodies: An Agency of the Department of Health

[372]

Medway NHS Trust Library

Medway Hospital
Windmill Road
Gillingham
Kent ME7 5NY
Telephone: 01634 407820
Fax: 01634 845640
Contact: Rhiannon Cox (Librarian)
Objectives and Purposes: To provide library and information services to NHS staff in North Kent and Medway and to support their education and training; also to provide a service to patients who require information about their health care or support groups
Stock and Subject Coverage: 11,000 books; 200 periodicals on general medical subjects
Services/Facilities: CD-ROM searches; photocopies; fax; word processing
Availability: By prior appointment, for reference use only (charges apply)
Hours: 08.30–21.00

[373]

MENCAP – The Royal Society for Mentally Handicapped Children and Adults

MENCAP National Centre
123 Golden Lane
London EC1Y 0RT
Telephone: 0171 454 0454
Fax: 0171 608 3254
Contact: Information department
Objectives and Purposes: To provide support and help for parents and carers of people with learning disabilities, to raise public awareness and to improve services for those affected

Services/Facilities: Support and practical help; education programmes; Gateway Service for leisure activities; holiday scheme; employment service; residential accommodation; further education colleges

Availability: To all those who have a need, and to professional and public enquirers

Hours: 09.30-17.30

Publications: MENCAP News (monthly)

Related Bodies: 7 Divisional Offices and 550 Local Societies

[374]

Ménières Society

98 Maybury Road
Woking
Surrey GU21 5HX

Telephone: Voice and Answerphone: 01483 740597; Voice and Minicom: 01483 771207

Fax: 01483 771207

Contact: Brenda Shield

Objectives and Purposes: To encourage research into manifestations of Ménières Disease; to disseminate information about advances in the field of research; to encourage contact between members; to co-operate with other organisations with similar objectives

Services/Facilities: Comprehensive pack sent to members, which specialises in Ménières Disease

Availability: To members

Hours: 09.00-17.00

Publications: Quarterly newsletter

[375]

Mental After Care Association (MACA)

25 Bedford Square
London WC1B 3HW

Telephone: 0171 436 6194

Fax: 0171 637 1980

Contact: Siobhan Parker (Information Officer)

Objectives and Purposes: To provide quality services in the community for people with mental health needs and their carers

Stock and Subject Coverage: Material on mental health, including legislation, DoH/SSI reports, and guidance on practice

Availability: For organisations use only

Publications: Series of information leaflets; annual report

[376]

Mental Health Services of Salford NHS Trust

Prestwich Hospital
Bury New Road
Manchester M25 7BL

Telephone: 0161 773 9121, ext 3244

Fax: 0161 772 3663

Contact: John Coulshed (Librarian); Christine Hyatt (Library Assistant)

Objectives and Purposes: To provide library and information services for Trust staff and students

Stock and Subject Coverage: 5,000 books; 55 periodicals. Covers psychiatry; psychology; sociology; health services management; substance abuse; forensic psychiatry; psychiatric nursing; psychogeriatrics; social work; psychotherapy; psychoanalysis; eating disorders; community care; mental handicap; psychopharmacology; and occupational therapy. Collection of reports and other documents

Services/Facilities: CD-ROM searches (MEDLINE and Psyclit) three current awareness services; photocopies (priced); interlibrary loans (priced)

Availability: Telephone and written enquiries accepted

Hours: 09.00-17.00

Publications: Current awareness bulletins (three)

Related Bodies: North West Health Services Librarians Association; Psychiatric Libraries Co-operative Scheme

[377]

Metamorphic Association

67 Ritherdon Road
London SW17 5951

Telephone and Fax: 0181 672 5951

Contact: Gaston Saint-Pierre (Director); Evelyn Jordan; Yvonne Napper

Objectives and Purposes: The teaching and practice of the metamorphic technique for self-healing and creative growth

Stock and Subject Coverage: Material related to the metamorphic technique

Services/Facilities: Regular weekend teaching courses (priced)

Availability: Telephone and written enquiries; personal visits are accepted

Hours: 09.00-17.00 Monday to Thursday

Publications: Information leaflet (3 per year); Journal of the Metamorphic Association (2 per year); Principles and Practice of the Metamorphic Technique (book); video and audio cassette. All publications priced

Related Bodies: Links with related organisations in Belgium, Netherlands, USA and Canada

[378]

Mid Kent Healthcare Trust, Maidstone Hospital Library

Postgraduate Centre
Maidstone Hospital
Hermitage Lane
Maidstone
Kent ME16 9QQ

Telephone: 01622 729000, ext 4647

Fax: 01622 721308

E-mail: maidstone.health@dm.krinfo.ch

Contact: Mrs Frances Ashworth (Head of Library Services); Miss Marie Hurt (Assistant Librarian)

Objectives and Purposes: To provide facilities for training and education for all hospital staff

Stock and Subject Coverage: 12,000 books; 260 periodicals, covering the whole range of health-related subjects
Services/Facilities: Online and CD-ROM searches; photocopies; fax (charges apply)
Availability: Subscription membership available to non-staff
Hours: 09.00-21.00 Monday, Wednesday and Thursday; 09.00-17.00 Tuesday and Friday
Publications: Newsletter
Related Bodies: South Thames Library and Information Service

[379]
Mid Sussex NHS Trust

Health Sciences Library
Princess Royal Hospital
Lewes Road
Haywards Heath
West Sussex RH16 4EX
Telephone: 01444 441881, ext 4463
Fax: 01444 451576
Contact: Mrs Janet Thorpe (Library Service Manager)
Objectives and Purposes: To provide a comprehensive service by helping all NHS staff make effective use of the evidence base of health care
Stock and Subject Coverage: 5,000 books; 125 periodicals. Covers all general disciplines of medicine and nursing
Services/Facilities: Online and CD-ROM searches; photocopies
Availability: By prior appointment, for reference use only
Hours: 09.00-17.00

[380]
Middlesex University, Faculty of Health Studies

Library
Chase Farm Hospital
Enfield
Middlesex EN2 8JL
Telephone: 0181 967 5982
Fax: 0181 367 4561
E-mail: d.hall@mdx.ac.uk
Contact: Dilys M Hall (Campus Learning Resources Manager)
Services/Facilities: Open learning collection
Availability: Reference access on request; subscription service available. Written/telephone requests accepted from registered users only
Hours: 09.30-18.00 (closes 16.00 on Friday)
Related Bodies: Faculty libraries at Royal Free Hospital. Associated libraries at Whittington Hospital, and North Middlesex Hospital. Part of Middlesex University Information and Learning Resource Services

[381]
Middlesex University Library

Royal Free Centre
Royal Free Hospital
Pond Street
London NW3 2QG
Telephone: 0171 794 0500, ext 3737
E-mail: sue26@mdx.ac.uk
Contact: Susan Hill (Librarian); Ian Ward (Library Assistant); Toni Spong (Library Assistant)
Objectives and Purposes: To provide library and information services for nursing and other health related disciplines
Stock and Subject Coverage: 15,000 books; 80 periodicals. Covers nursing and related topics
Services/Facilities: CD-ROM searches; photocopies (priced)
Availability: By prior appointment, for reference use only
Hours: 09.00-17.00 Monday and Friday; 09.00-19.00 Tuesday to Thursday

[382]
Midwives Information and Resource Service (MIDIRS)

9 Elmdale Road
Clifton
Bristol BS8 1SL
Telephone: 0117 925 1791
Fax: 0117 925 1792
E-mail: midirs@dial.pipex.com
World Wide Web: http://www.gn.apc.org/midirs
Contact: Sue Hawkins (Head of Information); John Loy and Kathy Levine (Information Officers)
Objectives and Purposes: To be a central source for the storing and dissemination of information relating to childbirth
Stock and Subject Coverage: Material on midwifery; pregnancy; childbirth; the newborn; and maternity care and services
Services/Facilities: Enquiry service using MIDIRS internal database and other external databases; photocopies (priced); document supply
Availability: Open to all by arrangement, but subject to a charge. No loans or visits. Initial contact by telephone
Hours: 09.00-17.00
Publications: MIDIRS Midwifery Digest (quarterly); annual directory. Full list on request

[383]
Milton Keynes General NHS Trust

Staff Library
Postgraduate Centre
Standing Way
Milton Keynes MK6 5LD
Telephone: 01908 660033, ext 2175
Fax: 01908 671977
Contact: L Maguire (Library Services Manager)

Objectives and Purposes: To provide health care information to local professionals and to students of the Sir Gordon Roberts School of Nursing and Midwifery. Member of the HeLIN network

Stock and Subject Coverage: 8,500 books; 200 periodicals covering medicine; nursing; allied health; midwifery; and general management

Services/Facilities: Online and CD-ROM searches; current awareness service; fax; photocopies (priced)

Availability: By prior appointment, for reference use only

Hours: 09.00-17.00

Publications: New books list; annual report; forthcoming titles

[384]
MIND (National Association for Mental Health)

15-19 Broadway
Stratford
London E15 4BQ

Telephone: 0181 519 2122;
Infoline: 0181 522 1728/0345 660163

Fax: 0181 522 1725

Contact: Angela Hendra (Head of Communications)

Objectives and Purposes: MIND is the leading mental health charity in England and Wales, working for everyone in mental distress, campaigning for the right to lead an active and valued life and promoting development of community based services

Stock and Subject Coverage: Material on all aspects of mental health; a hanging file system of press cuttings and research papers

Services/Facilities: Infoline; conferences and training; befriending; advocacy; drop-in centres; counselling

Availability: To all who need it

Hours: 09.15-16.45

Publications: Full list available

Related Bodies: Network of 220 local branches

[385]
Miscarriage Association

c/o Clayton Hospital
Northgate
Wakefield WF1 3JS

Telephone: 01924 200799

Fax: 01924 298834

Contact: Ruth Bender Atik (National Director);
Mrs Sue Ellis (Information Officer)

Objectives and Purposes: To provide information and support facilities for those affected by pregnancy loss; information is gathered about causes and treatments; the Association promotes good practice in the way pregnancy loss is managed in hospitals and in the community. A network of volunteer telephone contacts and support groups is maintained

Stock and Subject Coverage: A small reference library on all aspects of miscarriage

Services/Facilities: Information pack; factsheets and booklets; an internal database of research findings on miscarriage; network of telephone support contacts and support groups

Availability: Telephone and written enquiries; donations appreciated

Hours: 09.00-16.00

Publications: Quarterly newsletter; annual report

Related Bodies: Network of local groups

[386]
Mobility Information Service (MIS)

National Mobility Centre
Unit 2a
Atcham Estate
Shrewsbury SY4 4UG

Telephone: 01743 761889

Fax: 01743 761149

Contact: DG Griffiths MBE (Chief Officer);
FE Stone (Hon. Treasurer)

Objectives and Purposes: To provide information and advice on mobility to the disabled, with particular regard to vehicles and their adaptation

Stock and Subject Coverage: All Benefits Agency publications; manufacturers brochures on vehicles; wheelchair information; holiday location information

Services/Facilities: Internal database; photocopies

Availability: Freely available by visit or telephone; researchers by appointment

Hours: 10.00-17.00

Publications: Wheels Under You (by D Griffiths); road tests on production cars with reference to their adaptation

[387]
Moor Green

Moseley Hall Hospital
Alcester Road
Moseley
Birmingham

Telephone: 0121 449 6339

Contact: Mrs EA Wright (Clinical Manager);
Mrs TP Partridge (Head Occupational Therapist)

Objectives and Purposes: To enable people with brain injury to increase their levels of independence in all areas of their life, thereby assisting in social re-integration and an improved quality of life

Stock and Subject Coverage: Basic service information and a reference facility for staff use

Availability: Telephone and written enquiries accepted; visits by prior arrangement

Hours: 08.30-16.30

Publications: Leaflet; part of Trust annual report

Related Bodies: Southern Birmingham Community Health NHS Trust

[388]

Mount Vernon and Watford Hospitals NHS Trust, Watford

Library
Postgraduate Medical Centre
Watford General Hospital
Vicarage Road
Watford WD1 8HB
Telephone: 01923 844143
Fax: 01923 827216
Contact: Richard M Osborn (Library and
 Information Services Manager))
Objectives and Purposes: To supply information in
 support of the work and training of health care
 staff
Stock and Subject Coverage: 2,500 books; 200
 periodicals. Covers medicine, nursing and allied
 fields, with particular strengths in plastic, oral and
 maxillofacial surgery, and cancer care and
 treatment
Services/Facilities: Online and CD-ROM searches;
 fax; photocopies (priced)
Availability: By prior appointment, for reference use
 only
Hours: 09.00-17.00
Publications: Periodicals holdings list; annual report
Related Bodies: Partner library at Mount Vernon
 Hospital site; part of North Thames Regional
 Library and Information Service

[389]

Mount Vernon Postgraduate Medical Centre, Mount Vernon

Les Cannon Memorial Library
Mount Vernon Hospital
Rickmansworth Road
Northwood
Middlesex HA6 2RN
Telephone: 01923 844143
Fax: 01923 827216
E-mail: richard.m.osborn@dm.rs.ch
Contact: Richard M Osborn (Library and
 Information Services Manager)
Objectives and Purposes: To provide library and
 information services for staff and to make effective
 use of the knowledge and information base of
 health care
Stock and Subject Coverage: 2,500 books; 200 current
 periodicals covering all branches of health care.
 Particular strengths are in plastic, oral and
 maxillofacial surgery, and cancer care and
 treatment
Services/Facilities: CD-ROM searches; photocopies;
 word processing; fax
Availability: By prior appointment, for reference use
 only
Hours: 09.00-17.00
Publications: Periodicals holdings list; annual report
Related Bodies: Harefield Hospital Medical Library
 (0895 828947); partner library at Watford General
 Hospital

[390]

Multiple Births Foundation

Queen Charlotte's and Chelsea Hospital
Goldhawk Road
London W6 0XG
Telephone: 0181 740 3519
Fax: 0181 740 3041
E-mail: mbf@rpms.ac.uk
Contact: Dr Elizabeth Bryan MD FRCP (Medical
 Director); Jane Denton RGN RM (Nursing
 Director); Caroline Baldock (Head of
 Administration - primary contact); Barbara Read
 BSc (Family Services Co-ordinator)
Objectives and Purposes: To provide professional
 support to families with twins, triplets, and higher
 order births, both directly through specialist
 clinics and indirectly by informing those
 professionals involved in their care
Stock and Subject Coverage: Written and audiovisual
 material on all aspects of multiple pregnancy and
 birth. Extensive collection of 35mm slides
Services/Facilities: Keywords and listings of specialist
 papers; family support services; Preparing for
 Twins and Triplets (information pack); lecturers
 supplied
Availability: By prior appointment, for reference use
 only; some material available for loan, and some
 services are priced
Hours: 09.00-17.00
Publications: Quarterly newsletter; annual report;
 biennial Friends of the Multiple Births
 Foundation newsletter; full list on request
Related Bodies: Part of Institute of Obstetrics and
 Gynaecology Trust

[391]

Multiple Sclerosis Resource Centre (MSRC)

4a Chapel Hill
Stansted
Essex CM24 8AG
Telephone: 01279 817101
Fax: 01279 647179
Contact: John Simkins; Mike Patmore
Objectives and Purposes: To provide information,
 advice, support and counseling for people with
 MS, their families and carers
Stock and Subject Coverage: Material on all aspects of
 multiple sclerosis. Covers symptoms; daily living;
 self-help techniques; home managed therapies
Services: Telephone information, counselling, leaflets,
 etc. on research, therapies, benefits, self-help
 groups and therapy centres
Availability: Open access to all literature
Hours: 08.30-17.30
Publications: Pathways (quarterly magazine); various
 books and booklets (some for sale); list available
 on request

[392]
Multiple Sclerosis Society of Great Britain and Northern Ireland (MS Society)
25 Effie Road
Fulham
London SW6 1EE
Telephone: 0171 736 6267
Fax: 0171 736 9861
E-mail: info@mssociety.org.uk
World Wide Web: http://www.mssociety.org.uk
Contact: Information Officers
Objectives and Purposes: To promote research into finding the cause of and a cure for MS, and to encourage people with MS to come together in mutual support; to provide a welfare and support service for sufferers, carers and professionals
Stock and Subject Coverage: Material on multiple sclerosis and related issues
Services/Facilities: Internal database of research papers
Availability: Enquiries accepted by letter, telephone, fax or e-mail. No visits
Hours: 09.00-17.00
Publications: List available
Related Bodies: Network of 360 local branches; International Federation of Multiple Sclerosis Societies

[393]
Multiple Sclerosis Therapy Centres (Federation of)
Bradbury House
155 Barkers Lane
Bedford MK41 9RX
Telephone: 01234 325781
Fax: 01234 365242
Contact: Mrs V Woods
Objectives and Purposes: To provide information, training, support, etc. to the many therapy centres throughout the country which in turn provide therapy, support and information to multiple sclerosis sufferers and their families
Publications: Range of information booklets
Related Bodies: MS Therapy centres around the country

[394]
Muscle Power (MP)
6 Ashover Road
Chaddesden
Derby DE21 4JD
Telephone: 01332 730279
Fax: 01332 730279
E-mail: pmatthews@cix.compulink.co.uk
World Wide Web: http://www.globalnet.co.uk/~pmatthews/DisabilityNet/
Contact: Paul Matthews (General Secretary)
Objectives and Purposes: Muscle Power is a national organisation of people with neuromuscular impairments. It is established to promote the equality of people with neuromuscular impairments in society. It achieves this by disseminating information using a magazine, conferences, reports and an Internet service, called Disability Net
Services/Facilities: Disability Net contains hundreds of pages of information on many disability issues, including legislation, independent living, arts, education and employment. The magazine is produced four times a year and contains similar information, albeit with a focus on people with neuromuscular impairments. Internet publishing and advertising is available free to organisations of disabled people and as a chargeable service otherwise
Availability: The magazine is available to members and those interested in becoming members of Muscle Power. Disability Net is available for anyone on the Internet to access. Enquiries are preferred by electronic mail or alternatively by letter or telephone
Hours: 09.00-17.00
Publications: Quarterly magazine, occasional reports plus Disability Net Internet service

[395]
Muscular Dystrophy Group of Great Britain and Northern Ireland (MDG)
7-11 Prescott Place
London SW4 6BS
Telephone: 0171 720 8055
Fax: 0171 498 0670
Contact: Jane Halksworth and Jane Kenyon (Information Officers)
Objectives and Purposes: To fund research into possible treatments and cures for muscular dystrophy and allied neuromuscular conditions; to provide support services and equipment to alleviate the difficulties faced by people affected by these conditions
Stock and Subject Coverage: A small library consisting of literature relating to the muscular dystrophies and related neuromuscular conditions, plus some material on disability issues in general
Availability: Telephone and written enquiries; the collection is not designed for research purposes, but the Information Section does commission literature on relevant conditions, and produces a booklist
Hours: 09.00-17.00 (answerphone available out of hours)
Publications: In Focus (bi-annual newsletter); The Search (bi-annual magazine); annual report; miscellaneous other materials - list available
Related Bodies: Part of the European Alliance of Muscular Dystrophy Associations (EAMDA)

[396]
Myalgic Encephalomyelitis Association (ME Association)

Stanhope House
High Street
Stanford-le-Hope
Essex SS17 0HA
Telephone: 01375 642466
Fax: 01375 360256
World Wide Web:
    http://www.compulink.co.uk/~deepings
Contact: Mavis Moore (Information Services
    Manager)
Objectives and Purposes: To provide information and
    support to all those affected by Myalgic
    Encephalomyelitis (ME)
Stock and Subject Coverage: Small collection of books
    and periodicals on ME. Internal database
    containing medical papers, news cuttings and
    articles on ME and related issues
Services/Facilities: Free information to sufferers, carers
    and anyone wanting to know more about ME
Availability: Telephone and written enquiries;
    charges for some literature
Hours: 10.00-12.30 and 13.30-16.00
Publications: Quarterly journal; newsletter for group
    leaders; annual report
Related Bodies: Office in Belfast; Scottish Office in
    Glasgow; a network of self-help groups

[397]
Myasthenia Gravis Association (MGA)

Keynes House
Chester Park
Alfreton Road
Derby DE21 4AS
Telephone: 01332 290219
Fax: 01332 293641
Contact: Preston Keeling (Chief Executive)
Objectives and Purposes: To raise funds which will be
    used to support research into the management and
    care of the disease, to provide a national support
    network, and to increase public and medical
    awareness of the condition
Stock and Subject Coverage: A range of publications
    dealing with myasthenia gravis and associated
    conditions
Services/Facilities: Advice service for sufferers and
    their families/carers. National freephone helpline
    for urgent advice and/or help on 0800 919922
Availability: To anyone in need
Hours: 09.00-16.30
Publications: Quarterly newsletter, MGA News;
    various leaflets; annual report

[398]
Myotonic Dystrophy Support Group

175A Carlton Hill
Carlton
Nottingham NG4 1GZ
Telephone: 0115 987 0080
Contact: Mrs MA Bowler (National Co-ordinator)
Objectives and Purposes: To give help, advice,
    information and support to families and people
    with myotonic dystrophy
Stock and Subject Coverage: Information on myotonic
    dystrophy and congenital myotonic dystrophy
Services/Facilities: Advice and information for
    sufferers and their families
Availability: Telephone and written enquiries;
    material is freely supplied
Hours: 24 hours
Publications: Quarterly newsletter; annual report;
    range of information leaflets
Related Bodies: Affiliated with Muscular Dystrophy

[399]
*Naevus Support Group

58 Necton Road
Wheathampstead
St Albans AL4 8AU
Telephone: 01582 832853
Contact: Renate and John O'Neill (Founders)
Objectives and Purposes: To provide information on
    various types of birthmarks; to introduce parents
    of children with similar birthmarks to one
    another; to provide support; to answer queries on
    a personal basis; to be voluntary and independent,
    offering services freely
Stock and Subject Coverage: Material written for the
    Group by consultants in congenital melanocytic
    naevus, portwine stain, strawberry (haemangioma)
    mark and glaucoma (portwine stain-related)
Availability: Telephone and written enquiries;
    occasional visits
Hours: 24 hours
Publications: Bi-annual newsletter

[400]
Napier University, Canaan Lane Campus

74 Canaan Lane
Edinburgh EH10 4TB
Telephone: 0131 536 5616
Fax: 0131 536 5621
Contact: Alison Aiton (Senior Librarian)
Objectives and Purposes: To provide library and
    information services to the Faculty of Health Studies
Stock and Subject Coverage: Material on nursing;
    midwifery; health; psychology; and sociology
Services/Facilities: Photocopies
Availability: By appointment for bona fide
    researchers; membership available
Hours: 09.00-17.00

[401]

Napier University, Comely Bank Campus

13 Crewe Road South
Edinburgh EH4 2LD
Telephone: 0131 343 7918
Fax: 0131 343 7959
Contact: Librarian
Objectives and Purposes: To provide library and
information services for nurses and midwives
Stock and Subject Coverage: Material on nursing,
midwifery and allied health subjects
Services/Facilities: Journal article database
Availability: By prior appointment, for reference use
only
Hours: 09.00-21.00 (closes 16.15 on Friday);
09.00-12.00 on Saturday
Publications: Library guide
Related Bodies: Napier University

[402]

Napier University, Livingston Campus

Education Centre Library
St John's Hospital
Howden Road West
Livingston EH54 6PP
Telephone: 01506 422831
Fax: 01506 462535
Contact: Miss D Millar (Senior Librarian);
Ms Mari Porter and Ms Mary Ann Cox (Assistant
Librarians)
Objectives and Purposes: To provide library and
information services to Napier University staff
and students, and to local NHS Trust staff
Stock and Subject Coverage: Books, periodicals and
audiovisuals covering nursing; midwifery;
medicine, psychiatry and allied health subjects
Services/Facilities: CD-ROM searches; photocopies
(priced)
Availability: By prior appointment, for reference use
only; membership available
Hours: 09.00-21.00; 09.00-12.00 Saturday

[403]

Napier University, Melrose Campus

The Library
Melrose Campus
Education Centre
Borders General Hospital
Melrose TD6 9BD
Telephone: 01896 661620/661632
Fax: 01896 823346
E-mail: moira@bhsi.demon.co.uk
Contact: Moira Livingstone (Librarian)
Objectives and Purposes: To provide an effective,
efficient and comprehensive information function
to support Borders Health Board; to improve and
protect the health of the Borders population; to
support the learning needs of staff and students of
Napier University

Stock and Subject Coverage: 15,000 books; 230
periodicals covering medicine; nursing; mental
health; professions allied to medicine; health care
management; ethics; primary care; and social work
Services/Facilities: Online and CD-ROM searches
(MEDLINE, CINAHL, ASSIA); current awareness
service; photocopies
Availability: By prior appointment, for reference use
only
Hours: 09.00-21.00; 09.00-12.00 Saturday
Publications: Current Awareness Bulletin (monthly);
annual report

[404]

Narcolepsy Association UK (UKAN)

1 Brook Street
Stoke-on-Trent ST4 1JN
Telephone and Fax: 01782 416417
E-mail: keith@ukan.powernet.co.uk
Contact: Mr M Sergeant
Objectives and Purposes: To promote awareness of
narcolepsy and provide authoritative information
about it; to press for recognition of narcolepsy as a
disability; to encourage research into its causes and
treatment; to cooperate with overseas associations;
to help members to form self-help groups
Services/Facilities: Resource packs for persons wishing
to co-ordinate a self-help group
Publications: Quarterly newsletter; Medication for
Narcolepsy (Report); Narcolepsy: A Layman's
Guide (Report); Narcolepsy: Care and Treatment
(Report); various other booklets; annual report

[405]

National Abortion Campaign (NAC)

The Print House
18 Ashwin Street
London E8 3DL
Telephone: 0171 923 4976
Fax: 0171 923 4979
Contact: Anne Marie Keary (Chair); Carol Kearney
(Fundraiser); Liz Ketch (Campaign Worker)
Objectives and Purposes: To campaign for a woman's
decision on abortion, allowing abortion on request
Stock and Subject Coverage: Material on abortion,
contraception and fertility. Press cuttings library.
Journals and pamphlets for sale
Services/Facilities: Limited advice line; photocopies
(priced)
Availability: Freely available, by appointment, but
loans to members only
Hours: 09.30-17.30
Publications: Quarterly newsletter. Full list available

[406]

National Advisory Service for Parents of Children with a Stoma (NASPCS – The Charity for Incontinent and Stoma Children)

51 Anderson Drive
Valley View Park
Darvel
Ayrshire KA17 0DE
Telephone: 01560 322024
Contact: John Malcolm (Chairman)
Objectives and Purposes: To provide lay-term information for parents on their child's birth defect in terms of bladder and bowel disorders which can be fatal. To put parents in contact with one another for mutual support and to provide the children with their own organisation. To support the medical profession with information on these conditions. Practical day-to-day management of all aspects of coping with a child with a colostomy, ileostomy or urostomy
Stock and Subject Coverage: Material on children with serious bladder and bowel problems, including imperforate anus, Hirschsprung's Disease, cloacal exstrophy, exstrophy of the bladder and Eagle-Barrett Syndrome
Availability: All genuine enquiries welcomed
Hours: 24 hours (answerphone out of working hours)
Publications: Quarterly newsletter; contact list (for parents only); range of booklets
Related Bodies: International Ostomy Association

[407]

National Ankylosing Spondylitis Society (NASS)

3 Grosvenor Crescent
London SW1X 7ER
Telephone: 0171 235 9585
Fax: 0171 235 5827
World Wide Web: http://web.ukonline.co.uk/
members/nass/contents.htm
Contact: Fergus J Rogers; Sophie Hughes
Objectives and Purposes: Patient education and support for persons with ankylosing spondylitis
Availability: Telephone and written enquiries accepted; material available for purchase
Hours: 09.00–17.00
Publications: Guidebook for Patients; Living with Ankylosing Spondylitis; Stretch and Relax; Fight Back (exercise video); exercise and cassette tape; bi-annual newsletter for members
Related Bodies: Network of 100 local branches

[408]

National Association for Colitis and Crohn's Disease (NACC)

4 Beaumont House
Sutton Road
St Albans AL1 5HH
Telephone: 01727 830038; answerphone out of hours
Fax: 01727 844296
E-mail: nacc@nacc.demon.co.uk
Contact: Richard Driscoll (Director)
Objectives and Purposes: To provide general information about inflammatory bowel diseases for sufferers and to offer support to those affected, their families and friends; to promote research into the treatment, management and causes of these diseases and to publish worthwhile results
Stock and Subject Coverage: No library. A range of newsletters, booklets and leaflets
Services/Facilities: Information to sufferers and their families; listening service; distribution of welfare funds
Availability: Information available in response to enquiries. Donations appreciated
Hours: 09.00–17.00
Publications: Quarterly newsletter; annual report. Full list available
Related Bodies: Network of 61 area groups

[409]

National Association for the Relief of Paget's Disease (NARPD)

1 Church Road
Eccles
Manchester M30 0DL
Telephone: 0161 707 9225
Fax: 0161 789 6755
E-mail: 106064.2032@compuserve.com
Contact: Mrs PM Roberts (Administrator)
Objectives and Purposes: To offer information and support to those suffering from Paget's Disease, their families and carers; to encourage and fund relevant research; to raise awareness of the Disease among the medical profession and the public
Stock and Subject Coverage: General information leaflets for enquirers, members and sufferers
Availability: Telephone and written enquiries
Hours: 09.00–15.30 Monday to Thursday
Publications: Quarterly newsletter; annual report
Related Bodies: A network of regional groups

[410]

National Association of Counsellors, Hypnotherapists and Psychotherapists (NACHP)

Ffynnonwen
Llangwyryfon
Aberystwyth
Ceredigion SY23 4EY
Telephone and Fax: 01974 241376

Contact: DM Harrison

Objectives and Purposes: To maintain a register of therapists; to enforce a code of ethics and act as a regulatory body; and to provide a referral service

Services/Facilities: Register of members

Availability: Telephone and written enquiries

Hours: 09.00–17.00

Publications: Quarterly newsletter

Related Bodies: Associated with the British Complementary Medicine Association

[411]
National Association of Deafened People (NADP)

Ashby
26 Stubbs Wood
Chesham Bois
Buckinghamshire HP6 6EY

Telephone: 01494 724830

Fax: 01494 431932

E-mail: jcresswell@cix.compulunk.co.uk

Contact: Mrs Jenny Dunning (Administrator); Mrs Jean Cresswell (Hon. Secretary)

Objectives and Purposes: To provide a service of information and support for people with a profound acquired hearing loss

Availability: Telephone and written enquiries

Hours: Any time

Publications: Network (quarterly newsletter); annual report; various information booklets/packs. List available

[412]
National Association of Health Authorities and Trusts (NAHAT)

(1) Birmingham Research Park
Vincent Drive
Birmingham B15 2SQ

Telephone: 0121 471 4444

Fax: 0121 414 1120

(2) 26 Chapter Street
London SW1P 4ND

Telephone: 0171 233 7388

Fax: 0171 233 7390

World Wide Web: http://www.nahat.net

Contact: Jean Trainor (Deputy Director); Roslyn Wheeler (Membership Marketing Manager)

Objectives and Purposes: To communicate the views of the core membership on key NHS issues; to act as a forum for exchange of information between members; to provide information to members; to disseminate good practice; to promote a positive image of the NHS and a better understanding of what its managing bodies do

Availability: Telephone and written enquiries

Hours: 08.30–17.30

Publications: Various – list available

[413]
National Association of Theatre Nurses (NATN)

22 Mount Parade
Harrogate
North Yorkshire HG1 1BX

Telephone: 01423 508079

Fax: 01423 531613

Contact: The Librarian

Objectives and Purposes: To promote the role of the nurse and development of operating practice to ensure the delivery of high quality patient care during the perioperative period in any environment; to lead the theatre nursing profession; to support other personnel providing care within the operating department; to provide high quality professional support to the membership

Stock and Subject Coverage: Collection of specialist theatre periodicals

Services: Photocopies (at cost)

Availability: On written request addressed to the Librarian

Hours: 09.00–16.30

Publications: British Journal of Theatre Nurses (monthly); full list available on request

[414]
National Asthma Campaign

Providence House
Providence Place
London N1 0NT

Telephone: 0171 226 2260; Helpline at local call rate: 0345 010203

Fax: 0171 704 0740

Contact: Lindsey Taylor and Chris Butcher (Information enquiries)

Objectives and Purposes: An independent UK charity working to conquer asthma in partnership with asthma sufferers and all who share their concern, through a combination of research, education and support

Stock and Subject Coverage: Material on asthma and related allergies (excluding eczema)

Services/Facilities: Information and emotional support via a Helpline; information service for health professionals; network of self-help groups

Availability: Written enquiries only

Hours: 09.00–17.30 (Helpline: 09.00–21.00)

Publications: Asthma News (quarterly); health professionals journal; full list available on request

[415]
National Autistic Society (NAS)

276 Willesden Lane
London NW2 5RB

Telephone: 0181 451 1114

Fax: 0181 451 5865

E-mail: nas@clus1.ulcc.ac.uk

World Wide Web:
   http://www.oneworld.org/autism_uk
Contact: Tessa Hall (Information Officer)
Objectives and Purposes: To offer families and carers information, advice and support; to raise awareness; to provide training and promote research; to develop a range of educational and support services for those with autism, and their families and carers
Stock and Subject Coverage: Material on autism in general
Services/Facilities: In-house research database; photocopies
Availability: By prior appointment, for reference use only
Hours: 09.30-17.00
Publications: Communication (journal); Connection (newsletter); annual report

[416]
National Back Pain Association (NBPA)

   16 Elmtree Road
   Teddington
   Middlesex TW11 8ST
Fax: 0181 943 5318
Contact: Norma Montague
Objectives and Purposes: The promotion of 'healthy back' information; the prevention of back injury; research into the treatment of back problems
Stock and Subject Coverage: Small library of material on back pain for staff use; file of press cuttings
Availability: Written enquiries preferred; information pack (£2) available to visitors
Hours: 09.00-17.00
Publications: Quarterly newsletter; annual report; various books and leaflets
Related Bodies: Network of 40 local self-help groups

[417]
National Centre for Cued Speech (NCCS)

   29-30 Watling Street
   Canterbury
   Kent CT1 2UD
Telephone: 01227 450757
Fax: 01227 784407
Contact: Anthony Jefferson (Founder and Director)
Objectives and Purposes: To promote the benefits of cued speech, give introductory talks, and organise training courses
Hours: 09.30-17.00
Publications: Wide range of books, booklets and videos availabale for sale. Full list available

[418]
National Centre for Training and Education in Prosthetics and Orthotics (NCTEPO)

   University of Strathclyde
   Curran Building
   131 St James Road
   Glasgow G4 0LS
Telephone: 0141 52 4400, ext 3814
Fax: 0141 552 1283
E-mail: h.smart@strath.ac.uk
Contact: Heather Smart (Information Officer)
Objectives and Purposes: Education and training in prosthetics and orthotics, and relevant rehabilitation engineering
Stock and Subject Coverage: Material covering prosthetics and orthotics; rehabilitation engineering; seating for the disabled; wheelchairs. RECAL Information Services is a range of paper and computer based bibliographic guides to the relevant subject literature
Services/Facilities: Database searches; photocopies
Availability: Telephone and written enquiries; by prior appointment, for reference use only
Hours: 09.00-17.00
Publications: RECAL Current Awareness (fortnightly publication); RECAL Abstracts (twice yearly); RECAL Offline (bibliographic databases)

[419]
National Centre for Volunteering

   Carriage Row
   183 Eversholt Street
   London NW1 1BU
Telephone: 0171 388 9888
Fax: 0171 383 0448
E-mail: voluk@mcr.geonet.de
World Wide Web: http://www.vois.org.uk
Contact: Michael Stewart (Information and Library); Ruth Johnson (Corporate Communications)
Objectives and Purposes: To be the central authority for volunteering in the UK; aims to extend the quality, quantity, contribution and accessibility of volunteering throughout the UK; to anticipate, identify and exert influence upon policies, practices and other external factors likely to affect or be affected by volunteering
Stock and Subject Coverage: A collection of items including books and periodicals – all on volunteering related topics. Extensive collection of newspaper and journal articles
Services/Facilities: Database searches; photocopies
Availability: Telephone and written enquiries; visits by arrangement
Hours: 09.30-16.30
Publications: Volunteering Magazine. Full list available

[420]

National Childbirth Trust Library

Alexandra House
Oldham Terrace
London W3 6NH
Telephone: 0181 992 2616
Fax: 0181 92 5929
Contact: Patricia Donnithorne (Librarian);
Eileen Abbott (Assistant Librarian)
Objectives and Purposes: To offer information and
support in pregnancy, childbirth and early
parenthood, and to give every parent the chance
to make informed choices
Stock and Subject Coverage: Material on pregnancy;
birth; early parenthood; breast feeding; and UK
maternity services. Collections are aimed at the
lay person and include 1,500 books; 120
periodicals; 300 subject files; and surveys
Services/Facilities: Cochrane database on pregnancy
and childbirth (on disk); limited enquiry service
for non-members
Availability: By prior appointment, for reference use
only; charges for commercial users
Hours: 09.30-17.00
Publications: Maternity services reading list; Through
the Maze; a guide to sources of research based
information on pregnancy, birth and postnatal
care; series of leaflets, information sheets and
books on pregnancy, birth and early parenthood

[421]

National Children's Bureau

8 Wakley Street
London EC1V 7QE
Telephone: 0171 843 6000
Fax: 0171 278 9512
Contact: Lisa Payne; Jayne Parkin
Objectives and Purposes: To identify and promote the
interests of all children and young people, and to
improve their status in a diverse society; to
improve the co-ordination of services for children
and to ensure that those services are child-centred
Stock and Subject Coverage: 32,000 items including
government and statistical publications, journals
and grey literature on children and young people,
including child health; disability and illness; rights;
residential care; sex education; early childhood;
solvent and drug misuse
Services/Facilities: Enquiry line: 0171 843 6008
(10.00-12.00 and 14.00-16.00 Monday to Friday);
interlibrary loans
Availability: Reference library open to visitors by
appointment only (small charge is levied)
Hours: 10.00-17.00
Publications: ChildData (CD-ROM): Children in the
News; Highlight. Full list available

[422]

★National Council for One Parent Families (NCOPF)

255 Kentish Town Road
London NW5 2LX
Telephone: 0171 267 1361
Fax: 0171 482 4857
Contact: Wendy van den Hende
Objectives and Purposes: A campaigning organisation
providing an information service for lone parents
and the people working with them; provides
training courses for lone parents wishing to return
to work and for professionals who advise them
Availability: Telephone and written enquiries
Hours: 09.15-17.15
Publications: Various - list available (free to lone parents)

[423]

National Deaf Children's Society (NDCS)

15 Dufferin Street
London EC1Y 8PD
Telephone: 0171 250 0123
Fax: 0171 251 5020
Contact: Helen Wheatley (Information Worker)
Objectives and Purposes: To support parents and carers
of deaf children by providing information and
advice on all aspects of childhood deafness
Stock and Subject Coverage: 2,000 books and
pamphlets; 30 periodicals covering deafness;
audiology; education; and official publications
relating to children
Services/Facilities: Photocopies
Availability: Telephone and written enquiries; visits
by appointment, for reference use only
Hours: 10.00-16.00
Publications: Various - list available

[424]

National Eczema Society

163 Eversholt Street
London NW1 1BU
Telephone: 0171 388 4097
Fax: 0171 388 5882
Contact: Julie Braithwaite (Information Manager);
Mercy Jeyasingham (Director of Training,
Education and Information)
Objectives and Purposes: To improve the quality of life
for people with eczema and their carers. The
Society works to empower people with eczema to
receive the quality of treatment and care that they
have a right to expect
Stock and Subject Coverage: Material on the
management and treatment of eczema, and
general dermatology reference
Services/Facilities: Photocopies
Availability: Telephone and written enquiries
accepted; visits by appointment
Hours: 09.00-18.00 (answerphone at other times)
Publications: Quarterly journal; annual reports

[425]
National Endometriosis Society

50 Westminster Palace Gardens
1-7 Artillery Row
London SW1P 1RL
Telephone: Helpline: 0171 222 2776
Fax: 0171 222 2786
Contact: Sandra French (Director)
Objectives and Purposes: To support information and research on endometriosis
Hours: 10.30-16.00
Publications: Newsletter (3 per year); range of publications, leaflets, etc. (books for sale only). Full list available

[426]
National Foster Care Association (NFCA)

Leonard House
5-7 Marshalsea Road
London SE1 1EP
Telephone: 0171 828 6266
Fax: 0171 357 6668
Contact: Sarah Tisdall (Administration Manager); Carol Bexty (Policy Information Officer)
Objectives and Purposes: To provide advice, information, training and publications on all aspects of foster care
Stock and Subject Coverage: 2,000 books on foster care; adoption; child care; and after care
Services/Facilities: Database searches; photocopies (priced)
Availability: By prior appointment, for reference use only
Hours: 09.00-17.00
Publications: Foster Care magazine (quarterly); Foster Care Finance (twice yearly); annual report

[427]
National Heart Society (Heart Link)

'Heart Link' House
351 Fishponds Road
Eastville
Bristol BS5 6QG
Telephone: 0117 939 5512
Fax: 0117 939 5513
E-mail: rwall@heartlink.org.uk
World Wide Web: http://www.heartlink.org.uk
Contact: Richard Wall; Sheila Wall; John Frampton
Objectives and Purposes: A support group and registered charity for heart patients of all ages and their carers. Making information available in non-technical terms for all to understand. Offer rehabilitation facilities to heart patients and carers
Stock and Subject Coverage: We produce our own non-technical literature in connection with coronary heart disease. We do produce, on request only, more technical information and services
Services/Facilities: Internet information service

Availability: Access is open to anyone via phone/fax/e-mail/Internet. We do not charge for our services except in exceptional circumstances. Personal visits can be made to our offices by appointment
Hours: 24 hours
Publications: List available on request; quarterly News Magazine
Related Bodies: The organisation has national contacts and links throughout the world via the Internet with professional and non-professional bodies

[428]
National HIV Prevention Information Service

Health Education Authority
Hamilton House
Mabledon Place
London WC1H 9TX
Telephone: 0171 388 9855
Fax: 0171 388 9844
E-mail: nhpis@hea.org.uk
Contact: Kristina Bird (Senior Information Officer)
Objectives and Purposes: A free specialist information service on HIV health promotion serving professionals in England. Covers technical issues of transmission, policy (government, professional and local), epidemiology and local practice
Services/Facilities: In-house database
Related Bodies: Health Education Authority

[429]
National Institute for Biological Standards & Control (NIBSC)

Blanche Lane
South Mimms
Potters Bar
Hertfordshire EN6 3QG
Telephone: 01707 654753
Fax: 01707 646730
E-mail: enquiries@nibsc.ac.uk; pjohnson@nibsc.ac.uk
World Wide Web: http://www.nibsc.ac.uk
Contact: Phil Johnson
Objectives and Purposes: A research institution and national control laboratory for biologicals used in medicine; government sponsored; designated as a World Health Organization international laboratory for biological standards
Stock and Subject Coverage: 4,500 books; 350 periodicals (170 current) covering vaccines; blood products; AIDS; biochemistry; haematology; virology; microbiology; immunology and endocrinology
Services/Facilities: Online, CD-ROM and Internet searches; internal databases (services for staff only)
Availability: For reference use only, by prior arrangement
Hours: 09.00-17.00
Publications: Catalogue of Biological Standards and Reference Materials; annual report

[430]

National Institute for Medical Research

Library and Information Service
The Ridgeway
Mill Hill
London NW7 1AA
Telephone: 0181 959 3666
Fax: 0181 913 8534
E-mail: library@nimr.mrc.ac.uk
World Wide Web: http://www.nimr.mrc.ac.uk
Contact: RJ Moore (Librarian); JF Norman (Deputy Librarian)
Objectives and Purposes: To promote biomedical research
Stock and Subject Coverage: Material covering basic biomedical sciences
Availability: Staff only; others only in exceptional circumstances

National Institute of Medical Herbalists
see **Stop Press on page 156**

[431]

National Kidney Federation

6 Stanley Street
Worksop
Nottinghamshire S81 7HX
Telephone: 01909 487795
Fax: 01909 481723
E-mail: nkf@dial.pipex.com
Contact: Mrs Jenny Bartlam (Office and Administration Manager); Mrs Margaret Jackson (Patient Liaison and Publications Manager)
Objectives and Purposes: To represent patients' interests to government and the media; it is active in campaigning to increase treatment facilities and encourage the public to look on organ donation as the gift of life
Stock and Subject Coverage: Range of patient information leaflets
Services/Facilities: Advice and information centre for patients and families, students, professionals and the public
Hours: 09.00-17.00
Publications: Kidney Life (quarterly)

[432]

National Kidney Research Fund (NKRF)

3 Archers Court
Stukeley Road
Huntingdon
Cambridgeshire PE18 6XG
Telephone: 01480 454828
Fax: 01480 454683
Contact: Director General
Objectives and Purposes: To fund research into kidney disease and other ailments
Availability: Telephone and written enquiries

Hours: 08.30-18.00
Publications: Bi-annual newsletter
Related Bodies: Sister charity is the Kidney Foundation (at the same address)

[433]

National Library for the Blind (NLB)

Far Cromwell Road
Bredbury
Stockport SK6 2SG
Telephone: 0161 494 0217
Fax: 0161 406 6728
Contact: Margaret Bennett (Chief Executive); I Hoyle (External Affairs Manager)
Objectives and Purposes: To provide free, and post-free, lending services to the visually handicapped
Stock and Subject Coverage: 400,000 volumes, principally in Braille (also a large Moon collection, and large print section); includes 7,500 scores of music in Braille. Coverage is general fiction and non-fiction. Special collection for shared reading "Two Ways Collection". Children's collection of 3,500 titles
Services/Facilities: Lending service for books in Braille and Moon; advice on Braille standards
Availability: Free to all registered blind persons
Hours: 08.30-16.30 (answerphone out of hours)
Publications: Hands On (newsletter); NLB Bulletin (bi-monthly)

[434]

National Meningitis Trust

Fern House
Bath Road
Stroud
Gloucestershire GL5 3TJ
Telephone: 01453 751738
Fax: 01453 753588
Contact: Anne Marie Delrosa (Marketing Officer)
Objectives and Purposes: To provide free information to the public and health professionals; to fund research into the disease, provide information, raise awareness and educate people about meningitis, and to support sufferers and their families
Stock and Subject Coverage: Range of material on meningitis
Availability: Freely available, but prior appointments for visits are preferred. For written enquiries an s.a.e. is required
Hours: 09.00-17.00
Publications: List available on request

[435]

National Osteoporosis Society (NOS)

PO Box 10
Radstock
Bath BA3 3YB
Telephone: 01761 471771

Fax: 01761 471104
Contact: Mrs Rosemary Rowe (Information Officer)
Availability: Telephone and written enquiries
Hours: 09.00-17.30
Publications: Newsletter (4 per year); Osteoporosis
    Review (abstracts journal - 3 per year); range of
    booklets, leaflets, posters and teacher's pack - list
    available

[436]

National Perinatal Epidemiology Unit (NPEU)

Radcliffe Infirmary
Gibson Building
Woodstock Road
Oxford OX2 6HE
Telephone: 01865 224118
Fax: 01865 792270
E-mail: lesley.kumiega@perinat.ox.ac.uk
Contact: Lesley Kumiega (Information Officer)
Objectives and Purposes: To provide information
    which can promote effective use of resources in
    the perinatal health services
Stock and Subject Coverage: Ca. 1,200 books and
    papers, and 100 journals covering midwifery;
    obstetrics; statistics; epidemiology; research
    methodology; and clinical trials
Services/Facilities: Online searches; fax
Availability: Reference only, for all bona fide
    researchers; personal visits permitted; telephone,
    written, or e-mail enquiries accepted
Hours: 09.00-17.00
Publications: Annual report; some monographs
Related Bodies: Part of Oxford University, part of
    HeLIN

[437]

National Radiological Protection Board (NRPB)

Chilton
Didcot
Oxfordshire OX11 0RQ
Telephone: 01235 831600; Direct Line: 822649
Fax: 01235 833891
Contact: David Perry (Librarian)
Objectives and Purposes: Statutory body to advise on
    the health effects of radiation, both ionising and
    non-ionising (electromagnetic and optical)
Stock and Subject Coverage: Books, periodicals and
    technical reports on health physics; radiobiology;
    environmental protection, health and safety; and
    legislation. Full sets of the publications of the
    International Commission on Radiological
    Protection and the National Council on Radiation
    Protection and Measurements (NCRP)
Services/Facilities: Searches on in-house database;
    photocopies (priced)
Availability: By appointment; loans to other
    libraries/organisations; research facilities (priced)
Hours: 08.00-18.00

[438]

National Reye's Syndrome Foundation of the UK (NRSF)

15 Nicholas Gardens
Pyrford
Woking
Surrey GU22 8SD
Telephone: 01932 346843
Contact: Mr Gordon H Denney (Hon.
    Administrator); Mrs Gillian Denney
Objectives and Purposes: To provide funds for research
    into the cause, treatment, cure and prevention of
    Reye's Syndrome (a children's disease that affects
    the liver and brain) and Reye-like illnesses; to
    inform both the public and the medical
    communities; and to provide support for parents
    whose children have suffered from these diseases
Stock and Subject Coverage: A small stock of articles
    and periodicals relating to Reye's Syndrome and
    Reye-like illnesses
Services/Facilities: Free advice and information to
    parents and families; photocopies at cost
Availability: Telephone and written enquiries only
Publications: Newsletter; annual report

[439]

National Schizophrenia Fellowship (NSF)

28 Castle Street
Kingston-upon-Thames
Surrey KT1 2LA
Telephone: 0181 547 3937; Advice Service:
    0181 974 6814 (10.00-15.00)
Fax: 0181 547 3862
E-mail: nsf@natschiz.demon.co.uk
Contact: Bahrat Mehta (Chief Executive);
    Gary Hogman (Research and Communications
    Manager); Liz Felton (Director of Operations);
    Fiona Carr (Press and Publications Officer - main
    contact)
Objectives and Purposes: The leading national voluntary
    organisation that helps people with a severe mental
    illness, their families and carers. NSF campaigns
    for better services for the mentally ill, and
    provides support to over 8,000 people per week
    in England, Wales and Northern Ireland through
    its 280 community care projects. NSF also has
    over 160 self-help carer and 40 user support
    groups. NSF Scotland is a sister group, and NSF is
    a member of the World Schizophrenia Fellowship
    and the European Federation of Associations for
    families of the Mentally Ill (EUFAMI)
Stock and Subject Coverage: Material on mental illness
    in general, with specific information on severe
    mental illness, especially schizophrenia; press
    cuttings library
Services/Facilities: Photocopies (priced)
Availability: Telephone and written enquiries. Visits
    occasionally possible
Hours: 09.00-17.00 (Advice Service: 10.00-15.00)
Publications: NSF Today (quarterly); annual report;
    full list available on request

[440]
National Society for Epilepsy (NSE)

Chalfont St Peter
Gerrards Cross
Buckinghamshire SL9 0RJ
Telephone: 01494 873991
Fax: 01494 871927
World Wide Web:
    http://www.erg.ion.ucl.ac.uk/nsehome
Contact: Information Department
Objectives and Purposes: To advance the research, treatment, care, understanding and support for people with epilepsy, nationwide
Services/Facilities: Information and education services offering resources, training, and a helpline/telephone service; rehabilitation, assessment, respite care, medical care and outpatient services; residential care for those with intractable epilepsy
Availability: Telephone and written enquiries (one set of information leaflets/factsheets issued free - more copies 10p each); medical referral required for medical research
Hours: 09.00-17.15
Publications: Newsletter (3 per year); annual report
Related Bodies: Network of self-help groups around the country

[441]
National Society for Phenylketonuria (United Kingdom) Ltd (NSPKU)

7 Southfield Close
Willen
Milton Keynes MK15 9LL
Telephone: 01908 691653
Fax: 01908 691653 (make voice contact first)
E-mail: nspku@ukonline.co.uk
World Wide Web: http://web.ukonline.co.uk/nspku/
Contact: Simon Kimpton (Hon. Secretary)
Objectives and Purposes: The NSPKU is a parent support group. It receives little income from statutory sources and relies on the generosity of PKU families and the general public for the majority of its income. The Society provides the opportunity for parents to meet and share their experiences, distributes information, and promotes the educational, medical and social welfare of persons with PKU. The Society promotes and encourages Regional Support Groups around the country. Medical Representation - The Society is represented by a voluntary Medical Advisory Panel (MAP) made up of Medical Professionals and is supported by a permanent part-time dietitian. The MAP addresses issues relating to the treatment of PKU
Availability: By appointment; telephone and written enquiries accepted
Hours: 24-hour answering machine
Publications: Newsletters, booklets and leaflets all describing PKU and its treatment. All available by post. Full list on request
Related Bodies: Network of local support groups

[442]
National Society for Research into Allergy (NSRA)

PO Box 45
Hinckley
Leicestershire LE10 1JY
Telephone and Fax: 01455 851546
E-mail: allergy@dial.pipex.com
Contact: Mrs Eunice Rose
Objectives and Purposes: To help allergic persons and their families by means of an altered lifestyle, changed diet, and advice on ethical doctors, tests and treatments
Stock and Subject Coverage: Material giving information on all aspects of allergic disease; also covers intolerance
Availability: Visits by appointment
Hours: 09.00-17.00
Publications: Reaction (quarterly magazine); Elimination (diet book); annual report; various booklets

[443]
National Sports Medicine Institute (NSMI)

c/o Medical College of St Bartholomew's Hospital
Charterhouse Square
London EC1M 6BQ
Telephone: 0171 251 0583
Fax: 0171 251 0774
E-mail: m.p.spalding@mds.qmw.ac.uk
World Wide Web: http://www.nsmi.org.uk
Contact: Ms K Walter (Information and Publications Manager); Ms MP Spalding (Librarian and Information Officer)
Objectives and Purposes: To provide academic and administrative support for research and clinical practice in the fields of sports medicine, exercise physiology, sports nutrition and the prevention and treatment of sports injuries
Stock and Subject Coverage: 500 books; 180 periodicals covering all aspects of sports medicine, including nutrition; ergogenic aids; biomechanics; and public health
Services/Facilities: Sport Discus (CD-ROM database); literature searches; reference enquiries (time permitting); photocopies (priced); evening lecture series
Availability: Telephone, fax, e-mail and written enquiries; library for reference use only
Hours: 09.00-17.00 (open until 20.00 on Wednesday - October to June)
Publications: Sports Medicine Bulletin (monthly); Ergogenic Aids in Sport: a bibliography (bi-monthly); Sports Nutrition: a bibliography (bi-monthly); Sport Physiotherapy: a bibliography (bi-monthly); Fitness and Health Index: a bibliography (bi-monthly)

[444]
Neurofibromatosis Association

82 London Road
Kingston-upon-Thames
Surrey KT2 6PX
Telephone: 0181 547 1636 (answerphone out of
hours); 0181 974 8707 (Minicom available on
both numbers)
Fax: 0181 974 5601
Contact: Roberta Tweedy (Director); Mark Stevens
(Assistant Director)
Objectives and Purposes: To assist all those affected by
neurofibromatosis by: providing information,
advice and counselling; supporting research;
providing self-help regional organisations backed
by professional family support workers; and
fundraising to pay for the above
Services/Facilities: Information and advice; family
support contacts at Oxford (01865 226014);
Manchester (0161 276 6294); Guy's Hospital,
London (0171 955 5000); Newcastle-upon-Tyne
(0191 221 0763); and Glasgow (0141 201 0504).
Nottingham and Birmingham contacts will be
established in the near future - contact head office
for numbers
Availability: Telephone and written enquiries; visits
by appointment
Hours: 09.00-17.30
Publications: Neurofibromatosis News (quarterly);
annual report; range of factsheets, etc. (list
available)
Related Bodies: Network of 24 local groups; member
of Genetic Interest Group (GIG); International
Neurofibromatosis Association (INFA), and
Neurological Alliance

[445]
Newcastle General Hospital

Tomlinson Teaching Centre Library
Westgate Road
Newcastle-upon-Tyne NE4 6BE
Telephone: 0191 273 8811, ext 22545
Fax: 0191 219 5044
Contact: Ms Kati Russell (Librarian)
Objectives and Purposes: To contribute to the quality
of health care by ensuring that NHS staff, and staff
and students of the College of Health Studies
who require information in the course of their
work have access to and help in making effective
use of the knowledge and information base of
health care
Stock and Subject Coverage: 6,000 books; 150
periodicals covering medicine and nursing;
Hurrell Collection
Services/Facilities: Online and CD-ROM searches
(MEDLINE and CINAHL); photocopies; fax
Availability: By prior appointment, for reference only
Hours: 09.00-18.00 Monday to Wednesday;
09.00-17.00 Thursday and Friday
Publications: Bi-monthly newsletter; annual report
Related Bodies: Linked to other libraries in Health
Libraries North

[446]
Newham Healthcare NHS Trust

Newham Hospital
Glen Road
Plaistow
London E13 8RU
Telephone: 0171 363 8016; answerphone out of hours
Fax: 0171 363 8087
Contact: Angela Head (Librarian); Terry Visram
(Assistant Librarian); Sharon Devlin (Library
Assistant)
Objectives and Purposes: To provide library and
information services for users involved in health
care, medical and nursing education, based in
Newham
Stock and Subject Coverage: Books; journals; reports;
indexes; bibliographies. Covers health care, clinical
medicine; nursing; and social policy. Special
collection of careers information
Services/Facilities: Online and CD-ROM searches;
PC/printer available; photocopies; project binding
facility. Charges for photocopies and interlibrary
loans
Availability: Full service to staff; restricted service
(reference use only) to others depending on status.
Enquiries accepted by any means that is
convenient
Hours: 08.30-19.00 Monday and Tuesday;
08.30-17.00 Wednesday to Friday
Related Bodies: Satellite library at St Andrew's
Hospital, Devons Road, Bromley by Bow, London
E3 (unstaffed)

[447]
NHS Centre for Reviews and Dissemination (CRD)

University of York
York Y01 5DD
Telephone: 01904 433707
Fax: 01904 433661
E-mail: revdis@york.ac.uk
World Wide Web: http://nhscrd.york.ac.uk
Contact: Ask for the Information Service.
Trevor Sheldon (Director); Ian Watt
(Dissemination Manager); Julie Glanville
(Information Service Manager); Janette Boynton,
Susan Mottram, Andy Bond and Olwen Jones
(Information Officers)
Objectives and Purposes: The Centre provides the
NHS with information on the effectiveness and
cost-effectiveness of treatments and the delivery
and organisation of health care. CRD carries out
and commissions systematic reviews of the
effectiveness of health interventions and works to
improve access to research-based evidence on
effective health care and to disseminate key
messages from research to decision makers in the
NHS and users of the NHS
Stock and Subject Coverage: The library and
information service collects material relating to
health economics, systematic reviews and health
technology assessment, health policy and
developments in the organisation and

management of the NHS. There is also a collection of health economics working papers and health and health service statistics

Services/Facilities: CRD offers access to two online databases free of charge: a database of abstracts to quality assessed systematic reviews (DARE) and a database of detailed abstracts of economic evaluations (NHS Economic Evaluation Database)

Availability: Access to non-CRD or Centre for Health Economics staff is restricted to enquiries by telephone, fax, e-mail and mail. Material is not available for loan or reference. No charges are made for the enquiry service

Hours: The enquiry service is manned 09.00-17.15. Answerphone available outside those hours. The service is closed between Christmas and New Year and on Bank Holidays

Linked organisations: The NHS Centre for Reviews and Dissemination is part of the University of York, and a sibling organisation to the UK Cochrane Centre in Oxford. CRD has a library and information service for its staff and those of the Centre for Heath Economics. An external enquiry service about systematic reviews and economic evaluations is available for enquirers who do not work at the Centres

Publications: Effective Health Care bulletin series, CRD reports, Effectiveness Matters and a range of evidence based leaflets for patients and health care professionals. Databases of Practice and Service Development Initiatives involving nurses and PAMs. The Centre for Health Economics produces a discussion paper series. Lists of publications are available on request

[448]

NHS Executive Northern and Yorkshire

John Snow House
Durham University Science Park
Durham DH1 3YG
Telephone: 0191 301 1300
Fax: 0191 301 1468
E-mail: 106004.3101@compuserve.com
Contact: Mrs CM Smith (Librarian); Mrs C Graham (Assistant Librarian)
Objectives and Purposes: To manage and disseminate information to help the organisation fulfil its mission
Stock and Subject Coverage: NHS management information; some medical and general management texts; NHS Estates information; statistics
Services/Facilities: Photocopies
Availability: By prior appointment, for reference use only; telephone and written enquiries accepted
Hours: 09.30-16.30
Publications: Monthly bulletin; accessions list; government publications list
Related Bodies: DOH Libraries

[449]

NHS Executive Trent

Fulwood House
Old Fulwood Road
Sheffield S10 3TH
Telephone: 0114 282 0481
Fax: 0114 230 6956
World Wide Web: http://www.netlink.co.uk/ users/nhstrent/index.html
Contact: Mrs Glenis Roddis (Librarian)
Objectives and Purposes: To provide information for the staff at the regional office
Stock and Subject Coverage: Health Administration Library for HQ staff; collection of Health Circulars and Guidance; Department of Health and NHS Executive publications
Services/Facilities: Online searches; current awareness; photocopies
Availability: Telephone and written enquiries accepted
Hours: 08.30-17.00

Niemann-Pick Support Group

see **Stop Press on page 156**

[450]

North Hampshire Hospital (NHH)

Aldermaston Road
Basingstoke
Hampshire RG24 9NA
Telephone: 01256 313166
Fax: 01256 461129
E-mail: libnhh@internal.co.uk
Contact: Suzy Hollaway (Acting Librarian); Lesley Heath (Library Assistant)
Objectives and Purposes: A medical-acute hospital. Member of SWRLIN and HATRICS
Stock and Subject Coverage: Material on medicine and nursing in general
Services/Facilities: Online and CD-ROM searches; Cochrane Library; interlibrary loans; photocopies; fax; video viewer
Availability: By prior appointment, for reference use only (charges for searches and photocopies)
Hours: 09.00-17.00

[451]

North Hertfordshire NHS Trust Medical Library

Lister Hospital
Corey's Mill Lane
Stevenage
Hertfordshire SG1 4AB
Telephone: 01438 781092/314333, ext 4092
Fax: 01438 312498
E-mail: sklister@demon.co.uk
World Wide Web: http://www.sklister.demon.co.uk
Contact: Sally Knight; Julia Mackenzie

Objectives and Purposes: To support the educational needs of all staff in the acute unit and in the North Hertfordshire community

Stock and Subject Coverage: Material on medicine and allied disciplines

Services/Facilities: Photocopies; online and CD-ROM searches

Availability: Staff only

Hours: 09.00-17.00

Publications: Annual report

Related Bodies: North Thames Postgraduate Medical Regional Library and Information Unit

[452]
North Hertfordshire NHS Trust Nurses Library

Lister Hospital
Corey's Mill Lane
Stevenage
Hertfordshire SG1 4AB
Telephone: 01438 781092/314333, ext 4877
Fax: 01438 312498
E-mail: sklister@demon.co.uk
World Wide Web: http://www.sklister.demon.co.uk
Contact: Sally Knight; Julia Mackenzie
Objectives and Purposes: To provide information services for nursing staff
Stock and Subject Coverage: Material on medicine, nursing and allied disciplines
Services/Facilities: Photocopies; online and CD-ROM searches
Availability: By prior appointment, for reference use only (charges for searches and photocopies)
Hours: 09.00-17.00
Publications: Annual report
Related Bodies: North Thames HIS Consortium

[453]
North Manchester Postgraduate Medical Centre Library

North Manchester Healthcare NHS Trust
Delaunays Road
Crumpsall
Manchester M8 6RH
Telephone: 0161 720 2718/2722
Fax: 0161 720 2721
Contact: Mrs Deborah Dunton BA ALA (Librarian)
Objectives and Purposes: To provide a full library service (book and journal stock), information retrieval, interlibrary loans, etc. to hospital staff and local GPs
Stock and Subject Coverage: 2,500 books; 122 periodicals covering all aspects of medicine
Services/Facilities: MEDLINE on CD-ROM (priced); photocopies (priced)
Availability: By prior appointment, for reference only
Hours: 09.00-20.00 (closes 16.30 on Friday)

[454]
North Middlesex Hospital Trust

David Ferriman Library
Sterling Way
Edmonton
London N18 1QX
Telephone: Enquiries: 0181 887 2223;
Renewals: 0181 887 3006
Fax: 0181 887 2714
E-mail: libnm1@mdx.ac.uk
Contact: Ann Mason BA ALA (Librarian);
Steven Whitlam BA DipLib (Assistant Librarian - Computers); Deborah Parsons BA DipLib (Assistant Librarian - Nursing and Midwifery)
Objectives and Purposes: The David Ferriman Library will contribute to the quality of patient care by supporting education, training, practice and research of health care personnel, students and related staff via the provision of a multi-disciplinary library and information service. Member of North Thames Regional Library and Information Service (NTRLIS), and part of Middlesex University (contracted library)
Stock and Subject Coverage: The David Ferriman Library is a multi-disciplinary medical library and thus contains stock relating to medicine, nursing and the allied health professions. The collection contains approximately 12,000 books (8,500 titles), 200 journals and 40 newsletters
Services/Facilities: Photocopying, reservations, interlibrary loans, CD-ROM and networked databases (CINAHL, MEDLINE, Cochrane, etc.), online searching, Open Learning Centre; Internet access
Availability: The David Ferriman Library is open to any funded user. These include: All staff and students at the North Middlesex Hospital Trust; Staff and students in the Faculty of Health Studies at Middlesex University; Members of other organisations which make appropriate contributions to the library budget; Members of the local health authority. Paying membership is available at the price of £7 per month. Access to others may be available, please contact the library for information. Loans to members only and libraries within NTRLIS. Charges are made for photocopying and interlibrary loans
Hours: Termtime: 09.00-19.00 Monday, Tuesday and Thursday; 08.00-18.00 Wednesday; 09.00-18.00 Friday; 09.00-12.00. Vacation (Christmas, Easter, July and August): 09.00-18.00 Monday to Friday

[455]
North Staffordshire Medical Institute Library

Hartshill
Stoke-on-Trent ST4 7NY
Telephone: 01782 716198
Fax: 01782 715422
Email: pd89@dial.pipex.com
Contact: Library Manager

Objectives and Purposes: The provision of library and information services to staff of two NHS Trusts and one District Health Authority

Stock and Subject Coverage: 3,000 books; 330 current periodicals covering clinical medicine and health care management

Services/Facilities: Literature searches; document supply; photocopies; CD-ROM searches (all priced)

Availability: By prior appointment, for reference use only

Hours: 09.00–17.00 Monday, Wednesday and Thursday; 09.00–20.30 Tuesday; 09.00–16.30 Friday

Related Bodies: West Midlands Health Libraries Network

[456]
North Tees Medical Library

North Tees General Hospital
Hardwick
Stockton-on-Tees
Cleveland TS19 8PE

Telephone: 01642 617617, exts 4784/4789
Contact: Mrs Elizabeth Clemo (Librarian)
Objectives and Purposes: A multidisciplinary library serving all health service staff in the North Tees district, and staff/students at Durham and Teesside College of Health
Stock and Subject Coverage: 14,000 books; 150 periodicals covering medicine, nursing and allied subjects
Services/Facilities: CD-ROM searches (MEDLINE, CINAHL, ASSIA and Cochrane); photocopies (at cost)
Availability: By prior appointment, for reference use only
Hours: 09.00–18.00 Monday to Wednesday; 09.00–17.00 Thursday and Friday

[457]
North Thames Regional Library & Information Unit (RLIU)

Thames Postgraduate Medical & Dental Education
33 Millman Street
London WC1N 3EJ

Telephone: 0171 405 5667
Fax: 0171 405 5668
E-mail: sgodbolt@tpmde.ac.uk
World Wide Web:
http://www.nthames-health.tpmde.ac.uk/ntrl/
Contact: Shane Godbolt (Regional Librarian and Head of Unit); John Hewlett (Associate Regional Librarian)
Objectives and Purposes: North Thames RLIU is an innovative, small specialist unit which is part of North Thames Region's Directorate of Education and Training. The Unit's work is largely project based, providing professional leadership and co-ordination of library and information services for NHS funded libraries in the Region

Stock and Subject Coverage: Material on health care librarianship. The SatelLife libraries cover a whole range of health care
Services/Facilities: Current Awareness on behalf of LA Health Libraries Group
Hours: 09.00–17.00
Publications: North Circular (quarterly); annual report; Regional Documents Database; Union List of Serials
Related Bodies: Part of the Directorate of Education & Training, North Thames Regional Office, NHS Executive. The library network within the Region consists of over 120 information professionals and support staff with some 40 service points

[458]
North Thames (West) Health Information Service

Level 4
Lister Hospital
Corey's Mill Lane
Stevenage SG1 4AB

Telephone: 0345 678400; 0800 665544; 01438 314333, ext 4877
Contact: Sally Knight; Julie Mackenzie
Objectives and Purposes: To provide a health information service to the public in the geographic area covered by North Thames (West) Regional Health Authority
Stock and Subject Coverage: 400 books; 3,000 information folders on general medicine
Services/Facilities: Public information service
Hours: 09.00–12.30 and 13.00–17.00 (closes 14.30 on Friday)
Related Bodies: Hertfordshire Library Service; North Thames RHA; North Thames Regional Library Service; NHSE

[459]
North Tyneside Medical Library

Education Centre
North Tyneside General Hospital
North Shields
Tyne and Wear NE29 8NH

Telephone: 0191 293 2761
Fax: 0191 293 2763
Contact: Linda Snowdon (Librarian)
Objectives and Purposes: To provide library and information services to doctors in North Tyneside and other paramedical staff in the hospital
Stock and Subject Coverage: 4,000 books; 120 periodicals; 100 videos covering medicine in general
Services/Facilities: MEDLINE, CINAHL and Cochrane on CD-ROM; photocopies; computer facities
Availability: Only to medical staff in North Tyneside
Hours: 09.00–17.00

[460]

North West Anglia Health Authority (NWAHA)

St John's
Thorpe Road
Peterborough PE3 6JG
(also at a headquarters office in King's Lynn)
Telephone: 01733 882112
Fax: 01733 882299
E-mail: 100347.3276@compuserve.com
Contact: Dorothy Husband (Librarian/Intelligence
    Co-ordinator - contact name); Gill Curtis (Library
    Assistant)
Objectives and Purposes: North West Anglia Health
    Authority is responsible for working with health
    professionals and others in North Cambridgeshire
    and West Norfolk to improve the health of its
    residents
Stock and Subject Coverage: Health management and
    public health are the main foci of interest. The
    library holds books and reports (much grey
    literature), health service circulars and journals
Services/Facilities: None available to external users
Availability: Open to local researchers for reference if
    appointment is made in advance. A charge may be
    made for photocopying items
Hours: 09.00-17.00

[461]

North West Health Library and Information Service (NWHLIS)

Hamilton House
24 Pall Mall
Liverpool L3 6AL
Telephone: 0151 236 4620
Fax: 0151 236 2808
Contact: Mrs Linda Ferguson Kieran Lamb (Contact)
Objectives and Purposes: To plan and organise health
    services within the North West
Stock and Subject Coverage: 4,000 books; 50
    periodicals covering NHS administration. Special
    collections of public health reports; Department
    of Health circulars; and Department of Health
    publications
Services/Facilities: Online and CD-ROM searches;
    current awareness service
Availability: Telephone and written enquiries
    (telephone enquiry service provides information
    on the NHS to all callers); visits by appointment
    only
Hours: 09.00-17.00
Publications: New accessions bulletin; library guide

[462]

North Yorkshire Health Authority (NYHA)

Sovereign House
Kettlestring Lane
York YO3 4XF
Telephone: 01904 693322
Fax: 01904 691769

Contact: Mrs MJ Rees (Resource Centre Officer)
Objectives and Purposes: To improve the health of the
    population of North Yorkshire
Stock and Subject Coverage: 3,000 books; 50
    periodicals. Covers health care, especially public
    health, government health publications and
    evidence-based medicine
Services/Facilities: Internal database searches;
    photocopies
Availability: Telephone and written enquiries
    accepted; visits by prior arrangement
Hours: 09.30-17.30

[463]

Northern Devon Healthcare Trust

Library
North Devon District Hospital
Raleigh Park
Barnstaple
Devon EX31 4JB
Telephone: 01271 22692
Contact: Mrs Alison Housley (Librarian)
Objectives and Purposes: To meet the information
    needs of Trust staff, staff and students of Plymouth
    University, and other NHS personnel in North
    Devon
Stock and Subject Coverage: Material on medicine,
    nursing and allied professions
Services/Facilities: Online and CD-ROM searches;
    fax; photocopies (priced)
Availability: Telephone and written enquiries
    accepted, visits by prior arrangement
Hours: 09.00-17.00
Publications: Journal holdings list; library guide

[464]

Northern Ireland Association for Mental Health

80 University Street
Belfast BT7 1HE
Telephone: 01232 328474
Fax: 01232 234940
Contact: Pauline Rainey (Information Officer)
Objectives and Purposes: To promote dignity, choice,
    integration and participation for those with
    mental health needs living in the community
Stock and Subject Coverage: Information on all aspects
    of mental health
Services/Facilities: Free advice and information to the
    general public, mental health professionals and
    students; Beacon Centres
Availability: Telephone and written enquiries; visits
    welcomed
Hours: 09.00-17.00 (closes 16.30 on Friday)
Publications: Mental Health Matters (quarterly
    magazine); range of factsheets; annual review
Related Bodies: A network of Beacon Centre,
    Residential Schemes and branches throughout
    Northern Ireland

[465]

Northern Ireland Council for Voluntary Action (NICVA)

127 Ormeau Road
Belfast BT7 1SH
Telephone: 01232 321224
Fax: 01232 438350
E-mail: nicva@ncri.poptel.org.uk
Contact: Nadia Downing (Information Officer)
Objectives and Purposes: The umbrella body for voluntary, community and charitable groups in Northern Ireland, providing information, support and training on a wide range of issues
Stock and Subject Coverage: Material covering health and social services - general theory; strategic planning; community care; community health; reproduction; addictions; mental health; physical health; well-being; social services; etc. - all relating to Northern Ireland
Services/Facilities: Free advice and information to community and voluntary groups, the public, and students; photocopies; fax; current awareness service
Availability: Visits by appointment, for reference use only; telephone and written enquiries accepted; some services priced
Hours: 09.00-17.00
Publications: Shared Lines (monthly current awareness bulletin); Scope (magazine); annual report; miscellaneous publications - catalogue available on request

[466]

Northumberland Health Authority, Library and Information Service

East Cottingwood
Morpeth
Northumberland NE61 2PD
Telephone: 01670 514331, ext 2014
Fax: 01670 518873
Contact: Sue Hey (Librarian)
Objectives and Purposes: The provision/purchasing of health services for the people of Northumberland
Stock and Subject Coverage: Material covering health management and purchasing; health promotion; public health; communicable diseases; and environmental health
Services/Facilities: Online and CD-ROM searches; photocopies; fax; interlibrary loans; Internet access
Availability: Mainly to staff only; telephone and written enquiries from others accepted where possible
Hours: 09.00-16.30
Publications: Annual report; statistical rofile; community care plan
Related Bodies: Member of Health Libraries North

[467]

Northwick Park and St Mark's Hospital NHS Trust

John Squire Medical Library
Watford Road
Harrow
Middlesex HA1 3UJ
Telephone: 0181 869 3322
Fax: 0181 869 3332
Contact: Mike Kendall (Head Librarian); Jo Davey (Assistant Librarian); Tony Thomson (Assistant Librarian)
Objectives and Purposes: The provision of library and information services supporting patient care, continuing education and research conducted onsite
Stock and Subject Coverage: 10,000 books; 425 periodicals. Covers clinical medicine and biomedical sciences; nursing; health service management
Services/Facilities: CD-ROM searches; photocopies (priced)
Availability: By prior appointment, for reference use only
Hours: 09.00-18.00; 10.00-16.00 Saturday
Publications: Monthly bulletin; North Thames Current Awareness Bulletin
Related Bodies: Part of North Thames Regional Library and Information Network

[468]

Nottingham City Hospital Library

Postgraduate Education Centre
Hucknall Road
Nottingham NG5 1PB
Telephone: 0115 969 1169, ext 45736
Fax: 0115 962 7741
E-mail: mfxrm@unix.ccc.nottingham.ac.uk
Contact: Richard Marriott (Librarian)
Objectives and Purposes: To provide accurate and timely information in support of patient care, education, management and research to staff at the hospital
Stock and Subject Coverage: A broad range of books, periodicals and videos covering medicine and physiotherapy
Services/Facilities: CD-ROM searches (MEDLINE, CINAHL); Cochrane midwifery database; computer assisted learning packages; video player; photocopies (priced); fax
Availability: Normally to NHS staff only; telephone and written enquiries accepted
Hours: 09.00-17.00 (24-hour pass-key access for members)
Publications: Annual journals catalogue
Related Bodies: Close links with Greenfield Medical Library, Queens Medical Centre, and departmental libraries at Nottingham City Hospital (Oncology, Clinical Genetics)

[469]

Nottingham Healthcare NHS Trust

Medical Library
Duncan MacMillan House
Porchester Road
Mapperley
Nottingham NG3 6AA
Telephone: 0115969 1300, ext 40760
Contact: Brian Spencer (Librarian); Kate Hudson (Assistant Librarian); Carol Fisher (Senior Library Assistant)
Objectives and Purposes: To provide library and information services to staff and students of the Trust
Stock and Subject Coverage: Material on psychiatry. Small handwritten archive relating to the history of Mapperley Hospital
Services/Facilities: Photocopies (priced)
Availability: By prior appointment, for reference use only
Hours: 09.00-12.00 and 13.00-17.00 Monday and Wednesday; 09.00-18.00 Tuesday and Thursday; 09.00-16.30 Friday

[470]

Nottingham University, School of Nursing and Midwifery

Avenue House
Ashfield Avenue
Mansfield NG18
Telephone: 01623 28860
Fax: 01623 26796
E-mail: sarah.carlile@nottingham.ac.uk
Contact: Sarah Carlile
Objectives and Purposes: The education of nurses and midwives
Stock and Subject Coverage: 8,000 books; 67 periodicals. Covers nursing and midwifery, with some coverage of other fields such as psychology and sociology
Services/Facilities: Usual library services
Availability: By prior appointment, for reference use only; membership may be arranged
Hours: 08.30-16.30 (closes at 16.00 on Friday)
Publications: Newsletter; library skills pack
Related Bodies: Nottingham University Library

[471]

Nuffield Council on Bioethics

28 Bedford Square
London WC1B 3EG
Telephone: 0171 631 0566
Fax: 0171 323 4877
Contact: David Shapiro; Rachel Bartlett
Objectives and Purposes: To identify and define ethical questions raised by recent advances in biological and medical research, and to publish reports
Stock and Subject Coverage: A growing library of files on ca. 900 biological and medical topics containing cuttings from leading journals and newspapers

Availability: By prior appointment, for reference use only
Hours: 10.00-16.00
Publications: Genetic screening: ethical issues; Human Tissue: ethical and legal issues; Animal to Human Transplants: the ethics of xenotransplantation

[472]

Nuffield Institute for Health Information Resource Centre

71-75 Clarendon Road
Leeds LS2 9PL
Telephone: Enquiries: 0113 233 3946; HELMIS: 0113 233 6971
Fax: 0113 246 0899
E-mail: l.Bate@leeds.ac.uk; helmis@leeds.ac.uk
World Wide Web: http://www.leeds.ac.uk/library/gateway/gateway.html
Contact: Lorraine Bate (IRC Manager)
Objectives and Purposes: To provide information services relating to health and social care management, health policy and public health in the UK and internationally
Stock and Subject Coverage: 30,000 books; 300 periodicals covering health and social care management, health policy and public health (non-clinical aspects). Coverage includes developed and developing country material. The IRC is also a WHO European Region documentation centre
Services/Facilities: Health Management Information Services (HELMIS) produces two current awareness publications, provides literature searches, database searches and document delivery. The HELMIS database contains over 50,000 references; Internet access to the database is available to subscribers. The IRC also supports two other databases: UK Clearing House on Health Outcomes and EC Clearing House on European Health Systems Reform
Availability: Telephone and written enquiries; visits by appointment; HELMIS services available on a fee-for-service or subscription basis
Hours: 09.30-17.30 Monday; 08.30-19.00 Tuesday to Thursday (17.30 in vacation); 08.30-16.30 Friday
Publications: Health Management Update (10 per year - current awareness bulletin); Information Bulletin for Developing Health Systems (4 per year - current awareness bulletin)
Related Bodies: University of Leeds Library

[473]

Nuffield Orthopaedic Centre NHS Trust (NOC)

Girdlestone Memorial Library
Windmill Road
Headington
Oxford OX3 7LD
Telephone: 01865 227361
Fax: 01865 227362
E-mail: eve.hollis@orthopaedic-surgery.ox.ac.uk

Contact: Mrs Eve Hollis (Library Services Manager; Mr Derek Goodwin (Library Assistant))

Objectives and Purposes: Library in support of patient care in orthopaedics, and research into patient care in orthopaedics and related disciplines

Stock and Subject Coverage: 4,000 books; 120 periodicals covering orthopaedics; orthopaedic nursing; and rheumatology. Small collection of historical material, and Oxford University theses

Services/Facilities: Online and CD-ROM searches (Index Medicus, and CINAHL); photocopies; word processing facilities; fax; Internet access

Availability: By prior appointment, for reference use only (some charges are imposed)

Hours: 08.00-18.00

Publications: Annual periodicals list; welcome guide; annual report

Related Bodies: Oxford Orthopaedic Engineering Centre; Mary Marlborough Disability Centre

---

[474]
Office of Health Economics (OHE)

12 Whitehall
London SW1A 2DY

Telephone: 0171 930 9203

Fax: 0171 747 1419

Contact: Miss Janet Ogleby (Librarian), ext 1441

Objectives and Purposes: To promote research on the economic aspects of medical care

Stock and Subject Coverage: 600 books; 130 periodicals covering economics; general medicine; health care; and pharmacy. This is a joint library with the Association of the British Pharmaceutical Industry

Services/Facilities: Interlibrary loans; photocopies

Availability: Enquiries from other libraries welcome

Hours: 08.30-16.30

Publications: Details of OHE publications from the OHE Secretary, not the Library

Related Bodies: Supported by the Association of the British Pharmaceutical Industry

---

[475]
One Parent Families Scotland (OPFS)

13 Gayfield Square
Edinburgh EH1 3NX

Telephone: 0131 556 3899/4562

Fax: 0131 557 9650

E-mail: imaxwell@gn.apc.org

Contact: Sue Robertson (Director); Ian Maxwell (Information Officer)

Objectives and Purposes: Working towards a better understanding of the needs and strengths of lone parents in Scotland

Stock and Subject Coverage: Books, periodicals and cuttings on all aspects of single parents and their families

Hours: 09.00-16.00

Publications: One in Five (newsletter); range of publications - list available

---

[476]
Opportunities for People With Disabilities

1 Bank Buildings
Princes Street
London EC2R 8EU

Telephone and Fax: 0171 726 4961; Minicom: 0171 726 4963

Contact: David C Burgess LLb MA (Chief Executive)

Objectives and Purposes: To provide opportunities through training, preparation and guidance to help people with disabilities to secure and maintain worthwhile employment matched to their talents and aspirations

Services/Facilities: Advice on the process of job applications

Availability: To those who need it

Hours: 09.30-17.30

Publications: Being Positive about Disability (leaflet); annual report

Related Bodies: Regional centres around the country

---

[477]
Organon Laboratories Ltd, Information Department

Science Park
Milton Road
Cambridge CB4 4FL

Telephone: 01223 423445

Fax: 01223 424368

Contact: Brian Clements; Claire Binnie

Objectives and Purposes: Pharmaceuticals manufacturer

Stock and Subject Coverage: Books; periodicals and reprints covering gynaecology, especially contraception; infertility; and menopause

Services/Facilities: Online searches; photocopies; fax

Availability: To medical personnel only, by letter or telephone

Hours: 09.00-17.00

---

[478]
Oxford Brookes University, School of Occupational Therapy

Dorset House Library
58 London Road
Oxford OX3 7PE

Telephone: 01865 485261

Fax: 01865 69679

E-mail: jscroft@brookes.ac.uk

Contact: Mrs Sally Croft

Objectives and Purposes: To serve the information needs of the School

Stock and Subject Coverage: Material on occupational therapy and rehabilitation

Services/Facilities: Photocopies

Availability: By prior appointment, for reference use only

Hours: 09.00-18.00; 09.00-12.00 Saturday. Vacations: 09.00-15.00

Publications: Library guide; journals list
Related Bodies: Oxford Brookes University

---

[479]

Paediatric Research Unit (PRU)

Division of Medical and Molecular Genetics
Prince Philip Research Laboratories
8th Floor, Guy's Tower
UMDS, Guy's Hospital
London SE1 9RT
Telephone: 0171 955 4135
Fax: 0171 955 4644
E-mail: l.exton@umds.ac.uk
Contact: Lesley Exton (Information Officer)
Objectives and Purposes: To assist the research aim of
the Unit and to increase the sum of knowledge of
medical genetics and disorders of early human
development
Stock and Subject Coverage: 3,500 books; 55
periodicals covering medicine; genetics; and
disorders of early human development
Services/Facilities: Database searches; photocopies
(priced)
Availability: By prior appointment, for reference use
only; telephone and written enquiries accepted,
but it is preferred if researchers come in and do
their own work
Hours: 09.00-17.00 (reading room sometimes
required for departmental meetings, and therefore
subject to temporary closure)
Publications: Library guide; publications list

---

[480]

Pain Relief Foundation (PRI)

Rice Lane
Liverpool L9 1AE
Telephone: 0151 523 1486
Fax: 0151 521 6155
Contact: Dr D Bowsher; Mrs L Cossins; Mr D Emsley
Objectives and Purposes: To carry out research into
human chronic pain conditions
Availability: Telephone and written enquiries
Hours: 09.00-17.00

---

[481]

Pain Society

9 Bedford Square
London WC1 3RA
Telephone and Fax: 0171 636 2750
Contact: Dr T Nash (President); Dr PJD Evans (Hon.
Secretary); Mrs A Sexton (Secretary)
Objectives and Purposes: To relieve the suffering of
pain by the promotion of education, research and
training in the field of pain management.
Members come from a range of backgrounds, but
all have a professional commitment to pain
Stock and Subject Coverage: An internal database of
members, detailing their fields of interest and the
pain control clinics to which they are attached

Services/Facilities: Free information about local pain
control clinics is provided. Database searches and a
journal for members
Availability: Telephone and written enquiries;
enquiries from the public on pain-related matters
are welcomed, although individual cases cannot be
commented on in detail
Publications: Journal of the Pain Society of Great
Britain and Ireland (bi-annual journal); Pain
Control Clinics and the Relief of Pain (leaflet)
Related Bodies: This is the UK and Ireland Chapter
of the International Association for the Study of
Pain; links with regional groups in the UK and
with pain societies in other countries

---

[482]

Pancreatitis Supporters Network (PSN)

15 Mayfield Court
59b Mayfield Road
Moseley
Birmingham B13 9HS
Telephone and Fax: 0121 449 0667
E-mail: 100537.2144@compuserve.com
World Wide Web: http://ourworld.compuserve.com/
homepages/psnjimarmour
Contact: JA Armour
Objectives and Purposes: To raise awareness on the
condition known as pancreatitis; to put patients in
touch with specialists; to offer counselling,
benefits information and bankruptcy help
Stock and Subject Coverage: Material on pancreatitis in
general
Services/Facilities: Photocopies; fax; Internet
Availability: Telephone enquiries; visits by prior
appointment
Hours: 09.00-17.00
Publications: Information booklets, etc. on acute and
chronic disorders, and cancer of, the pancreas

---

[483]

Papworth Hospital NHS Trust Clinical Library Service

Papworth Everard
Cambridgeshire CB3 8RE
Telephone: 01480 830541, ext 4145/4245
Contact: Lyn Edmonds (Library Service Manager)
Objectives and Purposes: To provide comprehensive
library and information services to hospital staff
Stock and Subject Coverage: Books and periodicals
covering cardiothoracic medicine and surgery
Services/Facilities: MEDLINE, CINAHL, NMI and
Cochrane Library on CD-ROM; photocopies
Availability: By prior appointment, for reference use
only
Hours: 09.00-17.00
Publications: Library guide; new books list; current
journals list

[484]

Parkinson's Disease Society of the UK (PDS)

22 Upper Woburn Place
London WC1H 0RA
Telephone: 0171 383 3513
Fax: 0171 383 5754
Contact: Bridget McCall (Information Officer);
Helen Burrows (Information Officer)
Objectives and Purposes: To help all people with
Parkinson's Disease, their families, and
professionals who look after them through
welfare, research, education and information
Stock and Subject Coverage: Material on Parkinson's
Disease, disability, and related subjects
Availability: By prior appointment, for reference use
only; telephone and written enquiries
Hours: 09.00-17.00
Publications: Wide range - lists available
Related Bodies: Network of local groups

[485]

Partially Sighted Society

62 Salusbury Road
London NW6 6NS
Telephone and Fax: 0171 372 1551
Contact: Jo Beech; Angela Fitzgerald
Objectives and Purposes: To enable those with a major
irreversible sight loss to make the most effective
use of their minimal remaining sight to maximise
independence, safety and abilities
Stock and Subject Coverage: Large print advice and
information leaflets
Services/Facilities: Large print printing
Availability: By prior appointment, for reference use
only; telephone and written enquiries accepted
Hours: 09.30-17.00
Publications: Oculus (bi-monthly)

[486]

Patients on Intravenous and Nasogastric Nutrition Therapy (PINNT)

258 Wennington Road
Rainham
Essex RM13 9UU
Telephone: 01708 521907
Fax: 01708 521907
Contact: Carolyn Wheatley (General Secretary)
Objectives and Purposes: To provide support and
contact for people receiving artificial nutrition,
and a forum for problems, support and advice
Services/Facilities: Advice to members; holiday
facilities
Availability: Telephone enquiries welcome
Hours: 10.00-17.00
Publications: Quarterly journal; newsletters; holiday
guidelines; schools pack; medical alert cards
Related Bodies: Works closely with British
Association for Parenteral and Enteral Nutrition

[487]

Pembrokeshire NHS Trust

Medical and Nursing Libraries
Withybush General Hospital
Fishguard Road
Haverfordwest
Pembrokeshire SA61 2PZ
Telephone: 01437 773730
Fax: 01437 773726
Contact: Miss Arwen Jackson (Librarian);
Mrs Andrea Thomas (Library Assistant)
Objectives and Purposes: To provide library and
information services for staff of the Trust,
contributing to the quality of health care, and
furthering the postgraduate education of staff
Stock and Subject Coverage: A small library with
books, periodicals and videos on medicine, health
care and nursing
Services/Facilities: CD-ROM searches (MEDLINE
and CINAHL); interlibrary loans; photocopies;
video viewing facility
Availability: By prior appointment, for reference use
only; external enquiries handled as time permits
Hours: 08.30-16.30 (closes 16.00 on Friday)
Related Bodies: Postgraduate Department, University
of Wales College of Medicine, Cardiff

[488]

Pembury Hospital Health Link

Library
Education Centre
Pembury
Kent TN2 4QJ
Telephone: 01892 823535, ext 3119
Fax: 01892 823137
Contact: Jan Hurst; Jenny Barker
Objectives and Purposes: An information service
available to professionals, carers, relatives, patients
and the public for health and related enquiries
Stock and Subject Coverage: Database of support
groups; books, leaflets, etc.
Services/Facilities: Photocopies (priced)
Availability: Telephone and written enquiries
accepted; visits by arrangement
Hours: 08.30-16.30 (closes 16.00 on Friday)

[489]

Perthes Association

42 Woodlands Road
Guildford
Surrey GU1 1RW
Telephone: Helpline: 01483 306637; Administration:
01483 34431
Fax: 01483 503213
E-mail: perthes@cableol.co.uk
Contact: Lisa Avery (Director)
Objectives and Purposes: To help and advise sufferers
of osteochondritis, including Perthes Disease, and
also sufferers of multiple epiphyseal dysplasia
Stock and Subject Coverage: Booklets, leaflets, etc. on
osteochondritis and Perthes Disease

Services/Facilities: Equipment library for members; information packs (at cost to non-members)
Availability: By prior appointment, for reference use only; telephone and written enquiries preferred
Hours: 09.00-13.00 and 14.00-17.30
Publications: Quarterly newsletter; annual report

[490]
Peterborough Hospitals NHS Trust

Postgraduate Medical Centre
Peterborough District Hospital
Thorpe Road
Peterborough PE3 6DA
Telephone: 01733 874662
Fax: 01733 347142
E-mail: hlycett@petlib.demon.co.uk
Contact: Mrs HM Lycett (Librarian)
Objectives and Purposes: The provision of library and information services to hospital staff and local medical/dental professionals
Stock and Subject Coverage: 2,500 books; 107 periodicals on medicine in general
Services/Facilities: CD-ROM searches (MEDLINE and Cochrane); interlibrary loans; photocopies (priced)
Availability: By prior appointment, for reference use only
Hours: 09.00-17.00 (closes 16.30 on Friday)

[491]
PHLS Communicable Disease Surveillance Centre (CDSC)

61 Colindale Avenue
London NW9 5EQ
Telephone: 0181 200 6868
Fax: 0181 200 7868
E-mail: hheine@phls.co.uk
Contact: Hilary Heine (Information Manager); Hannah Bowers (Information Assistant)
Objectives and Purposes: To contribute to the role of the Public Health Laboratory Service in protecting the population from infection by the prevention and control of communicable disease through surveillance and independent advice, epidemiological investigation and research
Stock and Subject Coverage: Material on all aspects of communicable diseases; internal database maintained
Availability: Restricted to staff
Hours: 08.30-18.00
Publications: Communicable Disease Report (weekly); Eurosurveillance (in collaboration with counterpart agencies throughout Europe)
Related Bodies: Public Health Laboratory Service

[492]
Phobics Society

4 Cheltenham Road
Chorlton-cum-Hardy
Manchester M21 9QN
Telephone: 0161 881 1937
Contact: Mr H Fisher (Director); Ms Nicola Lidbetter
Objectives and Purposes: To help sufferers of all anxiety disorders (panic attacks, phobias, obsessive compulsive disorders, and general Anxiety Disorder)
Services/Facilities: Telephone advice, self-help literature, contacts lists and counselling to sufferers and their families/partners; self-help material provided (small charge to cover postage and printing)
Hours: 09.00-21.00
Publications: Self-help packs; quarterly reports

[493]
Pilgrim Hospital

Staff Library
Sibsey Road
Boston
Lincolnshire PE21 9QS
Telephone: 01205 364801, ext 2272
Contact: Mrs AL Willis (Senior Librarian); Mrs A Darling (Librarian)
Objectives and Purposes: A multidisciplinary mental health NHS Trust library serving staff, postgraduate medical and dental education, and nursing and midwifery education
Stock and Subject Coverage: 15,000 books; 250 periodicals. Covers mental health; general medicine; nursing, and related fields including NHS administration
Services/Facilities: Photocopies; literature searches
Availability: By prior appointment, for reference use only
Hours: 09.00-17.00 Monday and Wednesday
Related Bodies: Lincolnshire County Libary Hospital Library Network

[494]
Pinderfields Hospital Postgraduate Education Services Library

Pinderfields Hospital NHS Trust
Aberford Road
Wakefield WF1 4DG
Telephone: 01924 814546
Contact: Mrs Diane Llewellyn (Library Manager)
Objectives and Purposes: To support medical and allied health professionals in continuing education and training
Stock and Subject Coverage: Material on medicine; nursing; rehabilitation; and paramedical subjects
Services/Facilities: CD-ROM searches; photocopies (priced); fax
Availability: Freely available for reference
Hours: 08.30-17.00
Publications: Rehabilitation Bulletin (monthly)

[495]

Pituitary Foundation (Pit-Pat)

17-18 The Courtyard
Woodlands
Almondsbury
Bristol BS12 4NQ
Telephone: 01454 201612
Fax: 01454 616071
E-mail: soc-endoc@bristol.ac.uk
Contact: Ms Sue Thorn (Secretary); Miss Lisa Nock (Administrator)
Objectives and Purposes: To provide support to pituitary patients and their carers
Services/Facilities: Information leaflets and newsletter for patients and carers
Hours: 09.00–17.00
Publications: Range of information leaflets

[496]

Podiatry Association

19A High Street
Chelmsford
Essex CM1 1BE
Telephone and Fax: 01462 790371
E-mail: rgraham@podiatry.dungeon.com.uk
Contact: Mr R Graham (Secretary); Mr I Turbutt (Chairman)
Objectives and Purposes: To promote the highest standards of research, development and training in podiatric surgery. The Association trains specialists in podiatric surgery for employment within the NHS
Publications: The British Journal of Podiatric Medicine and Surgery (quarterly)
Related Bodies: Subsidiary organisations are The British College of Podiatry and The College of Foot Surgeons

[497]

Pontefract General Infirmary, Postgraduate Medical Centre Medical Library

Friarwood Lane
Pontefract
West Yorkshire WF8 1PL
Telephone: 01977 600600, ext 6638
Fax: 01977 606361
Contact: Miss Jane Smethurst (Librarian)
Objectives and Purposes: To contribute to the quality of patient care within Pontefract Health Trust by providing comprehensive library and information services in support of a fully-informed and knowledgeable health care workforce
Stock and Subject Coverage: Material on medicine and related health care subjects
Services/Facilities: MEDLINE searches; interlibrary loans; photocopies; fax; library 'bookshop' service
Availability: By prior appointment, for reference use only
Hours: 24 hours

Publications: Bi-monthly library bulletin; annual journal holdings list; handouts on literature searching, MEDLINE, etc.
Related Bodies: Part of Wakefield Library Service, and JHLS regional library system; linked with Leeds University Medical School Library; part of Yorkshire Regional (PGME) Group

[498]

Poole Hospital NHS Trust

Longfleet Road
Poole
Dorset BH15 2JB
Telephone: 01202 442101
Fax: 01202 442557
E-mail: phlib@dial.pipex.com
Contact: Mr JB Gill (Principal Librarian); Miss S Merner (Librarian)
Objectives and Purposes: Library support to the clinical, educational and management activities of NHS staff in East Dorset
Stock and Subject Coverage: 12,000 books; 150 journals covering medicine; nursing; and related professions
Services/Facilities: CD-ROM searches; photocopies; fax
Availability: Mainly to staff only, but external visitors may be admitted by prior appointment
Hours: 08.30–17.00
Publications: Nursing and Midwifery Index; annual journal holdings list
Related Bodies: Member of Wessex Regional Library and Information Network; linked to Royal Bournemouth Hospital Library

[499]

Portsmouth Hospitals NHS Trust Staff Library, Queen Alexandra Hospital

Postgraduate Centre
Queen Alexandra Hospital
Cosham
Portsmouth PO6 3LY
Telephone: 01705 286043
Fax: 01705 286886
Contact: Ms J Reeves (Librarian); Mrs T Wilson (Library Services Manager)
Objectives and Purposes: To contribute to high quality patient care through the provision of text-based information services in the context of direct patient care, education and research
Stock and Subject Coverage: Books, periodicals, pamphlets, reports, audiovisual materials covering most aspects of medicine; nursing; and health care management
Services/Facilities: Online searches; interlibrary loans; photocopies; fax; word processing facilities
Availability: By prior appointment, for reference use only
Hours: 08.30–17.00 (closes 16.00 on Friday)
Related Bodies: Member of WRLIN and HATRICS

[500]

Portsmouth Hospitals NHS Trust Staff Library, St Mary's Hospital

Education Centre
St Mary's Hospital
Milton Road
Portsmouth PO3 6AD
Telephone: 01705 822331, ext 4856
Fax: 01705 866920
E-mail: h26@soton.ac.uk
Contact: Mrs Tina Wilson (Library Services Manager)
Objectives and Purposes: To contribute to high quality patient care through the provision of text-based information services in the context of direct patient care, education and research
Stock and Subject Coverage: Books, periodicals, pamphlets, reports, databases and multimedia materials covering most aspects of health care
Services/Facilities: Online and CD-ROM searches; interlibrary loans; photocopies; computer-based learning facilities
Availability: By prior appointment, for reference use only
Hours: 08.30-17.00 (closes 16.00 on Friday)
Related Bodies: Queen Alexandra Hospital Library

[501]

Prader-Willi Syndrome Association UK (PWSA(UK))

2 Wheatsheaf Close
Horsell
Woking
Surrey GU21 4BP
Telephone: 01483 724784
Contact: Mrs Rosemary Johnson (Secretary and Welfare Officer)
Objectives and Purposes: Helping those who deal with Prader-Willi Syndrome
Stock and Subject Coverage: Materials on all aspects of Prader-Willi Syndrome
Services/Facilities: Advice to anyone; information and speakers can be provided; welfare visits; members receive quarterly newsletters
Availability: Freely available, by arrangement
Hours: 24 hours
Publications: Range of books and videos - list available

[502]

Premier Health NHS Trust

Library and Information Centre
St Michael's Hospital
Trent Valley Road
Lichfield
Staffordshire WS13 6EF
Telephone: 01543 414555, ext 2131
Fax: 01543 442031
E-mail: rosalyn@libinfo.demon.co.uk
Contact: Mrs Rosalyn Pitt
Objectives and Purposes: The provision of community and mental health care

Stock and Subject Coverage: 1,500 books; 36 periodicals relating to psychology/psychiatry and allied subjects
Services/Facilities: Online and CD-ROM searches; SDI service; current awareness; photocopies
Availability: By prior appointment, for reference use only; free full service to staff
Hours: 09.00-16.30
Related Bodies: Links with Psychiatric Libraries Cooperative Scheme and West Midlands Regional Health Libraries Network

[503]

Preston Acute Hospitals NHS Trust

Acute Divisions Library
Royal Preston Hospital
Sharoe Green Lane
Fulwood
Preston PR2 8HT
Telephone: 01772 710765
Contact: Amanda Beaumont (Librarian)
Objectives and Purposes: To provide an information service to the hospital
Stock and Subject Coverage: 3,125 books; 125 periodicals. Covers medicine; allied health disciplines; management
Services/Facilities: Database searches
Availability: Staff only
Hours: 09.00-17.00 (open until 19.00 on Tuesday)
Publications: Newsletter

[504]

Prince Philip Hospital, Multidisciplinary Library

Llanelli
Carmarthenshire SA14 8QF
Telephone and Fax: 01554 749301
E-mail: leeuwerke@cf.ac.uk or harryk@cf.ac.uk
Contact: Ann Leeuwerke (Librarian); Kathryn Harry (Library Assistant)
Objectives and Purposes: To contribute to the quality of health care by helping NHS staff to make effective use of the knowledge base of health care
Stock and Subject Coverage: 8,300 books; 110 periodicals covering mainly medicine and nursing, but also management and subjects allied to medicine
Services/Facilities: MEDLINE and Cochrane on CD-ROM; videos; multimedia; photocopies
Availability: By subscription
Hours: 08.30-16.30 Monday, Tuesday and Thursday; 08.30-20.00 Wednesday; 08.30-16.00 Friday
Publications: Accessions lists; annual report
Related Bodies: Part of Association of Welsh Health Libraries Network; All Wales Library and Information Extension Services (AWHILES)

[505]

Princess Alexandra Hospital, Postgraduate Medical Library

Parndon Hall
Hamstel Road
Harlow
Essex CM20 1QX
Telephone: 01279 827021
Fax: 01279 445101
E-mail: pamedlib@pamedlib.demon.co.uk
Contact: Mrs B Carter; Mrs J Leary
Objectives and Purposes: To provide library resources to junior doctors in training primarily, but also to other health professionals
Stock and Subject Coverage: 3,000 books; 175 periodicals covering general medicine
Services/Facilities: CD-ROM searches; fax; TV, video, fiche and slide viewing facilities; photocopies; interlibrary loans; literature searches; Internet access
Availability: By appointment, for reference use; telephone and written enquiries accepted
Hours: 09.00–17.00
Related Bodies: Part of North Thames Regional Library Network

[506]

Princess Elizabeth Hospital, Guernsey

Nurse Education Centre Library
Princess Elizabeth Hospital
Guernsey GY4 6UU
Telephone and Fax: 01481 707329
E-mail: pehlibry@guernsey.net
Contact: Valerie Lewington (Librarian)
Objectives and Purposes: To provide library and information services for the Nurse Education Centre and to be a health studies reference resource for all Guernsey people
Stock and Subject Coverage: Material on nursing and allied health subjects; some general medicine
Services/Facilities: Photocopies; literature searches
Availability: By prior appointment, for reference use only; membership available
Hours: 09.00–16.00
Publications: Newsletter; library guide

[507]

Princess Royal Hospital NHS Trust

Apley Castle
Telford TF6 6TF
Telephone: 01952 641222, ext 4440
Fax: 01952 243405
Contact: Ms C Padley (Librarian)
Objectives and Purposes: A multidisciplinary library for staff and students of the Trust, neighbouring Trusts, and health care students at Staffordshire University

Stock and Subject Coverage: 7,500 books; 50 current periodicals. Covers general medicine and health care
Services/Facilities: Photocopies
Availability: By arrangement
Hours: 09.00–17.00 (closes 16.30 on Friday)
Related Bodies: Site library of Staffordshire University

[508]

Progressive Supranuclear Palsy (PSP Europe) Association

The Old Rectory
Wappenham
Nr Towcester
Northamptonshire NN12 8SQ
Telephone: 01327 860342
Fax: 01327 860242
E-mail: 100572.30@compuserve.com
Contact: Maggie Rose (Counsellor); Bigadier Michael Koe (Chief Executive)
Objectives and Purposes: To promote research into progressive supranuclear palsy; to find the cause, effective treatment and eventual care; to promote awareness amongst the medical profession regarding this condition
Stock and Subject Coverage: Material on progressive supranuclear palsy and strategies for handling the disease
Services/Facilities: Computer database; fax; photocopies
Availability: Membership available; Advocacy leaflet freely available
Hours: Any time
Publications: Newsletter (3 per year, by subscription)

[509]

Psionic Medical Society

2 Windrush Close
Bramley
Guildford
Surrey GU5 0BB
Telephone and Fax: 01483 894710
Objectives and Purposes: The Society exists for research into chronic and 'incurable' disease, its prevention, and the advancement of, and training in, methods of diagnosis and treatments, including the homoeopathic, which are known to be free of toxic risk
Stock and Subject Coverage: Leaflets on psionic medicine
Availability: Written information on practitioners of psionic medicine; no visits
Publications: Journal of the Psionic Medical Society and the Institute of Psionic Medicine (yearly)

[510]

Psychiatric Rehabilitation Association (PRA)

Bayford Mews
Bayford Street
London E8 3SF
Telephone: 0181 985 3570
Fax: 0181 986 1334
Contact: The Secretary
Objectives and Purposes: To stimulate psychiatric
    patients towards greater initiative and social
    awareness; also seeks to improve attitudes towards
    the mentally ill, to promote research and to
    encourage a better understanding of the measures
    required to combat mental distress in the
    community
Stock and Subject Coverage: Material on community
    care and the rehabilitation of the mentally ill; also
    tape slide programmes and videos
Availability: Telephone and written enquiries
Hours: 09.00-17.00
Publications: Quarterly newsletter; full list available

[511]

Public Health Laboratory Service (PHLS)

61 Colindale Avenue
London NW9 5HT
Telephone: 0181 200 4400
Fax: 0181 200 7875
E-mail: phslib@demon.co.uk
Contact: Miss MA Clennett (Chief Librarian);
    Miss C Murphy (Head of Press and Publications)
Objectives and Purposes: To support the diagnosis,
    treatment and control of infectious and
    communicable diseases
Stock and Subject Coverage: 9,000 books; 500
    periodicals (220 current); reports, reprints and
    press cuttings covering medical microbiology and
    infectious diseases
Services/Facilities: MEDLINE on CD-ROM; online
    searches; photocopies; fax
Availability: By prior appointment, for reference use
    only for bona fide researchers; telephone and
    written enquiries accepted for quick reference
    enquiries; photocopies to other libraries (charges
    for photocopies, literature searches and extensive
    research)
Hours: 09.30-17.30
Publications: Annual directory; PHLS Microbiology
    Digest (quarterly); Communicable Disease Report
    (weekly); PHLS Library Bulletin (weekly); HIV
    Bulletin (monthly); Food and Environment
    Bulletin - the bulletins are a part of the Library
    Current Awareness service. Full list available on
    request
Related Bodies: 50 laboratories throughout England
    and Wales, mostly in hospitals (none have libraries)

[512]

Queen Elizabeth Hospital for Children

Sir Selwyn Selwyn-Clarke Library
Hackney Road
London E2 8PS
Telephone and Fax: 0171 608 6586
E-mail: cduncan@qeh.compulink.co.uk
Contact: Mr Colin Duncan (Librarian)
Objectives and Purposes: A library and information
    service providing access to literature on all aspects
    of paediatrics
Stock and Subject Coverage: 1,000 books; 82
    periodicals covering paediatrics; child welfare;
    psychology; and psychiatry. Also some coverage of
    immunology; genetics; gastroenterology; and
    family therapy
Services/Facilities: Online and CD-ROM searches;
    current awareness; photocopies
Availability: Telephone and written enquiries from
    other libraries (subject to time constraints)
Hours: 09.00-17.00
Publications: Accessions list; annual report
Related Bodies: Parent body is the Royal Hospitals
    NHS Trust; member of North Thames (East)
    Regional Library Network

[513]

Queen Elizabeth Hospital, Gateshead

Education Centre Library
Sheriff Hill
Gateshead
Tyne and Wear NE9 6SX
Telephone: 0191 487 8989, ext 2103
Fax: 0191 491 4061
Contact: Mrs Susan Austin (Assistant Librarian);
    Mrs Pat Kerr (Senior Library Assistant)
Objectives and Purposes: To provide library and
    information services and educational resources for
    hospital staff and students, and students of the
    University of Northumbria, Faculty of Health,
    Social Work and Education
Stock and Subject Coverage: 12,000 books; 110
    periodicals covering medicine; nursing; and allied
    health subjects. Several nursing/allied health
    indexes and abstracts (hard copy) are held
Services/Facilities: CD-ROM searches (MEDLINE,
    CINAHL); multimedia facilities; interlibrary loans
    (priced); network access to University of
    Newcastle facilities; photocopies (priced)
Availability: By prior appointment, for reference use
    only; external membership by subscription
Hours: 09.00-16.30 (closes 16.00 on Friday)
Related Bodies: University of Northumbria

[514]

Queen Elizabeth Hospital, Neuroscience Library

Nuffield House
Metchley Lane
Edgbaston
Birmingham B15 2TH
Telephone: 0121 472 1311
Fax: 0121 697 8300
E-mail: diane@bnclib.demon.co.uk
Contact: Diane Pritchatt (Librarian)
Objectives and Purposes: To provide a wide range of medical and clinical materials for staff use; to encourage and train staff to use IT; to facilitate postgraduate development and research; to support the staff with an information service
Stock and Subject Coverage: 2,000 books; 1,800 bound journals. Covers neurology; neurosurgery; neuropathology; neurophysiology; neuroimaging; and other neuroscience subjects
Services/Facilities: Online and CD-ROM searches; Internet access; photocopies (services for staff only)
Availability: By prior appointment, for reference use only
Hours: 09.00-17.00
Publications: Newsletter; library handouts

[515]

Queen Elizabeth II Hospital Postgraduate Medical Centre Library, East Hertfordshire NHS Trust (QEII Hospital Library)

Howlands
Welwyn Garden City
Hertfordshire AL7 4HQ
Telephone: 01707 365046/328111, exts 4565/4855
Fax: 01707 390425
E-mail: joan@qeliza.demon.co.uk
Contact: Joan Lomas (Librarian)
Objectives and Purposes: To provide library and information services for hospital staff
Stock and Subject Coverage: 5,000 books; 149 periodicals in a multidisciplinary collection related to the needs of an acute hospital
Services/Facilities: Online and CD-ROM searches; interlibrary loans; current awareness; literature searches; computerised catalogues; photocopies; fax. There is also a nursing library with 2,500 books and 20 periodicals - contact 01707 328111, ext 4387
Availability: Open to medical staff 09.30-17.15; out of hours access for doctors only
Hours: 09.30-17.15
Publications: Library Bulletin; Library Welcome leaflet; Library Databases Guide

[516]

Queen Margaret Hospital, Education Centre

Whitefield Road
Dunfermline
Fife KY12 0SU
Telephone: 01383 623623
Contact: Ms Marie Smith (Librarian); Mrs Isabel Cowan (Secretary)
Objectives and Purposes: To provide library and information services for hospital doctors and GPs
Stock and Subject Coverage: 1,500 books; 60 periodicals covering all aspects of medicine and surgery
Services/Facilities: MEDLINE on CD-ROM; photocopies
Availability: By prior appointment, for reference use only
Hours: 08.30-16.30

[517]

Queen Victoria Hospital Medical Library

Holtye Road
East Grinstead
West Sussex RH19 3DZ
Telephone: 01342 410210
Fax: 01342 317907
Contact: Mrs C Beddard (Librarian)
Objectives and Purposes: To provide information for medical and nursing staff
Stock and Subject Coverage: Books and periodicals on plastic surgery and burns care; maxillofacial surgery; ophthalmic surgery; and nursing
Services/Facilities: MEDLINE and NMI on CD-ROM; photocopies (priced)
Availability: Telephone and written enquiries; no visits possible
Hours: 09.00-17.00 (closes 13.00 on Thursday and Friday)

[518]

Queen's University of Belfast Medical Library

Institute of Clinical Science
Grosvenor Road
Belfast BT12 6BJ
Telephone: 01232 321487
Fax: 01232 247068
Contact: Richard Kimber (Medical Librarian)
Objectives and Purposes: To provide library and information services for the Faculty of Medicine
Stock and Subject Coverage: Collections covering medicine, nursing, social services, health management, and subjects related to medicine
Services/Facilities: Usual library facilities
Availability: Members of the university and NHS staff in Northern Ireland

Hours: 09.00-22.00; 09.00-12.30 Saturday
Related Bodies: This library is the central library of the Northern Ireland Health and Social Services Library

[519]
Radcliffe Science Library (RSL)

Parks Road
Oxford OX1 3QP
Telephone: 01865 272800
Fax: 01865 272821
E-mail: rsl.enquiries@bodley.ox.ac.uk
World Wide Web: http://www.bodley.ox.ac.uk
Contact: Dr P Leggate (Keeper of Scientific Books); Miss Y Hibbott (Medical Librarian)
Objectives and Purposes: The main scientific reference and research library of the University of Oxford. As a department of the Bodleian it receives material by legal deposit
Stock and Subject Coverage: 760,000 volumes; 32,000 periodicals (5,000 current) covering medicine; life sciences; and other scientific subjects
Services/Facilities: Photocopies; online and CD-ROM searches; microfiche reader/printer
Availability: By appointment, for bona fide researchers, through the Admissions Office (01865 270208); telephone and written enquiries accepted
Hours: 09.00-22.00 (termtime); 09.00-13.00 Saturday. Shorter hours in vacations
Related Bodies: Bodleian Library

[520]
Radionic Association Ltd (RA)

Baerlein House
Goose Green
Deddington
Banbury
Oxfordshire OX15 0SZ
Telephone and Fax: 01869 338852
Contact: Mrs P Golby (Secretary); Mrs C Lyons (Assistant Secretary)
Objectives and Purposes: A professional body repesenting its practising and lay members; it provides training through its School and promotes research into the efficacy of radionics; aims to raise public awareness and to disseminate information worldwide
Stock and Subject Coverage: Material on radionics and allied subjects (NB The library is not located at the Secretariat)
Availability: Library list available from the Librarian; telephone and written enquiries accepted
Hours: 09.30-13.30
Publications: Radionic Journal (2 per year); Register of Radionic Practitioners
Related Bodies: The School of Radionics; The Healing Education Trust

[521]
Randall Institute

26-29 Drury Lane
London WC2B 5RL
Telephone: 0171 465 5318
Fax: 0171 497 9078
E-mail: enid.kishna@kcl.ac.uk
World Wide Web: http://www.kcl.ac.uk/
Contact: Enid Kishna (Librarian)
Objectives and Purposes: An interdisciplinary biomedical research institute. It houses the Medical Research Council Muscle & Cell Motility Unit. The research interests are developmental biology; muscle and cell motility; and molecular structure
Stock and Subject Coverage: 131 periodicals and a small book collection
Services/Facilities: Photocopies
Availability: Telephone and written enquiries accepted; visits by prior appointment, for reference use only
Hours: 09.30-17.00
Publications: Medical Research Council newsletter; annual report
Related Bodies: Part of King's College, London

[522]
Raynaud's and Scleroderma Association

112 Crewe Road
Alsager
Cheshire ST7 2JA
Telephone: 01270 872776
Fax: 01270 883556
Contact: Mrs Anne Mawdsley MBE (Director); Mrs Diane Davies (Secretary); Mrs Jan Scott (Public Relations)
Objectives and Purposes: Aims to help sufferers of Raynaud's Disease and scleroderma by offering advice and information, facilitating communication between doctors and patients, and funding research
Stock and Subject Coverage: Range of patient literature on Raynaud's Disease and scleroderma
Services/Facilities: Free information to sufferers and their families/carers; fax; photocopies
Availability: Telephone and written enquiries
Hours: 09.00-17.00 (answerphone out of hours)
Publications: Quarterly newsletter; annual report. List available on request

[523]
Reach – The Association for Children with Hand or Arm Deficiency

12 Wilson Way
Earls Barton
Northamptonshire NN6 0NZ
Telephone and Fax: 01604 811041
Contact: Mrs Sue Stokes (National Co-ordinator); Mr Nigel Tarrant (Chairman - 0181 296 9966)

Objectives and Purposes: To provide contact and support for families with children having any form of hand or arm deficiency

Services/Facilities: Facilitating contact between families with children who have matching disabilities; help and advice about any aspects of upper limb deficiency; local group meetings organised; insurance cover for a child's "good arm" is provided as part of membership

Availability: Telephone and written enquiries; enquiries from professionals are welcomed

Hours: 24 hours

Publications: Within Reach (quarterly newsletter); factsheets; video

[524]
Redbridge Medical Library

King George Hospital
Barley Lane
Goodmayes
Essex IG3 8YB
Telephone: 0181 970 8239
Fax: 0181 970 8269
Contact: Ms HA Jackson (District Librarian)
Stock and Subject Coverage: Materials on medicine; psychiatry; health care management; general practice. Incorporates the Goodmayes Hospital Postgraduate Medical Centre library and the Barking Hospital collection
Services/Facilities: Online and CD-ROM searches; photocopies
Availability: Each request judged on its merits; charges for some services
Hours: 09.30–18.00

[525]
Restricted Growth Association (RGA)

PO Box 8
Countesthorpe
Leicester LE8 5ZS
Telephone and Fax: 0116 247 8913
Contact: Mrs Honor Rawlings (National Development Officer)
Objectives and Purposes: To remove the substantial social barriers experienced by individuals of restricted growth; to improve the quality of life and help to alleviate the fear and distress experienced by families when a child of restricted growth is born; to provide information on various aspects of day-to-day living, as well as social contact, mutual counselling, meetings and newsletters
Stock and Subject Coverage: Up-to-date information on limb lengthening procedures. Material on genetics; orthopaedics; obstetrics and gynaecology; weight problems and anaesthesia
Services/Facilities: Information to members and families; networking of family support
Availability: Telephone and written enquiries accepted
Hours: 09.00–17.00

Publications: Layman's Guide to Restricted Growth; Coping with Restricted Growth; newsletter; various information pamphlets

[526]
Richmond Twickenham & Roehampton Healthcare NHS Trust (RTR Healthcare NHS Trust or Queen Mary's, Roehampton)

Queen Mary's University Hospital
Roehampton Lane
London, SW15 5PN
Telephone: 0181 355 2093
Fax: 0181 355 2856
E-mail: halper@qmpgmc.ac.uk
Contact: Mrs Helen Alper (Librarian)
Objectives and Purposes: To contribute to the quality of health care by helping all NHS staff make effective use of the evidence base of health care. The Library supports: the continuing education of all staff; clinical practice; research; management; quality assurance and medical audit
Stock and Subject Coverage: Books and journals on all clinical specialities. Special collections: Burns, Plastic Surgery, Oral Surgery, Bioengineering and Rehabilitation. Also, a collection of photographs of the history of Queen Mary's, Roehampton
Services/Facilities: Self-service photocopying (after buying a card); online searching (free for Trust staff, charges for other customers); CD-ROM databases available for own searches; fax machine (at cost)
Availability: Open to members of RTR Trust, and other NHS staff on proof of identity. Others by arrangement. External users may pay to become members. All services are free to Trust staff, others may be charged for certain services. Enquiries are accepted by telephone, fax or letter
Hours: 09.00–17.00
Related Bodies: Part of South Thames Regional Library Servic

[527]
Royal Association for Disability and Rehabilitation (RADAR)

12 City Forum
250 City Road
London EC1V 8AF
Telephone: 0171 250 3222; Minicom: 0171 250 4119
Fax: 0171 250 0212
Contact: Information Department
Objectives and Purposes: A campaigning and advisory disability charity
Stock and Subject Coverage: Not a library, but RADAR produces ca. 100 publications connected with disability
Availability: Telephone and written enquiries to the Information Department; publications available for purchase only

Hours: Information Department lines open
10.00–16.00
Publications: Extensive range – list available
Related Bodies: RADAR is an umbrella body with
around 500 affiliated groups around the country

[528]

Royal Berkshire and Battle Hospitals NHS Trust (RBH)

Postgraduate Centre
Royal Berkshire Hospital
London Road
Reading RG1 5AN
Telephone: 0118 987 7848/7849
Fax: 0118 987 7032
Contact: Enid Forsyth (Library Manager);
Rachel McErlane (Deputy Librarian); Jill Duncan
(Assistant Librarian)
Objectives and Purposes: The provision of a clinical
and managerial library service for all Trust staff
Stock and Subject Coverage: 3,000 books; 150
periodicals covering acute medicine; health care
administration; and management
Services/Facilities: Online and CD-ROM searches;
fax; photocopies; networked MEDLINE and
CINAHL available across the site
Availability: Public may use reference facilities, by
prior appointment
Hours: 09.00–17.00
Related Bodies: Branches at Battle Hospital and the
Royal Berkshire Hospital Maternity Unit

[529]

Royal Bournemouth Hospital Library

Education Centre
Royal Bournemouth Hospital
Castle Lane East
Bournemouth BH7 7DW
Telephone: 01202 704270
Fax: 01202 704269
Contact: Mr JB Gill (Principal Librarian);
Ms S Dorey (Librarian)
Objectives and Purposes: To provide library and
information services to NHS staff and students in
East Dorset to support their work
Stock and Subject Coverage: 10,000 books; 150
periodicals. Covers medicine; nursing; and related
health care professions
Services/Facilities: CD-ROM searches; fax;
photocopies
Availability: By prior appointment, for reference use
only
Hours: 08.30–17.00
Publications: Annual journal holdings list
Related Bodies: Poole Hospital Library

[530]

Royal College of Anaesthetists (RCA)

48–49 Russell Square
London WC1B 4JY
Telephone: 0171 813 1900
Fax: 0171 813 1876
Contact: Sir Geoffrey de Deney (Chief Executive);
Mrs AM Jones (Director, Collegiate Affairs)
Objectives and Purposes: The examination body for
the speciality of anaesthetics, the College monitors
anaesthetic training and seeks to ensure that the
quality of service offered to patients is of the
highest standard. The principal aim of the College
is to further the science and art of anaesthetics and
to maintain standards
Hours: 09.00–17.30
Publications: Quarterly newsletter; annual report

[531]

Royal College of General Practitioners (RCGP)

Information Services Section
14 Prince's Gate
Hyde Park
London SW7 1PH
Telephone: 0171 581 3232
Fax: 0171 225 3047
E-mail: grichardson@rcgp.org.uk
World Wide Web: http://www.rcgp.org.uk
Contact: GM Richardson (Senior Information
Manager); V Whelan (Information Officer –
Enquiries); S Armstrong-Young (Librarian)
Objectives and Purposes: The promulgation of
education, research and quality in general practice.
Information Services provides the information
support for these objectives
Stock and Subject Coverage: 5,000 books; 400
periodicals covering general practice and primary
health care in the UK and abroad
Services/Facilities: Online and CD-ROM searches;
enquiry service; literature searches; photocopies
(all services priced)
Availability: By prior appointment, for reference use
only; telephone and written enquiries accepted,
but priority is given to members
Hours: 09.00–17.00
Publications: Information sheets; new books list;
serials holdings list

[532]

Royal College of Midwives (RCM)

15 Mansfield Street
London W1M 0BE
Telephone: 0171 872 5160
Fax: 0171 872 5101
Contact: Miss J Ions (Senior Library Assistant);
Miss L Moss (Secretary)
Objectives and Purposes: To further the art and science
of midwifery

Stock and Subject Coverage: 6,700 books; 2,000 official reports; 63 current periodicals; covering midwifery and related subjects; some microfiche items; Marion Rabl Collection

Services/Facilities: Bibliographic services; photocopies

Availability: By prior appointment, for reference use only; fees charged for bibliographies and photocopies

Hours: 09.30-12.30 and 14.00-16.45

Publications: Midwifery Index

[533]
Royal College of Nursing (RCN)

20 Cavendish Square
London W1M 0AB

Telephone: 0171 409 3333

Fax: 0171 491 3859

Contact: Library Information Desk; Tony Shepherd (Senior Librarian)

Objectives and Purposes: To promote the art and science of nursing. The library service supports the College and is the largest nursing library in Europe

Stock and Subject Coverage: Material on nursing and allied subjects plus related topics including psychology; sociology; management; and education. The Steinberg Collection of nursing research

Services/Facilities: Photocopies; CD-RTOM searches; internal database

Availability: By prior arrangement (requests in writing in the first instance)

Hours: 08.30-19.00 (10.00-19.00 on Wednesday). Vacations: 08.30-18.00

Publications: Nursing Bibliography (monthly); RCN Nurse Rom (CD-ROM)

Related Bodies: RCN Archives available to members at RCN Board Offices Site Library in Edinburgh (0131 662 1010) and RCN Belfast (01232 668236)

[534]
Royal College of Obstetricians and Gynaecologists (RCOG)

27 Sussex Place
Regents Park
London NW1 4RG

Telephone: 0171 772 6309

Fax: 0171 262 8331

Contact: Miss Patricia Want (Head of Library Services)

E-mail: librarian@rcog.org.uk

Objectives and Purposes: The encouragement of the study and the advancement of the science and practice of obstetrics and gynaecology

Stock and Subject Coverage: Extensive collection on obstetrics; gynaecology; and closely related subjects. Includes a rare books collection

Services/Facilities: Online and CD-ROM searches; fax; photocopies

Availability: By prior appointment, for reference use only; charges apply

Hours: 10.00-17.00

[535]
Royal College of Paediatrics and Child Health (RCPCH) (formerly British Paediatric Association)

5 St Andrew's Place
Regents Park
London NW1 4LB

Telephone: 0171 486 6151

Fax: 0171 486 6009

Contact: Miss P Davies (Publications Officer); James Kempton (Secretary)

Objectives and Purposes: To advance the art and science of paediatrics; to raise the standards of children's medical care; to advance the education of the public and medical practitioners in child health

Stock and Subject Coverage: 300 books; 500 pamphlets; 500 government documents; 100 periodicals; various reports and memoranda. Covers all areas related to paediatrics and child health

Availability: Telephone and written enquiries accepted; visits restricted

Hours: 09.00-17.00

Publications: Newsletter (4 per year); Archives of Disease in Childhood (monthly); yearly handbook; annual report

Related Bodies: 21 paediatric speciality groups are affiliated; details on request

[536]
Royal College of Physicians and Surgeons of Glasgow (RCPSG)

232-242 St Vincent Street
Glasgow G2 5RJ

Telephone: 0141 221 6072, ext 204

Fax: 0141 221 1804

E-mail: rcpsg@enterprise.net

Contact: James Beaton (Librarian); Carol Parry (Archivist)

Objectives and Purposes: Standard setting in medicine, surgery and dental surgery. The library itself dates to 1698, and is an important resource in the field of medical hsitory

Stock and Subject Coverage: Material on medicine, surgery and dentistry, history of medicine. Also a large archive, including papers of Sir William Macewen, Dr William Mackenzie and 50% of the papers of Sir Ronald Ross. Also minute books of Glasgow Medic-Chirurgical Society and various other medical societies

Services/Facilities: Photocopying; online searches

Availability: All registered doctors and dentists, as well as bona fide researchers. Personal visits welcome. Material for reference only. Charges made for photocopying, and ILL

Hours: 09.00-17.00

Publications: Annual report

[537]

Royal College of Physicians of Edinburgh (RCPEd)

9 Queen Street
Edinburgh EH2 1JQ
Telephone: 0131 225 7324
Fax: 0131 220 3939
E-mail: "name"@rcgp.ac.uk
Contact: Iain Milne (Librarian); Mr Robin Harbour
(Information Librarian)
Objectives and Purposes: To promote the highest
standards of medical practice in internal medicine
and related specialties; the Library exists to
support the College's role
Stock and Subject Coverage: 50,000 books on all
aspects of medicine, plus 1,100 periodicals and
1,000 manuscripts. Some material dates back to
the founding of the Library in 1681. All major
aspects of medicine and medical history are
covered
Services/Facilities: Online searches; photocopies;
interlibrary loans; current awareness; bibliographic
checking; historical and biographical searches
Availability: Available by appointment to bona fide
researchers
Hours: 09.00-17.00
Publications: List available

[538]

Royal College of Physicians of London (RCP)

11 St Andrew's Place
London NW1 4LE
Telephone: 0171 935 1174
Fax: 0171 487 5218
Contact: J Beckwith (Assistant Librarian - 1st contact);
G Davenport (Librarian); G Yeo (Archivist)
Objectives and Purposes: To sustain standards of
medical practice by promoting medical education
and research
Stock and Subject Coverage: General medical
collection; special History of Medicine collection;
Library of the Marquis of Dorchester (1606-80,
ca. 3,400 volumes); Evan Bedford Library of
Cardiology, 1971 (1,000+ items)
Services/Facilities: Online searches; photocopies
Availability: By prior appointment, for reference use
only for bona fide researchers; telephone and
written enquiries (priced)
Hours: 09.30-17.30
Publications: Evan Bedford Library of Cardiology
catalogue

[539]

Royal College of Psychiatrists (RCPsych)

17 Belgrave Square
London SW1X 8PG
Telephone: 0171 235 2351
Fax: 0171 245 1231
World Wide Web: http://www.demon.co.uk/rcpsych

Contact: EM Noakes (Librarian);
M Harcourt-Williams (Archivist)
Objectives and Purposes: To advance the science and
practice of psychiatry, to further public education
therein, to promote study and research into
psychiatry and all sciences and disciplines
connected with the understanding and treatment
of mental disorder
Stock and Subject Coverage: 7,500 books; 100
periodicals covering all aspects of psychiatry,
including the history of psychiatry
Services/Facilities: In-house database of College
policies; CD-ROM searches; photocopies
Availability: By prior appointment, for reference use
only; some services subject to charge
Hours: 09.30-16.30
Publications: List of Books Suitable for a Psychiatric
Library; Reading List for Trainees: Basic Sciences;
Reading List for Trainees: General Psychiatry;
Psychiatric Instruments and Rating Scales: a Select
Bibliography; Index to Statements, Guidelines and
Policy Documents of the College

[540]

Royal College of Surgeons of Edinburgh (RCSEd)

Nicolson Street
Edinburgh EH8 9DW
Telephone: 0131 527 1600
Fax: 0131 557 6406
E-mail: library@ercsed.ac.uk
World Wide Web: http://www.rcsed.ac.uk
Contact: Ms M Smith (College Librarian);
Miss G Johnstone (Assistant Librarian);
Miss AM Stevenson
Objectives and Purposes: The training, examination
and continuing professional education and
development of surgeons in the UK and overseas
Stock and Subject Coverage: Material on surgery, the
history of medicine and surgery - especially in
Scotland, and medical biography
Services/Facilities: Online and CD-ROM searches
(MEDLINE); interlibrary loans; history of medicine
and medical biography enquiries; photocopies; fax;
manufacture of slides for presentations
Availability: Mainly members only; Fellows of other
Royal Colleges may use the Library on a
reciprocal basis; other bona fide researchers by
prior appointment only
Hours: 09.00-17.00
Publications: Journal of the Royal College of
Surgeons of Edinburgh (bi-monthly); List of
Fellows; annual report

[541]

Royal College of Surgeons of England (RCSEng)

35-43 Lincoln's Inn Fields
London WC2A 3PN
Telephone: Direct: 0171 973 2137; College:
0171 405 3473
Fax: 0171 405 4438

E-mail: Library@rcseng.ac.uk

World Wide Web: http://www.rcseng.ac.uk

Contact: Mr IF Lyle (Librarian); Tina Craig (Deputy Librarian)

Objectives and Purposes: The advancement of surgery and the maintenance of standards of surgical care

Stock and Subject Coverage: Holdings include ca. 60,000 books and 3,000 journals (400 current) on all aspects of clinical surgery including surgical specialities and dental surgery; also anatomy, physiology and pathology. Medical biography and the history of medicine are widely collected. The large historical collection includes 57 items of incunabula. Special collections which consist of printed books, manuscripts and autograph letters include the Hunter-Baillie collection (1,500 items); John Hunter – his contemporaries and pupils (1,100); Lord Lister (250); Richard Owen (750); and Arthur Keith (300). Added to this are ca. 3,000 engraved portraits, 2,000 bookplates and 150 medals. The Library provides a photographic service based on the College's paintings and sculptures and its own holdings

Services/Facilities: Library catalogue from 1975 on Unicorn Library Management System; Current periodicals listed on the Library's Web page; MEDLINE on Silver Platter; photocopies; faxes; interlibrary loans; literature searches; historical enquiries

Availability: Open to bona fide researchers provided a prior appointment is made. The material is for reference use only. Charges are made for photocopies and faxes and there is a scale of charges for genealogical enquiries

Hours: 09.00-18.00

Publications: List of current periodicals; English books before 1701 in the Library of the RCS; Lives of the Fellows of the Royal College of Surgeons

[542]

Royal College of Surgeons of England, Faculty of Dental Surgery (FDS)

35-43 Lincoln's Inn Fields
London WC2 3PN

Telephone: 0171 405 3474

Fax: 0171 973 2183

E-mail: fds@rcseng.ac.uk

Contact: Mr Albert de Looze (Secretary)

Objectives and Purposes: A postgraduate training and examining body whose function is to promote high standards of practice and to advance the art and science of dental surgery

Stock and Subject Coverage: Books from pre-1800 onwards on the surgical and dental sciences

Availability: Telephone and written enquiries for fellows and members

Hours: 08.00-17.30

Publications: Bi-monthly newsletter; annual report

Related Bodies: Sister faculties in Ireland, Edinburgh and Glasgow

[543]

Royal College of Surgeons of England, Lumley Study Centre

35-43 Lincoln's Inn Fields
London WC2A 3PN

Telephone: Direct line: 0171 973 2109

Fax: 0171 973 2117

E-mail: lumley@rseng.ac.uk,

World Wide Web: http://www.rcseng.ac.uk

Contact: Mrs Leonie Jones (Lumley Librarian); Mr Don Liu (Lumley Assistant Librarian)

Objectives and Purposes: The Lumley Study Centre is a facility for multimedia teaching and educational resources in surgery and dentistry encompassing current books and journals as well as audio-visual material and computer assisted learning programs

Stock and subject coverage: Educational resources and materials in the fields of surgery and dentistry. Current books and journals published within the last ten years. Computer assisted learning and multimedia programs. Audiovisual programs illustrating basic sciences and techniques in surgical practice

Services/Facilities: MEDLINE network and access to Internet; photocopies

Availability: Facilities and services are available to Diplomates of the College, including the Faculty of Dental Surgery and the Faculty of General Dental Practitioners. Participants registered on RCSEng courses and those undertaking independent self-directed study in surgery and dentistry. Researchers with professional interest requiring information in surgery and dentistry

Hours: 09.00-17.00

Publications: Lumley Study Centre brochure; Audiovisual Catalogue; Multimedia Catalogue

[544]

Royal Cornwall Hospitals Trust

Medical Library
Cornwall Postgraduate Centre
RCH Treliske
Truro TR1 3LJ

Telephone: 01872 252610

Fax: 01872 78469

Contact: Mrs P Kitch (Librarian); Mrs S Richards (Senior Library Assistant)

Objectives and Purposes: To support education, training, clinical practice, management and research of health care practitioners in the district

Stock and Subject Coverage: 6,800 books; 190 periodicals; videos and CD-ROMs. Covers all aspects of medicine and health care

Services/Facilities: Online and CD-ROM searches; fax; Internet access; photocopies

Availability: By prior appointment, for reference use only

Hours: 09.00-17.30

Publications: Guide to services; journals holdings list; monthly bulletin

[545]
Royal Defence Medical College (RDMC)

Millbank
London SW1P 4RJ
Telephone: 0171 414 8230
Fax: 0171 414 8235
E-mail: library@milmed.demon.co.uk
Contact: Ms Joanne O'Brien (College Librarian)
Objectives and Purposes: Training of, and clinical
    support to, Defence Medical Services (DMS) staff
Stock and Subject Coverage: Current clinical material
Services/Facilities: Online searches for DMS staff
    only; fax and photocopies on reciprocal basis
    against BLDSC forms
Availability: By prior appointment, for reference use
    only; access is restricted, but telephone and
    written enquiries are accepted
Hours: 09.00–16.30
Publications: Journal

[546]
Royal Free Hospital School of Medicine, Medical Library

Rowland Hill Street
London NW3 2PF
Telephone: 0171 794 0500, exts 3201 (Librarian) or
    3203 (Enquiries)
Fax: 0171 794 3534
E-mail: fletcher@rfhsm.ac.uk
Contact: Ann Hobbs (Librarian); Betsy Anagnostelis
    and Pauline Summers (Assistant Librarians)
Objectives and Purposes: To support undergraduate
    and postgraduate medical education and medical
    research
Stock and Subject Coverage: 20,000 books; 400 current
    periodicals covering general medicine; special
    Psychiatry/Psychology Collection (the greater
    part of the former Friern Hospital Academic
    Centre Library)
Services/Facilities: Online searches (priced); mediated
    literature searches (priced); interlibrary loans
    (priced); current awareness (priced); bibliographic
    database advice; photocopies (priced); fax for
    urgent requests (priced)
Availability: By prior appointment, for reference use
    only for bona fide researchers; full membership
    restricted to staff and local health authority
    employees
Hours: 09.00–19.00; 09.00–13.00 Saturday
Publications: Guides to individual services;
    newsletters; journals holdings lists; annual report
Related Bodies: Part of the University of London

[547]
Royal Institute of Public Health and Hygiene (RIPHH)

28 Portland Place
London W1N 4DE
Telephone: 0171 580 2731
Fax: 0171 580 6157
E-mail: riphh@pobox.com
Contact: Grp Capt Roger Smith (Secretary);
    Mrs WA Moore (Deputy Secretary – Business);
    Mr P Bartlett (Information Officer – for enquiries)
Objectives and Purposes: An active educational,
    standard-setting and examining body concerned
    to advance the cause of health and hygiene across
    the complete spectrum of age in the settings of
    home, school, work and leisure
Stock and Subject Coverage: Small collection of
    general public health publications and Institute
    archives
Availability: By prior arrangement only
Hours: 08.30–16.30
Publications: Health and Hygiene (quarterly journal);
    Health Notes (members newsletter); Handbook
    (annual); Mortuary Practice and Safety: Handbook
    for Anatomical Pathology Technicians

[548]
Royal Liverpool and Broadgreen University Hospitals NHS Trust (RLBUH)

Library
Postgraduate Medical Centre
Royal Liverpool and Broadgreen University
Hospital
Thomas Drive
Liverpool L14 3LB
Telephone: 0151 282 6447
Fax: 0151 220 1618
Contact: Miss Julie E McKie BA (Librarian)
Objectives and Purposes: To provide a service which
    meets the information needs of PGMC members
    and to encourage the effective use of information
    by anyone interested in health care
Stock and Subject Coverage: 6,000 books; 77 journals;
    videos; multimedia. Covers medicine; nursing;
    management; geriatrics; paediatrics; psychiatry;
    sociology; cardiology; nervous system;
    gastroenterology; and orthopaedics
Services/Facilities: Online and CD-ROM searches;
    interlibrary loans; word processing; offprints
    collection; literature searches
Availability: Telephone and written enquiries
    accepted; associate membership avilable for a fee
Hours: 08.30–20.00; 09.30–12.00 Saturday
Related Bodies: Staff library on Royal site of RLBUH

[549]

*Royal National Institute for Deaf People (RNID)

330-332 Gray's Inn Road
London WC1X 8EE
Telephone: 0171 915 1553 (voice);
    Minicom: 0171 915 1443
Contact: Mary Plackett (Library Development
    Manager)
Objectives and Purposes: To enable deaf, hard of
    hearing and deaf/blind people to exercise their
    right to full citizenship and to enjoy equal
    opportunities. It does this by increasing awareness
    and understanding of deafness and deaf people,
    and campaigning to remove prejudice and
    discrimination by raising issues and promoting
    debate in the press, media and in Parliament
Stock and Subject Coverage: 10,000 books; 300
    periodicals covering human communication
    disorders
Services/Facilities: Reference facilities; photocopies;
    interlibrary loans
Availability: Freely available
Hours: 10:00-13.00 and 14.00-18.00

[550]

Royal National Institute for Deaf People (Scotland) (RNID Scotland)

9 Clairmont Gardens
Glasgow G3 7LW
Telephone: 0141 332 0343; Minicom: 0141 332 5023
Fax: 0141 296 8199
Contact: Dorothy Davidson (Information Officer)
Objectives and Purposes: To enable deaf, hard of
    hearing and deaf/blind people to exercise their
    right to full citizenship and to enjoy equal
    opportunities. It does this by increasing awareness
    and understanding of deafness and deaf people,
    and campaigning to remove prejudice and
    discrimination by raising issues and promoting
    debate in the press, media and in Parliament
Stock and Subject Coverage: RNID has a library in
    London
Services/Facilities: RNID Scotland provides a range of
    quality services for deaf people and those who
    work with them. These include: information;
    residential care; communication support and
    training
Hours: 09.00-17.00 (closes 16.30 on Friday)
Publications: Range of publications/factsheets - list
    available
Related Bodies: Head office in London; this is a
    regional office

[551]

Royal National Institute for the Blind (RNIB)

Resource Centre
224 Great Portland Street
London W1N 6AA
Telephone: 0171 388 1266
Fax: 0171 388 2034
E-mail: (name)@rnib.org.uk
Contact: Erika Jenkins
Objectives and Purposes: RNIB wants a world in
    which blind and partially sighted people enjoy the
    same rights, freedoms and responsibilities and
    quality of life as people who are fully sighted. Our
    task is to challenge blindness. We challenge the
    disabling effects of blindness by providing services
    to help people determine their own lives. We
    challenge society's actions, attitudes and
    assumptions. Many barriers are put in the path of
    blind or partially sighted people - our task is to
    dismantle them. And we challenge the underlying
    causes of blindness by helping to prevent, cure or
    alleviate it
Stock and Subject Coverage: A reference library with
    material on all aspects of blindness, visual
    impairment and associated subjects
Services/Facilities: The Resource Centre handles
    enquiries on benefit rights, education,
    employment, leisure, services for local societies,
    health, social and environmental services, multiple
    disability and physiotherapy support
Availability: Telephone and written enquiries
    accepted; visits by arrangement
Hours: 09.00-17.15
Related Bodies: RNIB Peterborough (PO Box 173,
    Peterborough PE2 6WS; 01733 370777); RNIB
    Scotland (10 Magdala Crescent, Edinburgh
    EH12 5BE; 0131 313 1498); RNIB Resource
    Centre Stirling (9 Viewfield Place, Stirling
    FK8 1NL; 01786 451752); RNIB Northern
    Ireland Service Bureau (40 Linenhall Street,
    Belfast BT2 8BG; 01232 329373)

Royal National Orthopaedic Hospital Trust

see **Stop Press on page 156**

[552]

Royal Oldham Hospital

Education Centre
Rochdale Road
Oldham OL1 2JH
Telephone: 0161 627 8463
Fax: 0161 627 8462
Contact: BA Foster (Librarian)
Objectives and Purposes: To provide a
    multidisciplinary library service to hospital staff
Stock and Subject Coverage: 4,000 books; 80 journals.
    Covers all aspects of medicine

Services/Facilities: MEDLINE searches; Internet access; photocopies; interlibrary loans; current awareness
Availability: By prior appointment, for reference use only; telephone and written enquiries accepted
Hours: 09.00-17.00
Publications: Newsletter; acquisitions list

[553]

*Royal Orthopaedic Hospital

Research and Teaching Centre
Woodlands
Northfield
Birmingham B31 2AP
Telephone: 0121 627 1627
Contact: Mrs JM Dawson (Librarian)
Objectives and Purposes: To provide information for research and teaching of orthopaedics, and related materials to trainees on the regional teaching programme and other interested staff and students working in the field of orthopaedics
Stock and Subject Coverage: 800 books; 60 periodicals covering all aspects of orthopaedics and some general medicine. Special archive of the history of the hospital
Services/Facilities: Online searches; current awareness; photocopies; fax
Availability: By prior appointment, for reference use only; telephone and written enquiries and personal visits are accepted; charges for some services
Hours: 08.30-18.00 (some flexibility is possible by arrangement)

[554]

Royal Pharmaceutical Society of Great Britain (RPSGB)

1 Lambeth High Street
London SE1 7JN
Telephone: 0171 735 9141
Fax: 0171 793 0232
E-mail: info.rpsgb@dial.pipex.com
Contact: Roy Allcorn (Manager, Information Centre); Roddy Morrison (Librarian); Austin Gibbons (Senior Information Pharmacist)
Objectives and Purposes: Professional and statutory body for practising pharmacists
Stock and Subject Coverage: 60,000 books; 400 periodicals. Covers pharmacy practice; pharmaceutics; therapeutics; drug actions, interactions and adverse effects; medicinal botany; herbal medicine; pharmacopeias and proprietary books (worldwide). Historical collection of herbals (many hand coloured)
Services/Facilities: Photocopies; online, Internet and CD-ROM searches; in-house database available
Availability: Available to members, pre-registration candidates and pharmacy students. Other bona fide researchers on payment of a fee. Loans to members only. Some services priced

Hours: 09.00-17.00 (10.00-17.45 on Thursday)
Publications: Monthly acquisitions bulletin and journal holdings list. Society catalogue of publications available on request

[555]

Royal Pharmaceutical Society of Great Britain (Scottish Department)

36 York Place
Edinburgh EH1 3HU
Telephone: 0131 556 4386
Fax: 0131 558 8850
E-mail: 101561.2226@compuserve.com
Contact: Mrs D Barker (Library Assistant); Dr LC Howden (Assistant Secretary)
Objectives and Purposes: A professional and statutory body for pharmacists and pharmacy
Stock and Subject Coverage: Books and periodicals covering pharmacology; toxicology; chemistry; botany; and the history of pharmacy. Historical collection of rare, illustrated botanical works, pharmacopoeias and herbals
Services: Photocopies (priced); fax; CD-ROMs
Availability: Telephone and written enquiries
Hours: 09.00-13.00 and 14.00-17.00
Related Bodies: Royal Pharmaceutical Society of Great Britain (in London)

[556]

Royal Society for the Prevention of Accidents (RoSPA)

Edgbaston Park
353 Bristol Road
Birmingham B5 7ST
Telephone: 0121 248 2000
Fax: 0121 248 2001
Contact: The Librarian
Objectives and Purposes: To enhance the quality of life by exercising power and influence for accident prevention
Stock and Subject Coverage: Material on occupational health and safety; food safety; safety education; water and leisure; home safety; and road safety
Services/Facilities: CD-ROM searches; literature searches; photocopies; fax
Availability: By prior appointment, for reference use only
Hours: 09.00-17.00
Publications: RoSPA Bulletin; Occupational Safety and Health; Water and Leisure; Safety Education; Staying Alive; Care on the Road. Full list available on request

[557]

Royal Society of Chemistry Library and Information Centre (RSC)

Burlington House
Piccadilly
London W1V 0BN
Telephone: 0171 437 8656
Fax: 0171 287 9798
E-mail: library@rsc.org
World Wide Web:
  http://chemistry.rsc.org/rsc/library.htm
Contact: Peter Hoey (Librarian); Nigel Lees (Senior Marketing Officer); Ron Hudson (Information Scientist); Nicola Best (Senior Library Assistant)
Objectives and Purposes: To provide a comprehensive chemical information service to members and the chemical community at large
Stock and Subject Coverage: Principally chemistry and related subjects, but includes biochemistry; medicinal chemistry; toxicology; health aspects of chemicals; pharmaceutical chemistry; biotechnology; health and safety. There is an excellent collection of 16th-19th century historical chemical books, including some medicinal texts
Services/Facilities: Online and CD-ROM searches; microfiche/microfilm reader printers; photocopies (preferential rates for members and subscribers)
Availability: Free access for members; others admitted with a letter of introduction from a member or head of department; a day charge may apply
Hours: 09.30-17.30
Publications: Quarterly list of new accessions; periodicals holdings (annual)

[558]

Royal Society of Medicine Library (RSM)

1 Wimpole Street
London W1M 8AE
Telephone: 0171 290 2940
Fax: 0171 290 2939
E-mail: library@roysocmed.ac.uk
Contact: David WC Stewart (Director of Information Services - Tel: 0171 290 2931; Fax: 0171 290 2978)
Objectives and Purposes: To offer a postgraduate research information service in biomedicine
Stock and Subject Coverage: 100,000 books; 10,000 periodicals (2,000 current) covering all fields of medicine. Extensive historical collections
Services/Facilities: Database searches; loans to members only; photocopies: fax
Availability: Members only, but short-term (one day, one week or one month) library membership can be arranged (for a fee)
Hours: 09.00-20.30; 10.00-17.00 Saturday
Publications: Current Medical Literature (20+ subject titles); Journal of the Royal Society of Medicine

[559]

Royal Society of Tropical Medicine and Hygiene

26 Portland Place
London W1N 4EY
Telephone: 0171 580 2127
Fax: 0171 436 1389
Contact: The Administrator
Objectives and Purposes: The objectives of the Society are to promote health and to advance the study, control and prevention of disease in man and animals in warm climates; to facilitate discussion and the exchange of information among those who are interested in tropical diseases, and generally to promote the work of those interested in these objectives
Availability: No library or information service. Written queries may be forwarded to an appropriate source
Hours: 10.00-17.00
Publications: Transactions of the Royal Society of Tropical Medicine and Hygiene (£130)

[560]

Royal Surrey County Hospital (RSCH)

Egerton Road
Guildford
Surrey GU2 5XX
Telephone: Direct line: 01483 464137
Fax: 01483 455888
E-mail: jhutch@easynet.co.uk
Contact: Jonathan Hutchins (Librarian); Anne Madgwick (Assistant Librarian)
Objectives and Purposes: To provide a library and information service to all NHS professionals within the West Surrey district. Part of South Thames Regional Library and Information Service
Stock and Subject Coverage: 8,000 books; 220 current periodicals; grey literature on health service provision
Services/Facilities: Photocopying; fax; online searching; Internet access; CD-ROM MEDLINE; and Cochrane Library
Availability: Available to all NHS staff within the District for loan or reference, and to others for reference. Affiliated membership to non-NHS personnel (contact Librarian for charges). Photocopying and interlibrary loans free to other libraries in South Thames: BL form to other institutions
Hours: 09.00-19.00 Monday to Wednesday; 09.00-17.00 Thursday and Friday

[561]

Royal United Hospital Bath NHS Trust (RUH Trust)

Library
Postgraduate Centre
Combe Park
Bath BA1 3NG
Telephone: 01225 824898
Fax: 01225 316575
Contact: David Rumsey (Head of Library Services)
Objectives and Purposes: To provide high quality information to Health Service staff
Stock and Subject Coverage: Material on health care and related subjects. Special collections on rheumatology and the history of medicine
Services/Facilities: Online and CD-ROM searches; fax; photocopies (priced)
Availability: By prior appointment, for reference use only; access limited for non-NHS staff
Hours: 09.00-17.30
Publications: Library guide; list of journal holdings

[562]

★RSI Association

Chapel House
152 High Street
Yiewsley
West Drayton
Middlesex UB7 7BE
Telephone: 01895 431134
Contact: Ron Mulelly (Hon. Secretary)
Objectives and Purposes: National support group for Repetitive Strain Injury sufferers
Stock and Subject Coverage: Material on repetitive strain injuries
Availability: Personal calls welcome
Hours: 14.00-16.00
Publications: Information pack (priced)

[563]

Rugby NHS Trust, Hospital of St Cross

Barby Road
Rugby
Warwickshire CV22 5PX
Telephone: 01788 572831, ext 2470
Fax: 01788 545274
Contact: Petra Meeson (Librarian)
Objectives and Purposes: Information support for the training and development needs of Trust staff
Stock and Subject Coverage: Material, including 40 periodicals, on medicine in general
Services/Facilities: MEDLINE on CD-ROM; photocopies
Availability: By prior appointment, for reference use only
Hours: 11.30-14.30

[564]

Russells Hall Hospital, Medical Library

Dudley Group of Hospitals NHS Trust
Dudley
West Midlands DY1 2HQ
Telephone: 01384 244253
Fax: 01384 244213
E-mail: rhmlib@dial.pipex.com
Contact: Barbara Bolton (Medical Librarian)
Objectives and Purposes: To provide library and information services to support the education of doctors and other health personnel
Stock and Subject Coverage: Material on general medicine; surgery; ENT; ophthalmology; vascular surgery; urology; anaesthesia; orthopaedics; respiratory disorders; gastroenterology; and cardiology
Services/Facilities: Database searches; Internet access; slide presentation making
Availability: By prior appointment, for reference use only; telephone and written enquiries accepted
Hours: 09.00-17.00
Publications: Newsletter; journal and video lists; information leaflet
Related Bodies: West Midlands Regional Library Network

[565]

Salford Royal Hospitals NHS Trust

Frank Rifkin Postgraduate Medical Centre
Hope Hospital
Stott Lane
Salford M6 8HD
Telephone: 0161 787 5405
Fax: 0161 787 5409
E-mail: li6mail@fs1.ho.man.ac.uk
World Wide Web:
    http://www.hop.man.ac.uk/lib/lib.html
Contact: Mrs V Haigh BA (Hons) ALA (Chief Librarian)
Objectives and Purposes: To provide postgraduate medical information for staff of the Trust
Stock and Subject Coverage: Material on medicine in general (but excluding nursing)
Services/Facilities: Online searches; photocopies
Availability: By prior appointment, for reference use only
Hours: 09.15-20.00; 09.00-13.00 on Saturday
Publications: Bi-monthly newsletter

[566]

Salisbury Health Care Trust

Library
Education Centre
Salisbury District Hospital
Salisbury SP2 8BJ
Telephone: 01722 336262, ext 4433
Fax: 01722 339690

E-mail: wll@soton.ac.uk
Contact: Miss Sue Henshaw (Head Librarian)
Objectives and Purposes: Health care provision for the local population
Stock and Subject Coverage: Material on all aspects of health care in the acute and community sectors
Services/Facilities: Online and CD-ROM searches; photocopies; computer and audiovisual facilities
Availability: By prior appointment, for reference use only; telephone and written enquiries accepted
Hours: 09.30-16.50
Publications: Newsletter; library guides

[567]
Sandwell Health Authority Public Health Department

Library
Lewisham Street
West Bromwich B71 4NA
Telephone: 0121 553 6151, ext 272; Nursing Library: 0121 553 1831, ext 3645 (Tuesday to Friday)
Contact: Rowena Gray (Librarian, Monday only); Julie Bush (Office Administrator)
Objectives and Purposes: To improve the health of local people; the Library supports this by providing such services as are needed by the staff in as pleasant and helpful a manner as possible
Stock and Subject Coverage: 5,000 books and other items. General medical texts and works on preventive medicine. The bulk of the stock is pamphlet material such as government reports, legislation, health authority reports, etc.
Services/Facilities: CINAHL on CD-ROM; photocopies; interlibrary loans
Availability: By prior appointment, for reference use only; telephone and written enquiries accepted
Hours: 08.45-16.45
Publications: Annual report; various technical reports
Related Bodies: Sandwell Healthcare NHS Trust

[568]
SANE

199-205 Old Marylebone Road
London NW1 5QP
Telephone: 0171 724 6520
Fax: 0171 724 6502
Contact: Enquiries to the Library; Ms Marjorie Wallace (Chief Executive)
Objectives and Purposes: A mental health charity concerned with serious mental illness. Its main aims are to raise awareness, via campaigning and media work; to care, by means of a national Telephone helpline (Saneline); to research, by establishing an international research centre
Stock and Subject Coverage: Material covering the whole range of mental health, including therapies; drugs; benefits; legal aspects; and arts. An abstracts database is available
Services/Facilities: Database searches for contacts across the country; abstract searches; telephone helpline for legal/emotional/professional support

Availability: Written enquiries only
Hours: 09.30-17.30; SANELINE available 14.00-24.00 every day of the year
Publications: Sanetalk (quarterly)

[569]
Schering Health Care Ltd

The Brow
Burgess Hill
West Sussex RH15 9NE
Telephone: 01444 232323
Fax: 01444 246613
World Wide Web: http://www.schering.co.uk
Contact: Miss E Watson (Medical Information Resources Manager); Mrs A Bennett (Library Assistant)
Objectives and Purposes: Pharmaceutical company specialising in contraception, HRT, leukaemia and diagnostics
Stock and Subject Coverage: 3,000 books; 120 periodicals on contraception; HRT; cancer; neurology; and diagnostics
Availability: A private company library. Telephone enquiries accepted in exceptional circumstances
Hours: 09.00-17.00

[570]
Schizophrenia Association of Great Britain (SAGB)

Bryn Hyfryd
The Crescent
Bangor
Gwynedd LL57 2AG
Telephone and Fax: 01248 354048
Contact: Mrs Gwynneth Hemmings (Director)
Objectives and Purposes: To help patients suffering from mental illness, and their families; to promote research into the biochemical factors involved in schizophrenia; to educate the public about schizophrenia
Stock and Subject Coverage: Books and periodicals on all aspects of schizophrenia
Services/Facilities: Free advice and information to sufferers and their families; information packs available; photocopies (at cost)
Availability: Visits by appointment; telephone and written enquiries accepted
Hours: 09.30-16.00
Publications: Newsletter (2 per year); information pack; various leaflets

[571]
Scoliosis Association UK (SAUK)

2 Ivebury Court
323-327 Latimer Road
London W10 6RA
Telephone and Fax: 0181 964 5343
Contact: Mrs Pauline Grey; Brenda Sullivan Saunders; Denise Aulsberry
Status: Registered charity

Objectives and Purposes: SAUK seeks to spread knowledge about scoliosis, alerting the public and those in contact with children and young people to the need for early diagnosis; working alongside the medical profession SAUK aims to fill any gaps left by busy hospital clinics in the provision of information and social welfare

Hours: 10.00-14.00

Services/Facilities: Information on all aspects of scoliosis

Publications: Range of publications, posters, leaflets, etc. - list available; annual report

---

[572]

SCOPE: for People with Cerebral Palsy (formerly The Spastics Society)

12 Park Crescent
London W1N 4EQ
Telephone: 0171 636 5020
Fax: 0171 436 2601
World Wide Web: http://www.scope.org.uk/
Contact: Sarah Lawson (Information Officer); Gary Birkenhead (Librarian)

Objectives and Purposes: To provide a range of services for people with cerebral palsy, their carers and families, including schools, residential care, information and careers advice. The Cerebral Palsy Helpline (0800 626216) is available seven days per week (Monday to Friday 11.00-21.00; Saturday and Sunday 14.00-18.00) for initial advice and counselling

Stock and Subject Coverage: Books and reports on cerebral palsy and related disabilities, and items on equipment and other organisations; various periodicals. Large reference stock, including DISSBASE; 55 current periodicals; Special collection: Clinics in Developmental Medicine, and Developmental and Child Neurology

Services/Facilities: Photocopies; student factsheet; telephone and written enquiries accepted; reference facilities

Availability: By prior appointment, for reference use only

Hours: 09.00-17.00

Publications: Disability Now (monthly); booklists

Related Bodies: 200 local groups

---

[573]

Scottish Association for Mental Health (SAMH)

Atlantic House
38 Gardners Crescent
Edinburgh EH3 8DQ
Telephone: 0131 229 9687
Fax: 0131 229 3558
Contact: Shona Barcus (Director); Cheryl Minto (Information Officer)

Objectives and Purposes: A voluntary organisation which campaigns for better hospital and community services; it seeks to increase

understanding of mental distress; it provides supported accommodation and training for employment for people with mental health problems

Stock and Subject Coverage: 5,500 items on all aspects of mental health

Services/Facilities: Photocopies; database searches; information pack

Availability: Telephone and written enquiries accepted visits by prior arrangement

Hours: 09.30-12.00 (other times by appointment only)

Publications: List available

Related Bodies: 23 local groups

---

[574]

Scottish Centre for Infection and Environmental Health (SCIEH)

Ruchill Hospital
Bilsland Drive
Glasgow G20 9NB
Telephone: 0141 946 7120
Fax: 0141 946 4359
E-mail: norman@scieh.tcom.co.uk
Contact: Mr N MacDonald (Librarian

Objectives and Purposes: To provide an information service for the staff of the Unit in the fields of epidemiology; communicable diseases; travel medicine; environmental health; infection control; and surveillance statistics

Stock and Subject Coverage: 3,000 books; 200 periodicals; collection of reports covering epidemiology; communicable diseases; travel medicine; environmental health; infection control; and surveillance statistics

Services/Facilities: Photocopies (priced)

Availability: By prior appointment, for reference use only for bona fide researchers; telephone and written enquiries accepted

Hours: 09.30-17.00

Publications: SCIEH Weekly Report; Answer (AIDS news supplement to weekly report); Salmonellosis: summary of isolations; various annual publications; annual report

---

[575]

Scottish Council on Alcohol (SCA)

166 Buchanan Street
Glasgow G1 2NH
Telephone: 0141 333 9677
Fax: 0141 333 1606
Contact: Mr Douglas T Allsop (Executive Director); Mrs Ann Furst (PR and Appeals Director); Mr Graham Dunn (Statistics Officer)

Objectives and Purposes: To provide confidential support and self-help services for individuals and families with drinking problems; to encourage all who drink to adopt healthier, safer and more sensible drinking styles; to provide an effective education and information service for young people; to train volunteer counsellors

Stock and Subject Coverage: Reference library containing books, periodicals, articles, reports and conference proceedings. Covers all aspects of alcohol use and misuse; other addictions; psychotherapy; HIV and AIDS; and counselling

Services/Facilities: Photocopies; fax; Alcohol Database

Availability: By prior arrangement

Hours: 09.00-17.00 (closes 16.30 on Friday)

Publications: Various - list available

Related Bodies: National network of 28 local agencies

[576]

Scottish Down's Syndrome Association (SDSA)

158-160 Balgreen Road
Edinburgh EH11 3AU

Telephone: 0131 313 4225

Fax: 0131 313 4285

Contact: Alison M Gilvray (Director); Cathie Rowan and Margaret Tollick (Development Officers); Pat Hernandez (Secretary - part time)

Objectives and Purposes: To provide information and support for people with Down's Syndrome and their families in Scotland, and for those who work with them. To secure better services and resources for people with Down's Syndrome in Scotland

Stock and Subject Coverage: Small collection of books, journals and videos on all aspects of Down's Syndrome, e.g. developmental, medical, educational, etc.

Services/Facilities: Photocopies; fax

Availability: Freely available to persons in Scotland; visits accepted; most material reference only

Hours: 09.00-17.00

Publications: SDSA News (quarterly - annual report in the summer issue); information series Living With Down's Syndrome (7 titles so far)

Scottish Drugs Forum

see **Stop Press on page 156**

[577]

Scottish Health Service Centre, Development Group

Crewe Road South
Edinburgh EH4 2LF

Telephone: 0131 332 2335

Fax: 0131 315 2369

E-mail: mdg@ednet.co.uk

Contact: Mrs Maureen Thom (Librarian); Miss Alison Clapham (Assistant Librarian)

Objectives and Purposes: To support the NHS in Scotland in becoming more effective by providing expert, relevant consultancy to Trusts, Health Boards and Management Executives, enabling the development of key individual capabilities and add value to the planning and delivery of health care in Scotland through the development of managerial capability and effectiveness across the service

Stock and Subject Coverage: 11,000 books/reports; 155 current periodicals covering all aspects of health care management and planning; general management; and community care. An in-house database of books and selected journal articles

Services/Facilities: CD-ROM and online searches; photocopies (priced); enquiries and loans

Availability: Postal service to Scottish Health Service employees; others may visit in person. Books available for loan, but periodicals are for reference only. Restricted service for those who are not withn NHS Scotland

Hours: 09.00-17.00 (closes 16.30 on Friday)

Publications: Current awareness bulletin; NHS in Scotland Directory

Related Bodies: Part of the Directorate of Human Resources of the NHS in Scotland Management Executive

[578]

Scottish Office Library

Room 050
St Andrews House
Edinburgh EH1 3DG

Telephone: 0131 244 2619

Fax: 0131 244 2618

E-mail: mmacdonald.so.sah@gtnet.gov.uk

Contact: Ms E Macdonald (Librarian); Ms H Widdall (Assistant)

Objectives and Purposes: To provide library and information services to staff of the Scottish Office, particularly in the fields of health, home affairs and social work

Stock and Subject Coverage: Material on health in general and health and safety (plus other non health-related collections)

Services/Facilities: Photocopies; online services for staff only

Availability: By prior appointment, for reference use only. Loans via the British Library and the Association of Scottish Health Science Libraries

Hours: 09.00-16.30

[579]

Scottish Poisons Information Bureau (SPIB)

The Royal Infirmary
Edinburgh EH3 9YW

Telephone: 0131 536 2300

Fax: 0131 536 2304

E-mail: 101574.424@compuserve.com

Contact: Mrs AM Good (Manager); Dr AT Proudfoot (Director)

Objectives and Purposes: To provide doctors and other health care professionals with up-to-date information to enable them to manage appropriately persons exposed to poisons

Services/Facilities: 24-hour telephoneservice for poisons information; TOXBASE - an online database with information on toxicity and management of poisoning with regard to 12,000 products and substances including drugs, household products, industrial chemicals and agrochemicals

Availability: Freely available within the NHS

Hours: 09.00-21.00 (telephone service and TOXBASE 24 hours)

Publications: Annual report

Related Bodies: National Poisons Information Service

[580]
Scottish Science Library (SSL)

National Library of Scotland
33 Salisbury Place
Edinburgh EH9 1SL

Telephone: 0131 226 4531, ext 3525

Fax: 0131 662 0644

Contact: Morag Nisbet (Head of Life Sciences)

Objectives and Purposes: To meet the information needs of the scientific, industrial and business communities in Scotland

Stock and Subject Coverage: The stock of the Library includes books; periodicals, abstracts, indexes and CD-ROMs in all scientific subjects, including medicine and business information

Services/Facilities: Enquiries; CD-ROM searches; photocopies

Availability: Reference only (ID required before admission); charges for value-added services

Hours: 09.30-17.00 Monday, Tuesday, Thursday and Friday; 10.00-20.30 Wednesday

Publications: SSL News (3 per year)

Related Bodies: Part of National Library of Scotland

[581]
Scottish Spina Bifida Association

190 Queensferry Road
Edinburgh EH4 2BW

Telephone: 0131 332 0743

Fax: 0131 343 3651

Contact: Mr Andrew Wynd (General Secretary)

Objectives and Purposes: To increase public understanding and awareness of individuals with spina bifida/hydrocephalus and allied disorders; it aims to secure special provision for their needs, and those of their families

Stock and Subject Coverage: A range of materials relating to spina bifida and hydrocephalus

Services: Family support service; photocopies

Availability: Telephone and written enquiries preferred; no loans or reference facilities

Hours: 09.30-16.00

Publications: Contact (quarterly magazine); annual report/yearbook

Related Bodies: Local branches throughout Scotland

[582]
Seacroft Hospital Postgraduate Centre

York Road
Leeds LS14 6UH

Telephone: 0113 264 8164, exts 3325/3675

Fax: 0113 232 6235

E-mail: rao51@dial.pipex.com

Contact: Frances Norton (Librarian); Andrew Pantin (Library Assistant)

Objectives and Purposes: To provide library and information services for hospital personnel and local GPs

Stock and Subject Coverage: 2,000 books; 60 periodicals on medicine; nursing; health care management; and statistics

Services/Facilities: Online and CD-ROM searches; fax; photocopies

Availability: To staff and local GPs

Hours: 09.00-17.00

[583]
Seasonal Affective Disorder Association (SADA)

PO Box 989
London SW7 2PZ

Telephone and Fax: 01903 814942 (administration and emergency use only)

Contact: Jenny Simmonds (Administrator)

Objectives and Purposes: To identify, help and advise on SAD; to educate health professionals; to heighten public awareness of the illness

Stock and Subject Coverage: Material on SAD in general

Services/Facilities: Enquiries; information pack (£5); helpline; lightbox hire scheme

Availability: Freely available

Publications: Information leaflets; newsletter (3 per year)

[584]
Sense: The National Deafblind and Rubella Association

11-13 Clifton Terrace
Finsbury Park
London N4 3SR

Telephone: 0171 272 7774

Fax: 0171 272 6012

Contact: Caroline Edwards (Information Officer)

Objectives and Purposes: To work and campaign for the needs of children and young adults who are deaf/blind, providing advice, support, information, and services for them, their families, carers and the professionals with whom they are involved; residential holiday schemes and educational programmes are arranged

Stock and Subject Coverage: A library (housed at Sense West; 0121 456 1564) of 3,000 books and periodicals covering deafblindness; deafness, blindness, multi-sensory impairment; multiple disability, communication and education. Other enquiries should be directed to headquarters

Services/Facilities: Fax; photocopies

Availability: Telephone and written enquiries; visits by appointment (at Sense Midlands; 0121 456 1564)

Hours: 09.00-17.00

Publications: Talking Sense (quarterly newsletter); annual report; Building a Future (leaflet); Making Contact

Related Bodies: National network of regional centres and branches

[585]

Sheffield Academic Press Ltd (SUBIS)

Mansion House
19 Kingfield Road
Sheffield S11 9AS

Telephone: 0114 255 4433

Fax: 0114 255 4626

E-mail: subis@sheffac.demon.co.uk

World Wide Web: http://www.shef-ac-press.co.uk

Contact: Mr D Chambers (Senior Editor)

Objectives and Purposes: The provision of a current awareness service and publication of books, journals and conference proceedings in biology and medicine

Stock and Subject Coverage: No library, but informal links with the University of Sheffield Library System

Services/Facilities: Customised current awareness services for companies, other publishers and charities; targeted mailing lists in biology and medicine

Availability: Telephone and written enquiries accepted; visits by prior arrangement

Hours: 09.00-16.00

Publications: Series of 97 current awareness bulletins – list and samples available

Related Bodies: Parent body is Sheffield Academic Press Ltd

[586]

Sheffield Children's Hospital NHS Trust

Illingworth Library
Floor F
Stephenson Unit
Sheffield S10 2TH

Telephone: 0114 271 7347

Fax: 0114 275 5364

E-mail: H.C.Needham@Sheffield.ac.uk

Contact: Dr RA Primhak (Hon. Librarian); enquiries to Mrs HC Needham and Mrs AV Seton (Library Assistants)

Objectives and Purposes: To provide library and information services for students and staff

Stock and Subject Coverage: 1,500 books; 30 periodicals covering paediatrics and general medicine

Services/Facilities: CD-ROM searches (MEDLINE and Cochrane); photocopies

Availability: By prior appointment, for reference use only; telephone and written enquiries accepted

Hours: 09.00-19.00 (closes 17.00 on Friday)

Related Bodies: University of Sheffield, Department of Paediatrics

[587]

Shiatsu Society of the United Kingdom

31 Pullman Lane
Godalming
Surrey GU7 1XY

Telephone and Fax: 01483 860771

Contact: Joy Martin (Administrator)

Objectives and Purposes: To be the national network for information on shiatsu, and the professional practitioners' association

Availability: Telephone, fax and written enquiries accepted. Information pack on request (A5 s.a.e. required)

Publications: Quarterly newsletter; list of registered practitioners

Related Bodies: Affiliated to the Institute of Complementary Medicine

[588]

Shingles Support Society (SSS)

41 North Road
London N7 9DP

Telephone: 0171 607 9661

Contact: Marian J Nicholson

Stock and Subject Coverage: Self-help and drug therapy sheets on shingles and post-herpetic neuralgia

Services/Facilities: List of contacts for self-help and mutual support

Availability: Information pack available (s.a.e. required; donation appreciated)

[589]

Shropshire Centre for Health Promotion

Trust Headquarters
Cross House
Shrewsbury SY5 6JN

Telephone: 01743 761242, ext 355

Fax: 01743 761601

Contact: Mrs Sue Lee (Resources Manager)

Objectives and Purposes: The promotion, protection and maintenance of good health and well-being

Stock and Subject Coverage: Material on all aspects of health promotion; health education; and some public health issues

Availability: Freely available

Hours: 09.00-16.30 (closes 15.30 on Friday)

[590]
Sickle Cell Society

54 Station Road
Harlesden
London NW10 4YA
Telephone: 0181 961 7795/4006
Fax: 0181 961 8346
Contact: J Richards (Administrator): B Campbell (Director)
Objectives and Purposes: To promote awareness of sickle cell disorders through talks, videos and publications; to provide financial help for sickle cell sufferers through welfare and the Bryan Jones Fund
Stock and Subject Coverage: Material on sickle cell disorders (videos, books and leaflets)
Availability: Telephone and written enquiries; visits by appointment
Hours: 09.00-17.00
Publications: Quartely newsletter; annual report; videos, books and leaflets

[591]
*Society and College of Radiographers (SCOR)

14 Upper Wimpole Street
London W1M 8BN
Telephone: 0171 935 5726
Fax: 0171 487 3483
Contact: Peter M Smith (Acting Chief Executive); Eleanor Ransom (Research Officer)
Objectives and Purposes: To promote and develop the science of radiography; the Society is the professional body for radiography, with specific responsibilities for professional and educational functions; the objectives include the regulation of employers and employees, and it is a trade union affiliated to the TUC
Stock and Subject Coverage: The library service is managed by the British Institute of Radiology Library and Information Service (36 Portland Place, London W1N 4AT; Tel: 0171 580 4085; Fax: 0171 255 3209). The College houses a special collection of theses prepared for the College's own postgraduate qualifications
Services/Facilities: Current awareness; literature searches; document delivery
Availability: By prior appointment, for reference use only
Hours: 10.00-17.00
Publications: Radiography (quarterly); Radiography Today (monthly); various ad hoc publications - details on application
Related Bodies: British Institute of Radiology Library and Information Service

[592]
Society for Endocrinology

17-18 The Courtyard
Woodlands
Almondsbury
Bristol BS12 4NQ
Telephone: 01454 616046
Fax: 01454 616071
E-mail: info@endocrinology.org
World Wide Web: http://www.endocrinology.org
Contact: Sue Thorn (Executive Director); Amanda Sherwood (Society Affairs Manager)
Objectives and Purposes: To promote the advance of endocrinology by observational, experimental or clinical studies. No library facility
Hours: 09.00-17.00
Publications: Journal of Endocrinology; Journal of Molecular Endocrinology; series of books
Related Bodies: British Endocrine Societies

[593]
Society for Medicines Research (SMR)

20 Queensberry Place
London SW7 2DZ
Telephone: 0171 581 8333
Fax: 0171 823 9409
Contact: Barbara Cavilla
Objectives and Purposes: To provide opportunities for those involved in drug research to meet for the reading of papers and discussion; the Society is concerned with all sciences relevant to the discovery and development of new medicines, and not simply the drug entity
Publications: Members newsletter (4 per year)

[594]
Society for Mucopolysaccharide Diseases (MPS Society)

55 Hill Avenue
Amersham
Buckinghamshire HP6 5BX
Telephone: 01494 434156
Fax: 01494 434252
E-mail: 101716.2774@compuserve.com
World Wide Web: http://www.vois.org/mps
Contact: Christine Lavery (Director); Joan Evans (Development Officer)
Objectives and Purposes: To provide support for families of children suffering from MPS; to raise public awareness about the condition; to encourage research into MPS diseases
Stock and Subject Coverage: Material on mucopolysaccahride diseases, bereavement support, anaesthetic risks and patterned inheritance
Services/Facilities: Free advice, advocacy and information to sufferers and their families; annual weekend conference; family holidays; teenage activity holiday

Availability: Telephone and written enquiries; visits by arrangement

Hours: 09.00–15.00

Publications: Quarterly newsletter; annual report; booklets on specific diseases (list available)

[595]

Society for the Autistically Handicapped (SFTAH)

199 Blandford Avenue
Kettering
Northamptonshire NN16 9AT

Telephone and Fax: 01536 523274

E-mail: autism@rmplc.co.uk

World Wide Web: http://www.rmplc.co.uk/eduweb/ sites/autism/index.html

Contact: K Lovett (Chairman); P Lovett (Secretary); T Pollard (Financial Secretary)

Objectives and Purposes: To promote understanding and awareness of autism; provide support for families and carers along with practical help where possible; to perceive the needs of those with autism and find appropriate services in health, education and social care

Stock and Subject Coverage: A large and comprehensive library covering all aspects of the autistic continuum

Services/Facilities: Advice for parents/carers/ professionals; 24-hour helpline; voicemail; training seminars and workshops

Availability: By prior appointment, for reference use only; enquiries by telephone, fax, e-mail or letter are accepted

Hours: 11.00–20.00 Monday to Saturday

Publications: Half-yearly newsletter; annual report

[596]

Society of Chiropodists and Podiatrists

53 Welbeck Street
London W1M 7HE

Telephone: 0171 486 3381

Fax: 0171 935 6359

Contact: Dr Georgina Stevens (Editorial and Public Relations Officer); Mr Michael Collins (Director of Professional Development)

Objectives and Purposes: An information service for members and for those interested in chiropody and state-registered chiropodists

Stock and Subject Coverage: Archive of the Journal of British Podiatric Medicine (formerly The Chiropodist)

Availability: Written enquiries preferred

Hours: 09.30–16.45

Publications: Journal of British Podiatric Medicine; The Foot; information leaflet

[597]

Society of Homoeopaths

2 Artizan Road
Northampton NN1 4HU

Telephone: 01604 21400

Fax: 01604 22622

E-mail: fran@gn.apc.org

Contact: Mary Clarke (General Secretary)

Objectives and Purposes: To develop and maintain high standards for the practice of homoeopathy; maintain a register of professional practitioners; to promote public awareness of the profession; to promote and support education and training in homoeopathy

Stock and Subject Coverage: UK Register of Professional Homoeopaths; archives on homoeopathic medicine and the work of the Society

Services/Facilities: Information about the work of members, and about the discipline in general

Availability: By arrangement

Hours: 09.30–17.00

Publications: The Homoeopath (quarterly); newsletter (quarterly); annual report

[598]

Society of Occupational Medicine (SOM)

6 St Andrew's Place
Regents Park
London NW1 4LB

Telephone: 0171 486 2641

Fax: 0171 486 0028

E-mail: 1100637.2012@compuserve.com

World Wide Web: http://www.ed.ac.uk/~rma/som.html

Contact: Dr PJJ Ryan (Hon. Secretary)

Objectives and Purposes: The protection of the health of people at work and the prevention of occupational disease and injuries. The Society constitutes a forum for the membership and stimulates interest in research and education in occupational medicine

Services/Facilities: Guidelines and advice on topics relevant to occupational medicine; usual office facilities available

Availability: Telephone and written enquiries; visits by appointment, for reference use only

Hours: 09.00–17.00

Publications: Journal of Occupational Medicine; quarterly newsletter

[599]

Society of Public Health

28 Portland Place
London W1N 4DE

Telephone: 01652 601117 (Mrs JE Graham, Secretary)

Contact: Dr PA Gardner (Hon. Secretary - for written contact - 31 Battye Avenue, Huddersfield HD4 5PW)

Objectives and Purposes: To give independent epidemiological advice on matters which directly or indirectly affect the public; to maintain close links with all other organisations which represent public health physicians and practitioners; to maintain and enhance its position as an advisory body to Government and its Departments; to take the lead in the training of those working in the clinical preventive field of Community Health

Stock and Subject Coverage: No library. Small collection of booklets and conference proceedings, which are available for sale

Services/Facilities: Suitable literature can be supplied on matters pertaining to public health (for a fee, and after discussion of the needs); speakers can be provided for relevant events

Availability: No visits; telephone and written enquiries accepted

Publications: Public Health (6 per year); quarterly newsletter; miscellaneous booklets and conference proceedings

[600]
Solihull Hospital Library

Education Centre
Lode Lane
Solihull B91 2JL
Telephone: 0121 711 4455, ext 3252
Fax: 0121 685 5054
Contact: Mrs B Bird (Librarian)
Stock and Subject Coverage: Range of books, and 70 current periodicals in a multidisciplinary collection covering medicine; nursing; management; and allied professions
Services/Facilities: MEDLINE on CD-ROM; photocopies
Availability: No public access
Hours: 09.00–17.00

[601]
Solvent Abuse Resource Group (SARG)

28 Penny Street
Blackburn
Lancashire BB1 6HL
Telephone: 01254 677493
E-mail: sarg@airtime.co.uk
World Wide Web:
    http://www.airtime.co.uk/users/sarg/
Contact: Keith Owen (Coordinator/Development Officer); John Verit (Solvent Abuse Community Worker)
Objectives and Purposes: Provides free and confidential help, information and guidance to users, parents, friends - in fact anyone who is interested or concerned about the issue of solvent and other substance misuse by young people
Stock and Subject Coverage: Specific solvent misuse information - leaflets, books, videos and other resources along with some more general drug information

Services/Facilities: Internet link available by negotiation
Availability: General open availability - particularly to locally based groups. No charges
Hours: 09.30–16.30
Publications: Annual Report; business plan - produced annually

[602]
South Bank University, Redwood College of Health Studies

Harold Wood Education Centre
Harold Wood Hospital Grounds
Gubbins Lane
Harold Wood
Essex RM3 0BE
Telephone: 0171 815 5982
Fax: 0171 815 5906
E-mail: fieldw@sbu.ac.uk
Contact: WE Field; DJ Whatmough
Objectives and Purposes: To supply and satisfy material/learning needs for students and staff
Stock and Subject Coverage: Material on nursing and health-related subjects
Services/Facilities: CD-ROM searches; hardcopy indexes; interlibrary loans; photocopies; Internet access
Availability: Telephone and written enquiries accepted
Hours: 08.30–19.30 (closes 17.00 on Friday)
Related Bodies: South Bank University

[603]
South Devon Health Care Trust

The Library
Medical Centre
Torbay Hospital
Torquay
Devon TQ2 7AA
Telephone: 01803 654704
Fax: 01803 616395
E-mail: pamela@pamprior.demon.co.uk
Contact: Mrs Pam Prior
Objectives and Purposes: To provide multidisciplinary library and information services to all Trust employees, and an information service for patients and their carers
Stock and Subject Coverage: 7,000 books; 200 periodicals. Covers medicine, nursing and allied professions
Services/Facilities: Online and CD-ROM searches; Internet access; fax; photocopies
Availability: By prior appointment, for reference use only
Hours: 08.30–17.15

[604]
South Kent Hospitals NHS Trust, Education Centre Library

William Harvey Hospital
Kennington Road
Willesborough
Ashford
Kent TN24 0LZ

Telephone: 01233 633331, ext 8413
Fax: 01233 613597
Contact: Mr W Jones (Head of Library Services)
Objectives and Purposes: To provide quality library and information services to Trust employees
Stock and Subject Coverage: 5,000 books; 127 periodicals on clinical medicine; nursing; and allied health
Services/Facilities: Online and CD-ROM searches; fax; photocopies
Availability: By prior appointment, for reference use only (charges may be made)
Hours: 09.00–17.00
Related Bodies: Postgraduate Medical Library, Buckland Hospital, Dover

[605]
South Manchester University Hospitals NHS Trust

Medical Library
Withington Hospital
Nell Lane
West Didsbury
Manchester M20 2LR

Telephone: 0161 447 3878
Fax: 0161 447 3879
E-mail: library@fs1.wph.man.ac.uk
Contact: Miss E Jordan (Hospital Librarian); Ms D Wright (Assistant Librarian)
Stock and Subject Coverage: 7,000 books; 250 periodicals covering general medicine, nursing, dentistry, and related topics such as pharmacy and pharmacology
Services/Facilities: Online and CD-ROM searches; photocopies; interlibrary loans; fax
Availability: Via interlibrary loans
Hours: 09.00–20.30 Monday, Tuesday and Thursday; 09.00–17.30 Wednesday and Friday
Publications: Monthly current awareness list
Related Bodies: Postgraduate Medical Library, Wythenshawe Hospital

[606]
South Staffordshire Medical Centre Library (SSMC)

The Royal Wolverhampton Hospitals NHS Trust
New Cross Hospital
Wolverhampton WV10 0QP

Telephone: 01902 643109
Fax: 01902 723037
Contact: Miss JH Paterson (Medical Librarian); Mrs E Sheppard (Library Assistant)
Objectives and Purposes: To provide library and information services to all medical, paramedical, dental and veterinary staff in the West Midlands and Staffordshire areas
Stock and Subject Coverage: Books and 200 periodicals on all aspects of medicine
Services/Facilities: Online and CD-ROM searches; photocopies
Availability: Telephone and written enquiries, at the Librarian's discretion
Hours: 09.00–17.00 (closes 16.30 on Friday)
Related Bodies: Wolverhampton and Midland Counties Eye Infirmary

[607]
South Tyneside Postgraduate Medical Centre Library

District Hospital
Harton Lane
South Shields
Tyne and Wear NE34 0PL

Telephone: 0191 454 8888, ext 2572
Fax: 0191 427 0096
E-mail: mduffy@stpgmc.demon.co.uk
Contact: Mrs M Duffy BA ALA (Librarian)
Objectives and Purposes: To provide efficient, effective library and information services for doctors, dentists and other health care workers in South Tyneside
Stock and Subject Coverage: 4,000 books; 120 periodicals; audiovisual materials covering medicine, psychiatry and the NHS
Services/Facilities: Online and CD-ROM searches; current awareness services; fax; photocopies (priced); interlibrary loans
Availability: Telephone and written enquiries accepted; visits by prior arrangement
Hours: 09.3–17.00 (closes 16.30 on Friday)

[608]
South Warwickshire Medical Education Centre

Medical Library
John Turner Building
Warwick Hospital
Lakin Road
Warwick CV34 5BW

Telephone: 01926 495321, ext 4287
Fax: 01926 400895
Contact: Mr NP Harden (Librarian); Mrs A Walton
Stock and Subject Coverage: Material covering medicine and health care
Services/Facilities: Online and CD-ROM searches; photocopies (priced)
Availability: Telephone and written enquiries accepted; visits by prior appointment, for reference use only
Hours: 09.00–17.30
Related Bodies: St Michael's Hospital Medical Library is a branch Library

[609]

Southampton Health Library and Information Service (SOHLIS)

Staff Library
Royal South Hants Hospital
Brintons Terrace
Southampton SO14 0YG
Telephone: 01703 825714
Fax: 01703 234020
Contact: Ms R Noyes; Ms C Shemilt; Miss C Allen;
Mr S Gilbert; Mrs A Peckham
Stock and Subject Coverage: 7,000 books; 254
periodicals covering general medicine and
surgery; with particular interest in psychiatry,
radiotherapy, cancer, dermatology and health
management
Services/Facilities: Online and CD-ROM searches;
current awareness service; photocopies
Availability: By prior appointment, for reference use
only (for a fee)
Hours: 09.00-17.30
Publications: Member of SWRLIN and HATRICS

[610]

Southend Medical Centre Library

Education Centre
Southend Hospital
Prittlewell Chase
Westcliff-on-Sea
Essex SS0 0RY
Telephone: 01702 435555, ext 2620
Fax: 01702 221081
E-mail: ian@smclib.demon.co.uk
Contact: Mr I Mather (District Medical Librarian);
Mrs L Thres and Mrs R Syers (Assistant Medical
Librarians); Mrs G Bronze (Senior Library
Assistant)
Objectives and Purposes: To deliver access on equal
terms for all NHS staff to the knowledge base to
further appropriate and effective health care
Stock and Subject Coverage: 1,200 books; 130
periodicals; audiovisual materials covering general
medicine
Services/Facilities: CD-ROM and online searches;
CAL facility; photocopies; fax; interlibrary loans
Availability: Telephone and written enquiries
accepted; value-added services are priced
Hours: 08.30-18.00 (closes 16.00 on Friday)
Publications: Monthly newsletter
Related Bodies: North East Thames Regional Library
Service

[611]

Southern General Hospital (Glasgow) NHS Trust

Central Library
1345 Govan Road
Glasgow G51 4TF
Telephone: 0141 201 2163
Fax: 0141 201 2133
E-mail: char@jbeaton.demon.co.uk

Contact: Charlotte Boulnois; Mary Robins
Objectives and Purposes: To provide effective and
up-to-date information to help all NHS staff to
make effective use of the knowledge base of
health care
Stock and Subject Coverage: 4,000 books; 120
periodicals. Covers all aspects of medicine, nursing
and allied professions, with an emphasis on
neurology, neurosurgery and spinal injuries
Services/Facilities: Online and CD-ROM searches;
photocopies (priced)
Availability: By prior appointment, for reference use
only
Hours: 09.00-19.00 (closes 17.00 on Friday)

[612]

Southmead Library and Information Service

Southmead Hospital
Westbury-on-Trym
Bristol BS10 5NB
Telephone: 0117 959 5333
Fax: 0117 959 5529
E-mail: ce62@pipex.dial.com
Contact: Caroline Plaice (Library Manager);
Lesley Greig (Senior Assistant Librarian);
Lynne Cholmondeley (Assistant Librarian -
Nursing); Keren Lilley (Assistant Librarian -
Outside Contracts); Bev Murray (Assistant
Librarian - Patients Library Service)
Objectives and Purposes: To provide a dynamic,
efficient and pertinent library and information
services to all users; to provide support for clinical
practice, research, continuing education, audit and
management development, within available
resources
Stock and Subject Coverage: 7,050 books; 297
periodicals. Covers renal medicine; orthopaedics;
paediatrics; immunology; NHS management; and
public health
Services/Facilities: Online and CD-ROM searches
(MEDLINE and CINAHL); Internet access;
photocopies (priced); CAL; word processing; fax
Availability: By prior appointment, for reference use
only
Hours: 08.00-17.30 (open until 19.00 on Thursday)
Publications: Library guide; journals holdings list
Related Bodies: National Blood Service Library; Avon
Health Authority; NHS Executive South and West
Regional Office

[613]

Spinal Injuries Association (SIA)

Newpoint House
76 St James's Lane
Muswell Hill
London N10 3DF
Telephone: 0181 444 2121
Fax: 0181 444 3761
E-mail: sia@spinali.demon.co.uk
World Wide Web: http://jgrweb.com/sia/
Contact: Information Officers

Objectives and Purposes: To provide support and services for those paralysed by spinal cord injury (paraplegia and tetraplegia) and their families and friends

Stock and Subject Coverage: Material covering all aspects of living with spinal cord injury. A small video collection of relevant material

Services/Facilities: Photocopies; telephone counselling; holiday facilities

Availability: Telephone and written enquiries accepted

Hours: 09.30-17.30

Publications: Bi-monthly newsletter; annual report; Moving Forward: A Guide to Living with Spinal Cord Injury. Full list available

Related Bodies: Member of the British Council of Organisations of Disabled People, and of Rights Now

[614]
St Albans City Hospital Library

Waverley Road
St Albans AL3 5PN
Telephone: 01727 897347
Fax: 01727 852015
Contact: Mrs EM Trounce (Library and Information Services Manager)
Objectives and Purposes: Multidisciplinary library and information services for health service staff working for the Trust and in the local community
Stock and Subject Coverage: Material covering all aspects of medicine and health
Services/Facilities: CD-ROM searches; fax; photocopies
Availability: By prior appointment, for reference use only
Hours: 09.00-17.00
Publications: Library guide; library bulletin (bi-annual)
Related Bodies: Hemel Hempstead Hospital Library

[615]
St Christopher's Hospice, Halley Stewart Library

51-59 Lawrie Park Road
Sydenham
London SE26 6DZ
Telephone: 0181 778 9252
Fax: 0181 776 9345
E-mail: denise@stchris.ftech.co.uk
Contact: Denise Brady; Jan Smith
Objectives and Purposes: To improve the quality of life of people with advanced cancer, motor neurone disease or AIDS
Stock and Subject Coverage: 3,000 books; 3,000 articles/pamphlets covering terminal care; palliative care; death and dying; ethics; hospices; bereavement; and pastoral care
Services/Facilities: Small bookshop of specialised literature
Availability: Telephone and written enquiries accepted (literature searches may be charged for if they are complex); visits by appointment, for reference use only
Hours: 09.00-17.00

Publications: Directory of Hospice Services in the UK
Related Bodies: Hospice Information Service

[616]
St George's Hospital Medical School

Library
Hunter Wing
Cranmer Terrace
London SW17 0RE
Telephone: 0181 725 5441
Fax: 0181 767 4696
E-mail: s.gove@sghms.ac.uk
World Wide Web:
http://www.sghms.ac.uk/library/sthome.htm
Contact: Ms S Gilbert (Readers Advisor); Mrs S Gove (Librarian); Ms M Logan-Bruce (Deputy Librarian); Mrs J Yeoh (Healthcare Sciences Faculty)
Objectives and Purposes: The provision of information services to hospital staff and NHS Trusts
Stock and Subject Coverage: 32,000 books; 795 periodicals covering all aspects of health care, but especially strong in psychiatry; clinical psychology; medical sociology; nursing studies; health care management and education; medical statistics; and care of the elderly. Special historical collection
Services/Facilities: Multimedia; online and CD-ROM searches (MEDLINE and CINAHL); fax; photocopies; word processing; scanner
Availability: Telephone and written enquiries; visits by prior appointment for reference use only (subject to a charge)
Hours: 09.00-21.00; 09.30-12.30 Saturday
Publications: Monthly newsletter and accessions list; annual report; instructional leaflets
Related Bodies: Branch libraries at Atkinson Morley Hospital and Bolingbroke Hospital. Joint Faculty of Health Sciences with Kingston University

[617]
St Helens and Knowsley Postgraduate Medical Centre

Whiston Hospital
Prescot
Merseyside L35 5DR
Telephone: 0151 430 1759
Fax: 0151 430 1312
Contact: Mrs T Jackson
Objectives and Purposes: To promote and advance the study of medicine, dentistry and allied sciences
Stock and Subject Coverage: Books and periodicals on general medicine and dentistry. Special collection of pathological specimens. Tape-slide collection on anaesthetics
Services/Facilities: MEDLINE searches; fax; photocopies (priced)
Availability: By prior appointment, for reference use only (charges for some services)
Hours: 08.30-18.00 (closes 17.00 on Friday)
Publications: Library handbook

[618]

St Michael's Hospital Medical Library

St Michael's Road
Warwick CV34 5QW
Telephone: 01926 406789
Fax: 01926 406702
Contact: Mr NP Harden
Objectives and Purposes: To provide library and
  information services for doctors in training and
  other staff of South Warwickshire Mental Health
  Services
Stock and Subject Coverage: Material on psychiatry;
  psychology; and mental health
Services/Facilities: Photocopies (priced)
Availability: Telephone and written enquiries
  accepted; visits by prior arrangement
Hours: 09.00-12.30 Wednesday and Friday only
Related Bodies: South Warwickshire Medical
  Education Centre Library

[619]

St Thomas' Hospital Library

North Wing, Ground Floor
Lambeth Palace Road
London SE1 7EH
Telephone: 0171 928 9292, ext 2507
Fax: 0171 922 8251
Contact: Diane Finlayson; Ruth Nicholson
Objectives and Purposes: To provide recreational
  reading and health information to patients, and
  management information to staff
Stock and Subject Coverage: Management and NHS
  administration. Special collection on consumer
  health information
Services/Facilities: CD-ROM searches; photocopies
Availability: Reference use only
Hours: 08.30-17.00

[620]

Stafford District General Hospital, Postgraduate Medical Centre Library

Weston Road
Stafford ST16 3SA
Telephone: 01785 230638
Fax: 01785 230639
Contact: Mrs LI Brain (Library Services and
  Information Assistant)
Objectives and Purposes: To provide educational
  facilities and resources for postgraduate doctors
  and consultants
Stock and Subject Coverage: 3,500 books; 120
  periodicals covering medicine and allied health
  subjects (excluding nursing). There is a growing
  audiovisual collection
Services/Facilities: CD-ROM searches; photocopies;
  slide-making facilities
Availability: Telephone and written enquiries
  accepted; visits by arrangement

Hours: 10.00-18.00
Publications: Library guide; various information sheets

[621]

Steroid Aid Group (SAG)

PO Box 220
London E17 3JR
Contact: Mrs B Copestake (Co-ordinator)
Objectives and Purposes: Advice, information and
  counselling for patients on prescribed steroids; a
  self-help group for patients, by patients
Availability: Written enquiries only (s.a.e. required)
Publications: Information and advice sheets for
  members; newsletter (3 or 4 per year)

[622]

Stillbirth and Neonatal Death Society (SANDS)

28 Portland Place
London W1N 4DE
Telephone: 0171 436 7940; Helpline: 0171 436 5881
Fax: 0171 436 3715
Contact: Mary El-Rayes (Director)
Objectives and Purposes: To provide support to
  bereaved parents and their families through a
  Helpline, publications, information service and
  over 200 local groups and contacts; to increase
  awareness of issues surrounding stillbirth
Stock and Subject Coverage: Material on pregnancy;
  baby bereavement; stillbirth/neonatal
  death/miscarriage
Services/Facilities: Helpline: 0171 436 5881
Availability: Reference use only
Hours: 09.00-17.00
Publications: List available on request

[623]

Stoke Mandeville Hospital NHS Trust

Wilfred Stokes Library
Mandeville Road
Aylesbury
Buckinghamshire HP21 8AL
Telephone: 01296 315428
Fax: 01296 315437
Contact: Ms J Kelson (Library Services Manager);
  Ms B Hylton (Assistant Librarian)
Objectives and Purposes: To provide high quality
  library and information services supporting the
  clinical, educational and research activities of all
  members
Stock and Subject Coverage: 3,500 books; 100
  periodicals. Covers general medicine. Special
  collection of materials on spinal cord injuries
Services/Facilities: Photocopies (priced); telephone
  and written enquiries accepted (as time permits)
Availability: By prior appointment, for reference use
  only
Hours: 08.30-17.00
Related Bodies: Member of HeLIN

[624]

Stroke Association

CHSA House
Whitecross Street
London EC1Y 8JJ
Telephone: 0171 490 7999
Fax: 0171 490 2686
Contact: Advisory Service, or Research Secretary
Objectives and Purposes: To work to prevent stroke illness and help those who suffer from it and their families
Services/Facilities: Advisory service for patients/carers and local information centres
Hours: 09.00-17.00
Publications: Stroke News; full list available
Related Bodies: Affiliated stroke clubs

[625]

Sussex Postgraduate Medical Centre Library

Brighton General Hospital
Elm Grove
Brighton BN2 3EW
Telephone: 01273 696011, exts 3702/3704
Fax: 01273 690032
Contact: Mrs Judy Lehmann (District Librarian); Miss Sharon Springham (Deputy Librarian)
Objectives and Purposes: To provide information and resources to all health care staff in Brighton, nursing students at the Institute, and (for reference only) to patients, relatives and the public
Stock and Subject Coverage: 16,000 books; 320 periodicals covering clinical medicine; nursing; NHS management; and all other aspects of health care, including physiotherapy and speech therapy. Also houses a History of Medicine Collection,
Services/Facilities: Online and CD-ROM searches; contents page service; interlibrary loans; fax; photocopies (priced)
Availability: Open to all, but reference use only for non-members (membership available for a fee); telephone and written enquiries accepted; membership available
Hours: 08.30-17.00 Monday and Friday; 08.30-20.00 Tuesday and Thursday; 08.30-18.00 Wednesday
Publications: The District Librarian edits IN-SET - The Newsletter of the South Thames (East) Regional Library Service (4 per year)
Related Bodies: Part of South Thames (East) Regional Library Service; Brighton University Institute of Nursing

[626]

Swindon and Marlborough NHS Trust

Princess Margaret Hospital
Swindon
Wiltshire SN1 4JU
Telephone: 01793 426200
Fax: 01793 426712

Contact: Miss HL Spurrier (Librarian)
Objectives and Purposes: A district general hospital
Stock and Subject Coverage: 4,800 books; 167 current periodicals. Covers medicine in general
Services/Facilities: Photocopies
Availability: By prior appointment, for reference use only
Hours: 09.00-17.15

[627]

Tameside Postgraduate Centre

Tameside General Hospital
Fountain Street
Ashton under Lyne OL6 9EW
Telephone: 0161 331 6341
Fax: 0161 331 6345
Contact: Mrs S Harrison (Secretary)
Objectives and Purposes: To provide library and information services for the education and support of local medical professionals
Stock and Subject Coverage: 3,000 books; 60 periodicals. Covers medicine in general
Availability: Members only
Hours: 09.00-17.00 (closes 16.00 on Friday)
Publications: Accessions list

[628]

Tavistock Library

Tavistock Centre
120 Belsize Lane
London NW3 5BA
Telephone: 0171 447 3776
Fax: 0171 447 3734
E-mail: info@tavilibdemon.co.uk
Contact: Ms Margaret Walker (Librarian); Ms Angela Haselton (Deputy Librarian); Ms Helen Oliver (Assistant Librarian)
Objectives and Purposes: To provide library and information services to support the training, research and clinical work of the Tavistock and Portman NHS Trust
Stock and Subject Coverage: 26,000 books; 720 periodicals; 700 audiovisual items covering psychology (with emphasis on psychotherapy, psychoanalysis and counselling); social work; and education
Services: Photocopies; online and CD-ROM searches
Availability: By prior appointment, for reference use only (fee charged)
Hours: 09.00-17.30. Termtime: 09.00-19.30 Monday to Thursday

[629]

Thyroid Eye Disease (TED)

Lea House
21 Troarn Way
Chudleigh
Devon TQ13 0PP
Telephone: 01626 852980
Contact: Mrs Sally Mitchell (Founder President)

Objectives and Purposes: To provide information, care and support to those affected by thyroid eye disease. Can provide copies of articles written by members of the medical profession
Availability: Statistical information available free to medical professionals and researchers; telephone and written enquiries accepted
Hours: 09.00-16.00
Publications: Bi-monthly newsletter; patients information (newsletter articles 10p each)

---

[630]

Toxoplasmosis Trust (TTT)

61-71 Collier Street
London N1 9BE
Telephone: 0171 713 0663 (office); Helpline: 0171 713 0599
Fax: 0171 713 0611
Contact: Christine Asbury (Director); Sue Heap (Support and Information Officer)
Objectives and Purposes: To educate those most at risk from this infection, in particular pregnant women and people with impaired immunity, and to provide support and information to those affected, their families, and carers
Stock and Subject Coverage: Library of research papers on all aspects of toxoplasmosis and of other publications on other issues of relevance to sufferers. A record of case histories is maintained
Services/Facilities: Comprehensive range of factsheets and leaflets; support network of local groups co-ordinated; telephone helpline
Availability: Telephone and written enquiries
Hours: 09.30-17.30
Publications: Newsletter (3 per year); information leaflets and factsheets; annual report

---

[631]

Tracheo Oesophageal Fistula Support Group (TOFS)

St George's Centre
91 Victoria Road
Netherfield
Nottingham NG4 2NN
Telephone and Fax: 0115 940 0694
Contact: David Dobbs (Chairman); Christine Shepherd (Vater Co-ordinator); Sue Dobbs
Objectives and Purposes: To provide contact between Tof families; to share management problems and solutions; to raise funds for equipment and research; to promote and spread information about Tof to new families and professionals
Stock and Subject Coverage: Tof information - leaflets and videos
Availability: Telephone and written enquiries accepted
Hours: 10.00-15.00 Monday to Thursday
Publications: List available

---

[632]

Tuberous Sclerosis Association (TSA)

Little Barnsley Farm
Catshill
Bromsgrove
Hereford and Worcester B61 0NQ
Telephone: 01527 871898
Fax: 01527 579419
E-mail: 101740.2252@compuserve.com
World Wide Web: http://users.ox.ac.uk/~jesu0132/tsa
Contact: Mrs Janet Medcalf (National Secretary); Mrs Ann Hunt (Family Care Work); Anne Carter (Appeals and Publicity Officer)
Objectives and Purposes: To support individuals with Tuberous Sclerosis and their carers; to educate professionals and the general public about tuberous sclerosis; to raise funds to encourage research into the causes and management of TS
Services/Facilities: Free advice and information to families; benevolent fund for needs arising from the condition; family care officer; information packs
Availability: Telephone and written enquiries accepted; videos available for loan/hire/purchase; annual subscription £10
Hours: 09.00-18.00
Publications: Newsletter - 3 per year; annual report; series of factsheets; medical brochure. Full list on request
Related Bodies: Part of Tuberous Sclerosis International (TSI); member of the Genetics Interest Group of the Neurological Alliance

---

[633]

Twins and Multiple Births Association (TAMBA)

PO Box 30
Little Sutton
South Wirral L66 1TH
Telephone and Fax: 0151 348 0020
World Wide Web: http://www.surreycc.gov.uk/tamba/
Contact: Gina Siddons (Administrator)
Objectives and Purposes: To support families with twins, triplets or more, individually, through Twins Clubs and specialist support groups; to promote public and professional awareness of their needs
Stock and Subject Coverage: Medical and educational information relating to twins and higher multiples
Services/Facilities: Information amd educational material on twins and higher multiple births from conception to adolescence; information packs for parents, professionals and students
Availability: Telephone and written enquiries accepted only (s.a.e. required)
Hours: 09.00-14.00 (answerphone out of hours)
Publications: List available

---

[634]

UK Cochrane Centre

Summertown Pavilion
Middle Way
Oxford OX2 7LG
Telephone: 01865 516300
Fax: 01865 516311
E-mail: general@cochrane.co.uk
Contact: Ms Carol Lefebvre (Information Specialist)
Status: Part of NHS Research and Development Programme
Objectives and Purposes: Facilitating the preparation, maintenance and dissemination of systematic reviews of the effects of health care, using electronic media
Related Bodies: Part of the International Cochrane Collaboration consisting of several Cochrane Centres and many individuals worldwide; closely associated with the NHS Centre for Reviews and Dissemination in York

[635]

UK Thalassaemia Society (UKTS)

107 Nightingale Lane
London N8 7QY
Telephone: 0181 348 0437
Fax: 0181 348 2553
E-mail: ukts@easynet.co.uk
Contact: Mr Costas Paul; Miss Katie Yiannikou
Objectives and Purposes: To bring families of sufferers together; to educate people by giving talks; to create awareness of the condition; to provide information about the condition; to raise funds for research; to offer counselling; to aim for the relief of persons suffering from thalassaemia
Services/Facilities: Free advice and information services; photocopies (priced); fax (at cost)
Availability: Telephone and written enquiries accepted; visits by appointment
Hours: 09.00-17.00
Publications: Booklets available for purchase. Full publications list available on request

[636]

Ulster Cancer Foundation

40-42 Eglantine Avenue
Belfast BT9 DX
Telephone: 01232 663281; Helpline: 01232 663439
Fax: 01232 660081
Contact: Arlene Spiers (Head of Education and Care Services); Ruth Campbell (Co-ordinator, Cancer Information Service)
Objectives and Purposes: To provide a telephone helpline and call-in service. Information is available on all aspects of cancer. Counselling is provided by nurse counsellors with experience in cancer care. It is confidential and open to anyone concerned about cancer
Stock and Subject Coverage: Small library, and an up-to-date resource centre of information on cancer

Services/Facilities: Information, support and counselling; Helpline; photocopies (priced)
Availability: Available to all who need it. Access for health professionals and students
Hours: 09.30-12.30 (and 14.00-16.00 Monday and Wednesday)
Publications: List available

[637]

United Bristol Healthcare NHS Trust (UBHT)

Bristol Royal Infirmary
Bristol BS2 8HW
Telephone: 0117 928 2043
Fax: 0117 928 2192
E-mail: postgrad-lib@bccnc.org.uk
Contact: Chrissy Jones (Library and Information Services Manager)
Stock and Subject Coverage: Multidisciplinary postgraduate library with 2,000 books and 140 periodicals; patient and staff recreational library service; patient information
Services: Photocopies; fax
Availability: Telephone and written enquiries accepted; visits by arrangement
Hours: 08.30-17.00
Publications: Library guide; quarterly report; PILLS (Patient Information Leaflet and Literature Service) Guide

[638]

United Kingdom Transplant Support Authority (UKTSA)

Fox Den Road
Stoke Gifford
Bristol BS12 6RR
Telephone: 0117 975575
Fax: 0117 975 7577
Contact: Mr Trevor T Jones Bsc Msc CertMHS MHSM (Librarian)
Objectives and Purposes: UKTSA is a special health authority operating within the NHS. It provides a 24-hour support service to all transplant units in the UK and the Republic of Ireland for the matching and allocation of organs for transplantation
Stock and Subject Coverage: Books and periodicals relating to transplantation and immunology. The Authority maintains the National Transplant Database, which is also used to produce reports/audits of the success of transplantation
Services/Facilities: Members of the public who require transplantation information services should contact the Authority's Publicity Services Section
Availability: Enquiries by letter or fax are preferred
Hours: By arrangement
Publications: Annual reports; audit reports

[639]

United Medical and Dental School (UMDS)

(1) Medical Library
St Thomas' Hospital
Lambeth Palace Road
London SE1 7EH
Telephone: 0171 928 9292, ext 2367
Fax: 0171 401 3932
E-mail: library@umds.ac.uk

(2) Wills Medical Library
Guys Hospital
London Bridge
London SE1 9RT
Telephone: 0171 955 4234
Fax: 0171 357 0458
E-mail: library@umds.ac.uk

(3) FS Warner Dental Library
Guys Hospital
London Bridge
London SE1 9RT
Telephone: 0171 955 4238

World Wide Web:
http://www.umdsac.uk/elsewhere/library
Contact: Andrew Baxter (Acting Librarian/Systems);
Angela Gunn (Reader Services Librarian);
David Hodgson (Cataloguing and Acquisitions Librarian)
Objectives and Purposes: To educate students in medicine and dentistry, postgraduate students in medicine, dentistry and the mental health sciences, and research in the biomedical sciences
Stock and Subject Coverage: Material, including 1,000 periodicals, covering general medicine, dentistry and the basic medical sciences. The dental library also has a video collection. Special collections: books by staff of Guy's; history of medicine
Services: Online searches; current awareness; photocopies
Availability: By prior appointment, for reference use only
Hours: Termtime: 09.00-20.45; 09.00-16.45 Saturday. Vacations: 09.00-19.00 Monday to Friday (Dental Library closes at 19.00)
Publications: Annual report; periodicals list

[640]

University College Chester School of Nursing and Midwifery

The Library
Nurse Education Centre
Arrowe Park Hospital
Upton
Wirral
Merseyside L49 5PE
Telephone: 0151 678 5111, ext 2115
Fax: 0151 604 7174
Contact: Mrs Christine Holly
Objectives and Purposes: To provide nursing library services

Stock and Subject Coverage: Materials on nursing; psychology; sociology; management and the NHS
Services/Facilities: CD-ROM searches (self-service); photocopies; interlibrary loans. Charges apply
Availability: Telephone and written enquiries accepted; visits by prior arrangement
Hours: 08.30-18.00 (closes 16.30 on Monday and Friday, and closes 12.30-13.00 in times of staff shortages)
Related Bodies: A site library of University College Chester

[641]

University College London, Clinical Sciences Library

1 University Street
London WC1E 6JJ
Telephone: 0171 209 6079
Fax: 0171 380 7727
E-mail: library@ucl.ac.uk
World Wide Web: http://www.ucl.ac.uk/library/
Contact: Garry Peacock (Site Librarian);
Louise Chitre (Senior Library Assistant)
Objectives and Purposes: A university medical school library
Stock and Subject Coverage: Books, periodicals, videos, CD-ROMs and multimedia items covering clinical medicine
Services/Facilities: Networked CD-ROMs; photocopies
Availability: Day reading tickets available (maximum 2 per academic year); by appointment with the Librarian for longer periods (usually a charge applies)
Hours: 09.00-21.00
Related Bodies: Branch of University College London Library

[642]

University College London, Department of Human Communication Science

Library
Chandler House
2 Wakefield Street
London WC1N 1PG
Telephone: 0171 837 0113, ext 3554
Fax: 0171 713 0861
E-mail: angela.douglas@ucl.ac.uk
World Wide Web: http://www.ucl.ac.uk/HCS/
Contact: Angela Douglas; Colin Graham;
Clive Culliford
Objectives and Purposes: To train students in the broader curriculum of speech sciences. Serves as the National Centre for Speech Sciences
Stock and Subject Coverage: Material on speech therapy; language disorders; voice disorders; linguistics; neurology; psychology; special needs. Special Test collection for speech therapists in clinics and schools

Services/Facilities: Online searches; photocopies (priced); fax; specialist bibliographies
Availability: Membership available
Hours: 09.15-19.00 (closes 18.00 on Monday and Thursday, and 17.00 on Friday)
Publications: List available
Related Bodies: Part of University College London

[643]

University College London, Institute of Orthopaedics

Royal National Orthopaedic Hospital Trust
Brockley Hill
Stanmore
Middlesex HA7 4LP
Telephone: 0181 954 2300
Fax: 0181 954 3213
Contact: Dr PF Smith
Objectives and Purposes: To contribute to studies of disorders of the locomotive system
Stock and Subject Coverage: Material on orthopaedics; spinal injuries
Services/Facilities: Photocopies
Availability: Open to bona fide researchers, by prior appointment
Hours: 09.00-17.00
Related Bodies: University College London

[644]

University College London, Science Library

Gower Street
London WC1E 6BT
Telephone: 0171 387 7050
Fax: 0171 380 7727
E-mail: library@ucl.ac.uk
World Wide Web: http://www.ucl.ac.uk/library/
Contact: Diana Mercer (Life Sciences Librarian)
Objectives and Purposes: To support the research and teaching of the Faculty of Life Sciences
Stock and Subject Coverage: Material on pre-clinical medicine and related biomedicine areas. Printed material increasingly supplemented with electronic material
Services/Facilities: Networked CD-ROMs, including BIOSIS; photocopies
Availability: Day reading tickets available (maximum 2 per academic year); by appointment with the librarian for longer periods (usually a charge applies)
Hours: 09.30-18.45
Related Bodies: Branch of University College London Library

[645]

University College Suffolk

Nursing Library
Education Centre
Ipswich Hospital
Ipswich IP4 5PD
Telephone: 01473 702547
Fax: 01473 710757
Contact: Deirdre Griffin (Librarian); Heather Arculeo (Library Assistant)
Objectives and Purposes: To support staff and students pursuing nursing and health care-related courses
Stock and Subject Coverage: 110,000 books; 60 periodicals; 350 videos. Covers nursing; midwifery; radiography; radiotherapy, and related subjects
Services/Facilities: Online and CD-ROM searches (priced); photocopies (priced)
Availability: By appointment, for reference use only
Hours: 08.30-16.30 (closes 14.30 on Wednesday and 16.00 on Friday)

[646]

★University of Aberdeen, Medical School Library

Polwarth Building
Foresterhill
Aberdeen AB25 2ZD
Telephone: 01224 681818, ext 52488
Fax: 01224 685157
E-mail: medlib@aberdeen.ac.uk
Contact: Dr PD Lawrence (Faculty Librarian); Mrs W Pirie (Site Librarian)
Objectives and Purposes: To supply access to information relevant to the needs of staff and students and to staff of the local hospitals, Trusts, health boards and GPs
Stock and Subject Coverage: Books, periodicals and electronic media covering clinical medicine and pre-clinical medical sciences. Some historical (pre-1900) material
Services/Facilities: MEDLINE and EMBASE on CD-ROM; computer assisted learning; interlibrary loans; fax; photocopies
Availability: Open access, but loans to members only. Charges for some services
Hours: 08.45-22.00 Monday to Thursday; 08.45-20.00 Friday; 09.00-17.00 Saturday; 14.00-17.00 Sunday. Hours may differ in vacations
Related Bodies: Aberdeen University Library

[647]

University of Birmingham, Barnes Library

Edgbaston
Birmingham B15 2TT
Telephone: 0121 414 3567
Fax: 0121 414 5855
E-mail: library@bham.ac.uk
Contact: SR Jean Scott (Barnes Librarian)

Objectives and Purposes: To provide library and information services to meet the research and teaching needs of staff and students; also limited support for postgraduate medical and dental education in the West Midlands RHA

Stock and Subject Coverage: Books and periodicals covering clinical and pre-clinical medicine and biological science; University of Birmingham thesis collection; Historical Collection of 5,000 volumes, including a special collection of books on the plague

Services/Facilities: Photocopies

Availability: By prior appointment, for reference use only

Hours: 09.00-21.00 Monday to Thursday; 09.00-19.00 Friday; 09.00-18.00 Saturday. Shorter hours in vacations

Related Bodies: Part of University of Birmingham Information Services; site library at the School of Dentistry

---

[648]

University of Bristol Dental Library

Dental Hospital
Lower Maudlin Street
Bristol BS1 2LY

Telephone: 0117 928 4419

Contact: Ms A Farrell (Dental Librarian); Ms G Kingham (Library Assistant)

Objectives and Purposes: To provide library and information services on oral and dental science

Stock and Subject Coverage: 5,700 books; 50 current periodicals; theses; 40 tape slide programmes; 84 video cassettes

Services/Facilities: Online access to University Library catalogues; interlibrary loans; photocopies; audiovisual viewing facilities

Availability: Telephone and written enquiries accepted, as time permits

Hours: 09.00-17.00

Related Bodies: Branch of the University of Bristol Medical Library

---

[649]

University of Bristol Medical Library

School of Medical Sciences
University Walk
Bristol BS8 1TD

Telephone: 0117 928 7945

Fax: 0117 929 0185

E-mail: j.scherr@bris.ac.uk

Contact: Ms Jennifer Scherr (Science/Engineering/Medical Librarian)

Objectives and Purposes: To provide library and information services in medicine for University members and other eligible users

Stock and Subject Coverage: 117,000 volumes in pre-clinical and clinical subjects at undergraduate and research level. Strongroom Collection (1478-1799), comprising 1,900 18th Century volumes and 300 earlier volumes. Nineteenth

Century Collection, 14,000 volumes. Mineral Waters and Spa Collection, 285 volumes. Parry Collection (1755-1822), 900 early medical works

Services/Facilities: Online and CD-ROM searches; photocopies

Availability: By prior appointment, for reference use only

Hours: Termtime: 08.45-21.00; 08.45-13.00 Saturday. Vacations: 08.45-18.30 Monday to Friday

Publications: Library guides

Related Bodies: Part of University of Bristol Library

---

[650]

University of Central England in Birmingham (UCE)

Nursing and Midwifery Library
Westbourne Road
Edgbaston
Birmingham B15 3TN

Telephone: 0121 331 6011/2

Fax: 0121 331 6012

E-mail: peter.ebrey@uce.ac.uk

Contact: Jane Richards (Faculty Librarian); Peter Ebrey (Subject Librarian)

Objectives and Purposes: To support nursing and health related education across a wide level

Stock and Subject Coverage: 70,000 books; 250 periodicals; 12 CD-ROM services. Specialist core collections held to support teaching programmes

Services/Facilities: Photocopies; CD-ROM searches; fax; Internet access

Availability: On payment of a fee

Hours: 08.30-21.00 (closes 17.00 on Friday); 10.00-17.00 Saturday. Vacations: 09.00-17.00

Publications: List available

Related Bodies: Other UCE site libraries

---

[651]

University of Central Lancashire, Sharoe Green Site Library

Sharoe Green Building
Preston PR1 2HE

Telephone: 01772 711226

Fax: 01772 719383

Contact: Helen Cooper (Site Information Officer); Adele Dunn and Caroline Melling (Senior Learning Resource Assistants)

Objectives and Purposes: To serve the needs of nursing students, and other students in related fields

Stock and Subject Coverage: Books, periodicals and multimedia in nursing and health related topics

Services/Facilities: CD-ROM searches; photocopies

Availability: By prior appointment, for reference use only

Hours: 08.45-17.30 (open until 19.00 on Monday; closes 16.30 on Friday)

Related Bodies: Other University sites around Lancashire

[652]

University of Derby Library

Chevin Avenue
off Western Road
Mickleover
Derby DE3 5GX
Telephone: 01332 622222
Fax: 01332 514323
E-mail: d.w.hiscock@derby.ac.uk
Contact: Gordon Brewer (Librarian); Richard Finch
    (Reader Services Librarian); David Hiscock
    (Subject Advisor, Health and Community Studies)
Objectives and Purposes: Providing library and
    information services to support teaching and
    research in the university
Stock and Subject Coverage: Multidisciplinary, but
    including health collections on nursing; health
    care; occupational therapy; radiography and
    radiotherapy; psychology; social work
Services/Facilities: Photocopies; online and CD-ROM
    searches; current awareness
Availability: Freely available for reference. Loans to
    members (membership available for a fee)
Hours: 08.45-21.00 Monday to Thursday;
    08.45-17.00 Friday; 10.00-17.00 Saturday;
    13.00-17.00 Sunday. Vacations: 09.00-17.00
    Monday to Friday
Related Bodies: Cedars Site Library, Whitaker Road,
    Derby

[653]

University of Derby, Cedars Site Library

Whittaker Road
    Derby DE3 6AP
Telephone: 01332 622222
Fax: 01332 298403
E-mail: d.w.hiscock@derby.ac.uk
World Wide Web:
    http://www.derby.ac.uk/library/homelib.html
Contact: David Hiscock (Subject Advisor, Health and
    Community Studies); Annabel Caulton (Senior
    Library Assistant)
Objectives and Purposes: Providing library and
    information services to support teaching and
    research in the university
Stock and Subject Coverage: Material on occupational
    therapy and arts therapies
Services/Facilities: Photocopies; online and CD-ROM
    searches; current awareness
Availability: Freely available for reference. Loans to
    members (membership available for a fee)
Hours: 08.45-19.00 Monday and Thursday;
    08.45-17.00 Tuesday, Wednesday and Friday.
    Restricted hours in vacations
Related Bodies: University of Derby Library

[654]

University of Dundee, Ninewells Medical School Library

Ninewells Hospital and Medical School
Dundee DD1 9SY
Telephone: 0101382 660111, exts 2515/2519
Fax: 01382 566179
E-mail: d.a.orrock@dundee.ac.uk
Contact: DA Orrock
Objectives and Purposes: The provision of
    bibliographic and medical resources for medical
    staff and students
Stock and Subject Coverage: Material covering all
    medical subjects
Services/Facilities: CD-ROM searches on MEDLINE;
    BIDS; photocopies
Availability: By prior appointment, for reference
    only (full service to those who subscribe and
    become members)
Hours: 09.00-22.00; 12.00-17.00 Saturday. Shorter
    hours in vacations
Related Bodies: Part of Dundee University Library

[655]

University of Dundee, School of Nursing and Midwifery, Fife Campus

Forth Avenue
Kirkcaldy
Fife KY2 5YS
Telephone: 01592 268888, ext 230
Fax: 01592 642910
Contact: Miss Elinor Skedgell; Mrs Donna Duff
Objectives and Purposes: To provide library and
    information services to students in health care
Stock and Subject Coverage: 20,000 books and
    audiovisual items; 160 periodicals. Covers nursing;
    midwifery; dentistry; health topics; general
    management and education
Services/Facilities: Online and CD-ROM searches
    (CINAHL, MEDLINE, ASSIA, HEBS and
    Cochrane); photocopies
Availability: Loans to staff, students and registered
    Fife health employees; reference facilities for others
Hours: 08.45-21.00 (closes 16.30 on Friday)
Publications: Current awareness list
Related Bodies: University of Dundee

[656]

University of Edinburgh, Erskine Medical Library

George Square
Edinburgh EH8 9XE
Telephone: 0131 650 3684
Fax: 0131 650 6841
E-mail: emlsd1@srv1.lib.ed.ac.uk
Contact: Philip Vaughan (Medical Librarian);
    Ms I McGowan (Reader Services); Ms J Martin
    (Bibliographic Services)

Stock and Subject Coverage: Materials covering clinical
    and pre-clinical medicine
Services/Facilities: Online and CD-ROM searches;
    photocopies
Availability: External users admitted for a fee
Hours: 09.00-22.00 Monday to Thursday;
    09.00-17.00 Friday and Saturday; 14.00-19.00
    Sunday. Shorter hours in vacations
Related Bodies: Branches at Western General
    Hospital, City Hospital, Royal Edinburgh
    Infirmary and University of Edinburgh Psychiatry
    Library. Part of Edinburgh University Library

[657]

University of Greenwich School of Health Library

Elizabeth Raybould Centre
Bow Arrow Lane
Dartford DA2 6PJ
Telephone: 0181 331 9164
Fax: 0181 331 9986
E-mail: j.morgan@greenwich.ac.uk
Contact: Jean Morgan
Objectives and Purposes: Education and training for
    health and social care, nursing and midwifery
Stock and Subject Coverage: Material on nursing;
    midwifery; health and social care. Special interest
    in mental health and learning disabilities
Services/Facilities: CD-ROM searches; photocopies
    (priced)
Availability: By prior appointment, for reference use
    only
Hours: 08.30-17.00 (open until 18.30 on Monday
    and Wednesday)

[658]

University of Hertfordshire, Learning Resources Centre

Hatfield Campus
College Lane
Hatfield
Hertfordshire AL10 9AB
Telephone: 01707 284678
Fax: 01707 284666
E-mail: C.Cox@herts.ac.uk or
    L.Woolgrove@herts.ac.uk
World Wide Web: http://www.herts.ac.uk
Contact: Chris Cox; Linda Woolgrove
Objectives and Purposes: An institution of higher
    education which is involved in health education
    in a major way
Stock and Subject Coverage: Hatfield Campus
    Learning Resources Centre serves a number of
    academic disciplines, including nursing, midwifery,
    child health, learning disabilities, mental health,
    social work, social sciences, psychology,
    biosciences, physiotherapy, radiography and
    medical imaging. There are large book collections
    and over 700 current journals related to the health
    areas

Services/Facilities: Photocopies; online searches; fax
Availability: The Centre is open for reference
    purposes only, but the CD-ROM database
    network is not available to users outside the
    university. Self-service photocopying is available,
    but there is a charge for this service. No written
    or telephone enquiries can be accepted
Hours: Termtime: 08.30-21.30; 13.00-18.00
    weekends. Vacations: 09.00-18.00

[659]

University of Leeds Medical & Dental Library

Level 7
Worsley Building
University of Leeds
Leeds LS2 9JT
Telephone: 0113 2335549
Fax: 0113 2334381
E-mail: medical.library@leeds.ac.uk
World Wide Web:
    http://www.leeds.ac.uk/library/medintr.html
Contact: Anne M.K. Collins (Medical Librarian)
Objectives and Purposes: To support the teaching and
    research of the Faculty of Medicine, Dentistry and
    Health, and the needs of clinical staff in the local
    NHS Trusts
Stock and Subject Coverage: Large collections of books
    and journals on all aspects of Medicine and
    Dentistry Special Collections include the original
    Library of Leeds General Infirmary, and the
    Library of the West Yorkshire Medical Chirurgical
    Society
Services/Facilities: Self-service photocopying;
    CD-ROM databases including MEDLINE
    (available to members only)
Availability: During termtime the Library is open to
    staff and students of the University, and many
    employees of local NHS Trusts. Bona fide
    researchers should apply in writing about access to
    the Library. Enquiries by telephone, e-mail, and
    letter will be dealt with when time is available.
    Material is only available for loan to full members
    of the Library. Photocopying, and mediated
    literature searches are available for a fee
Hours: 09.00-21.00 (closes 17.00 on Friday, and
    earlier closing in vacations); 10.00-13.00 Saturday
Related Bodies: The Medical & Dental Library is part
    of the Leeds University Library. Related units are:
    St James's Medical and Healthcare Library -
    provides Library facilities for University and NHS
    personnel working at St James Hospital. Leeds
    General Infirmary Healthcare Library, High Royds
    Healthcare Library - provide Library facilities to
    staff and students at the School of Healthcare
    Studies. Leeds Medical Information - compile and
    publish bibliographic current awareness services,
    and provide tailored information services to the
    Faculty of Medicine, Dentistry and Health

[660]

University of Leicester, Clinical Sciences Library

Leicester Royal Infirmary
PO Box 65
Leicester LE2 7LX
Telephone: 0116 252 3104
Fax: 0116 252 3107
E-mail: clinlib@leicester.ac.uk
World Wide Web: http://www.le.ac.uk
Contact: Ms Louise Jones (Librarian);
   Miss JoanneDunham (Deputy Librarian);
   Mrs Sue Spriggs (Toxicology Librarian)
Objectives and Purposes: To provide library and
   information services in medicine and
   health-related subjects to staff and students, and
   other health professionals in Leicestershire
Stock and Subject Coverage: 12,000 books; 550
   periodicals covering medicine, nursing and allied
   health. Houses the Leicester Medical Society
   Library - a collection of historical texts
Services/Facilities: Online and CD-ROM searches;
   interlibrary loans; database of articles on ethnic
   health in the UK; photocopies
Availability: Visits by appointment, for reference use
   only (some charges apply)
Hours: 09.00-22.00; 09.00-18.00 Saturday;
   14.00-21.00 Sunday
Related Bodies: Part of University of Leicester Library

[661]

University of Liverpool Library

Harold Cohen Library
Ashton Street
Liverpool L69 3DA
Telephone: 0151 794 5407
Fax: 0151 794 5417
E-mail: ql23@liverpool.ac.uk
World Wide Web:
   http://www.liv.ac.uk/Library/libhomep.html
Contact: Mr GJ Smith (Medical Librarian)
Objectives and Purposes: To support the research and
   teaching activities of the University and
   co-operative schemes within the library profession
Stock and Subject Coverage: General collection on
   medicine, dentistry, veterinary science and
   professions allied to medicine
Services/Facilities: Online and CD-ROM searches;
   current awareness service (priced); interlibrary
   loans; photocopies (colour available; priced)
Availability: By prior appointment, for reference use
   only. Charges for value-added services
Hours: 09.00-19.00; 09.00-13.00 Saturday
Publications: Newsletter. Full list available
Related Bodies: Branch libraries for certain subjects

[662]

University of Newcastle upon Tyne, Medical and Dental Library

Medical School
Framlington Place
Newcastle upon Tyne NE2 4HH
Telephone: 0191 222 7750/7609
Fax: 0191 222 8102
E-mail: helen.macfarlane@newcastle.ac.uk
World Wide Web:
   http://www.ncl.ac.uk/library/medindex.html
Contact: Mrs Helen MacFarlane BA DipLib ALA
   (Medical Librarian)
Objectives and Purposes: An academic library
   supporting teaching and research interests
   primarily of the Faculty of Medicine
Stock and Subject Coverage: 40,000 books; 900 current
   periodicals; 325 videos. Covers medicine;
   dentistry; and the biomedical sciences.
Services/Facilities: Networked CD-ROM services
   (MEDLINE, PsychLit, Biological Abstracts,
   Cochrane); photocopies (colour available); online
   searches; PC cluster; interlibrary loans (charges
   apply for mediated searches, photocopies and
   interlibrary loans)
Availability: By written application to the Medical
   Librarian; charges may apply
Hours: Termtime: 09.00-22.00; 09.00-16.30
   Saturday; 11.00-17.30 Sunday. Vacations:
   09.00-21.00; 09.00-13.00 Saturday
Publications: Union List of Medical Periodicals in the
   Northern Region (annual, £15)
Related Bodies: A Division of Newcastle University
   Library

[663]

University of Northumbria at Newcastle

Information Service
Coach Lane Campus
Coach Lane
Newcastle-upon-Tyne NE7 7XA
Telephone: 0191 227 4137
Fax: 0191 227 4419
E-mail: graham.walton@unn.ac.uk
World Wide Web: http://www.unn.ac.uk
Contact: Pam Bailey (Departmental Librarian);
   Hugh Hedley (Subject Librarian); David Peacock
   (Senior Librarian)
Objectives and Purposes: To provide library and
   information services to staff and students of the
   Faculty of Health, Social Work and Education and
   to other health staff
Stock and Subject Coverage: Material covering health,
   social work and education. Specialist collections in
   nursing; occupational therapy; and physiotherapy
Services/Facilities: Current awareness service;
   in-house database of journal articles, plus
   CINAHL, MEDLINE, ASSIA, etc.
Availability: Freely available for reference use

Hours: Termtime: 09.00-21.00 Monday to Thursday; 09.00-17.00 Friday; 09.30-17.00 Saturday. Vacation: 09.00-17.00 Monday to Friday
Related Bodies: University of Northumbria at Newcastle Information Services

[664]

University of Paisley, Department of Nursing, Midwifery and Healthcare

Paisley Campus
Royal Alexandra Hospital
Paisley PA2 9PN
Telephone: 0141 887 9111, ext 4127
Fax: 0141 887 4962
Contact: Veronica Harry MA Msc (Sub-Librarian, Health); Katrina Dalziel BA (Assistant Librarian)
Objectives and Purposes: To provide library and information services for Paisley University and the Royal Alexandra Hospital
Stock and Subject Coverage: 5,000 books; 170 periodicals. Covers nursing; midwifery; health care; medicine; and education
Availability: By arrangement with the Librarian
Hours: 08.30-18.00 (closes 16.00 on Friday)

[665]

University of Portsmouth, School of Health Studies

Library
St Mary's Hospital
Newport
Isle of Wight PO30 5TG
Telephone: 01983 534479
Fax: 01983 822105
Contact: Mrs R Painter (Librarian); Mrs J Hillier (Library Assistant)
Objectives and Purposes: The education and training of student nurses and other health professionals
Stock and Subject Coverage: 7,500 books; 35 periodicals covering all aspects of nursing and allied subjects
Services/Facilities: CD-ROM searches; current awareness service; literature searches; photocopies
Availability: By prior appointment, for reference use only; telephone and written enquiries are accepted
Hours: 08.30-16.30 (closes 16.00 on Friday)
Related Bodies: Frewen Library at the University of Portsmouth; member of Wessex Regional Libraries Information Network

[666]

University of Salford, Bury Campus

Academic Information Services
Talbot Grove
Bury
Lancashire BL9 6PH
Telephone: 0161 705 3316
Fax: 0161 761 6793
Contact: David Andrew

Objectives and Purposes: To provide library and information services to the Faculty of Health Care and Social Work Studies and to the Department of Midwifery
Stock and Subject Coverage: 7,000 books; 40 periodicals. Covers nursing and midwifery
Services/Facilities: CD-ROM searches; photocopies
Availability: Telephone and written enquiries accepted; visits by prior arrangement
Hours: 08.30-16.30

[667]

University of Sheffield Health Sciences Library, Northern General Hospital

Herries Road
Sheffield S5 7AV
Telephone: 0114 271 4902
Fax: 0114 243 8255
E-mail: hsl.ngh@sheffield.ac.uk
World Wide Web: http://www.shef.ac.uk/~lib/libsites/hslindex.html
Contact: John van Loo (Librarian); Susan Nicholls (Assistant Librarian)
Objectives and Purposes: To develop collections and resources and provide comprehensive information services in the health sciences in support of teaching, learning and research within the University and health services in Sheffield
Stock and Subject Coverage: 8,000 books; 250 periodicals covering medicine and nursing
Services/Facilities: Online and CD-ROM searches (MEDLINE, CINAHL, ASSIA, NMI, NurseRom, SportDiscus); photocopies
Availability: External membership, for a fee, at the Librarian's discretion
Hours: 09.00-20.00 (closes 17.00 on Friday); 09.00-13.00 Saturday. Reduced hours in vacations
Related Bodies: Part of University of Sheffield Library; linked with Health Sciences Library, Royal Hallamshire Hospital

[668]

University of Sheffield Health Sciences Library, Royal Hallamshire Hospital

Glossop Road
Sheffield S10 2JF
Telephone: 0114 271 2030
Fax: 0114 278 0923
E-mail: hsl.rhh@sheffield.ac.uk
Contact: John van Loo (Librarian); Fionna MacGillivray (Assistant Librarian)
Objectives and Purposes: To develop collections and resources and provide comprehensive information services in the health sciences in support of teaching, learning and research within the University and health services in Sheffield
Stock and Subject Coverage: 30,000 books; 500 periodicals. Covers medicine; dentistry; and nursing

Services/Facilities: Online and CD-ROM searches (MEDLINE, CINAHL, NMI, SportDiscus); photocopies
Availability: External membership, for a fee, at the Librarian's discretion
Hours: Termtime: 09.00-21.30 (closes 17.00 on Friday); 09.00-13.00 Saturday. Vacations: 09.00-19.00 (closes 17.00 on Friday); 09.00-12.30 Saturday
Related Bodies: Part of University of Sheffield Library; separate branch at Northern General Hospital, Huntsman Building

[669]

University of Southampton Library, Biomedical Sciences

Basset Crescent East
Southampton SO16 7PX
Telephone: 01703 594215
Fax: 01703 593007
E-mail: illbs@southampton.ac.uk
World Wide Web: http://www.soton.ac.uk/~library/
Contact: Miss AM Norman (Branch Librarian); Dr PL Royle
Objectives and Purposes: To support the University's work in teaching and research in the field of biomedical sciences
Stock and Subject Coverage: Books; periodicals; abstracts and indexing journals covering biology; biochemistry; physiology; human nutrition; pharmacology; human morphology; medicine (undergraduate)
Services/Facilities: Photocopies; loans (registered users only)
Availability: Open access, but some services only available to registered users
Hours: 09.00-22.00 Monday to Thursday; 09.00-18.00 Friday; 09.00-17.00 Saturday; 12.00-21.00 Sunday
Related Bodies: Part of University of Southampton Library; member of SWRLIN

[670]

University of Southampton Library, Health Sciences

South Academic Block
Mailpoint 16
Southampton General Hospital
Tremona Road
Southampton SO17 1BJ
Telephone: 01703 796541
Fax: 01703 798939
E-mail: acl@soton.ac.uk
World Wide Web: http://www.soton.ac.uk/~library/hs-home.htm
Contact: Mr Andrew Lobb (main contact); Mrs Pip Beck; Mrs Elizabeth Robertson
Objectives and Purposes: To serve the health sciences information needs of Southampton University, and NHS staff in the South and West Region

Stock and Subject Coverage: 20,000 books; 500 periodicals; audiovisual materials. Covers clinical medicine and most related disciplines
Services/Facilities: Photocopies; mediated online searches
Availability: Staff and students only
Hours: 09.00-22.00 Monday to Thursday; 09.00-18.00 Friday; 09.00-17.00 Saturday; 14.00-18.00 Sunday
Publications: Current periodicals list
Related Bodies: Part of University of Southampton Library; member of SWRLIN and WRLIN

[671]

University of Southampton, South and West Health Care Libraries Unit

South Academic Block
Southampton General Hospital
Tremona Road
Southampton SO16 6YD
Telephone: 01703 796543
Fax: 01703 785648
E-mail: ca.fowler@soton.ac.uk
World Wide Web: http://www.soton.ac.uk/~library/swhclu.html
Contact: Ms CA Fowler (Regional Services Librarian)
Objectives and Purposes: To support the work of all libraries serving the NHS in the South and West Region
Availability: At the discretion of the Librarian
Hours: 09.00-22.00 Monday to Thursday; 09.00-18.00 Friday; 09.00-17.00 Saturday; 14.00-18.00 Sunday
Publications: SWRLIN Directory of Libraries; SWRLIN News. Full list available
Related Bodies: Linked with SWRLIN

[672]

University of St Andrews Library

North Street
St Andrews
Fife KY16 9TR
Telephone: 01334 462281
Fax: 01334 462282
E-mail: library@st-and.ac.uk
World Wide Web: http://www-library.st-and.ac.uk/main.html
Contact: University library
Objectives and Purposes: NF Dumbleton MA ALA (Librarian); Reference Librarians on 01334 462286
Stock and Subject Coverage: Material on pre-clinical medicine, including some early medical books (library collection dates from 1642)
Services/Facilities: Online and CD-ROM searches; photocopies
Availability: Bona fide researchers admitted by appointment; external membership available
Hours: 08.45-22.00 (closes 18.00 on Friday); 09.00-17.00 Saturday; 13.00-19.00 Sunday. Shorter hours in vacations

University of Teesside
see **Stop Press on page 157**

---

[673]
University of the West of England (UWE)

Library, Faculty of Health and Social Care
Glenside Campus
Blackberry Hill
Stapleton
Bristol BS16 1DD
Telephone: 0117 975 8404
Fax: 0117 975 8402
E-mail: jl-nichols@wpg.uwe.ac.uk;
l-weeks@wpg.uwe.ac.uk
World Wide Web: http://www.uwe.ac.uk/library/
Contact: Liz Weeks ALA (Campus Librarian);
Jan Nichols (Subject Librarian)
Objectives and Purposes: To serve the Faculty of
Health and Social Care and local health care
professionals
Stock and Subject Coverage: 45,000 books; 350
periodicals; large audiovisual collection; bones and
models. Covers nursing, midwifery, physiotherapy
and radiography
Services/Facilities: CD-ROM and online searches;
photocopies; fax; current awareness; enquiries;
interlibrary loans
Availability: By prior appointment, for reference use
only; membership available
Hours: 09.00-20.30 (closes 19.00 on Friday; opens
10.00 on Wednesday); 09.30-16.00 Saturday
Related Bodies: Other campus libraries at Bath,
Gloucester, Swindon and St Matthias, Bristol

---

[674]
*University of Wales College of Medicine Library (UWCM)

The Sir Herbert Duthie Library
University Hospital of Wales
Heath Park
Cardiff CF4 4XN
Telephone: 01222 742874
Fax: 01222 743651
E-mail: lancaster@cf.ac.uk (Librarian);
pritchard@cf.ac.uk (Deputy Librarian)
Contact: Mr JM Lancaster (Librarian);
Mr SJ Pritchard (Deputy Librarian and Contact)
Objectives and Purposes: Undergraduate and
postgraduate medical, dental and nursing
education; the Library also supports the College's
extensive biomedical research programmes and
provides full library and information services to
NHS staff and GPs throughout South Glamorgan;
in addition UWCM co-ordinates a network of
Postgraduate Medical Centre libraries throughout
Wales
Stock and Subject Coverage: 42,000 books; 1,000
periodicals covering medicine; nursing; dentistry;
the basic medical sciences and related areas
including professions allied to medicine, and

relevant parts of the social sciences. Also, an
extensive collection of video material and a large
collection of dental photographs. A historical
collection of 2,000 volumes
Services/Facilities: Online and CD-ROM searches;
photocopies; PC facilities; user education
programmes; self-service binding facility
Availability: By prior appointment, for reference use
only; external membership is available by
subscription
Hours: October to July: 09.00-21.00; 09.00-17.00
Saturday. August to September: 09.00-19.00;
09.00-12.30 Saturday
Publications: UWCM Libraries Guide; annual report;
Russia and Wales: Essays on the State Involvement
in Health Care (Cole, JH and Lancaster, JM);
History of Medicine Society of Wales (1994)
Related Bodies: Branch/outlier libraries at: Dental
Library, Heath Park, Cardiff CF4 4XY; Medical
Library, Cardiff Royal Infirmary, Newport Road,
Cardiff CF2 1SZ; Cochrane Library, Llandaff
Hospital NHS Trust, Penarth CF64 2XX; Violet
Hughes Memorial Library, Velindre Hospital,
Whitchurch, Cardiff CF4 4XY

---

[675]
University of Wales Swansea, Department of Nursing, Midwifery and Health Care

Morriston Hospital
Swansea SA6 6NL
Telephone: 01792 703767; Librarian: 01792 703754
Fax: 01792 799230
E-mail: s.m.storey@swansea.ac.uk
Contact: Stephen Storey (Librarian)
Objectives and Purposes: To provide library and
information services for nurse education
Stock and Subject Coverage: Range of material on
nursing
Services/Facilities: Photocopies; Internet access; BIDS
searches; word processing
Availability: By prior appointment, for reference use
only
Hours: 08.30-20.30 (open until 21.00 on Monday;
closes 16.00 on Friday)
Related Bodies: University of Wales Swansea

---

[676]
University of Wolverhampton, Burton Site

Nurse Education Centre
Burton Hospital
Belvedere Road
Burton-on-Trent
Staffordshire DE13 0RB
Telephone: 01283 66333, ext 2237
Contact: Liz Watson (Site Librarian);
Annette Newton; Dorothy Wilkinson
Objectives and Purposes: To support the students and
academic staff in relation to nursing and
midwifery fields

Stock and Subject Coverage: 6,000 books; 55 periodicals. Covers nursing and midwifery
Services/Facilities: CD-ROM searches; interlibrary loans; photocopies
Availability: By prior appointment, for reference use only; membership available
Hours: 08.15-17.00 (closes 16.00 on Friday)
Related Bodies: Other site libraries

[677]
University of Wolverhampton, Manor Site

Manor Hospital
Pleck Road
Walsall
West Midlands WS2 9PS
Telephone: 01922 721172, ext 7181
Contact: Shirley Towe (Site Librarian); Ann Roadway; Julie Jackson
Objectives and Purposes: To support the students and academic staff in relation to nursing and midwifery fields
Stock and Subject Coverage: 10,000 books; 50 periodicals. Covers nursing and midwifery
Services/Facilities: CD-ROM searches; interlibrary loans; photocopies
Availability: By prior appointment, for reference use only; membership available
Hours: 08.15-17.00 (closes 16.00 on Friday)
Related Bodies: Other site libraries

[678]
University of Wolverhampton, New Cross Site

Education Centre
New Cross Hospital
Wolverhampton WV10 0QP
Telephone: 01902 307999, ext 2649
Fax: 01902 306072
Contact: Pam Collins (Senior Librarian); Kirstin Ewart; Sheila Scribrer
Objectives and Purposes: To support the students and academic staff in relation to nursing and midwifery fields
Stock and Subject Coverage: 20,000 books; 150 periodicals; 200 videos; 200 open learning packs. Covers nursing and midwifery
Services/Facilities: CD-ROM searches; interlibrary loans; photocopies
Availability: By prior appointment, for reference use only; membership available
Hours: 09.00-17.00 (closes 16.30 on Friday)
Related Bodies: Other site libraries

[679]
University of Wolverhampton, Russells Hall Site

Esk House
Russells Hall Hospital
Dudley
West Midlands
Telephone: 01384 456111, ext 2594
Contact: Gill Williamson (Site Librarian); Ann Colley; Linda Howes
Objectives and Purposes: To support the students and academic staff in relation to nursing and midwifery fields
Stock and Subject Coverage: 12,000 books; 65 periodicals. Covers nursing and midwifery
Services/Facilities: CD-ROM searches; interlibrary loans; photocopies
Availability: By prior appointment, for reference use only; membership available
Hours: 08.15-17.00 (closes 16.00 on Friday)
Related Bodies: Other site libraries

[680]
Urostomy Association (UA)

Buckland
Beaumont Park
Danbury
Essex CM3 4DE
Telephone and Fax: 01245 224294
Contact: Mrs Angela Cooke (National Secretary)
Objectives and Purposes: To assist people who are about to undergo or who have undergone surgery resulting in a Urinary Diversion/Ileal Conduit; to assist with counselling as may be necessary with regard to appliances, housing, work situations, marital problems and assisting them to resume as full a life as possible with every confidence
Availability: Telephone and written enquiries accepted
Hours: 09.00-17.00 (answerphone available out of hours)
Publications: Journal (3 per year); range of leaflets and booklets (free); a video is available for purchase

[681]
Vegan Society

Donald Watson House
7 Battle Road
St Leonards-on-Sea
East Sussex TN37 7AA
Telephone: 01424 427393
Fax: 01424 717064
World Wide Web:
   http://www.veg.org/orgs/veganSocUk
Contact: Richard Farhall (General Secretary)
Objectives and Purposes: To promote veganism and vegan diets
Stock and Subject Coverage: Material on vegan nutrition; health; and animal rights
Availability: Telephone and written enquiries

Hours: 09.00-17.30
Publications: The Vegan (quarterly journal); Vegan
  Nutrition; Animal-Free Shopping

[682]
*Victoria Infirmary, Glasgow, NHS Trust

Langside Road
Glasgow G42 9TY
Telephone: 0141 201 5760
Fax: 0141 649 2206
Contact: Mrs A Clackson (Librarian)
Stock and Subject Coverage: 1,000 books; 150
  periodicals; slides; videos covering medicine;
  surgery; laboratory medicine; professions allied to
  medicine (physiotherapy, occupational therapy and
  speech therapy)
Services/Facilities: CD-ROM searches; photocopies
  (priced)
Availability: Telephone and written enquiries
  accepted; visits by arrangement
Hours: 09.00-17.00
Publications: The Victoria Infirmary of Glasgow
  1890-1990: A centenary history (Slater, SD and
  Dow, DA)

[683]
Vitiligo Society

19 Fitzroy Square
London W1P 5HQ
Telephone: 0171 388 8905
Fax: 0171 388 0487
Contact: Michael Wadsworth (Administrator);
  Mrs Maxine Whitton (Chair)
Objectives and Purposes: A support group offering
  advice to people with vitiligo (a skin condition in
  which patches of skin turn white through loss of
  pigment); to inform, educate and fund research
Services/Facilities: Free advice service to enquirers
  (limited in the case of non-members)
Availability: Telephone and written enquiries only
  (s.a.e. appreciated)
Hours: 09.00-17.00 (answerphone available out of
  hours)
Publications: Quarterly newsletter; annual report;
  range of information leaflets

[684]
Wales Council for the Blind

3rd Floor, Shand House
20 Newport Road
Cardiff CF2 1YB
Telephone: 01222 473954
Fax: 01222 455710
Contact: Vanessa Webb (Director and Development
  Officer); Rebecca Thomas (Administrator);
  Deborah David (Clerical Officer)
Objectives and Purposes: To enable and empower
  visually impaired people by monitoring services in
  Wales, promoting services where they do not

exist, encouraging improvement in standards of
  services, supporting voluntary efforts, and
  co-ordinating statutory and voluntary efforts in
  Wales
Stock and Subject Coverage: 400 books; 50 periodicals
  covering all aspects of visual impairment
Services/Facilities: Free advice and information;
  translation into Braille; database searches;
  awareness training; resource packs
Availability: Freely available
Hours: 09.00-17.00
Related Bodies: Network of local branches
  throughout Wales

[685]
Wales Council for the Deaf (WCD)

Glenview House
Court House Street
Pontypridd
Mid Glamorgan CF37 1JW
Telephone: 01443 485687 (voice); Minicom:
  01443 485686
Fax: 01443 408555
Contact: Mr Norman B Moore
Objectives and Purposes: The main aim of the Council
  is to support all activities of people with hearing
  loss in Wales with the object of enabling these
  people to lead fuller and more independent lives
Stock and Subject Coverage: Various publications and
  videos on hearing impairment
Services/Facilities: Interpreting agency and laminating
  services
Availability: Telephone and written enquiries only
Hours: 09.00-17.00
Publications: Wales HI Magazine (quarterly);
  Volunteer Handbook; Text Terminal Users
  Directory (annual); annual report

[686]
Walsall Hospitals NHS Trust

Postgraduate Medical Centre Library
Manor Hospital
Moat Road
Walsall WS2 9PS
Telephone: 01922 721172, ext 6628
Fax: 01922 656612
Contact: Mrs C Thomas (Medical Librarian)
Objectives and Purposes: To provide an information
  service to medical staff in the local area
Stock and Subject Coverage: 1,500 books; 120
  periodicals covering all medical subjects
Services/Facilities: CD-ROM searches (MEDLINE);
  photocopies
Availability: By prior appointment, for reference use
  only
Hours: 09.00-17.00

[687]

Wellcome Centre for Medical Science

183 Euston Road
London NW1 2BE
Telephone: 0171 611 8722
Fax: 0171 611 8726
E-mail: infoserv@wellcome.ac.uk
Contact: Mrs S Hernando (Head of Information Service)
Objectives and Purposes: To help medical science to flourish by promoting better public understanding of science and by facilitating a more informed approach to science policy making
Stock and Subject Coverage: 9,000 books/reports; 500 periodicals; 700 videos covering popular science; public understanding of science; science policy
Services/Facilities: In-house databases on sources of medical research funding and science policy information news
Availability: Freely available for reference
Hours: 09.45–17.00; 09.00–13.00 Saturday
Publications: IS News (quarterly newsletter)
Related Bodies: Part of Wellcome Trust

Wellcome Institute for the History of Medicine

see **Stop Press on page 157**

---

[688]

Wellhouse NHS Trust Libraries and Information Service

(1) Medical Library
Edgware General Hospital
Edgware
Middlesex HA8 0AD
Telephone: 0181 732 6603
Fax: 0181 952 7113

(2) Medical Library
Barnet General Hospital
Wellhouse Lane
Barnet
Hertfordshire EN5 3DJ
Telephone: 0181 732 4834
Fax: 0181 732 4678
E-mail: guy@medlib.demon.co.uk

Contact: Tom Roper; Guy Robinson (Librarian); David Clay (Assistant Librarian)
Objectives and Purposes: To provide information to support education, research and clinical practice of NHS staff in the Wellhouse NHS Trust
Stock and Subject Coverage: Material on all fields of medical and nursing information (books, journals and databases). Particularly strong GP Collection at Barnet
Services/Facilities: Online, Internet and CD-ROM searches; photocopies; free loans and reference facilities

Availability: Primarily to Trust staff. Personal and telephone enquiries are accepted. (Charges made for some interlibrary loans)
Hours: 09.00–17.00

---

[689]

★Welsh Health Common Services Authority EstateCare Group (WHCSA EstateCare)

Crickhowell House
Pierhead Street
Capital Waterside
Cardiff CF1 5XT
Telephone: 01222 502164
Fax: 01222 502508
Contact: Miss HK George (Librarian)
Objectives and Purposes: The provision of architectural, engineering, quantity surveying, landscape and site inspectorate services, project management, specialist engineering such as x-ray, sterilizers, etc. Property management and estate appraisal
Stock and Subject Coverage: 2,500 books; 79 periodicals; several microfile systems containing technical documents and a collection of trade literature relating to the design, operation and maintenance of health service buildings and estates. Also NHS Estates documents
Services/Facilities: Enquiry service; reference
Availability: To persons in the health care field, normally for reference only. Visits and loans by arrangement
Hours: 09.00–17.00
Publications: Library bulletin; list of periodicals; Care by Design: The Community Hospitals of Wales

---

[690]

★Welsh Office Library

Cathays Park
Cardiff CF1 3NQ
Telephone: 01222 825388
Fax: 01222 823122
Contact: David Allum (Chief Librarian); Ms Dinah Roberts (Deputy Librarian and Health Subject Specialist)
Status: Government department
Stock and Subject Coverage: The medicine and health care section of the collection is limited to non-clinical, strategic and administrative aspects of the NHS in Wales
Services/Facilities: Online and CD-ROM searches; microfiche; fax; photocopies
Availability: By prior appointment, for reference use only
Hours: 08.30–17.00 (closes 16.30 on Friday)
Publications: Current awareness bulletin (monthly); monthly and annual checklists of Welsh Office publications

[691]

West Cheshire Postgraduate Medical Centre

Countess of Chester Hospital
Liverpool Road
Chester CH2 1BQ
Telephone: 01244 383676
Fax: 01244 364105
Contact: Mrs ER Fletcher (Librarian);
Mrs R Brennan (Assistant Librarian)
Objectives and Purposes: Medical education for
hospital doctors, GPs and dentists
Stock and Subject Coverage: 3,000 books; 130
periodicals covering all aspects of medicine and
dentistry
Services/Facilities: CD-ROM searches; slide
production; fax; photocopies (all services charged
at a nominal fee)
Availability: Primarily for doctors and dentists, but
paramedics and nurses have access for study
purposes
Hours: 09.00-20.00
Publications: Annual report

[692]

West Dorset NHS Trust

Staff Library
Postgraduate Medical Centre
Dorset County Hospital
Princes Street
Dorchester DT1 1TS
Telephone: 01305 213248
Fax: 01305 213359
Contact: Anne Rampersad (Library Services
Manager); Patricia Graham (Assistant Library
Services Manager)
Objectives and Purposes: A hospital library for the
needs of its staff to assist them with information
required to help with patient care and for
health-related research
Stock and Subject Coverage: Material covering
medicine; surgery; nursing; health-related sciences;
and the NHS
Services/Facilities: CD-ROM searches; photocopies;
fax
Availability: By prior appointment, for reference use
only (may be subject to a fee)
Hours: 09.00-17.00 (closes 16.30 on Friday)
Publications: List available on request
Related Bodies: Part of WRLIS

[693]

West Glamorgan Health Information and Library Service (WGHILS)

Staff Library
Singleton Hospital
Sketty
Swansea SA2 8QA
Telephone: 01792 205666, ext 5281
Fax: 01792 285127

E-mail: engel@cf.ac.uk
Contact: Colin Engel (Library Services Manager)
Objectives and Purposes: To supply the information
needs of NHS staff in the area
Stock and Subject Coverage: Material on all clinical
specialties, with emphasis on the South West Wales
sub-regional specialties, e.g. cardiology; burns and
plastics; and cancer. Coverage also for pre-clinical
areas of special research significance, e.g. medical
physics
Services/Facilities: Translations
Availability: By arrangement. There are mutual
service relationships with the Association of Welsh
Health Librarians and the All Wales Health
Information Library Extension Service
Hours: 08.30-17.00
Publications: This is the editorial office for the
Newsletter of Association of Welsh Health
Librarians
Related Bodies: WGHILS comprises five libraries
linked in confederacy: Singleton, Morriston,
Neath and Cefn Coed Hospitals and the Iechyd
Morgannwg Health library

[694]

West Kent Postgraduate Medical Centre Library

Farnborough Hospital
Orpington
Kent BR6 8ND
Telephone: 01689 814305/6
Fax: 01689 861218
Contact: Mrs S Tarbox (Head of Library Services);
Mrs M Fiander and Mrs G Hernon (Library
Assistants)
Objectives and Purposes: To provide high quality
services to all staff of Bromley Hospitals NHS
Trust and to reflect the day-to-day needs of staff
in order to carry out the job, their ongoing
educational needs and information on the
changing aspects of the NHS
Stock and Subject Coverage: 5,000 books; 100
periodicals. Covers all medical topics
Services/Facilities: Online and CD-ROM searches
(MEDLINE, CINAHL, ClinPsych and Cochrane);
photocopies (priced); fax; word processing
Availability: Staff only
Hours: 09.00-17.00
Publications: Newsletter
Related Bodies: South Thames Region Library and
Information Service

[695]

West London Health Care NHS Trust

Coombs Library
St Bernard's Wing
Uxbridge Road
Southall
Middlesex UB1 3EU
Telephone and Fax: 0181 967 5009
Contact: Mr P Valentine (Library Services Manager)

Objectives and Purposes: To support the work of Trust and community staff in education and training, research and patient care; main field of interest is mental health

Stock and Subject Coverage: Material on mental health (special collection); nursing; public health; and management

Services/Facilities: Photocopies; database searches; word processing

Availability: Staff only

Hours: 09.00-17.00

Publications: Current awareness bulletin

[696]
West Middlesex University Hospital NHS Trust

Twickenham Road
Isleworth
Middlesex TW7 6AF

Telephone: 0181 565 5968

Fax: 0181 565 5408

E-mail: library@wmuhnhst.co.uk

World Wide Web: http://www.nthames-health. tpmde.ac.uk/ntrl/Ania.htm

Contact: Mrs Patricia Bowen (Librarian); Mr James Riste (Assistant Librarian); Mrs Madhulike Bahde (Assistant Librarian)

Objectives and Purposes: A multidisciplinary library for Trust employees and students at Charing Cross and Westminster Medical School

Stock and Subject Coverage: Material on all aspects of medicine and health care

Services/Facilities: CD-ROM and online searches; Internet access; scanning; fax; photocopies

Availability: Restricted to staff and students

Hours: 09.00-20.00 (closes 17.00 on Thursday and Friday)

Related Bodies: Charing Cross and Westminster Medical School; North Thames Regional Library and Information Service

[697]
West Suffolk Hospitals NHS Trust

Clinical Resource Centre and Library
Hardwick Lane
Bury St Edmunds
Suffolk IP33 2QZ

Telephone: 01284 713343

Fax: 01284 713113

E-mail: 100445.3112@compuserve.com

Contact: Mrs Lynette Last (Assistant Librarian); Mrs Valerie Wallis (Interlibrary Loans)

Objectives and Purposes: To ensure the provision of a quality and cost-effective library service to Trust staff

Stock and Subject Coverage: Collection of clinical and NHS-related material

Services/Facilities: Database searches; interlibrary loans; photocopies; fax

Hours: 08.30-17.00 (closes 21.00 on Thursday and 16.00 on Friday)

Publications: Monthly current awareness list

Related Bodies: Anglia and Oxford Regional Libraries Group

[698]
Western Health and Social Services Board/Western Area College of Nursing (WH&SSB/WACN)

Library
Multidisciplinary Education Centre
Altnagelvin Area Hospital
Glenshane Road
Londonderry
Northern Ireland BT47 1JB

Telephone: 01504 45171, ext 3725

Fax: 01504 49334

Contact: Mr F O'Deorain (Library Services Manager); Ms S Hodgson (Nursing College Librarian)

Objectives and Purposes: A library and document supply service to support the education, continuing professional development, and direct patient/client care for nursing, medical, paramedical, social work and management staff

Stock and Subject Coverage: 8,500 books; 120 periodicals; audiovisual items covering health care management; nursing; postgraduate medical education; and social work

Services/Facilities: Online and CD-ROM searches (MEDLINE, CINAHL, etc.); information files on NHS management and nursing topics; fax; photocopies

Availability: Freely available for reference use; visits by appointment

Hours: 09.00-17.30 Monday; 09.00-21.30 Tuesday to Thursday; 09.00-17.00 Friday

Publications: Current awareness lists; accessions lists

Related Bodies: Part of the Northern Ireland Health and Social Services Library, whose central library is the Queen's University Belfast Medical Library

[699]
Weston Area Health Trust (WAHT)

Staff Library
Weston General Hospital
Grange Road
Uphill
Weston-super-Mare BS23 4TQ

Telephone and Fax: 01934 647166

E-mail: diane@wahtlib.demon.co.uk

Contact: Mrs D Smithson (Librarian); Mrs T Babell (Assistant Librarian)

Objectives and Purposes: Multidisciplinary library for a small general hospital

Stock and Subject Coverage: 5,000 books; 60 periodicals covering all aspects of medicine and nursing, and some management

Services/Facilities: CD-ROM searches; fax; photocopies

Availability: By prior appointment, for reference use only

Hours: 09.00-17.00

Publications: Library guide; Beginner's Guide to MEDLINE and CINAHL

---

[700]

Wharfedale General Hospital Postgraduate Medical Library

Newall Carr Road
Otley
West Yorkshire LS21 2LY

Telephone: 0113 292 6072

Fax: 01943 468314

Contact: Mrs VK Williams (Librarian)

Objectives and Purposes: To provide library and information services for hospital staff and local GPs

Stock and Subject Coverage: 1,500 books; 60 periodials on medicine

Services/Facilities: Online and CD-ROM searches; fax; photocopies

Availability: Access free to all. Material available for loan to hospital staff. Charges made for some services

Hours: 09.00-17.00

Related Bodies: Part of the United Leeds Teaching Hospitals NHS Trust

---

[701]

Whitchurch Postgraduate Medical Centre Library

Whitchurch Hospital
Cardiff CF4 7XB

Telephone: 01222 693191, ext 6382

Fax: 01222 520170

Contact: Mrs Jean Walkden (Librarian)

Objectives and Purposes: To provide information and support to staff of South Glamorgan Health Authority on psychiatry and allied subjects

Stock and Subject Coverage: 1,900 books; 95 periodicals covering psychiatry; psychology; mental handicap; addiction; psychotherapy; some social work and allied therapies

Services/Facilities: Online and CD-ROM searches; fax; photocopies

Availability: By prior appointment, for reference use only

Hours: 09.00-17.00

---

[702]

Whittington Hospital Library

Highgate Hill
London N19 5NF

Telephone: 0171 288 5049

Fax: 0171 288 5770

Contact: Miss Jane Stephen (Librarian)

Objectives and Purposes: To support staff working in the hospital

Stock and Subject Coverage: 8,000 books; 200 periodicals covering general medicine; surgery; and nursing

Services/Facilities: Online searches

Availability: To employees of the Whittington Hospital NHS Trust and Camden and Islington Community Services Trust

Hours: 09.00-20.00 (closes 17.00 on Friday and 13.00 on Saturday)

---

[703]

Williams Syndrome Foundation Ltd (incorporating Infantile Hypercalcaemia)

The Little Ruin
Edge Road
Edge
Stroud GL6 6NE

Telephone and Fax: 01452 812277

E-mail: 101752.1563@compuserve.com

Contact: Mr Mike Adlam (Chairman); Mrs Valerie Adlam

Objectives and Purposes: The WS Foundation has been set up to help parents of children with WS/Infantile Hypercalcaemia by providing information about the condition, by putting parents in touch with each other, by enabling their children to meet, by acquiring background information to assist research, and by stimulating interest particularly among the medical profession. It funds research projects and holidays for WS families

Availability: Telephone and written enquiries

Hours: 10.00-16.00

Publications: Newsletter; magazine; miscellaneous items

---

[704]

Winchester and Eastleigh Healthcare NHS Trust

Healthcare Library
Royal Hampshire County Hospital
Romsey Road
Winchester
Hampshire SO22 5DG

Telephone: 01962 824680

Fax: 01962 824659

E-mail: rhclib@interalpha.co.uk

Contact: Miss Brenda Goddard (Library and Information Services Manager)

Objectives and Purposes: To support the objectives of the Trust and of King Alfred's School of Health and Community Studies by providing a quality professional library and information service

Stock and Subject Coverage: Material covering health care; medicine, nursing and related topics; NHS management

Services/Facilities: Online and CD-ROM searches; fax; photocopies

Availability: Access and reference free to all; membership available

Hours: 08.30-17.00 (closes 16.30 on Friday)
Publications: Library Guide

[705]
Winterton Medical Library

Winterton Hospital
Sedgefield
Stockton on Tees
Cleveland TS21 3EJ
Telephone: 01740 620521, ext 4140
Contact: Ms Claire Masterman (Librarian); Mrs Verna Siddle (Library Assistant)
Objectives and Purposes: To provide library and information services for all NHS Trust staff in South Durham
Stock and Subject Coverage: 2,200 books; 22 periodicals. Main coverage is psychiatry, but also covers psychology, nursing and occupational therapy. File of DataStar literature searches. Small collection of tapes and slides
Services/Facilities: Photocopies (priced); online searches
Availability: Telephone and written enquiries accepted; visits by prior arrangement
Hours: 08.30-17.00 (opens 13.00 on Wednesday; closes 16.30 on Friday)
Related Bodies: Part of Health Libraries North

[706]
★Wirral Postgraduate Medical Centre (Clatterbridge Hospital)

Bebington
Merseyside L63 4JY
Telephone: 0151 334 4000, ext 4404
Fax: 0151 334 6379
Contact: Miss Audrey W Hall (Librarian)
Objectives and Purposes: To provide library and information services for medical staff at Clatterbridge and at the sister site of Arrowe Park Hospital
Stock and Subject Coverage: 1,600 books; 70 periodicals on medicine in general
Services/Facilities: MEDLINE on CD-ROM; photocopies
Availability: By prior appointment, for reference use only
Hours: 09.00-17.00
Related Bodies: Arrowe Park Hospital

[707]
Women in Medicine (WIM)

21 Wallingford Avenue
London W10 6QA
Telephone: 0181 960 7446
Contact: Susan Schonfield (Central Contact); Jo Crowe (Secretary)
Objectives and Purposes: To provide support and a political voice for women doctors and medical students
Availability: Publications for sale to anyone enquiring

Publications: Planning and Pitfalls (comprehensive information and career guide); Job-Sharing in General Practice; A Family-Friendly Employment Policy; newsletter (6 per year)

[708]
Women's Health (WH)

52 Featherstone Street
London EC1Y 8RT
Telephone: 0171 251 6333; Helpline: 0171 251 6580
Fax: 0171 608 0928
Contact: Ms B Fernandez (Information Officer)
Objectives and Purposes: To provide information in a supporting manner, helping women to make informed decisions about their health
Stock and Subject Coverage: 1,200 books; 160 periodicals; 3,500 folders containing information on all aspects of women's health
Services/Facilities: Helpline; photocopies
Availability: Freely available for reference; telephone, fax and written enquiries accepted
Hours: 10.00-16.00 (closed on Tuesday)
Publications: Quarterly newsletter; annual report; range of information leaflets for sale (send s.a.e. for list)

[709]
Women's Health Information and Support Centre (WHISC)

Junction 7
Hazelwood Road
Northampton NN1 1LG
Telephone: 01604 39723
Contact: Mary Stamp
Objectives and Purposes: A women's health organisation with information on physical, emotional, social and sexual health; the information is available in different languages
Stock and Subject Coverage: A variety of leaflets, books and videos on subjects dealing with women's health
Services/Facilities: Pregnancy testing; advice in setting up support groups and courses; teenage pregnancy awareness project; library facility; translations; photocopies
Availability: Telephone and written enquiries; visits by appointment; charges made for photocopies and some leaflets; discretionary donations for pregnancy testing
Hours: 'Drop In' days on Monday and Wednesday (10.00-15.00); Telephone enquiries throughout the week

[710]
Women's Nutritional Advisory Service (WNAS)

PO Box 268
Lewes
East Sussex BN7 2QN
Telephone: 01273 487366
Fax: 01273 487576
Contact: Cheryl Griffiths (PR Assistant)

Objectives and Purposes: A nutritional advisory service covering PMS; menopausal problems; Irritable Bowel Syndrome; preconceptual care; and fatigue

Availability: Tailor-made programmes (priced); information packs available on receipt of A5 s.a.e. and four 1st class stamps (state topic of interest)

Hours: 09.00-17.30

Publications: List available. Vitamin and mineral supplements by mail order

---

[711]
Worcester Royal Infirmary NHS Trust

Charles Hastings Postgraduate Medical Centre Library
Ronkswood Branch
Newtown Road
Worcester WR5 1HN

Telephone: 01905 760602

Fax: 01905 767834

Contact: Mrs C Spencer-Bamford (Medical Librarian)

Objectives and Purposes: To provide a general medical library

Stock and Subject Coverage: 870 books; 110 journals covering general medicine

Services/Facilities: CD-ROM searches; photocopies (priced)

Availability: Restricted to bona fide medical staff; reference only

Hours: 09.00-17.00

Publications: Charles Hastings Postgraduate Journal (2 per year)

---

[712]
Worcestershire Health Authority (WHA)

The Library
Department of Public Health Medicine
Isaac Maddox House
Shrub Hill Road
Worcester WR4 9RW

Telephone: 01905 760000, ext 31273

Fax: 01905 26156 (mark 'fao Library')

E-mail: phm@phwhc.demon.co.uk

Contact: Mrs Jane Portman (Librarian/Information Officer)

Objectives and Purposes: To supply health service information to Health Service managers and other staff, in particular consultants and trainees in public health medicine

Stock and Subject Coverage: 5,000 books; 30 periodicals, mostly concerned with Health Service management; health care purchasing; and public health medicine

Services/Facilities: Online searches; photocopies

Availability: By prior appointment, for reference use only for persons from the West Midlands Region

Hours: 09.00-12.00 Monday and Tuesday

Publications: Weekly accessions newsletter

Related Bodies: Part of West Midlands Health Libraries Network

---

[713]
Worthing Postgraduate Medical Centre

Homefield Road
Worthing
West Sussex BN11 2HY

Telephone: 01903 285025

Fax: 01903 203815

E-mail: sue@merriott.demon.co.uk

Contact: Susan J Merriott (Library Services Manager)

Objectives and Purposes: To support the work and continuing education of all members of staff within the Worthing health district

Stock and Subject Coverage: 10,000 books; 144 periodicals. Covers general medicine; nursing and health service management

Services/Facilities: Online and CD-ROM searches; Internet access; current awareness service; fax; photocopies

Availability: By prior appointment, for reference use only

Hours: 09.00-17.00

---

[714]
Wotton Lawn Library

Horton Road
Gloucester GL1 3HY

Telephone: 01452 395720

Fax: 01452 395757

Contact: Angela Perrett

Objectives and Purposes: A mental health library and information service for Gloucestershire

Stock and Subject Coverage: Material on mental health; learning disabilities; and psychology

Services/Facilities: CD-ROM searches; Internet access

Availability: By prior appointment, for reference use only

Hours: 09.00-16.30

Publications: Monthly current awareness bulletin

Related Bodies: Severn NHS Trust

---

[715]
Wrexham Medical Institute

John Spalding Library
Croesnewydd Road
Wrexham LL13 7YP

Telephone: 01978 291100, ext 7455

Fax: 01978 290346

Contact: Mrs Mary McKeon (Senior Librarian); Mr Richard Bailey (Assistant Librarian)

Objectives and Purposes: To provide library and information services for medical professionals

Stock and Subject Coverage: 4,000 books; 200 periodicals. Covers medicine in general. Large collection of videos on medical topics

Services/Facilities: Literatute searches; photocopies (priced); interlibrary loans (priced)

Availability: By prior appointment for reference use only

Hours: Staffed 08.30-17.00 (16.30 on Friday)

Publications: Various library guides; holdings lists; quarterly newsletter
Related Bodies: Member of NHS Regional Library Service for Wales

[716]

Wynne Davies Postgraduate Medical Centre Library

The Alexandra Healthcare NHS Trust
Woodrow Drive
Redditch B98 7UB
Telephone: 01527 503030, ext 4646
Fax: 01527 518489
Contact: Miss Samantha Lloyd (Medical Librarian); Mrs Sarah Parnell (Library Assistant)
Objectives and Purposes: To assist consultants, hospital doctors, trainees and GPs with clinical information and medical education information requirements
Stock and Subject Coverage: 2,000 books; 90 periodicals on postgraduate medicine
Services/Facilities: MEDLINE searches; current awareness service; access to BMA Library; photocopies
Availability: By prior appointment, for reference use only
Hours: 08.30-15.30 Monday; 09.00-17.00 Tuesday to Thursday; 08.30-16.00 Friday
Publications: Library guide; MEDLINE guide; newsletter; current awareness bulletin
Related Bodies: Part of West Midlands Regional Library Network

[717]

York Health Library and Information Service

3rd Floor, Administrative Block
York District Hospital
York YO3 7HE
Telephone: 01904 454301
Fax: 01904 454330
E-mail: k.smith@pulse.york.ac.uk
Contact: Mrs KM Smith (Senior Librarian); Mr DIL Jenkins (Assistant Librarian); Mrs C Bycroft (Interlibrary Loans); Mrs L Wrigglesworth (Periodicals)
Objectives and Purposes: To locate, collect, organise and disseminate information whilst educating the staff and students in the effective use of literature services, plus providing an environment and the facilities for study
Stock and Subject Coverage: Material on medicine; nursing; management; and health-related subjects
Services/Facilities: CD-ROM searches (MEDLINE, CINAHL, ASSIA); online searching of NHS Project Register System, and Cochrane; photocopies
Availability: By prior appointment, for reference use only
Hours: 09.15-20.00 Monday and Wednesday; 09.15-16.30 Tuesday, Thursday and Friday
Publications: Library guide; periodicals holdings list; library exercises

Related Bodies: Northern and Yorkshire Region Department of Postgraduate Medical Education, York University, and York Health Services NHS Trust

[718]

Zion Community Health and Resource Centre

Zion Crescent
Hulme
Manchester M15 5ZY
Telephone: 0161 226 5412
Fax: 0161 227 9862
Contact: Nicky Lidbetter
Services/Facilities: Telephone advice and literature to sufferers of anxiety disorders, and their families; free counselling; free massage service; free relaxation classes (Wednesday, 15.30-16.30)
Hours: 13.00-15.00 Wednesday)
Publications: Zion Anxiety Group Newsletter (bi-monthly)

Stop Press

The following details were received too late to be included in the main alphabetical sequence of the *Guide*

[719]

Anaesthetic Research Society (ARS)

c/o Dr PM Hopkins, Honorary Secretary
Anaesthetic Research Society
St James University Hospital
Leeds LS9 7TF
Telephone: 0113 206 5274
Fax: 0113 206 4140
Contact: Professor L Strunin (President); Dr D Rowbotham (Treasurer); Dr PM Hopkins (Hon. Secretary)
Objectives and Purposes: To present and discuss ongoing research in anaesthesia and related subjects
Availability: Non-members wishing to present to the Society must be sponsored by a member. Membership restricted to those who have successfully presented an abstract which has been approved by the Society
Hours: 09.00-17.00
Publications: Abstracts published 3 times per year in the British Journal of Anaesthesia

[720]

Association of Optometrists (AOP)

90 London Road
London SE1 6LN
Telephone: 0171 261 9661
Fax: 0171 261 0228
E-mail: aoptom@atlas.co.uk
World Wide Web: http://www.assocoptom.co.uk
Contact: Ian Hunter BSc FCOptom (Secretary General)

Objectives and Purposes: To represent the interests of all individual optometrists in the UK; to provide facilities for the defence of the members and their representation on UK and European bodies, including government
Publications: Optometry Today (fortnightly); annual report

[721]
Health Promotion Wales/Hybu Iechyd Cymru (HPW)

Ffynnon-Las
Ty Glas Avenue
Llanishen
Cardiff CF4 5DZ
Telephone: 01222 752222 (direct lines: 681245/681226)
Fax: 01222 756000
E-mail: sue_t@hpwales.demon.co.uk
Contact: Ms S Thomas (Librarian); Mrs S Davies (Senior Library Assistant); Mrs J Howells (Library Assistant)
Objectives and Purposes: To promote good health and prevent ill-health in Wales
Stock and Subject Coverage: 8,000 books and reports; 135 periodicals; 300 videos. Covers all aspects of health promotion including coronary heart disease, substance abuse, women's health, schools and young people, nutrition, physical fitness, epidemiology, public health and statistics. World Health Organization Documentation collection
Services/Facilities: CD-ROM searches; enquiries; photocopies (priced)
Availability: By appointment, for reference use. Membership available
Hours: 09.00-17.00
Publications: Various. List available
Related Bodies: Association of Welsh Health Librarians; Consortium of Welsh Library and Information Services

[722]
National Institute of Medical Herbalists

56 Longbrook Street
Exeter EX4 6AH
Telephone: 01392 426022
Fax: 01392 498963
E-mail: herbmed@dial.pipex.com (address for European Journal of Herbal Medicine)
Objectives and Purposes: Professional body of qualified herbalists
Services/Facilities: Information on herbal medicine in general, and on how to contact a practitioner
Availability: Telephone and written enquiries accepted
Hours: 09.00-17.00
Publications: Information leaflets; practitioners register

[723]
Niemann-Pick Support Group

Linden Bank
2 Linden Crescent
Hawick
Roxburghshire TD9 9LQ
Telephone: 01450 371155
Fax: 01450 370356
Contact: Susan Green (Volunteer Co-ordinator)
Objectives and Purposes: To provide support to parents of children with the metabolic disease Niemann-Pick; support is via letter, telephone and a newsletter. The Group aims to keep parents informed of recent research and to help them make contact with other parents in a similar situation, and to raise awareness of NPD among professionals
Services/Facilities: Free advice and information to parents of children with NPD; letter and telephone support
Availability: Telephone and written enquiries are accepted; no visits
Hours: 24-hour helpline
Publications: Newsletter (3 per year); annual report; information leaflet

[724]
Royal National Orthopaedic Hospital Trust, Nurse Education Library

Brockley Hill
Stanmore
Middlesex HA7 4LP
Telephone: 0181 954 2300, ext 216
Contact: Hilary Isham BSc ALA
Objectives and Purposes: To provide a full information service for all non-medical staff of the Trust, and for students
Stock and Subject Coverage: 3,000 books; 50 periodicals; 50 videos. Covers orthopaedics and related fields
Services/Facilities: Photocopies; CD-ROM searches
Availability: Open to bona fide researchers, by prior appointment
Hours: 09.00-17.00
Related Bodies: University College London, Institute of Orthopaedics

[725]
Scottish Drugs Forum (SDF)

Shaftesbury House
5 Waterloo Street
Glasgow G2 6AY
Telephone: 0141 221 1175
Fax: 0141 248 6414
Contact: Irene Hendry (Information Officer); David Liddell (Director)
Status: Company limited by guarantee

Objectives and Purposes: To facilitate the development of a comprehensive range of services to meet the needs of drug users and their families in Scotland; to act as a national body to represent the interests of those directly affected by drug use

Stock and Subject Coverage: A small collection of books, reports, periodicals, press cuttings and government reports relating to all aspects of drug use and drug services

Services/Facilities: Online database; fax; photocopies

Availability: Telephone and written enquiries; visits by appointment, for reference use only

Hours: 09.30-16.30

Publications: Monthly newsletter; annual report; conference reports; policy statements; Drugfax. Full list available

Related Bodies: Regional offices in Edinburgh and Dundee

---

[726]
University of Teesside Library and Information Services

Library and Information Services
Borough Road
Middlesbrough TS1 3BA
Telephone: 01642 342100
Fax: 01642 342190
E-mail: i.baird@tees.ac.uk
World Wide Web: http://www.tees.ac.uk/
Contact: Ian Butchart (Director of Library and Information Services); Iain Baird (Subject Information Team Leader - Health)

Objectives and Purposes: To facilitate access to all forms of information in order to support learning, research and other University activities

Stock and Subject Coverage: Printed and computer based information in nursing, midwifery, occupational therapy, physiotherapy and radiography within the context of a university library

Services/Facilities: Online searches; photocopies

Availability: Free to University staff and students. Others can use the services for a fee

Hours: 08.00-21.00 (closes 17.00 Friday); shorter hours at weekends and in vacations

Related Bodies: Three directly managed School of Health site libraries at: Darlington Memorial Hospital, Dryburn Hospital in Durham and Bishop Auckland Hospital. Also make resources available through three multidisciplinary sites at: South Cleveland Hospital Middlesbrough, North Tees Hospital in Stockton and Hartlepool General Hospital

---

[727]
Wellcome Institute for the History of Medicine

The Library
183 Euston Road
London NW1 2BE
Telephone: 0171 611 8582
Fax: 0171 611 8369
E-mail: library@wellcome.ac.uk
World Wide Web: http://www.wellcome.ac.uk
Contact: David Pearson (Librarian); Wendy Fish (Head of Reader Services); Julia Sheppard (Archivist)

Objectives and Purposes: Founded on the collection of Sir Henry Wellcome. The Wellcome Trust was set up to support research in medicine and allied subjects, and in the history of medicine. It is one of the primary centres for the study of medical history, nationally and internationally, and its holdings have been steadily developed to support that role

Stock and Subject Coverage: The subject focus is the history of medicine but this is widely interpreted and includes much material on the history of science and mankind in a broader sense. Includes ca. 66,000 pre-1851 printed books, over 7,000 pre-1901 western manuscripts, extensive collections of 20th Century manuscripts and archives (The Contemporary Medical Archives Centre), ca. 14,000 non-European manuscripts and printed books, and a large iconograph collection (56,000 images are available on a videodisc)

Services/Facilities: Photocopies (priced); photography

Availability: Freely available for reference use

Hours: 09.45-17.15 (open until 19.15 on Tuesday and Thursday); 09.45-13.00 Saturday

Publications: Various. List available on request

Related Bodies: The Wellcome Trust

APPENDIX
Medical Resources on the World Wide Web

An important new feature in this edition of the *Guide* is the inclusion of World Wide Web addresses on many entries. It is appropriate, therefore, to supplement this new information by supplying references here to a variety of sites on the Web which offer useful information, or further links to relevant information, in the field of medicine and health care.

By its very nature, the World Wide Web is a dynamic entity. No list such as this one can ever aim to be complete or up-to-date because new sites appear every day; some disappear; and some change address. The addresses given in this Appendix reflect the editor's view of what were the most useful sites for users of this *Guide* at the time of compilation. In order to address the above-stated problem of constantly changing details - and as (I hope) a useful gesture aimed at cutting down the amount of time spent keying in Web addresses - I have created a dedicated Web site at:

http://www.geocities.com/Paris/1716/medlink.htm

This site provides hotlinks to the addresses mentioned here. It is my intention to maintain the site regularly, updating the addresses as appropriate. Input and feedback from users would be most helpful in keeping this site up-to-date, so should anyone, at any time, wish to suggest additions or modifications, please feel free to e-mail me (peter.dale@bl.uk, or the alternative address on the site itself) and I will carefully consider every suggestion.

Editor's choice

If pressed to nominate what is currently the most potentially useful Web site for users of this *Guide*, I would recommend the very comprehensive listing of health resources found on the Nahat site at:

http://nahat.net

This provides links to all NHS organisations on the Web (plus contact details for others who do not have a Web presence), UK teaching hospitals and a wide range of other medical resources. This site is truly a goldmine of healthcare information.

General sites

Other useful and comprehensive listings of medical resources (mainly based in, or aimed at, the United Kingdom) can be found at:

http://www.cs.man.ac.uk/mig/people/medicine/uk.medicine.html
http://www.hop.man.ac.uk/misc/medres.html
http://www.bubl.bath.ac.uk/BUBL/medical.html

Organising Medical Networked Information (OMNI):
http://omni.ac.uk

A good list of resources for librarians is found at:
http://www.epi.bris.ac.uk/rd/links/

Still in the realm of general coverage, the Medical Matrix at:
http://www.slackinc.com/matrix/
is well worth a visit.

A useful medical encyclopaedia can be found at:
http://www.globalmedic.com/ang/frm_enc_2.htm

Cochrane information is available at:
http://hiru.mcmaster.ca/cochrane/default.htm

Disease/condition specific sites

http://www.community-care.org.uk/health/
provides a detailed listing of resources covering specific diseases and conditions.

There is a list of cancer help groups and associations at:
http://kryton.cr.man.ac.uk/help/groups.htm

Disability information

In the field of disability, the very comprehensive Disability Net site at:
http://globalnet.co.uk/~pmatthews/DisabilityNet
is an invaluable resource.

Support groups for a wide range of disabilities and medical conditions can be tracked down at:
http://www.charitynet.org/

In this same field, a very good address list of contacts can be found at:
http://www.hensa.ac.uk/dyslexia/groups/skill/orgslist.html
The presentation may be a little cluttered, but it is a most useful source of addresses.

Search engines

If none of the above sites produces the information that you are looking for, it is always worth visiting one of the search engines and simply keying in the keywords that are of interest to you.

Several of the search engines allow searching by subject category, and some of them offer good listings of the main sites in a category on the search engine page itself. The most impressive example of this is Yahoo. Although not restricted to UK coverage, the Yahoo search engine has an extremely comprehensive coverage of health resources at:
http://www.yahoo.com/Health/

If you require information on a specific medical condition you should take a look at the list given at:
http://www.yahoo.com/Health/Diseases_and_Conditions

If it is important to restrict your search to UK coverage, they have a UK-specific engine at:
http://yahoo.co.uk/Regional/Countries/United_Kingdom/Health

Similarly, several of the other search engines allow you to search under a Medical subdirectory. My favourite engines include:
http://www.altavista.digital.com
http://www.infoseek.com
http://ultra.infoseek.com
http://www.lycos.com
http://www.excite.com

Usenet News

Another good source of information (but not for the faint-hearted) is Usenet News, where individuals post articles, opinions, questions and answers, etc. Searching here can be likened to panning for gold; there may well be gold in there, but it is buried amongst a great deal of what can only be described as dross. A special service on the Web enables you to enter keywords and let a robot scan all the newsgroups on your behalf. You will still have to sort the gold from the dross, but this service does make things a great deal easier. You can find it at:
http://www.search.com

Mailing lists

The Mailbase service co-ordinates an extensive list of mailing lists for discussion groups, general "can anybody help me with this query?" questions, etc. There is a general medical list, and many specialist lists. Full details are at:
http://www.mailbase.ac.uk

Other useful Web sites

I would also recommend the following sites, the content of which should be apparent from their names:

British Medical Journal
http://www.bmj.com/bmj/

Department of Health
http://www.open.gov.uk/doh/dhhome.htm

Department of Health Press Release Menu
http://www.coi.gov.uk/coi/depts/GDH/GDH.html

Health Services Research Super Highway
http://www.york.ac.uk/~jmm7/places.htm

Healthnet
http://www.healthnet.org/hnet/hnet.html

Internet Resources on Public Health
http://www.epi.mh-hannover.de/(eng)/public.health.links.html

Medscape (full text articles from a selection of journals)
http://www5.medscape.com/

MedWeb: Electronic Newsletters and Journals
http://www.cc.emory.edu/WHSCL/medweb.ejs.html

NHS Centre for Reviews and Dissemination
http://www.york.ac.uk/inst/crd/

Reuters Health Information Service
http://www.reutershealth.com

UK Clearing House on Health Outcomes
http://www.leeds.ac.uk/nuffield/infoservices/UKCH/

The Virtual Hospital
http://indy.radiology.uiowa.edu/

ORGANISATION ACRONYM INDEX

The following is an index of those libraries and organisations who are sometimes known by an acronym. This is **not** a complete listing of the organisations included in the *Guide*. For the full listing please refer to the Organisation Index

A

B

ORGANISATION INDEX

C

SUBJECT INDEX

Note: Index refers to entry numbers and not to page numbers. General coverage of broad disciplines such as medicine, nursing and surgery is ***not*** indexed here.

F

Family planning . . . . [209] [276] [314]
 see also Contraception; Preconception
 care

Fear *see* Phobias

Female medical staff . . . . [370] [707]

Fertility (human) . . . [146] [215] [319] [342] [405]

Fibromyalgia . . . . [211]

Food allergy . . . . [213]

Food poisoning . . . . [78]

Foot disorders . . . . [73] [349]

Forensic medicine . . . . [64] [214]

Forensic psychiatry . . . . [120] [376]

Foster care . . . . [426]

Fragile X Syndrome . . . . [219]

G

Gall stones . . . . [78]

Gastroenterology . . . . [115] [548] [564]
 in children . . . . [512]

Gaucher's Disease . . . . [227]

General practice (medicine) . . . . . . [531] [688]

Genetics . . . . [164] [342] [361]
      [366] [367] [479] [525]
 in children . . . . [512]

Geriatrics . . . . [11]-[16] [24] [79]
     [153] [226] [331] [548]

Gerontology . . . . [11]-[16] [79] [110] [265] [331]

Gifted children . . . . [230]

Gilbert's Syndrome . . . . [78]

Glaucoma . . . . [312]

Glycogen Storage Disease . . . . [32]

Growth disorders . . . . [525]
 in children . . . . [148] [503] [525]

Guide dogs (for the blind) . . . . [241]

Guillain-Barré Syndrome . . . . [243]

Gynaecology . . . . [477] [525] [535]
 see also Midwifery; Obstetrics

H

Haematology . . . . [51] [429]

Haemochromatosis . . . . [244]

Haemophilia . . . . [245]

Hair loss . . . . [246]

Hand deficiency (in children) . . . . [523]

Head noise *see* Tinnitus

Head surgery . . . . [69]

Healing . . . . [158]

Health and safety *see* Occupational health

Health care librarianship . . . . [457]

Health economics . . . . [332] [447] [474]

Health education *see* Health promotion

Health physics . . . . [437]

Health policy . . . . . [170] [350] [472] [687] [690]

Health promotion . . . . [212] [251]-[256]
     [264] [299] [331] [350]
 in Avon . . . . [45]
 in Leeds . . . . [335]
 in Northumberland . . . . [466]
 in Scotland . . . . [253]
 in Shropshire . . . . [589]
 in Wales . . . . [721]

Health research . . . . [140] [447]

Health service management . [150] [313] [350] [616]
 buildings/estates . . . . [689]
 see also NHS management

Health statistics . . . . [157]

Health visiting . . . . [257]

Hearing aids . . . . [259]

Hearing impairment . . . . [260] [685]
 see also Deafness

Heart disease . . [80] [145] [161] [208] [252] [289]
   [427] [538] [548] [564] [693] [721]
 nursing . . . . [274]

Heartburn . . . . [78]

Hepatitis . . . . [78]

Herbal medicine . . . . [81] [554] [722]

Herpes viruses . . . . [267]

Hiatus hernia . . . . [78]

Hirschsprung's Disease . . . . [406]

History of Medicine . . . . [282] [536] [537] [538]
    [540] [541] [561] [639] [727]

HIV *see* AIDS

Hodgkin's Disease . . . . [271] [339]

Holistic medicine . . . . [82]

Home safety . . . . [556]

Homoeopathic medicine . . [83] [278] [509] [597]

Hormone disorders . . . . [592]

Hormone replacement therapy . . . . . [186] [569]

Hospices . . . . [615]
 see also Terminal care

HRT *see* Hormone replacement therapy

Huntington's Disease . . . . [284]

Hydrocephalus . . . . [581]

Hygiene *see* Occupational health

Hyperactivity . . . . [11] [285]

Hypercalcaemia . . . . [703]

Hyperlipidaemia . . . . [208]

Hypnosis *see* Hypnotherapy

Hypnotherapy . . . . [84] [410]

I

Identification (by bracelets, etc.) of medical
 conditions . . . . [364]

Ileal conduit . . . . [680]

Ileostomy . . . . [287]
 in children . . . . [406]

181

HAVE YOU MISSED OUT?

If your organisation/library is not listed in this edition of *Guide to Libraries and Information Sources in Medicine and Healthcare* (or you know of any organisation/library that should be included) then complete this form (photocopy this page) and send it to us at the address below. Entries are included in the *Guide* free of charge and all suggested entries will be considered carefully by the editor for inclusion in the next edition.

Name of Organisation   _____

Abbreviation *(if any) by which* _____
organisation is generally known

Address - *including postcode*   _____
_____
_____

Telephone   _____

Fax   _____

E-Mail   _____

WWW page   _____

Key Staff - *including name for enquiries* _____
_____

Objectives and / or purposes - _____
please state concisely the purpose of _____
your organisation and its field of _____
interest _____
_____
_____
_____

Stock and subject coverage - _____
If your organisation has a library _____
please detail the subjects covered _____
and the types of material held _____
_____
_____
_____

Services - *please* _____
list special services and facilities _____
provided for readers, e.g. photocopying, _____
translating services, online searching, _____
fax machines _____
_____
_____

Please turn over >

Availability - *is access available to all bona fide researchers or restricted to certain groups? Is material available for loan or reference? Are charges made?*

_____
_____
_____
_____
_____
_____
_____
_____

Hours of availability

_____
_____
_____
_____
_____

Publications - *details of any regular publications (title, publisher, frequency and date) including annual reports, yearbooks, directories, etc., and any important recent non-recurring works*

_____
_____
_____
_____
_____

Related Bodies - *please provide brief details, e.g. does your organisation have any subordinate or related institutions? Is it part of a larger body? Provide hierarchial charts or publicity material explaining the structure of your organisation (if already available)*

_____
_____
_____
_____
_____
_____

Please tick this box if you do not   ❑
want to receive mailings on other
related products and services

Name of person completing entry   _____

Signature   _____

Return this form to: Paul Wilson, Room 121, The British Library, Science Reference and Information Service, 25 Southampton Buildings, London WC2A 1AW. Tel: 0171-412 7472 or Fax: 0171-412 7947. If you have any queries you can contact the editor on (e-mail address) peter.dale@bl.uk